Custom Edition

SECONDARY METHODS

With contributions by:

Richard Kellough

Noreen Kellough

R. Bruce Williams

Steven E. Dunn

Taken from:

Secondary School Teaching: A Guide to Methods and Resources, Second Edition
by Richard Kellough and Noreen Kellough

Brain-Compatible Learning for the Block
by R. Bruce Williams and Steven E. Dunn

PEARSON

Custom
Publishing

**CHAPTER 13   Assessing Teaching Effectiveness
and Continued Professional Development   324**

Taken from: *Secondary School Teaching: A Guide to Methods and Resources,* Second Edition
by Richard Kellough and Noreen Kellough

I

ORIENTATION TO TEACHING AND LEARNING IN TODAY'S SECONDARY SCHOOLS

Part I responds to your needs concerning:

- Creation of your professional resources file.
- Development of a personal instructional strategies repertoire.
- Expectations, responsibilities, competencies, and fundamental teaching behaviors of a secondary school classroom teacher.
- Guidelines for recognizing and providing for student differences.

- Home, school, and community connections.
- Teaching for positive character development.
- The importance of developing an eclectic teaching style.
- The realities of public secondary school classroom teaching today and the diversity of students and types of schools.
- The teacher as a reflective decision maker.

Reflective Thoughts

During one school year, you will make literally thousands of decisions, many of which can and will affect the lives of students for years to come. You may see this as an awesome responsibility, which it is.

History brims with examples of how relatively few but positive moments with a truly caring and knowledgeable teacher can drastically alter for the better the life of a student who until then had a history of mostly negative experiences.

A teacher who, for all students, uses only one style of teaching in the same classroom setting day after day is shortchanging students who learn better another way.

Traditional teaching techniques—such as the lecture, which assumes that students are homogeneous in terms of background, knowledge, motivation, learning styles, and facility with the English language—are ineffective in many of today's secondary school classrooms.

Like intelligences, teaching style is neither absolutely inherited nor fixed. Your teaching style will change, develop, and emerge throughout your career.

A nontraditional school schedule alone—without quality individualized attention to the individual needs of the students—seems to be of no value in addressing the needs of students who are at risk of dropping out of school.

Today's movement to transform schools into caring and responsive learning environments has as its sole purpose that of helping all students make the transitions necessary to succeed in school and in life.

Exemplary schools are those that are rooted in celebrating and building upon the diverse characteristics and needs of students. To become and to remain exemplary, they must be in a continual mode of inquiry, reflection, and change.

To hold high, although not necessarily identical, expectations for all students is to promote respect for diversity.

The advantage of utilizing a combination of practices concurrently is usually a greater way to help all students succeed in school than using any singular practice by itself.

1

Teaching and Learning in Today's Secondary Schools

You have probably begun reading this book because you are interested in a career in secondary school teaching. Whether you are in your early twenties and starting your first career or older and beginning a new career, this book is for you—that is, for any person interested in becoming a secondary school classroom teacher.

If you are now in a program of teacher preparation, perhaps near the completion of the program you will be offered your first teaching contract. If that happens, you will be excited and eager to sign the contract and begin your new career. Yet after the initial excitement, you will

have time to reflect. Many questions will then begin to form in your mind. If in a multiple-school district, to which school will I be assigned? Will it be a comprehensive high school, a ninth-grade center, a junior high school, or a middle school? Will it be a traditional school, or will it be a **magnet school,** that is, a school that specializes in a particular academic area, or a career academy, a magnet program that specializes in preparing students with career-oriented curriculum? For example, Austin High School (Houston, TX) specializes in preparing students for the teaching professions; Murry

3

Bergtraum High School (New York, NY) for business careers; Chicago High School (Chicago, IL) for the Agricultural Sciences; Renaissance High School (Detroit, MI) emphasizes college admissions for all its graduates; and Fremont High School (Oakland, CA) houses six separate academies, one each for architecture, business and government, electronics, health and bioscience, media, and arts and education. The Illinois Math and Science Academy (Aurora, IL) is a *residential school* that specializes in preparing specially selected students for careers in mathematics and science. Or it might be a partnership school, that is, a school that has entered into a partnership agreement with community business and industry to link school studies with the workplace.[1] Or a tech-prep high school, that is, one that has a curriculum that is articulated with the first two years of college, leading to an associate of applied science degree.[2] Or a fundamental school that specializes in teaching basic skills. Or a charter school that is an independent public school freed from rules but accountable for results.[3] Or a for-profit school, a public school that is operated by a for-profit company. Or an International Baccalaureate School, that is, one with a curriculum approved by the International Baccalaureate Organization (IBO), a worldwide nonprofit educational foundation that is based in Switzerland.[4] Or a special transitional school such as New York City's Liberty High School, a one-year school designed to help recent immigrant students feel welcome and self-assured and to succeed in learning to read and write in English.[5] It might also be an independent school (a private school without religious affiliation), a church-affiliated school, or an alternative high school.[6] Or perhaps it is another type or a combination of these, such as a for-profit charter school or a charter-magnet-fundamental school. Although in different ways and with various terminology, the historical practice of providing different routes for students with different needs and different vocational and academic aspirations continues.

Will it be a school that has its start in the fall, as is traditional, or will it be a year-round school? Which subjects will I be assigned to teach? What specific grade levels will I have? How many different preparations will I have? Will I be a member of a teaching team? What supervision and extra-curricular responsibilities might I have? What will the students be like? What will their parents or guardians be like? How will I get along with the rest of the faculty? What textbooks or media program will I use, and when can I expect to see them? How should I prepare? How *can* I prepare when there are so many unanswered questions? What school district policies do I need to learn about? What support services can I expect? How extensive are the school's rules and regulations? Will my teaching assignment be split between departments? Will the department chairperson like me? Will there be an orientation for new and beginning teachers? How can I prepare for students I know nothing about?

Those questions, and many others, are often the concerns of beginning teachers. To guide you through this initial experience and to help answer some of your questions, this chapter offers a first glimpse into today's world of secondary school classroom teaching. This chapter and the two that follow in Part I provide a basis for your planning and selecting learning activities presented in subsequent chapters. Enjoy your quest toward becoming the best classroom teacher you can be.

Upon completion of this chapter you should be able to:

1. Define *secondary school,* and describe similarities and differences between the middle school, junior high school, and high school.
2. Describe essential characteristics that characterize a school as being exemplary.
3. Describe the middle school concept and its contributions to secondary education.
4. Describe similarities and differences between the exemplary middle school and the traditional junior high school.
5. Describe the purposes and characteristics of the school-within-a-school concept.

---

[1] Some schools belong to the National Network of Partnership 2000 Schools. For information, contact the Center on School, Family, and Community Partnerships, The Johns Hopkins University, 3506 North Charles Street, Baltimore, MD 21216. Phone (410) 516-8807 or fax (410) 516-8890. See also M. G. Sanders, "Improving School, Family, and Community Partnerships in Urban Middle Schools," *Middle School Journal* 31(2):35–41 (November 1999), and W. Johnson et al., "Texas Scholars," *Phi Delta Kappan* 79(10):781–783 (June 1998).

[2] See, for example, B. L. Brown, *Tech Prep: Is It Working? Myths and Realities* (Columbus, OH: ERIC Clearinghouse on Adult, Career, and Vocational Education, 1998).

[3] B. V. Manno et al., "Beyond the Schoolhouse Door," *Phi Delta Kappan* 81(10):736–744 (June 2000), p. 737. Connect to the charter school home pages via the United States Charter School website at http://www.uscharterschools.org/. For additional information and for a copy of the *National Charter School Directory,* contact the Center for Education Reform (CER) at (800) 521-2118; see the website at http://edreform.com/research/css9697.htm.

[4] IBO offers a Primary Years Program (for children ages 3 to 12), a Middle Years Program (for students ages 11 to 16), and a Diploma Program for students in the final two years of high school. See the IBO site http://www.ibo.org.

[5] See B. Schnur, "A Newcomer's High School," *Educational Leadership* 56(7):50–52 (April 1999).

[6] See, for example, "Alternative Schools: Caring for Kids on the Edge," *Northwest Education* 3(4) (Summer 1998). See also Nevada Virtual High School, the nation's first full service interactive on-line high school open to students everywhere, at http://www.nvvhs.org/.

6. Describe current trends, problems, and issues in United States public secondary school education.

Before going further, let us define what is meant by the term **secondary school.** A secondary school is any school that houses students in some combination of what traditionally have been known as grades 7 through 12. However, as you shall learn, some middle schools, which may have students at the eighth-grade level, also house students in grade 6 and even grade 5. So, for this book, our definition of secondary school includes middle schools, junior high schools, and high schools.

ORIENTATION

The rapid and dramatic changes occurring throughout modern society, as well as what has been learned in recent years about intelligence and learning, are reflected in the equally rapid and dramatic changes occurring in today's secondary schools. The school in which you soon will be teaching may bear little resemblance to the school that you attended in its curriculum, its student body, its methods of instruction, or its physical appearance. From the moment you set foot onto a secondary school campus during this program for teacher preparation and later, when you obtain your first paid teaching job, you will want to keep your sensory input channels wide open and alert, to learn as much as you can about the school, its organization, its students, and its support staff. Although it is only the beginning to your learning about teaching, this book does offer information and resources that you will want to refer to time and again, long after the initial course for which it is used is over.

Orientation Meetings: Start of the School Year

As a beginning teacher, you will likely be expected to participate in orientation meetings—meetings designed to help you get off to a good beginning. When not in meetings you will have time to prepare your assigned classroom(s) for instruction.

Some school districts start the school year with a districtwide orientation, whereas others schedule on-site orientations at each school. Many school districts do both, with perhaps a districtwide morning meeting followed by school on-site meetings in the afternoon. Such meetings provide you the opportunity to meet other teachers and establish new collegial friendships and professional relationships. Many school districts sponsor beginning teacher induction programs that provide special assistance to new teachers. Of course, the scheduling and planning of orientation meetings will vary, district by district and school by school. The objectives for all orientation meetings, however, should be similar to those in the following paragraphs.

You should become familiar with the district's (or school's) written statement of its unique beliefs and goals—its *statement of mission* (or philosophy or vision)—and what that statement means to the people affiliated with the district or school. [*Note:* Although the terms *mission statement, philosophy statement,* and *vision statement* are often used interchangeably, and while in our opinion the first two are synonymous, the vision statement is or should be a statement of intention that goes beyond the immediate mission of the school and gives future direction to the school's stated mission.] See sample mission statements shown in Figures 1.1a and 1.1b.

You will be encouraged to become familiar with the policies of the school and district. Numerous policies often cover a wide range. There are policies for procedures relating to students who are injured at school; for what to do during natural disasters, such as earthquakes, floods, and severe storms; regarding students who need to take prescribed medications; for finding illegal drugs and weapons; for parking on campus; for leaving campus during the school day; for classroom conduct; for school programs, field trips, and parties in the classroom; for mandatory testing and grading practices; for completing absentee and tardy forms; for sending students to the office; and for chaperoning and sponsoring student activities. And these examples are just the beginning.

You will learn about the myriad forms that teachers must fill out. There are forms for injuries that occur while at school, for textbook loans, for key loans, for attendance, for student academic deficiencies, for sponsoring student activities, for field trips, for working with students who have special needs, and for referrals of students for misbehavior, to name just a few.

You will learn about the approved curriculum that defines what teachers are to teach and what students are to learn. This means that you must familiarize yourself with the academic benchmarks, courses of study, curriculum guides, resource units, teacher's manuals, student textbooks, media programs, and supplementary materials—all of which should reflect the school's mission statement and approved curriculum. You will learn about the school or district plan for monitoring, assessing, and supervising implementation of the curriculum; mandatory testing for achievement; and available resource materials and equipment, as well as the procedures for reserving and using them.

You will learn about the school library/media resource center, its personnel and procedures, and you will meet district and school personnel and become familiar with the many services that support you in the classroom. You will meet campus security personnel, resource officers, and other ancillary personnel and learn about their functions and locations.

As a student in a program for teacher preparation, you may be expected to participate in an orientation

- It is the mission of Appling Middle School (Bartlett, TN) to teach all students the skills necessary to accept personal responsibility and to live as productive citizens in a changing world.
- Understanding that diversity is our strength, we at Broughal Middle School (Bethlehem, PA) believe that all students (a) deserve a quality education regardless of race, gender, or socioeconomic status, (b) can learn and achieve increased academic levels of success, and (c) should celebrate their uniqueness and that of others. Further, the staff, along with parents and community members, will empower all students to achieve their full potential by (a) meeting students' individual needs through a caring and encouraging environment, (b) providing the educational opportunities needed to meet established academic standards, develop new skills, enhance communication skills, think critically, engage in creative problem solving and decision making, and interact responsibly in preparation for lifelong personal growth, (c) developing instructional strategies, techniques, or adaptations to motivate students and assure proper learning, and (d) encouraging good citizenship through the development of self-discipline, the growth of responsibility, and the respect for self and others.
- The purpose of Columbia Middle School (Sunnyvale, CA) is to provide every student with a comprehensive, relevant learning experience that is the foundation for productive citizenship in a constantly changing and diverse society.
- At Mansfield Middle School (Storrs, CN), we implement an open-ended curriculum which embraces not only mastery of basic skills, but also higher level thinking and learning. We present material in heterogeneously grouped classes whenever possible. Support service, computer, and enrichment staff assist the regular classroom teacher in providing academic support and challenge to students. Children have opportunities to make choices and accept consequences, to explore a wide range of school activities, to value the process of inquiry, to solve problems, and to sustain effort. We are flexible in our methods of assessment so that achievements of children with different learning styles can be measured appropriately. We want students to become responsible citizens. We emphasize cooperation and concern for others and respect for individual and cultural differences. We foster communication among the participants within our school community and beyond.

Figure 1.1a
Sample middle school mission statements. (Reprinted by permission.)

- It is the mission of Antelope Union High School (Wellton, AZ) to create a safe learning environment where students learn to be responsible, thoughtful, self-reliant, productive citizens capable of adapting to and competing in a rapidly changing world community.
- It is the mission of Bloomington High School (Bloomington, IL) to prepare students for the challenges of a demanding global society. This responsibility is shared by faculty, staff, parents/guardians, and most importantly—students. We believe in providing educational equity for our dynamic and diverse population. As responsible citizens, our students will face challenges that require increasingly complex problem-solving skills and the ability to adapt and apply knowledge. Accordingly, our responsibility is to assist all students in mastering the knowledge and skills for successful, independent, and lifelong learning. Further, we help students acquire effective communication skills needed for individual interaction and collaboration. Finally, we accept the responsibility to inspire our students to achieve their full potential.
- It is the mission of Sacramento High School (Sacramento, CA) to enable our students to succeed in a rapidly changing world. We expect our students to develop a positive vision for themselves and to become responsible, independent, self-directed learners, and effective communicators who make informed and ethical decisions.
- It is the mission of Sehome High School (Bellingham, WA), a community committed to excellence, to assure all students will learn and apply knowledge, skills, and attitudes necessary for productive citizenship, lifelong learning, and success in the changing workplace by sharing responsibilities in a quality, student-centered environment.

Figure 1.1b
Sample high school mission statements. (Reprinted by permission.)

meeting at your college or university. The meeting may be held at the beginning of the program or just before the beginning of your field experiences, or both. Perhaps this meeting will be a function of one of your college or university courses. You will receive your school assignment, the name of the school and the school district, the school's location, the date when you should report to that assignment, the name of your cooperating teacher(s), the grade level(s), the subject(s), and perhaps the name of your college or university supervisor. You will probably be encouraged to follow many of the objectives just discussed as well as to meet other teacher candidates.

When you arrive at your assigned school, and after introductions have been made, you should begin to become familiar with the school campus and the way that the school is organized. Walk around the campus, perhaps with a copy of the school map, and learn the location of your classroom. Also locate the nearest restrooms for girls, for boys, and for faculty men or women. You may be loaned one or several keys—one for the classroom, one for the faculty restroom, and perhaps one for a faculty workroom. Become familiar with such areas as the teachers' workroom, the faculty room, and the faculty lunch room (which may or may not be a single area—a large, comprehensive high school may have several faculty rooms scattered about the campus).

Thoroughly investigate this campus environment. Where do students eat their lunches? Is there a multipurpose room—a room used for lunch as well as for educational purposes? Is there a school nurse? Where is the nurse's room? When is the nurse available? Where is the nearest first aid and emergency equipment? How do you notify maintenance personnel quickly and efficiently? Where are the written procedures for fire drills and other emergencies? Where is information about the school's emergency warning system? Is there a plan posted in a conspicuous place for all to see? Where are the various administrative offices? Where are the counseling and guidance offices? Is there an office of student activities? Where are the library, the media center, the resources room, gymnasium(s), and the auditorium? Where are textbooks stored, and how are they checked out and distributed? Where is the attendance office? Are there resource specialists, and if there are, what are their functions and where are their offices located?

At an orientation session, you may meet the department chairperson or the team leader and members of that team. How can you discover where those persons are to be found at various times during the school day? Where are teaching materials and laboratory supplies kept, and how do you obtain them? Have you located your faculty mailbox and the place to check in or out when you arrive at school or leave at the end of the day? What procedures do you follow if you are absent because of illness or if you know you are going to arrive late? Do you have the necessary phone numbers? Not least in importance, if you drive a vehicle to school, where do you park? Otherwise, what is the best local transportation available for getting to and from school each day?

After becoming familiar with the school campus and obtaining answers to some of your more urgent questions, you will want to focus your attention on the various school schedules and particularly your own teaching schedule.

The School Calendar Year: Conventional and Year-Round

School years vary from state to state, from district to district, and from school to school. Most school years begin in mid- to late-August or early September and continue through late May or mid-June. However, to accommodate more students without a significant increase in capital costs and to better sustain student learning, an increasing number of schools are eliminating the traditional long summer break by switching to year-round education (YRE or YRO for year-round operation), which, by the way, has been around for more than half a century.[7] Nevertheless, whether the school follows a year-round schedule or not, for teachers and students in United States the school year still approximates 180 days.

In a school with year-round operation, a teacher might teach for three-quarters of the year and be off for one-quarter or teach in a 45/15 program, which means nine weeks of school (45 days) "on track" followed by three weeks of school (15 days) "off track" throughout the year. In the widely-used 45/15 arrangement, teachers and students are on tracks, referred to as A Track, B Track, and so on, with starting and ending times that vary depending on the track and time of year. At any one time there is always at least one track that is on vacation. At that time while some students literally are out of school and on vacation, others may choose to participate in voluntary intersession programs consisting of classes designed for remediation, exploration, or enrichment.

Beginning about 8:00 a.m., the school day lasts until about 3:00 or 4:00 p.m. District and state laws vary, but generally teachers are expected to be in the classroom no less than 15 minutes prior to the start of school and to remain in their classrooms no less than 15 minutes after final dismissal of students.

Drawing upon studies of adolescent sleep patterns as well as the need to find ways to deal with crowded schools or to cut transportation expenses by reducing the number of buses and drivers needed, some schools are experimenting with later than usual starting times or, because no single schedule can accommodate the desires and needs of everyone, with multiple starting times.[8]

---

[7]See, for example, N. R. Brekke, *Year-Round Education: Does It Cost More?* (Madison, WI: Consortium for Policy Research in Education, 1997); J. Curry et al., *Year-Round Schools Evaluation, 1996–97* (Austin, TX: Publication Number 96.10, Austin Independent School District, 1997); C. C. Kneese, "Review of Research on Student Learning in Year-Round Education," *Journal of Research and Development in Education* 29(2):60–72 (Winter 1996); M. McCord, "Bursting at the Seams: Financing and Planning for Rising Enrollments," *School Business Affairs* 63(6):20–23 (June 1997); and, K. Rasmussen, "Year-Round Education," *Education Update* 42(2):1, 4–5 (March 2000).

[8]See, for example, M. Lawton, "For Whom the School Bell Tolls," *School Administrator* 56(3):6–12 (March 1999), and the several related articles in the January 1999 issue of *Phi Delta Kappan* 80(5).

Teaching Teams

Traditionally, elementary school teachers taught their groups of children in their self-contained classrooms for most of the school day and junior high and senior high school teachers taught their subject disciplines as often as seven or eight times each day to as many groups of students. At all levels, teachers taught in their assigned classrooms while fairly isolated from other teachers and school activities—not unlike the parallel play of preschool children, that is, playing side-by-side but not really together. In some schools, that is still the case. Increasingly, however, teachers at all levels are finding themselves members of a collaborative **teaching team** in which several teachers work together to reflect, plan, and implement a curriculum for a common cohort of students. (*Note:* A distinction must be made between teaching teams and team teaching; **team teaching** refers to two or more teachers simultaneously providing instruction to students in the same classroom. Members of a teaching team may participate in team teaching.)

The teaching team may comprise only a few teachers, for example, all 7th-grade teachers of a particular middle school, or the 10th- and 11th-grade teachers of history and English at a particular high school, or the teachers who teach the same cohort of seventh-grade students in English/reading/language arts and in history/social studies/geography at a middle-level school. Sometimes teaching teams are comprised of one teacher each from English/reading/language arts (known also as *literacy*), history/social studies/geography, mathematics, and science. These four areas are known as the **core curriculum.** In addition to teachers of the core subjects, specialty-area teachers may be part of the team, including teachers of physical education, the visual and performing arts, and even special education teachers and at-risk specialty personnel or school counselors. As a visiting or continuing member of this interdisciplinary team organization (ITO), a team may invite a community-resource person (e.g., the vignette of Figure 1.5) to join them. Because the core and specialty subjects cross different disciplines of study, these teams are commonly called interdisciplinary teaching teams or simply **interdisciplinary teams.**[9]

The School-Within-a-School (SWAS)

An interdisciplinary teaching team and its common cohort of students is referred to as the **school-within-a-school** (also called village, pod, academy, family, house, or team), where each team of teachers is assigned each day to the same cohort of students for a common block of time.[10] Within this block of time, teachers on the team are responsible for the many professional decisions necessary, such as how school can be made developmentally responsive (i.e., most meaningful) to students' lives, what specific responsibilities each teacher has each day, what guidance activities need to be implemented, which students need special attention, and how students will be grouped for instruction. Members of such a team become "students of their students" and thereby build the curriculum and instruction around their students' interests, perspectives, and perceptions. Because they "turn on" learning, the school and its classrooms become exciting places to be and to learn. (In contrast, "symptoms of turned-off learning include students' seeming inability to grasp concepts, to exert effort, or to display enthusiasm; repeated lateness or absence; boredom; and work that is sloppy or of poor quality.")[11]

The SWAS concept helps students make important and meaningful connections among disciplines. It also provides them with both peer and adult group identification, which provides an important sense of belonging. In some schools, using an arrangement called **looping** (also referred to as banding, multiyear grouping, multiyear instruction, multiyear placement, and teacher–student progression), the cohort of students and teachers remain together as a group for several or for all the years a student is at that school. Although looping can be found at all levels of schooling, its use is most prevalent in the primary grades and in some middle schools.[12]

The advantages to being a member of a teaching team in a SWAS environment are numerous. For example, the combined thinking of several teachers creates an expanded pool of ideas, enhances individual capacities for handling complex problems, and provides intellectual stimulation and emotional support. The combination of talents produces an energy that has a positive impact on the instructional program. A beginning teacher who joins a team has the benefit of support from more experienced teammates. When a team member is absent, other members of the team work closely with the substitute, resulting in less loss of instructional time for students. More and better planning for students occurs as teachers discuss, argue, and reach agreement on behav-

---

[9]See, for example, P. Spies, *Interdisciplinary Teams for High Schools,* Fastback 416 (Bloomington, IN: Phi Delta Kappa Educational Foundation, 1997).

[10]See, for example, S. R. Sabo, "A Blueprint for Change. A Learner–Focused Curriculum Drove the Design of Minnesota's Chaska High School," *Techniques: Making Education and Career Connections* 73(2):16–19 (February 1998).

[11]The phrases "students of their students" and "turn on learning" are borrowed from C. A. Grant and C. E. Sleeter, *Turning on Learning* (Upper Saddle River, NJ: Prentice Hall, 1989), p. 2.

[12]See, for example, J. Grant, I. Richardson, and C. Forsten, "In the Loop," *School Administrator* 57(1):30–33 (January 2000), and A. Pyle, "In the Loop," *Middle Ground* 1(1):15 (August 1997).

ioral expectations, curriculum emphasis, instructional approaches, media, and materials.[13]

Teachers' Daily Schedules

For many secondary school teachers, the school day consists of the traditional seven or eight periods, each lasting about 50 minutes. This traditional schedule includes teaching three or four classes before lunch and three or four following lunch. One of these periods is a preparation period, sometimes referred to as the conference or planning period. Most teachers are quite busy during their preparation periods, reading and grading student papers, preparing class materials, organizing the classroom, meeting in conferences, or preparing instructional tools.

Common Planning Time

For an interdisciplinary team to plan effectively and efficiently, members must meet frequently. This is best accomplished when they share a **common planning time,** preferably a minimum of four hours a week.[14] This means that in addition to each member's daily preparation time (discussed in the next section), members of a team share a common planning time to plan curriculum and to discuss the progress and needs of individual students within the cohort.

Each team assigns a member to be team facilitator, or **lead teacher.** The lead teacher organizes the meetings and facilitates discussions during the common planning time. Usually, this teacher also acts as a liaison with the administration to assure that the team has the necessary resources to put its plans into action. A team's lead teacher (or another member designated by the team) may also serve on the school leadership team, a group of teachers and administrators, and sometimes students, designated by the principal or elected by the faculty (and student body) to assist in the leadership of the school. Sometimes, in lieu of a traditional site principal, the school leadership team *is* the leadership for the school.[15]

Nontraditional Scheduling

To maximize the learning time, to allow for more instructional flexibility, and to accommodate common planning time for teachers, an increasing number of schools are using some form of **block scheduling.** Block scheduling means that, for at least part of the school day or part of the week, blocks of time ranging from 70 to 140 or more minutes replace the traditional structure of 50-minute-long classes. The possible variations are nearly limitless.[16]

For example, for some schools, the school year consists of three 12-week-long trimesters, and each school day is divided into five 70-minute-long class periods. Such a schedule is referred to as a *5 × 7 block plan.* Some schools use a *4 × 4 block plan,* whereby students take four 85–90-minute-long *macroperiods* (or *macroclasses*) each day, each semester.[17] Other schools use an *alternating day block plan,* sometimes called the A-B plan, where classes meet every other day for the entire school year for 90-minute blocks.[18]

Using extended periods, or macroperiods, lengthens the time each day that students are in a course, simultaneously reducing the number of courses taken at one time. The macroperiod allows the teacher to supervise and assist students with assignments and project work as well as with their reading, writing, thinking, and study skills. Macroperiods provide more time for student inquiry and for interactive and interdisciplinary thematic instruction that might otherwise be difficult or impossible to accomplish in shorter class periods.

Block Scheduling: Advantages and Disadvantages

Consistently reported in the research of schools using block scheduling—where students and teachers work together in longer but fewer classes at a time—is greater satisfaction among teachers and administrators and improvement in both the behavior and the learning of all students.[19] Students do more writing, pursue issues in greater depth, enjoy classes more, feel more challenged, and gain deeper understandings. In addition, assumedly because each teacher teaches fewer courses during a semester and is responsible for fewer students, student–teacher interaction is more productive. Teachers get to know the students better and are therefore able to respond to a student's needs with greater care. Additionally, researchers report more course credits completed,

---

[13]R. J. McCarthy, *Initiating Restructuring at the School Site,* Fastback 324 (Bloomington, IN: Phi Delta Kappa Educational Foundation, 1991), p. 11.

[14]See, for example, A. C. Howe and J. Bell, "Factors Associated with Successful Implementation of Interdisciplinary Curriculum Units." *Research in Middle Level Education Quarterly* 21(2):39–52 (Winter 1998), and L. Mann, "Finding Time to Collaborate," *Education Update* 42(2):1, 3, 8 (March 2000).

[15]See, for example, D. Barnett et al., "A School Without a Principal," *Educational Leadership* 55(7):48–49 (April 1998).

[16]For sample schedules, see R. L. Canady and M. D. Rettig, "The Power of Innovative Scheduling," *Educational Leadership* 53(3):4–10 (November 1995).

[17]See, for example, R. B. Cobb, S. Abate, and D. Baker, "Effects on Students of a 4 × 4 Junior High School Block Scheduling Program," *Education Policy Analysis Archives* 7(3) (1999); and D. W. Mutter et al., "Evaluation of 4 × 4 Block Schedules," *ERS Spectrum* 15(1):3–8 (Winter 1997).

[18]See, for example, M. D. DiRocco, "How an Alternating–Day Schedule Empowers Teachers," *Educational Leadership* 56(4):82–84 (December 1998/January 1999).

[19]See, for example, S. Black, "Learning on the Block." *American School Board Journal* 185(1):32–34 (January 1998).

equal or better mastery and retention of material, and a significant reduction in suspension and dropout rates ostensibly because the school climate is positive with fewer discipline problems.[20] Most teachers using block scheduling report they accomplish more in each class session.[21]

Other reported benefits of the block plans over a traditional seven- or eight-period daily schedule are that in one school year the total hours of instruction is significantly greater, and, because planning periods are longer, there is more time for teachers to plan and to interact with parents and guardians.

There are also benefits to taxpayers. During one school year teachers teach more courses and potentially more students, thereby decreasing the number of faculty needed. In addition, fewer textbooks are needed. For example, instead of all 11th-graders taking history for an entire year, half of them take it the first semester and half the second, thereby reducing the number of textbooks needed by one-half.

Block scheduling arrangements often produce serendipitous benefits. For example, students may not have to carry as many books—not an insignificant benefit in this day of heavy books in dangerously heavy backpacks—and may go to their lockers fewer times a day to exchange textbooks and materials between blocks. In many schools, except perhaps in physical education and vocational education, student lockers are not used at all. Also, the reduction of bells ringing from as many as eight times a day to perhaps only two or three times a day or not at all creates less disturbance.

Because students are not roaming halls for three to five minutes five or six times a day, teachers can more easily supervise unstructured time and thereby have better control over the unplanned and subtle message systems within schools referred to as the **hidden curriculum.** The messages of the hidden curriculum are the school climate, the feelings that are projected from the teacher and other adults to students and from the students to one another, not only in classrooms but before and after school, at social events, school programs, club meetings, and in the halls, restrooms, lunch areas, and other places on the school campus that are not monitored as closely as are the classrooms.

Nontraditional school schedules are not without their problems. Problems that sometimes arise from block scheduling are: (a) content coverage in a course may be less than that which was traditionally covered; (b) teachers may be unhappy, especially teachers of foreign languages, English, and mathematics if classes meet

less frequently than in the traditional one period a day, five days a week schedule;[22] (c) there may be a mismatch between content actually covered and that expected by state-mandated tests and the dates those tests are administered to students; (d) community relations problems may occur when students are out of school and off campus at nontraditional times; and (e) when the instructional strategy is inappropriate (e.g., the teacher uses a dull lecture for the entire length of a macroperiod) students are likely to become bored, restless, and mischievous. The latter is certainly not insignificant as dull, boring, uninspired teaching is probably the root-cause for many secondary students becoming disenfranchised from school.

Using a *modified block schedule,* some schools have successfully combined schedules, thus satisfying teachers who prefer block scheduling and those who prefer a traditional schedule. A modified block schedule can provide both traditional, 40-minute periods (sometimes called *split-block periods*) that meet daily and longer blocks. A modified block schedule centers on a seven or eight 45- or 40-minute-period day along with alternate longer blocks. In a modified block schedule all students might start the day with a 30- or 40-minute-long first period which serves as a homebase (known also as homeroom or *advisor–advisee*) time. From there, some students continue the morning attending traditional-length periods while others move into a morning block class. Throughout the day, teachers and students may pass from block classes to those of traditional length or vice versa.

Some schools use a *flexible block schedule*. The daily schedule is a seven-period day with all seven classes meeting on Monday. Periods one through four meet for 75 minutes, while periods five through seven meet for 30 minutes. Periods one through four meet for 105 minutes each on Tuesdays and Thursdays, and periods five through seven meet for 120 minutes each on Wednesdays and Fridays. A 30-minute homebase period is held at the same time each day, perhaps the first thing in the morning or immediately after lunch.

In short, there is little doubt that longer blocks of instructional time with students is a positive factor contributing to students' meaningful learning, especially when combined with some form of year-round education and the use of project-based learning and interdisciplinary thematic instruction.

---

[20]See, for example, T. L. Shortt and Y. V. Thayer, "Block Scheduling Can Enhance School Climate," *Educational Leadership* 56(4):76–81 (December 1998/January 1999).
[21]R. Jones, "Wake Up," *Executive Educator* 17(8):14–18 (August 1995).

---

[22]See, for example, S. L. Kramer, "What We Know About Block Scheduling and Its Effects on Math Instruction, Part II," *NASSP* (National Association of Secondary School Principals) *Bulletin* 81(587):69–82 (March 1997), and M. Hamdy and T. Urich, "Perceptions of Teachers in South Florida Toward Block Scheduling," *NASSP* (National Association of Secondary School Principals) *Bulletin* 82(596):79–92 (March 1998).

Striving to Present Quality Education for All Students

Nontraditional scheduling is part of the effort to restructure schools in a way that will deliver quality education for all students. The curriculum of a *quality education school* is one seen by students as having meaning and usefulness in their lives and is delivered by activity-oriented instruction. Rather than dictating procedures, ordering students to work, and berating them when they do not, in a quality school the teachers provide a stimulating learning environment and are seen by students as being encouraging and helpful. Unfortunately, as many educators fear and as stated by Tomlinson,[23]

> for many teachers, curriculum has become a prescribed set of academic standards, instructional pacing has become a race against a clock to cover the standards, and the sole goal of teaching has been reduced to raising student test scores on a single test, the value of which has scarcely been questioned in the public forum.

School Organization Affects Learning

Sometimes it may appear that more energy is devoted to organizational change (*how* the curriculum is delivered) than to school curriculum (*what* is taught). However, the two are inseparable. School organization has a direct effect on what students learn; if it didn't, educators wouldn't be spending so much valuable time trying to restructure their schools to effect the most productive (and cost-effective) delivery of the curriculum. Exemplary schools establish and maintain a climate of constant modification. They are in a continual process of inquiry, reflection, and change.

Organizational changes are often referred to as *school restructuring*, a term that has a variety of connotations, including site-based management, collaborative decision making, school choice, personalized learning, integrated curricula, and collegial staffing. School restructuring has been defined as "activities that change fundamental assumptions, practices, and relationships, both within the organization and between the organization and the outside world, in ways leading to improved learning outcomes."[24] No matter how it is defined, educators agree on the following point: the design and functions of schools should reflect the needs of young people of the twenty-first century rather than a nineteenth century factory-like, assembly line, "one-size-fits-all" model.

Exemplified by efforts mentioned in the preceding discussions, the movement to year-round operation and the redesigning of schools into smaller cohorts of teachers and students represents a movement that is becoming increasingly common across the country. With this redesign, the intention is that schools will better address the needs and capabilities of each unique student. To that end, a number of specific trends are shown in Figure 1.6. As a teacher in the twenty-first century, you will undoubtedly help accomplish many of those changes.

Middle Schools and Junior High Schools

When you receive your state teaching credential, you may or may not be certified to teach at the middle school level. In some states an elementary school credential certifies a person to teach in any grade, kindergarten through grade eight. In some states a secondary school credential certifies a person to teach a particular subject at any grade level, kindergarten through grade 12. In other states such a credential qualifies a person to teach only grades 7 through 12. At least 33 states provide a middle school teaching credential to candidates who have successfully completed a program specifically designed to prepare teachers for that level.

At this point you should note that there are two sometimes quite different types of schools, both of which may be called middle schools. One is the traditional junior high school with perhaps a few minor changes, such as changing its name to "middle school." The second is the exemplary middle school, which is, as shown in Table 1.1, quite different from the traditional junior high school. To understand the significance of what has become known as the middle school concept, certain background information may prove helpful.

The Middle School Concept and Philosophy

Used historically from about 1880, the term **junior high school** most commonly refers to schools having grades seven and eight or grades seven, eight, and nine, in which a program is designed to approximate the type of education commonly found in traditional high schools. Thus, a junior high school might be considered a "not-quite-yet-but-trying-to-be" high school. Students graduating from a junior high school often would then move on to a **senior high school.**

The term **middle school** gained favor as a result of the movement away from the concept of "junior" high school. Reasons for the reorganization away from the concept of junior high school and the adoption of a middle school education include: (a) to provide a program specifically designed for students of the 10–14 age group, (b) to set up a more effective transition between the elementary school and the high school, and (c) to move ninth graders to the high school or, as has happened in some school districts in recent years, to a

---

[23]C. A. Tomlinson, "Reconcilable Differences? Standards-Based Teaching and Differentiation," *Educational Leadership* 58(1):7 (September 2000).
[24]D. T. Conley, "Restructuring: In Search of a Definition," *Principal* 72(3):12 (January 1993).

Table 1.1 Summary of Differences between Middle Schools and Traditional Junior High Schools

	Junior High School	*Middle School*
Most common grade span organization	7–8 or 7–9	6–8
Scheduling	Traditional 50-minute periods. six-period day	Flexible, usually block
Subject organization	Departmentalized	Integrated and thematic; interdisciplinary, usually language arts, math, science, and social studies
Guidance/counseling	Separate sessions with counselor on individual basis or as needed; full-time counselors	Adviser-advisee relation between teacher and student in homeroom or homebase
Exploratory curriculum	Electives by individual choice	Common "wheel" of experiences for all students
Teachers	Subject-centered; grades 7–12 certification	Interdisciplinary teams; student-centered; grades K–8 or 6–8 certification
Instruction	Traditional; lecture; skills and repetition	Thematic units; discovery techniques; study skills
Athletics	Interscholastic sports emphasizing competition	Intramural programs emphasizing participation

location designed solely for ninth graders, known as a *ninth-grade center* or *academy*.[25,26]

Although any combination of grades five through nine may be included in a middle school, the trend and the most common configuration is grades six through eight. The trend of including sixth graders and excluding ninth graders is a reflection of the recommendation of the National Middle School Association in its official position paper, *This We Believe*.[27] The trend continues.

The term **middle level education** identifies school organizations based on a philosophy that incorporates curricula and instructional practices specifically designed to meet the needs of students ages 10–14. This philosophy is referred to as the *middle school concept*. The notion that greater and more specific attention should be given to the special needs of young adolescents became known as the *middle school movement*. Basic to the movement is the continued belief that middle school teachers need specialized training to work most effectively with young adolescents.[28]

School Restructuring and Students at Risk

Although the focus in Chapter 2 is on specifics about working with particular groups of students, it is appropriate at this time to say a few words about school restructuring efforts and students at risk. **At risk** is the term used by educators when referring to students who have a high probability of dropping out of formal school before finishing high school. The National Institute on the Education of At-Risk Students defines an at-risk student as one who "because of limited English proficiency, poverty, race, geographic location, or economic disadvantage, faces a greater risk of low educational achievement or reduced academic expectation."[29] Many students, at any one time, have risk factors from more than one of these categories.[30]

---

[25]K. Brooks and F. Edwards, *The Middle School in Transition: A Research Report on the Status of the Middle School Movement* (Lexington, KY: College of Education, University of Kentucky, 1978).
[26]See, for example, the story of Oregon City High School, a ninth-grade-only school since 1990, in C. Paglin and J. Fager, *Grade Configuration: Who Goes Where?* (Portland, OR: Northwest Regional Educational Laboratory, 1997), pp. 29–31; the West Orange High School (Orlando, FL) Ninth Grade Center, opened in 1993, on the Internet at http://mac.ae10.ocps.k12.fl.us/sch/hwo/9TH/INDEX.HTM; the Scott County Schools (Georgetown, KY) Ninth Grade Center, opened in 1996, on the Internet at http://www.scott.k12.ky.us/9th/ 8thhistory.html; and the ninth grade academy at James F. Rhodes High School (Cleveland, OH) and at Hartford Public High School (Hartford, CN) both of which opened in 1999.
[27]National Middle School Association, *This We Believe* (Columbus, OH: Author, 1982, reissued in 1995).

---

[28]See, for example, Chapter 5 ("Expert Teachers for Middle Grades Schools: Pre-service Preparation and Professional Development," pp. 94–120) of A. W. Jackson and G. A. Davis, *Turning Points 2000: Educating Adolescents in the 21st Century* (New York: Teachers College Press, 2000).
[29]See http://www.ed.gov/offices/OERI/At-Risk/.
[30]See, for example, D. E. Matus, "Humanism and Effective Urban Secondary Classroom Management," *Clearing House* 72(5):305–307 (May/June 1999).

It has been estimated that by year 2020, the majority of students in the public schools in the United States will be at-risk.[31] A nontraditional school schedule alone, without quality, personalized attention to each student, may be of no value in addressing the needs of students who are at risk of not finishing school.

Today's movement to transform schools into caring and responsive learning environments has as its sole purpose that of helping all students, perhaps especially those at risk, to make the transitions necessary to succeed in school and in life.

Responsive School Practices for Helping All Students Succeed

Because of the enormous diversity of students, the advantage from utilizing a combination of practices concurrently is usually greater in helping all students succeed in school than is the gain from using any singular practice by itself. The reorganization of schools and the restructuring of school schedules, then, represent only two of the efforts to help all students make successful transitions.

Other important responsive practices (including attitudes) are: (a) a perception, shared by all teachers and staff, that all students can learn when they are given adequate support, although not all students need the same amount of time to learn the same thing; (b) high, although not necessarily identical, expectations for all students; (c) personal attention, adult advocacy, scheduling and learning plans to help students learn in a manner by which they best learn—research clearly points out that achievement increases, students learn more, and students enjoy learning and remember more of what they have learned when individual learning styles and capacities are identified and accommodated; there are learning style traits known to significantly discriminate between students who are at risk of dropping out of school and students who perform well, discussed in Learning Modalities and Learning Styles in Chapter 2; (d) engagement of parents and guardians as partners in their child's education; (e) extra time and guided attention to basic skills—such as those of thinking, writing, and reading—rather than on rote memory; (f) specialist teachers and smaller classes; (g) peer tutoring and cross-age coaching; and

(h) attention and guidance in the development of coping skills.

THE FUNDAMENTAL CHARACTERISTIC OF EXEMPLARY EDUCATION

Wherever and however the students are housed, and regardless of other responsive practices, in the end it is the dedication, commitment, and nature of the understanding of the involved adults—the teachers, administrators, bus drivers, cooks, grounds crew, security staff, custodial staff, and support personnel—that remains the incisive element. That, in our opinion, is the fundamental characteristic of exemplary education—to celebrate and build upon the diverse characteristics and needs of students. In fact, it is the title of the next chapter.

Committed Teachers

Secondary school teachers represent myriad individual personalities—perhaps impossible to capture in generalizations. Let us imagine that a teaching colleague mentions that Pat Gomez, in room 34, is a "fantastic teacher," "one of the best teachers in the district," "super," and "magnificent." What might be some of the characteristics you would expect to see in Pat's teaching behaviors?

We can expect Pat to: (a) be understanding of and committed to the school's mission statement; (b) know the curriculum and how best to teach it; (c) be enthusiastic, motivated, and well organized; (d) show effective communication and interpersonal skills; (e) be willing to listen to the students and to risk trying their ideas; (f) be accepting and caring about all students; and (g) to be a reflective and responsible decision maker.

Students need teachers who are well organized and who know how to establish and manage an active and supportive learning environment, even with its multiple instructional demands. Students respond best to teachers who provide leadership and who enjoy their function as role models, advisers, mentors, and reflective decision makers.

Reflective Decision Making

During any school day, as a teacher you will make hundreds of nontrivial decisions, many of them instantaneously. In addition, you will have already made many decisions in preparation for the teaching day. During one school year a teacher makes literally thousands of decisions, many of which can and will affect the lives of her or his students for years to come. As in the nearly poetic words of Brown and Moffett, "We [teachers]

[31]R. J. Rossi and S. C. Stringfield, "What We Must Do for Students Placed at Risk," *Phi Delta Kappan* 77(1):73–76 (September 1995). See also the several related articles in the theme issue, "The Changing Lives of Children," *Educational Leadership* 54(7) (April 1997).

influence students in myriad, unperceived ways that affect them and the lives of people with whom they interact like the widening circles extending from a stone tossed into a tranquil pond."[32] This may seem to be an awesome responsibility; indeed it is.

Initially, of course, you will make errors in judgment, but you will also learn that your students are fairly resilient and that there are experts available who can guide you to help ensure that the students are not harmed severely by your mistakes. You can learn from your errors. Keep in mind that the sheer number of decisions you make each day will mean that not all will be the best decisions that could have been made had you had more time and better resources for planning.

Good Teaching Is as Much An Art as It Is a Science

Although pedagogy is based on scientific principles, good classroom teaching is as much an art as it is a science. Few rules apply to every teaching situation. In fact, decisions about the selection of content, instructional

objectives and materials, teaching strategies, a teacher's response to student misbehavior, and the selection of techniques for assessment of the learning experiences are all the result of subjective judgments. Although many decisions are made at a somewhat unhurried pace when you are planning for your instruction, many others will be made intuitively and *tout de suite*. Once the school day has begun, there is rarely time for making carefully thought-out judgments. At your best, you base your decisions on your teaching style, which, in turn, is based on your knowledge of school policies, pedagogical research, the curriculum, and the unique characteristics of the students in your classroom. You will also base your decisions on instinct, common sense, and reflective judgment. The better your understanding and experience with schools, the curriculum, and the students, and the more time you give for thoughtful reflection, the more likely it will be that your decisions will result in the students meeting the educational goals. You will reflect upon, conceptualize, and apply understandings from one teaching experience to the next. As your understanding about your classroom experience accumulates, your teaching will become more routinized, predictable, and refined.

---

[32]J. L. Brown and C. A. Moffett, *The Hero's Journey* (Alexandria, VA: Association for Supervision and Curriculum Development, 1999), p. 24.

EXERCISE 1.1
Conversation with a Classroom Teacher

Instructions: The purpose of this exercise is to interview one or more teachers, perhaps one who is relatively new to the classroom and one who has been teaching for ten years or more. Use the following questions. You may duplicate blank copies of this form. Share the results with others in your class.

1. Name and location of school _____
   _____

2. Grade span of school _____

3. Date of interview _____

4. Name and grade level (and/or subject) of interviewee _____
   _____

5. In which area(s) of the school's curriculum do you work? _____
   _____

6. Why did you select teaching as a career? _____
   _____
   _____
   _____
   _____
   _____

7. Why are you teaching at this grade level? _____
   _____
   _____
   _____
   _____
   _____

8. What preparation or training did you have? _____
   _____
   _____
   _____
   _____
   _____

9. What advice about preparation can you offer? _____

_____

_____

_____

_____

10. What do you like most about teaching? _____

_____

_____

_____

_____

_____

11. What do you like least about teaching? _____

_____

_____

_____

_____

_____

12. What is the most important thing to know to be an effective classroom teacher? _____

_____

_____

_____

_____

_____

13. What other specific advice do you have for those of us entering teaching at this level?

_____

_____

_____

_____

_____

The Principal Can Make a Difference

As a new or visiting member of the faculty, one of your tasks is to become familiar with the administrative organization of your school and district.

One person significantly responsible for the success of any school is its principal. What are the characteristics of an effective school principal? See Figure 1.2. Perhaps foremost is that the principal has a vision of what a quality school is and strives to bring that vision to life. School improvement is the effective principal's constant theme.[33]

---

[33]See, for example, G. N. Tirozzi, "The Artistry of Leadership: The Evolving Role of the Secondary School Principal," *Phi Delta Kappan* 82(6):434–439 (February 2001).

* Admonishes behaviors rather than personalities.
* Advocates a school of problem solvers rather than of blamers and faultfinders.
* Assures a base of community support for the school, its students, its faculty, and its mission.
* Emphasizes the importance of making everyone feel like a winner.
* Encourages people when they have made a mistake to say "I'm sorry," rather than making them feel compelled to cover their mistakes.
* Ensures that school policies are closely and collaboratively defined and clearly communicated.
* Ensures that staff and students receive proper and timely recognition for their achievements.
* Ensures that teachers' administrative chores and classroom interruptions are limited only to those that are critically important to student learning and effective functioning of the school.
* Establishes a climate in which teachers and students share the responsibility for determining the appropriate use of time and facilities.
* Follows up promptly on recommendations, concerns, and complaints.
* Fosters professional growth and development for teachers, with opportunities for visitations, demonstrations, conferences, workshops, and projects.
* Has a vision of what an exemplary school is and strives to bring that vision to life.
* Involves teachers, parents, and students in decision making and goal setting.
* Is an advocate for teachers and students.
* Is positive in her or his outlook.
* Keeps everyone well-informed of events and of successes.
* Spends time each day with students.

Figure 1.2
Key characteristics of exemplary school principals.

The principal establishes a climate in which teachers and students share the responsibility for determining the appropriate use of time and facilities. Because exemplary educators today believe in the innate potential of every student, rather than of dumbing down standards and expectations, they modify the key variables of time, grouping, and instructional strategies to help individual students achieve mastery. It is nearly impossible to do so without a supportive and positive thinking school principal.[34] (Sometimes, instead of having a school principal, the responsibility traditionally held by the person in that position is shared by a site-based management team or school-site council.)[35]

In addition to the school principal there will be vice- or assistant principals and persons with specific responsibilities and oversight functions, such as student activities, school discipline and security, transition programs, and curriculum and instruction. (Some large schools have the school-site principal plus persons designated as grade-level principals.[36]) Sometimes teachers who are department chairs or designated team leaders may also serve administrative functions. However, the principal is (or should be) the person with the final responsibility for everything that happens at the school. Where principals used to debate whether they were leaders or managers, today there is no debate—to be most effective the principal must be both.

TELECOMMUNICATIONS NETWORKS, MEMBERS OF THE COMMUNITY, AND PARENT ORGANIZATIONS: VEHICLES FOR OBTAINING AND SHARING IDEAS AND INFORMATION

Today's exemplary educators are making major efforts to enhance the connections between the home, school, local, and global communities to promote the success of all students.

Home and School Connections

It is well known that parental and family involvement in a student's education can have a positive impact on the student's achievement at school. For example, when parents or guardians of at-risk students get involved, the student benefits with more consistent attendance at school, more positive attitudes and actions, better grades, and higher test scores.

Although not all schools have a parent organization, when school principals were given a list of community

---

[34]B. J. Omotani and L. Omotani, "Expect the Best," *Executive Educator* 18(8):27, 31 (March 1996).
[35]See, for example, D. Barnett et al., p. 48.
[36]For example, housing approximately 1,300 students, First Colony Middle School (Sugar Land, TX) has, in addition to its school-site principal, principals for each grade level, sixth through eighth.

groups or organizations and asked to assess the influence each group had exerted on their school, the group that had the most influence was the parent–teacher organization (PTO) or parent–teacher association (PTA).[37] Recognizing the positive effect that parent and family involvement has on student achievement and success, the National PTA published *National Standards for Parent/ Family Involvement Programs.*[38]

Many schools have adopted formal policies about home and community connections. These policies usually emphasize that parents/guardians should be included as partners in the educational program, that teachers and administrators will inform parents/ guardians about their child's progress, about the school's family involvement policy, and about any programs in which family members can participate. Some schools are members of the *National Network of Partnership 2000* schools. Efforts to foster parent/guardian and community involvement are as varied as the people who participate, and include: (a) student– teacher–parent contracts and assignment calendars, sometimes available via the school's web page on the Internet; (b) home visitor programs; (c) involvement of community leaders in the classroom as mentors, aides, and role models;[39] (d) newsletters, workshops,[40] and electronic hardware and software for parents/ guardians to help their children; (e) homework hotlines; (f) regular phone calls[41] and personal notes home about a student's progress; (g) enrollment of not only students but of entire families as members of a learning team;[42] and (h) involvement of students in community service learning.[43]

Service Learning

With service learning, students can learn and develop through active participation in thoughtfully organized

---

[37]J. W. Valentine et al., *Leadership in Middle Level Education. Vol. 1: A National Survey of Middle Level Leaders and Schools* (Reston, VA: National Association of Secondary School Principals, 1993), p. 98.

[38]See P. Sullivan, "The PTA's National Standards," *Educational Leadership* 55(8):43–44 (May 1998). For a copy of the standards, contact the National PTA, 330 N Wabash Ave., Chicago, IL 60611-3690. Phone (312) 670-6782; Fax (312) 670-6783.

[39]See, for example, the "Hand in Hand" web page http://www.handinhand.org.

[40]See, for example, T. Whiteford, "Math for Moms and Dads," *Educational Leadership* 55(8):64–66 (May 1998).

[41]See, for example, C. Gustafson, "Phone Home," *Educational Leadership* 56(2):31–32 (October 1998).

[42]Such is the case at Metropolitan Regional Career and Technical Center, a public high school in Providence, RI. See R. Allen, "Forging School–Home Links," *Education Update* 42(7):1, 4, 8 (November 2000).

[43]See: B. Kleiner and C. Chapman, *Youth Service–Learning and Community Service among 6th- through 12th-Grade Students in the United States: 1996–1999. Statistics in Brief.* ED439086 (Washington, DC: National Center for Education Statistics, 2000); and the May 2000 theme issue, "service learning," of *Phi Delta Kappan,* 81(9).

- Big Dummy's Guide to Service-Learning at http:// www.fiu.edu/~time4chg/Library/bigdummy.html.
- Links for Service-Learning at http:// www.bbrook.k12.nj.us/servlink.htm.
- National Service-Learning Cooperative Clearinghouse at http://www.nicsl.coled.umn.edu.

Figure 1.3
Internet sources on community service learning.

and curriculum-connected experiences that meet community needs. (See Figure 1.3 for Internet sources of additional information and descriptions of community service projects.)

Community members, geographic features, buildings, monuments, historic sites, and other places in a school's geographic area constitute one of the richest instructional laboratories that can be imagined. In order to take advantage of this accumulated wealth of resources, as well as to build school–community partnerships, once hired by a school you should start a file of community resources. For instance, you might include files about the skills of the students' parents or guardians and other family members, noting which ones could be resources for the study occurring in your classroom. You might also include files on various resource people who could speak to the class, on free and inexpensive materials, sites for field trips, and what other communities of teachers, students, and adult helpers have done.

It is a good idea to start your professional resources file now, and keep it going throughout your professional career; for that, see Figure 1.4. Many resource ideas and sources are mentioned and listed throughout this book.

Telecommunications Networks

Teachers are increasingly turning to the Internet to guide their students toward becoming autonomous thinkers, effective decision makers, and life-long learners. To make their classrooms more student-centered, collaborative, interdisciplinary, and interactive they are increasingly turning to telecommunications networks and to the community. For example, see the vignette, Interdisciplinary Thematic Instruction at West Salem Middle School, that follows. Webs of connected computers allow teachers and students from around the world to reach each other directly and gain access to quantities of information previously unimaginable. Students using networks learn and develop new inquiry and analytical skills in a stimulating environment and gain an increased appreciation of their role as world citizens. Sample websites and addresses are shown in Figure 1.5; others are indicated throughout this guide.

A professional resources file is a project that you can begin now and continue throughout your professional career. Begin your resources file either on a computer database program or on color-coded file cards that list: (1) the name of the resource; (2) how and where to obtain the resource; (3) description of how to use the resource; and (4) evaluative comments about the resource.

Organize the file in a way that makes the most sense to you now. Cross-reference or color-code your system to accommodate the following categories of instructional aids and resources.

- Articles from print sources
- Compact disc titles
- Computer software titles
- Games
- Guest speakers and other community resources
- Internet resources
- Media catalogs
- Motivational ideas
- Pictures, posters, graphs
- Resources to order
- Sources of free and inexpensive materials
- Student worksheets
- Test items
- Thematic units and ideas
- Unit and lesson plans and ideas
- Videocassette titles
- Videodisc titles
- Miscellaneous

Figure 1.4
Beginning my professional resources file.

- *Classroom Connect* http://www.wentworth.com. Resources for teachers; links to schools.
- *Council of the Great City Schools* http://cgcs.org. Descriptions of programs and projects in large urban schools.
- *Education links* http://www.execpc.com/~dboals/k-12.html.
- *Education World* http://www.education-world.com. Electronic version of *Education Week*.
- *ENC* http://www.enc.org. Eisenhower National Clearinghouse for Mathematics and Science.
- *FedWorld* http://www.fedworld.gov. Access to information from government agencies.
- *GEM, the Gateway to Educational Materials* http://www.thegateway.org/index.html. Federal government's effort to provide access to Internet-based educational materials.
- *GlobaLearn* http://www.globalearn.org/. Students interact with remote expedition teams.

- *Global Schoolnet Foundation* http://www.gsn.org/. Global resources and links.
- *GLOBE* (Global Learning and Observations to Benefit the Environment) *Program* http://www.globe.gov. An international environmental science and education partnership.
- *Homeschool Resources* http://mint.net~caronfam/links.htm.
- *HomeworkCentral* http://www.homeworkcentral.com. For lesson plans and subject research.
- *Kathy Schrock's Guide for Educators* http://www.capecod.net/schrockguide/ for resources and information on education.
- *Learning Network* http://www.learningnetwork.com/. Wealth of informational resource links for teachers, students, administrators, and parents.
- *Library of Congress* http://lcweb.loc.gov/homepage/lchp.html. National Digital Library life history manuscripts from the WPA Federal Writers' Folklore Project, Civil War photographs, early motion pictures, legal information, and research sources.
- *ClubMid* http://www.ClubMid.phschool.com. Middle grades network.
- *Cross City Campaign for Urban School Reform* http:www.crosscity.org.
- *MiddleWeb* http://www.middleweb.com/. Focuses on middle schools.
- *National Consortium for School Networking* http://cosn.org.
- *Novagate reference site* http://www.novagate.com/novasurf/onlinereference.html
- *On-Line Books* http://digital.library.upenn.edu/books/.
- *Study Web* http://www.studyweb.com. Place for students and teachers to research topics.
- *Teachers Helping Teachers* http://www.pacificnet.net/~mandel/.
- *Teacher Talk* http://education.indiana.edu/cas/tt/tthmpg.html. Mostly for middle school and high school teachers.
- *21st Century Teachers* http://www.21ct.org. Teachers for teachers' exchange.
- *United Nations' CyberSchool Bus* http://www.un.org/Pubs/CyberSchoolBus/. Curriculum units and projects, databases on U.N. member states, and global trends.
- *United States Department of Education* http://www.ed.gov/index.html.
- *Virtual Reference Desk, for Educators* http://thorplus.lib.purdue.edu/reference/.
- *Yahoo's Education Index* http://www.yahoo.com/Education/tree.html.

Figure 1.5
Sample Internet sites for teachers and students.

SCHOOL VIGNETTE
Interdisciplinary Thematic Instruction at West Salem Middle School*

What began as an isolated, single-grade, telecommunications-dependent project for students at West Salem Middle School (Wisconsin) developed into a longer-term, cross-grade interdisciplinary program of students and adults working together to design and develop a local nature preserve. Students began their adventure by interacting with explorer Will Steger as he led the International Arctic Project's first training expedition. Electronic on-line messages, via the Internet, allowed students to receive and send messages to Will and his team in real time. Students delved into the Arctic world, researching the physical environment and the intriguing wildlife, reading native stories and novels about survival, keeping their own imaginary expedition journals, learning about the impact of industrialized society on the Arctic, and conversing with students from around the world. But something very important was missing—a connection between the students' immediate environment and the faraway Arctic.

West Salem Middle School's focus became the local 700-acre Lake Neshonoc, an impoundment of the LaCrosse River, a tributary of the Mississippi. Although many students had enjoyed its recreational opportunities, they had never formally studied the lake. The Neshonoc Partners, a committee of parents, community leaders, teachers, students, and environmentalists, was established to assist in setting goals, brainstorming ideas, and developing the program for a year's study of the lake. Right from the start, students showed keen interest in active involvement in the project. A second committee, involving parents, students, and the classroom teacher, met during lunch time on a weekly basis to allow for more intensive discussions about the lake and the overall project.

The team of teachers brainstormed ideas to further develop an interdisciplinary approach to the study of Lake Neshonoc. Special activities, including an all-day "winter survival" adventure, gave students a sense of what the real explorers experience. Students learned about hypothermia, winter trekking by cross-country skiing, and building their own snow caves.

For several weeks, students learned about the ecosystem of Lake Neshonoc through field experiences led by local environmentalists and community leaders. Guest speakers told their stories about life on the lake and their observations about the lake's health. Student sketchbooks provided a place to document personal observations about the shoreline, water testing, animal and plant life, and the value of the lake. From these sketchbooks, the best student creations were compiled to create books to share electronically with students with similar interests in schools from Russia, Canada, Missouri, South Carolina, Nevada, Wisconsin, and Washington, D.C. The opportunity to share findings about their local watershed sparked discussions about how students can make a difference in their own community. Comparative studies gave students a chance to consider how humans and nature impact other watersheds.

West Salem students worked with the local County Parks and Recreation Department to assist in developing a sign marking the new County Park where the nature sanctuary would reside. Students brainstormed design ideas and then constructed a beautiful redwood sign with the help of a local technical educational teacher. Today the sign is a symbol of the partnership that has been established between the students and the community. It is a concrete reminder that together we can work for the common good of the community and the environment. Students celebrated the study of the lake with a closure. Will Steger, along with community leaders, parents, school board members, and staff, commended the students for what is sure to be the start of a long and enduring relationship—a partnership created out of common respect and appreciation for the value of our ecosystem.

Source: J. Wee, "The Neshonoc Project: Profiles in Partnership," *World School for Adventure Learning Bulletin* (Fall 1993):2–3. Adapted by permission.

THE EMERGENT OVERALL PICTURE

Certainly, no facet of education receives more attention from the media, causes more concern among parents and teachers, or gets larger headlines than that of a decline (factual or fanciful) in students' achievement in the public schools. Reports are issued, polls taken, debates organized, and blue-ribbon commissions are formed. Community members write letters to local editors about it, news editors devote editorial space to it, television anchors comment about it, and documentaries and specials focus on it in full color. We read, "Students Play Catch-Up on Basic Skills," and "U.S. Students Lag Behind Other Nations," and so on. What initiated this attention that began more than a quarter-century ago and continues today? We are not sure, but it has never been matched in its political interest and participation, and it has affected and continues to affect both the public schools and the programs in higher education that are directly or indirectly related to teacher preparation and certification.[44]

In response to the reports, educators, corporations and local business persons, and politicians acted. Around the nation, their actions resulted in:

- Changes in standards for teacher certification. For example, model standards describing what prospective teachers should know and be able to do in order to receive a teaching license were prepared and released in 1992 by the Interstate New Teacher Assessment and Support Consortium (INTASC), a project of the Council of Chief State School Officers (CCSSO), in a document titled *Model Standards for Beginning Teacher Licensing and Development.* Representatives of at least 36 states and professional associations—including the National Education Association (NEA), the American Federation of Teachers (AFT), the American Association of Colleges for Teacher Education (AACTE), and the National Council for the Accreditation of Teacher Education (NCATE)—comprise the group. The standards are performance-based and revolve around a common core of principles of knowledge and skills that cut across disciplines. The INTASC standards were developed to be compatible with the National Board for Professional Teaching Standards (NBPTS).[45] Specifically addressing middle level in-

struction, in 1997 the NBPTS released 11 categories of standards for certification as a Middle Childhood/ Generalist. The 11 categories are (1) knowledge of students, (2) knowledge of content and curriculum, (3) learning environment, (4) respect for diversity, (5) instructional resources, (6) meaningful applications of knowledge, (7) multiple paths of knowledge, (8) assessment, (9) family involvement, (10) reflection, and (11) contributions to the profession.[46]

- Development of national education standards for all major subject areas.
- Emphasis on education for cultural diversity and ways of teaching language minority students.
- Emphasis on helping students make effective transitions from one level of schooling to the next and from school to life, with an increased focus on helping students make connections between what is being learned and real life, as well as connections between subjects in the curriculum and between academics and vocations.
- Emphasis on rising test scores, reducing dropout rates (that is, the rate of students who do not complete high school nor receive the equivalent degree), increasing instructional time, and changing curricula.
- Formation of school–home–community connections.
- New requirements for a high school diploma.[47]
- School restructuring to provide more meaningful curriculum options.

Key Trends and Practices Today

Key trends and practices today are listed in Figure 1.6.

Problems and Issues That Plague the Nation's Schools

Major problems and issues plague our nation's schools, some of which are shown in Figure 1.7. Some of these are discussed in subsequent chapters (see index for topic locations). Perhaps you and members of your class can identify other issues and problems faced by our nation's schools.

---

[44]See, for example, G. I. Maeroff (ed.), *Imaging Education: The Media and School in America* (New York: Teachers College Press, 1998).

[45]For copies of the INTASC document, contact CCSSO, One Massachusetts Ave. NW, Suite 700, Washington, DC 20001; (202) 3367-7048. See footnote 7 page 58 of this text.

---

[46]Access the standards at http://www.nbpts.org/nbpts/standards/ mc-gen.html. You may want to compare the 11 standards of the NBPTS document with the 22 competencies that are presented in Chapter 3 of this book and with the 22 "components of professional practice" in C. Danielson, *Enhancing Professional Practice: A Framework for Teaching* (Alexandria, VA: Association for Supervision and Curriculum Development, 1996).

[47]Many of the changes for high school graduation have involved adding a fourth year of English, a third year of mathematics, and assorted computer, arts and community service requirements, and in at least 18 states the passing of a standardized achievement test.

- Changing high school graduation requirements to include mandatory passing of a state-wide standardized achievement test.
- Deemphasizing or eliminating traditional curriculum tracking and instead providing meaningful curriculum options with multiple pathways for academic success.
- Dividing the student body and faculty into cohorts, that is, the house or academy concept, and using nontraditional scheduling.
- Facilitating students' social skills as they interact, relate to one another, solve meaningful problems, develop skills in conflict resolution, and foster peaceful relationships and friendships.
- Facilitating the developing of students' values as related to their families, the community, and schools.
- Holding high expectations, although not necessarily the same expectations, for all students by establishing goals and assessing results against those goals.
- Integrating the curriculum.
- Involving parents/guardians and communities in the schools.
- Involving students in self-assessment.
- Providing students with the time and the opportunity to think and be creative, rather than simply memorizing and repeating information.
- Redefining giftedness to include nonacademic as well as traditional academic abilities.
- Teaching and assessing for higher-order thinking skills.
- Using heterogeneous small-group learning, peer coaching, and cross-age tutoring as instructional strategies.
- Using the Internet in the classroom as a communication tool and learning resource.
- Using occupations to contextualize learning and instruction to vitalize a school-to-work transition.

Figure 1.6
Key trends and practices in today's secondary schools.

- Bias, prejudice, harassment, and violence in schools.[48]
- Buildings in need of repair and upgrading.[49]
- Controversy over maintaining both a developmentally appropriate yet academically rigorous curriculum.[50]
- Continuing controversy over books and their content.
- Continuing controversy over values, morality, and sexuality education.
- Controversy created by the concept of teaching less content but teaching it better.
- Controversy over the concept of a national curriculum with national assessments.[51]
- Controversy over high-stakes testing and the potential for an increased number of high school students who do not graduate.[52]
- Continued debate over the value of traditional ability grouping and curriculum tracking.[53]

---

[48]See, for example, S. L. Wessler, "Sticks and Stones," *Educational Leadership* 58(4):28–33 (December 2000/January 2001).

[49]See, for example, C. Rowand, *How Old Are America's Public Schools?* (Washington, DC: ED426586, National Center for Education Statistics, 1999).

[50]See, for example, J. R. Belair and P. Freeman, "Providing a Responsive and Academically Rigorous Curriculum," *Middle School Journal* 32(1):5–6 (September 2000).

[51]See, for example, A. Kohn, "Fighting the Tests: A Practical Guide to Rescuing Our Schools," *Phi Delta Kappan* 82(5):349–357 (January 2001).

[52]See, for example, P. Schmidt, "Colleges Prepare for the Fallout from State Testing Policies," *Chronicle of Higher Education* 46(20): A26–A28 (January 21, 2000); J. Spritzler, "Students, Parents, and Teachers Say, 'Take This Test and Shove It!' " *Paths of Learning: Options for Families & Communities,* 3:46–47 (Winter 2000); S. Ohanian, "News from the Test Resistance Trail," *Phi Delta Kappan* 82(5):363–366 (January 2001); and M. Sadowski, "Are High-Stakes Tests Worth the Wager?" *Harvard Education Letter* 16(5):1–5 (September/October 2000).

[53]See, for example, T. Loveless, *The Tracking and Ability Grouping Debate, Volume 2, Number 8* (Washington, DC: Thomas B. Fordham Foundation, 1998).

- Controversy over student uniforms and dress codes.[54]
- Identification and development of programs that recognize, develop, and nurture talents in all our youths.[55]
- Low ratio of counselors to students.
- Recruiting and retaining school administrators.[56]
- Retention in grade versus social promotion.[57]
- Using standardized test scores and statistics to judge and reward the performance of schools.
- Scarcity of teachers of color to serve as role models for minority students.[58]
- School security and the related problem of weapons, crime, violence, and drugs on school campuses and in nearby neighborhoods.[59]
- Schools that are too large.[60]
- Shortage of qualified teachers, especially in certain subjects and for schools located in areas of high poverty.[61]
- The education of teachers on how to work effectively with students who may be too overwhelmed by personal problems to focus on learning and to succeed in school.
- The number of students at risk of dropping out of school, especially Hispanics for whom the dropout rate has hovered around 30 percent for more than a quarter century.[62]

Figure 1.7
Problems and issues that plague the nation's secondary schools.

[54]See, for example, K. A. White, "Do School Uniforms Fit?" *School Administrator* 57(2):36–40 (February 2000), and B. Dowling-Sendor, "Disagreeing over Dress," *American School Board Journal* 188(1):16–17, 55 (January 2001).

[55]See, for example, J. Fulkerson and M. Horvich, "Talent Development: Two Perspectives," and J. VanTassel-Baska, "The Development of Academic Talent," both in *Phi Delta Kappan* 79(10):756–759 and 760–763 (respectively) (June 1998).

[56]See, for example, M. Pierce, "Portrait of the 'Super Principal'," *Harvard Education Letter* 16(5):6–7 (September/October 2000) and D. A. Gilman and B. Lanman-Givens, "Where Have All the Principals Gone?" *Educational Leadership* 58(8):72–77 (May 2001).

[57]See, for example, K. Kelly, "Retention vs. Social Promotion: Schools Search for Alternatives," *The Harvard Education Letter* 15(1):1–3 (January/February 1999).

[58]M. S. Lewis, *Supply and Demand of Teachers of Color* (Washington, DC: ED390875, ERIC Clearinghouse on Teaching and Teacher Education, 1996). See also "The Need for Minority Teachers" in P. R. Rettig and M. Khodavandi, *Recruiting Minority Teachers: The UTOP Program* (Bloomington, IN: Fastback 436, Phi Delta Kappa Educational Foundation, 1998), pp. 13–21.

[59]Intended to alert teachers and parents to the warning signs exhibited by troubled youth is *Early Warning–Time Response: A Guide to Safe Schools*. Written by the National Association of School Psychologists and released in August, 1998, the guide is available free by calling 1(877)4ED-PUBS or from the Internet at http://www.ed.gov/offices/OSERS/OSEP/earlywrn.html.

[60]Although researchers repeatedly have reported that small schools (less than 800 students for a secondary school) are at least equal to and often superior to large ones on most measures, still in today's urban and suburban settings high school enrollments of 2,000–3,000 students are common. See K. Cotton, "School Size, School Climate, and Student Performance," *Close-Up Number 20* (Portland, OR: Northwest Regional Educational Laboratory, 1996). [On-line 2/10/00] http://www.nwrel.org/scpd/sirs/10/c020.html; "Flash Facts Issue #1-Small Schools," on the Cross City Campaign website [On-line 1/1/01] http://www.crosscity.org/pubs/flashfacts.htm; S. Klonsky and M. Klonsky, "In Chicago: Countering Anonymity Through Small Schools," *Educational Leadership* 57(1):38–41 (September 1999); M. A. Raywid, *Current Literature on Small Schools* (Charleston, WV: ED425049, ERIC Clearinghouse on Rural Education and Small Schools, 1999); and, from the Bank Street College of Education research, see "Small Schools: Great Strides," [On-line 1/1/01] http://www.bankstreet.edu. See also J. Schoenlein, "Making a Huge High School Feel Smaller," *Educational Leadership* 58(6):28–30 (March 2001).

[61]See, for example, R. M. Ingersoll, "The Problem of Out-of-Field Teaching," *Phi Delta Kappan* 79(10):773–776 (June 1998), and L. Olson, "Finding and Keeping Competent Teachers," *Quality Counts 2000: Education Week* 19(28):12–18 (January 13, 2000).

[62]See, for example, P. Kaufman et al., *Dropout Rates in the United States, 1998*. Statistical Analysis Report (Washington, DC: ED438381, National Center for Education Statistics, 2000).

SUMMARY

In beginning to plan for developing your teaching competencies, you have read an overview of today's secondary schools and of the characteristics of some of the adults who work there, of trends and practices, and of problems and issues that continue to plague our nation's schools. That knowledge will be useful in your assimilation of the content explored in chapters that follow, beginning in the next chapter with the characteristics of secondary school students, how they learn, and strategies to use to effectively work with them.

Despite the many blue-ribbon commissions, writers, and politicians that have and continue to vilify the failures of public school education, thousands of committed teachers, administrators, parents, and members of the community struggle daily, year after year, to provide students with a quality education. Throughout the remaining chapters of this text many exemplary secondary schools and school programs are recognized and identified by name.

ADDITIONAL EXERCISES

See the companion website http://www.prenhall.com/ kellough for the following exercises related to the content of this chapter:

- Attending a Parent–Teacher or Parent–Teacher–Student Organization Meeting
- Interviewing a Teacher Candidate

QUESTIONS FOR CLASS DISCUSSION

1. How would you know if you were at an exemplary school? Describe at least three characteristics of an exemplary middle school or high school. Is it possible for a traditional junior high or high school to also be an exemplary school? Explain why or why not.
2. One of the fastest growing demographic groups in the United States is the prison population. With more than one million individuals incarcerated, the United States now has the highest prison population in the world. The relationship between incarceration and education is perhaps more than coincidental: 82 percent of the country's prisoners are school dropouts. We spend roughly five times as much money to house a prisoner as we do to educate a child. Do you believe that this is the way it should be in the United States? Explain why or why not. If not, what can be done about it?
3. Identify at least six differences between the exemplary middle school and the traditional junior high school.
4. From your point of view, what societal influences affect today's youth? Are crime, gangs, drugs, and images of professional athletes and musicians among those influences? Explain the effects.
5. Select one of the Reflective Thoughts from the opening of Part I (page 2) and that is specifically related to the content of this chapter, research it and write a one page essay explaining why you agree or disagree with the thought. Share your essay with members of your class for their thoughts.
6. It is estimated that approximately half a million young people are being kept out of the public schools and taught at home, perhaps double the number that were home-schooled just a decade ago. Why do you suppose so many parents are choosing to keep their children out of school? Some school districts are reaching out to home-schooling parents and offering services such as textbooks, library privileges, and testing. What do you think about the trend toward home schooling and its effects on children? Describe how secondary schools in your geographic area are cooperating with home schooling.
7. It has been predicted that by the year 2020, for-profit corporations will run 20 to 30 percent of U.S. public schools. (See page 67 of the February 7, 2000, issue of *Business Week* magazine.) Are, in fact, for-profit public schools increasing in number from the approximately 200 such schools in the year 2000? Why or why not, do you suppose, is the for-profit public school alternative growing in popularity?
8. How do high school graduation requirements and standards compare from one high school to another and from one region of the country to another? For instance, does a high school graduate's grade point average represent the same thing regardless of the high school? What do university and college admissions officers look for today when screening high school graduates' applications for admission? Is the SAT score of greater or lesser importance today than it was a decade ago? Do you believe traditional letter grades of A, B, C, and D may become relics of the past? Explain why or why not.
9. From your current observations and fieldwork as related to this teacher preparation program, clearly identify one specific example of educational practice that seems contradictory to exemplary practice or theory as presented in this chapter. Present your explanation for the discrepancy.
10. Do you have other questions generated by the content of this chapter? If you do, list them along with ways answers might be found.

FOR FURTHER READING

Battista, M. T. "The Mathematical Miseducation of America's Youth: Ignoring Research and Scientific Study in Education." *Phi Delta Kappan* 80(6):425–433 (February 1999).

Ben-Avie, M. "Secondary Education: The School Development Program at Work in Three High Schools." *Journal of Education for Students Placed at Risk* 3(1):53–70 (1998).

Blassingame, K. M. "SCANS Success Story." *Techniques: Connecting Education and Careers* 75(1):32–34 (January 2000).

Boyer, E. *The Basic School: A Community for Learning*. Princeton, NJ: The Carnegie Foundation for the Advancement of Teaching, 1995.

Carnegie Council on Adolescent Development. *Great Transitions: Preparing Adolescents for a New Century*. Washington, DC: Author, 1995.

Cloud, J. P. "School Community Partnerships that Work." *Social Studies Review* 37(2):45–48 (Spring/Summer 1998).

Downs, A. "Successful School Reform Efforts Share Common Features." *Harvard Education Letter* 16(2):1–5 (March/April 2000).

Duke, D. L. *A Design for Alana: Creating the Next Generation of American Schools*. Fastback 468. Bloomington, IN: Phi Delta Kappa Educational Foundation, 2000.

Finn, C. E., Jr., Manno, B. V., and Vanourek, G. *Charter Schools in Action: Renewing Public Education*. Princeton, NJ: Princeton University Press, 2000.

Gallagher, J. "Teaching in the Block." *Middle Ground* 2(3):10–15 (February 1999).

George, P. S. "The Evolution of Middle Schools." *Educational Leadership* 58(4):40–44 (December 2000/January 2001).

Gibbs, W. W., and Fox, D. "The False Crisis in Science Education." *Scientific American* 281(4):87–92 (October 1999).

Glasser, W. *The Quality School*. New York: Harper & Row, 1990.

Hackman, D. G., and Waters, D. L. "Breaking Away from Tradition: The Farmington High School Restructuring Experience." *NASSP* (National Association of Secondary School Principals) *Bulletin* 82(596):83–92 (March 1998).

Hannaford, B., Fouraker, M., and Dickerson, V. "One School Tackles the Change to Block Scheduling." *Phi Delta Kappan* 82(3):212–213 (November 2000).

Hansen, D., Gutman, M., and Smith, J. "Scheduling AP Classes in a 2×4 Block Schedule." *Phi Delta Kappan* 82(3):209–211 (November 2000).

Hope, W. C. "Service Learning: A Reform Initiative for Middle Level Curriculum." *Clearing House* 72(4):236–238 (March/April 1999).

Jordan, W. J., McPartland, J. M., Legters, N. E., and Balfanz, R. "Creating a Comprehensive School Reform Model: The Talent Development High School with Career Academies." *Journal of Education for Students Placed at Risk (JESPAR)* 5(1–2):159–181 (2000).

Kohn, L. "Quest High School's Mission and the 'Fully Functioning Person.' " In Freiberg, H. J. (ed.). *Perceiving, Behaving, Becoming: Lessons Learned*. Alexandria, VA: Association for Supervision and Curriculum Development, 1999.

Kommer, D. "Is it Time to Revisit Multiage Teams in the Middle Grades?" *Middle School Journal* 30(3):28–32 (January 1999).

Lounsbury, J. H. "The Middle School Movement: A Charge to Keep." *Clearing House* 73(4):193 (March/April 2000).

Lucas, S. R. *Tracking Inequality: Stratification and Mobility in American High Schools*. New York: Teachers College Press, 1999.

Manning, M. L. "A Brief History of the Middle School." *Clearing House* 73(4):192 (March/April 2000).

National Commission on Excellence in Education. *A Nation at Risk: The Imperative for Educational Reform*. Washington, DC: Government Printing Office, 1983.

National Middle School Association. *This We Believe: Developmentally Responsive Middle Level Schools*. Columbus, OH: National Middle School Association, 1995.

Nelson, B., et al. *The State of Charter Schools, 2000*. National Study of Charter Schools. Fourth-Year Report (Washington, DC: ED437724, Office of Educational Research and Improvement, 2000).

Neuschatz, M., and McFarling, M. "Background and Professional Qualifications of High-School Physics Teachers." *Physics Teacher* 38(2):98–104 (February 2000).

O'Neil, J. "Fads and Fireflies: The Difficulties of Sustaining Change." *Educational Leadership* 57(7):6–9 (April 2000).

Queen, J. A. "Block Scheduling Revisited." *Phi Delta Kappan* 82(3):214–222 (November 2000).

Ravitch, D. *Left Back: A Century of Failed School Reform*. New York: Simon & Schuster, 2000.

Reeves, K. "The Four-Day School Week." *School Administrator* 56(3):30–34 (March 1999).

Schnitzer, D. K., and Caprio, M. J. "Academy Rewards." *Educational Leadership* 57(1):46–48 (September 1999).

Schwartz, W., ed. *New Trends in Language Education for Hispanic Students*. ERIC/CUE Digest Number 155. New York: ED442913, ERIC Clearinghouse on Urban Education, 2000.

Secretary's Commission on Achieving Necessary Skills (SCANS). *SCANS Report*. Washington, DC: United States Department of Labor, 1992.

Sizer, T. R. *Horace's School: Redesigning the American High School*. New York: Houghton Mifflin, 1992.

Slavin, R. E. "Putting the SCHOOL Back in School Reform." *Educational Leadership* 58(4):22–27 (December 2000/January 2001).

Wahlstrom, K. L. "The Prickly Politics of School Starting Times." *Phi Delta Kappan* 80(5):345–347 (January 1999).

Wise, A. E. "Creating a High-Quality Teaching Force." *Educational Leadership* 58(4):18–21 (December 2000/January 2001).

2

Celebrating and Building upon the Diverse Characteristics and Needs of Secondary School Students

The bell rings, and the students enter your classroom, a kaleidoscope of personalities, all peerless and idiosyncratic, each a packet of energy with different focuses, experiences, dispositions, and learning capacities, differing proficiencies in use of the English language—different challenges. What a challenge it is to understand and to teach 30 or so unique individuals all at once and to do it for six hours a day, five days a week, 180 days a year! What a challenge it is today to be a secondary school teacher. To prepare yourself for this challenge, consider the information provided in this chapter about the diverse characteristics and

needs of teenagers, for it is well known that their academic achievement is greatly dependent upon how well their other developmental needs are understood and satisfied.

Upon completion of this chapter you should be able to:

1. Demonstrate developing skills in recognizing, celebrating, and building upon student diversity.
2. Demonstrate an understanding of the significance of the concepts of learning modalities, learning styles, and learning capacities, and their implications for appropriate educational practice.

3. Demonstrate an understanding of the three-phase learning cycle and types of learning activities that might occur in each phase.

4. Demonstrate an awareness of appropriate curriculum options and instructional practices for specific groups of secondary school learners.

5. Demonstrate your developing knowledge of practical ways of attending to students' individual differences while working with a cohort of students.

6. Demonstrate the concept of *multilevel instruction* and how you would use multilevel instruction in your teaching.

DIMENSIONS OF THE CHALLENGE

At any age young people differ in many ways: physical characteristics, interests, home life, intellectual ability, learning capacities, motor ability, social skills, aptitudes and talents, language skills, experience, ideals, attitudes, needs, ambitions, hopes, and dreams. Having long recognized the importance of these individual differences, educators have made many attempts to develop systematic programs of individualized and personalized instruction. In the 1920s there were the "programmed" workbooks of the Winetka Plan. The 1960s brought a multitude of plans, such as IPI (Individually Prescribed Instruction), IGE (Individually Guided Education), and PLAN (Program for Learning in Accordance with Needs). The 1970s saw the development and growth in popularity of individual learning packages and the Individualized Education Program (IEP) for students with special needs. Although some of these efforts did not survive the test of time, others met with more success; some have been refined and are still being used. Today, for example, Maryville Middle School (Maryville, TN) and Celebration School (Celebration, FL) are just two of the schools who report success using personalized learning plans for all students, not only those with special needs.[1]

Furthermore, for a variety of reasons (e.g., learning styles and learning capacities, modality preferences, information-processing habits, motivational factors, and physiological factors) all persons learn in their own way and at their own rate. Interests, background, innate and acquired abilities, and a myriad of other influences, shape how and what a person will learn. From any particular learning experience no two persons ever learn exactly the same thing.

The Classroom in a Nation of Diversity and Shifting Demographics

Central to the challenge is the concept of **multicultural education,** the recognition and acceptance of students from a variety of backgrounds. An important goal of this concept

> is to educate citizens who can participate successfully in the workforce and take action in the civic community to help the nation actualize its democratic ideals . . . Schools should be model communities that mirror the kind of democratic society we envision [where] the curriculum reflects the cultures of the diverse groups within society, the languages and dialects that students speak are respected and valued, cooperation rather than competition is fostered among students and students from diverse racial, ethnic and social-class groups are given equal status.[2]

The variety of individual differences among students requires that classroom teachers use teaching strategies and tactics that accommodate those differences. To most effectively teach students who are different from you, you need skills in: (a) establishing a classroom climate in which all students feel welcome and that they can learn and are supported in doing so; (b) techniques that emphasize cooperative and social-interactive learning and that deemphasize competitive learning (topics of Chapters 8 and 9); (c) building upon students' learning styles, capacities, and modalities; and (d) strategies and techniques that have proven successful for students of specific differences. The last two are topics of this chapter.

To help you meet the challenge, a wealth of information is available. As a licensed teacher you are expected to know it all, or at least know where you can find all necessary information and to review it when needed. Certain information you have stored in memory will surface and become useful at the most unexpected times. While concerned about all students' safety and physical well being, you will want to remain sensitive to each student's attitudes, values, social adjustment, emotional well-being, and cognitive development. You must be prepared not only to teach one or more subjects but also to do it effectively with students of different cultural backgrounds, diverse linguistic abilities, and different learning styles, as well as with students who have been identified as having special needs. It is, indeed, a challenge! The statistics that follow make this challenge even more clear.

The traditional two-parent, two-child family now constitutes only about 6 percent of U.S. households. Approximately one-half of the children in the United States

---

[1]See C. McCullen, "Using Data to Change Instruction," *Middle Ground* 4(3):7–9 (February 2001), and the Celebration School website at http://www.cs.osceola.k12.fl.us.

[2]J. A. Banks, "Multicultural and Citizenship Education in the New Century," *School Administrator* 56(6):8–10 (May 1999). [On-line 3/19/00 at http://www.aasa.org/SA/may9901/htm.]

will spend some years being raised by a single parent. Between one-third and one-fourth of U.S. children go home after school to places devoid of any adult supervision. And, on any given day, it is estimated that as many as a quarter million children have no place at all to call home. Even with all the nation's resources and wealth, it is estimated that about 10 percent of the children in the United States have a mental illness[3] and about one out of every five children live in poverty, two facts that are unforgivable in the wealthiest nation in the world.[4]

By the year 2050, the U.S. population is predicted to reach 400 million (from 2001's approximately 283 million), a population boom that it is expected to be led by Hispanics and Asian Americans. Although, long before then, minority youths in the school-age population throughout the United States will average close to 40 percent. A steady increase in interracial marriages and interracial babies may challenge today's conceptions of multiculturalism and race.[5]

The United States truly is a multilingual, multiethnic, multicultural nation. In many large school districts, as many as 100 languages are represented, with as many as 20 or more different primary languages found in some classrooms. An increasing ethnic, cultural, and linguistic diversity is affecting schools all across the country, not only the large urban areas but also traditionally homogeneous suburbs and small rural communities.

The overall picture that emerges is a diverse student population that challenges teaching skills. Teachers who traditionally have used direct instruction (see Chapter 6) as the dominant mode of instruction have done so with the assumption that their students were relatively homogeneous in terms of experience, background, knowledge, motivation, and facility with the English language. However, no such assumption can be made today in classrooms of such cultural, ethnic, and linguistic diversity. *As a classroom teacher today, you must be knowledgeable and skilled in using teaching strategies that recognize, celebrate, and build upon that diversity.* In a nutshell, that is your challenge.

STYLES OF LEARNING AND IMPLICATIONS FOR TEACHING

Classroom teachers who are most effective are those who adapt their teaching styles and methods to their students, using approaches that interest the students, that

are neither too easy nor too difficult, that match the students' learning styles and learning capacities, and that are relevant to the students' lives. This adaptation process is further complicated because each student is different from every other one. All do not have the same interests, abilities, backgrounds, learning styles and capacities, or proficiency with the English language. As a matter of fact, not only do students differ from one another, but each student can change to some extent from one day to the next. What appeals to a student today may not have the same appeal tomorrow. Therefore, you need to consider both the nature of students in general (e.g., methods appropriate for a particular middle school sixth grade class are unlikely to be the same as those that work best for a group of high school seniors) and each student in particular. Since you probably have already experienced a recent course in the psychology of learning, what follows is only a brief synopsis of our current knowledge about learning.

Learning Modalities

Learning modality refers to the sensory portal (or input channel) by which a student prefers to receive sensory reception (modality preference), or the actual way a student learns best (modality adeptness). Some students prefer learning by seeing, a *visual modality;* others prefer learning through instruction from others (through talk), an *auditory modality;* while many others prefer learning by doing and being physically involved, the *kinesthetic modality,* and by touching objects, the *tactile modality.* A student's modality preference is not always that student's modality strength.

While primary modality strength can be determined by observing students, it can also be mixed and it can change as the result of experience and intellectual maturity. As one might suspect, modality integration (i.e., engaging more of the sensory input channels, using several modalities at once or staggered) has been found to contribute to better achievement in student learning. We return to this concept in Part II of this book.

Because many secondary school students, particularly young adolescents of middle school age, neither have a preference nor a strength for auditory reception, teachers in general and of middle school students in particular should severely limit their use of the lecture method of instruction, that is, of too much reliance on formal teacher talk. Furthermore, instruction that uses a singular approach, such as auditory (e.g., talking to the students), cheats students who learn better another way. This difference can affect student achievement. A teacher, for example, who only talks to the students or uses discussions day after day is shortchanging the education of learners who learn better another way, who are, for example, tactile, kinesthetic, and visual learners.

[3]N. Shute, "Children in Anguish: A Call for Better Treatment of Kids' Mental Ills" [On-line 1/8/01 at http://www.usnews.com/usnews/issue/010115/kids.htm.]

[4]H. Hodgkinson, "Educational Demographics: What Teachers Should Know," *Educational Leadership* 58(4):9 (December 2000/January 2001).

[5]See "race facts," in Hodgkinson, pp. 8–9.

Finally, if a teacher's verbal communication conflicts with his or her nonverbal messages, students can become confused and even resentful, and this too can affect their learning. And when there is a discrepancy between what the teacher says and what that teacher does, the teacher's nonverbal signal will win every time. Actions do speak louder than words! A teacher, for example, who emphasizes the importance of students getting their assignments in on time but then takes forever to read, evaluate, and return those same papers to the students is using inappropriate modeling. Or, as another example, a teacher who has just finished a lesson on the conservation of energy and does not turn off the room lights upon leaving the classroom for lunch, has, by his or her inappropriate modeling behavior, created cognitive disequilibrium and sabotaged the real purpose for the lesson. And yet another example, a teacher who asks students to not interrupt others when they are on task but who repeatedly interrupts students when they are on task, is confusing students with that teacher's contradictory words and behavior. A teacher's job is not that of confusing students. To avoid this, think through what it is that you really expect from your students and then ensure that your own verbal and nonverbal behaviors are consistent with those expectations.[6]

As a general rule, most young adolescents (students of middle school age) and many high school students prefer and learn best by touching objects, by feeling shapes and textures, by interacting with each other, and by moving things around. In contrast, learning by sitting and listening is difficult for many of them.

Some learning style traits significantly discriminate between students who are at risk of not finishing school and students who perform well. Students who are underachieving and at risk need: (a) frequent opportunities for mobility; (b) options and choices; (c) a variety of instructional resources, environments, and sociological groupings, rather than routines and patterns; (d) to learn during late morning, afternoon, or evening hours, rather than in the early morning; (e) informal seating, rather than wooden, steel, or plastic chairs; (f) low illumination, because bright light contributes to hyperactivity; and (g) tactile/visual introductory resources reinforced by kinesthetic (i.e., direct experiencing and whole-body activities)/visual resources, or introductory kinesthetic/visual resources reinforced by tactile/visual resources.[7]

Regardless of the subject(s) you intend to teach and regardless of whether it is at the middle school or high school level, you are advised to use strategies that integrate the modalities. When well designed, thematic units and project-based learning incorporate modality integration. In conclusion, when teaching any group of students of mixed learning abilities, modality strengths, language proficiency, and cultural backgrounds, integrating learning modalities is a must for the most successful teaching.

Learning Styles

Related to learning modality is **learning style,** which can be defined as independent forms of knowing and processing information. While some secondary school students may be comfortable with beginning their learning of a new idea in the abstract (e.g., visual or verbal symbolization), most need to begin with the concrete (e.g., learning by actually doing it). Many students prosper while working in groups, while others prefer to work alone. Some are quick in their studies, whereas others are slow, methodical, cautious, and meticulous. Some can sustain attention on a single topic for a long time, becoming more absorbed in their study as time passes. Others are slower starters and more casual in their pursuits but are capable of shifting with ease from subject to subject. Some can study in the midst of music, noise, or movement, whereas others need quiet, solitude, and a desk or table. The point is this: students vary in not only their skills and preferences in the way knowledge is received, but also in how they mentally process that information once it has been received. This latter is a person's style of learning.

Classifications of Learning Styles

It is important to note that learning style is *not* an indicator of intelligence, but rather an indicator of how a person learns. Although there are probably as many types of learning styles as there are individuals, David Kolb describes two major differences in how people learn: how they perceive situations and how they process information.[8] On the basis of perceiving and processing and earlier work by Carl Jung on psychological types,[9] Bernice McCarthy has described four major learning styles, which are presented in the following paragraphs.[10]

The *imaginative learner* perceives information concretely and processes it reflectively. Imaginative learners learn well by listening and sharing with others, integrating the ideas of others with their own experiences. Imaginative learners often have difficulty adjusting to traditional teaching, which depends less on classroom

---

[6]T. L. Good and J. E. Brophy, *Looking in Classrooms,* (8th ed.) (New York: Addison Wesley Longman, 2000), p. 127.
[7]R. Dunn, *Strategies for Educating Diverse Learners,* Fastback 384 (Bloomington, IN: Phi Delta Kappa Educational Foundation, 1995), p. 9.

[8]D. A. Kolb, *Experiential Learning: Experience as the Source of Learning and Development* (Upper Saddle River, NJ: Prentice Hall, 1984).
[9]C. G. Jung, *Psychological Types* (New York: Harcourt Brace, 1923).
[10]See B. McCarthy, "A Tale of Four Learners: 4MAT's Learning Styles," *Educational Leadership* 54(6):47–51 (March 1997).

interactions and students' sharing and connecting of their prior experiences. In a traditional classroom, the imaginative learner is likely to be an at-risk student.

The *analytic learner* perceives information abstractly and processes it reflectively. The analytic learner prefers sequential thinking, needs details, and values what experts have to offer. Analytic learners do well in traditional classrooms.

The *common sense learner* perceives information abstractly and processes it actively. The common sense learner is pragmatic and enjoys hands-on learning. Common sense learners sometimes find school frustrating unless they can see immediate use to what is being learned. In the traditional classroom the common sense learner is likely to be a learner who is at risk of not completing school, of dropping out.

The *dynamic learner* perceives information concretely and processes it actively. The dynamic learner also prefers hands-on learning and is excited by anything new. Dynamic learners are risk takers and are frustrated by learning if they see it as being tedious and sequential. In a traditional classroom the dynamic learner also is likely to be an at-risk student.

The Three-Phase Learning Cycle

To understand conceptual development and change, researchers in the 1960s developed a Piaget-based theory of learning where students are guided from concrete, hands-on learning experiences to the abstract formulations of concepts and their formal applications. This theory became known as the *three-phase learning cycle*.[11] Long a popular strategy for teaching science, the learning cycle is useful in other disciplines as well.[12] The three phases are: (1) the *exploratory hands-on phase,* where students can explore ideas and experience assimilation and disequilibrium that lead to their own questions and tentative answers; (2) the *invention* or *concept development phase,* where, under the guidance of the teacher, stu-

dents invent concepts and principles that help them answer their questions and reorganize their ideas (i.e., the students revise their thinking to allow the new information to fit); and (3) the *expansion* or *concept application phase,* another hands-on phase in which students try out their new ideas by applying them to situations that are relevant and meaningful to them.[13] During application of a concept the learner may discover new information which causes a change in the learner's understanding of the concept being applied. Thus, as discussed further in Chapter 9, the process of learning is cyclical.

Recent interpretations or modifications of the three-phase cycle include McCarthy's 4MAT.[14] With the 4MAT system, teachers employ a learning cycle of instructional strategies to try and reach each student's learning style. As stated by McCarthy, in the cycle, learners

sense and feel, they experience, then they watch, they reflect, then they think, they develop theories, then they try out theories, they experiment. Finally, they evaluate and synthesize what they have learned in order to apply it to their next similar experience. They get smarter. They apply experience to experiences.[15]

In this process they are likely to be using all four learning modalities.

To evince *constructivist learning theory,* that is, that learning is a process involving the active engagement of learners who adapt the educative event to fit and expand their individual world view (as opposed to the behaviorist pedagogical assumption that learning is something done to learners)[16] and to accentuate the importance of student self-assessment, some variations of the learning cycle include a fourth phase, an *assessment phase.* However, because we, the authors of this book, believe that assessment of what students know or think they know should be a continual process, permeating all three phases of the learning cycle, we reject any treatment of assessment as a self-standing phase.

---

[11]See R. Karplus, *Science Curriculum Improvement Study,* Teacher's Handbook (Berkeley, CA: University of California, 1974).

[12]See, for example, M. M. Bevevino, J. Dengel, and K. Adams, "Constructivist Theory in the Classroom: Internalizing Concepts through Inquiry Learning," *Clearing House* 72(5):275–278 (May/June 1999), on using the learning cycle in a history lesson about WWI; A. Colburn and M. P. Clough, "Implementing the Learning Cycle," *Science Teacher* 64(5):30–33 (May 1997); E. A. Kral, "Scientific Reasoning and Achievement in a High School English Course," *Skeptical Inquirer* 21(3):34–39 (May/June 1997); A. C. Rule, *Using the Learning Cycle to Teach Acronyms, a Language Arts Lesson* (ERIC Clearing House on Reading, English, and Communication, Indiana University, Bloomington, IN, ED383000, 1995); and J. E. Sowell, "Approach to Art History in the Classroom" *Art Education* 46(2):19–24 (March 1993).

[13]The three phases of the learning cycle are comparable to the three levels of thinking described variously by others. For example, in Elliot Eisner's *The Educational Imagination* (Macmillan, 1979), the levels are referred to as "descriptive," "interpretive," and "evaluative."

[14]For information about 4MAT, contact Excel, Inc., 23385 W. Old Barrington Road, Barrington, IL 60010, (847) 382-7272, or at 6322 Fenworth Ct., Agoura Hills, CA 91301, (818) 879-7442, or via the Internet at http://www.excelcorp.com/4mataboutlong.html.

[15]B. McCarthy, "Using the 4MAT System to Bring Learning Styles to Schools," *Educational Leadership* 48(2):33 (October 1990).

[16]R. DeLay, "Forming Knowledge: Constructivist Learning and Experiential Education," *Journal of Experiential Education* 19(2):76–81 (August/September 1996).

Learning Capacities:
The Theory of Multiple Intelligences

In contrast to learning styles, Gardner introduced what he calls *learning capacities* exhibited by individuals in differing ways.[17] Originally and sometimes still referred to as *multiple intelligences,* or *ways of knowing,* capacities thus far identified are:

- *Bodily/kinesthetic:* ability to use the body skillfully and to handle objects skillfully.
- *Interpersonal:* ability to understand people and relationships.
- *Intrapersonal:* ability to assess one's emotional life as a means to understand oneself and others.
- *Logical/mathematical:* ability to handle chains of reasoning and to recognize patterns and orders.
- *Musical:* sensitivity to pitch, melody, rhythm, and tone.
- *Naturalist:* ability to draw on materials and features of the natural environment to solve problems or fashion products.
- *Verbal/linguistic:* sensitivity to the meaning and order of words.
- *Visual/spatial:* ability to perceive the world accurately and to manipulate the nature of space, such as through architecture, mime, or sculpture.

As discussed earlier, and as implied in the presentation of McCarthy's four types of learners, many educators believe that many of the students who are at risk of not completing school are those who may be dominant in a cognitive learning style that is not in synch with traditional teaching methods. Traditional methods are largely of McCarthy's analytic style: information is presented in a logical, linear, sequential fashion. Traditional methods also reflect three of the Gardner types: verbal/linguistic, logical/mathematical, and intrapersonal. Consequently, to better synchronize methods of instruction with learning styles, some teachers and schools have restructured the curriculum and instruction around Gardner's learning capacities,[18] or around Sternberg's Triarchic Theory.[19]

- ERIC link to multiple intelligences resources at http://www.indiana.edu/~eric_rec/ieo/bibs/multiple.html
- Howard Gardner's Project Zero website at http://pzweb.harvard.edu/HPZpages/Whatsnew.html
- Resources on learning styles at http://www.d.umn.edu/ student/loon/acad/strat/lrnsty.html

Figure 2.1
Internet resources on learning styles and multiple intelligences.

Sternberg identifies seven metaphors for the mind and intelligence (geographic, computational, biological, epistemological, anthropological, sociological, and systems) and proposes a theory of intelligence consisting of three elements: analytical, practical, and creative.[20]

See the sample classroom scenario Using the Theory of Learning Capacities (Multiple Intelligences) and Multilevel Instruction. Internet resources on learning styles and multiple intelligences are shown in Figure 2.1.

From the preceding information about learning you must realize at least two important facts:

1. *Intelligence is not a fixed or static reality, but can be learned, taught, and developed.* This concept is important for students to understand, too. When students understand that intelligence is incremental, something that is developed through use over time, they tend to be more motivated to work at learning than when they believe intelligence is a fixed entity.[21]

2. *Not all students learn and respond to learning situations in the same way.* A student may learn differently according to the situation or according to the student's ethnicity, cultural background, or socioeconomic status.[22] A teacher who, for all students, uses only one style of teaching, or who teaches to only one or a few styles of learning, day after day is short-changing those students who learn better another way. As emphasized by Rita Dunn, when students do not learn the way we teach them, then we must teach them the way they learn.[23]

---

[17]For Gardner's distinction between "learning style" and "intelligences," see H. Gardner, "Multiple Intelligences: Myths and Messages," *International Schools Journal* 15(2):8–22 (April 1996), and the many articles in the "Teaching for Multiple Intelligences" theme issue of *Educational Leadership* 55(1) (September 1997).

[18]For example, see G. Gallagher, "Multiple Intelligences," *Middle Ground* 1(2):10–12 (October 1997).

[19]See, for example, R. J. Sternberg, "Teaching and Assessing for Successful Intelligence," and L. English, "Uncovering Students' Analytic, Practical, and Creative Intelligences: One School's Application of Sternberg's Triarchic Theory," *School Administrator* 55(1):26–27, 30–31, and 28–29 (respectively), (January 1998).

---

[20]See Sternberg, pp. 26–27, 30–31.

[21]See, for example, R. J. Marzano, "20th Century Advances in Instruction," in R. S. Brandt (ed.), *Education in a New Era,* Chap. 4, (Alexandria, VA: ASCD Yearbook, Association for Supervision and Curriculum Development, 2000), p. 76.

[22]See P. Guild, "The Culture/Learning Style Connection," *Educational Leadership* 51(8):16–21 (May 1994).

[23]Dunn, 1995, p. 30.

CLASSROOM VIGNETTE
Using the Theory of Learning Capacities
(Multiple Intelligences) and Multilevel Instruction

In one middle school classroom, during one week of a six-week thematic unit on weather, students were concentrating on learning about the water cycle. For this study of the water cycle, with the students' help the teacher divided the class into several groups of three to five students per group. While working on six projects simultaneously to learn about the water cycle: (1) one group of students designed, conducted, and repeated an experiment to discover the number of drops of water that can be held on one side of a new one-cent coin versus the number that can be held on the side of a worn one-cent coin; (2) working in part with the first group, a second group designed and prepared graphs to illustrate the results of the experiments of the first group; (3) a third group of students created and composed the words and music of a song about the water cycle; (4) a fourth group incorporated their combined interests in mathematics and art to design, collect the necessary materials, and create a colorful and interactive bulletin board about the water cycle; (5) a fifth group read about the water cycle in materials they researched from the Internet and various libraries; and (6) a sixth group created a puppet show about the water cycle. On Friday, after each group had finished, the groups shared their projects with the whole class.

MEETING THE CHALLENGE: RECOGNIZING AND PROVIDING FOR STUDENT DIFFERENCES

Assume that you are a history teacher and that your teaching schedule consists of four sections of U.S. history. Three sections meet daily for 50 minutes each day. The fourth section follows a block schedule of 100 minutes two days a week and 40 minutes for one day a week. Furthermore, assume that students at your school are tracked (as they are in many secondary schools). Of your three classes that follow the traditional schedule, one is a so-called college-prep class with 30 students. Another is a regular-education class with 35 students, three of whom have special needs because of disabilities. The third is a sheltered English class with 13 students, six Hispanics with limited proficiency in English, one student from Russia and two from the Ukraine all three of whom have very limited proficiency in English, and four Southeast Asians, two with no ability to use English. The class that follows the block schedule is a regular education class of 33 English-proficient students. Again, for all four sections, the course is U.S. history. Will one lesson plan using lecture and teacher-directed discussion as the primary instructional strategies work for all four sections? The answer is an emphatic no! How do you decide what to do? Before you finish this book we hope the answer to that question will become clear to you.

First consider the following general guidelines, most of which are discussed in further detail in later chapters as designated.

Instructional Practices That Provide for Student Differences: General Guidelines

To provide learning experiences that are consistent with what is known about ways of learning and knowing, consider the recommendations that follow and refer to them during the preactive phase of your instruction.

- As frequently as is appropriate, and especially for skills development, plan the learning activities so they follow a step-by-step sequence from concrete to abstract.
- Communicate with students in a clear, direct, and consistent manner.
- Concentrate on using student-centered instruction, by using project-centered learning, discovery and inquiry strategies, simulations, and role-play.
- Establish multiple learning centers within the classroom.
- Maintain high expectations, although not necessarily identical, for every student; establish high standards and teach toward them without wavering (emphasized throughout the book).
- Make learning meaningful by integrating learning with life, academic with vocational, helping each student successfully make the transitions from one level of learning to the next, one level of schooling to the next, and from school to life beyond formal schooling (emphasized throughout the book).
- Provide a structured learning environment with regular and understood procedures.

- Provide ongoing and frequent monitoring of individual student learning (*formative assessment* as discussed throughout the book).
- Provide variations in meaningful assignments, with optional due dates, that are based on individual student abilities and interests.
- Use direct instruction to teach to the development of observation, generalization, and other thinking and learning skills.
- Use interactive computer programs and multimedia.
- Use multilevel instruction.
- Use reciprocal peer coaching and cross-age tutoring.
- Use small-group and cooperative learning strategies.
- With students, collaboratively plan challenging and engaging classroom learning activities and assignments.

Because social awareness is such an important and integral part of a student's experience, exemplary secondary school programs and many of their practices are geared toward some type of social interaction. Indeed, learning is a social enterprise among learners and their teachers. Although many of today's successful instructional practices rely heavily on social learning activities and interpersonal relationships, each teacher must be aware of and sensitive to individual student differences. For working with specific learners, consider the guidelines that follow and refer back to these guidelines often during your preactive phase of instruction.

Recognizing and Working with Students with Disabilities

Students with disabilities (referred to also as *exceptional students* and **special needs students**) include those with disabling conditions or impairments in any one or more of the following categories: mental retardation, hearing, speech or language, visual, emotional, orthopedic, autism, traumatic brain injury, other health impairment, or specific learning disabilities. To the extent possible, students with special needs must be educated with their peers in the regular classroom. Public Law 94-142, the Education for All Handicapped Children Act (EAHCA) of 1975, mandates that all children have the right to a free and appropriate education, as well as to nondiscriminatory assessment. (Public Law 94-142 was amended in 1986 by P.L. 99-457, in 1990 by P.L. 101-476 at which time its name was changed to Individuals with Disabilities Education Act (IDEA), and it was amended in 1997 by P.L. 105-17.) Emphasizing normalizing the educational environment for students with disabilities, this legislation requires provision of the least-restrictive environment (LRE) for these students. An LRE is an environment that is as normal as possible.

Teachers today know that students with disabilities fall along a continuum of learner differences rather than as a separate category of student.[24] Because of their wide differences, students identified as having special needs may be placed in the regular classroom for the entire school day, called *full inclusion* (as is the trend[25]). Those students may also be in a regular classroom the greater part of the school day, called *partial inclusion,* or only for designated periods. Although there is no single, universally accepted definition of the term, **inclusion** is the concept that students with disabilities should be integrated into general education classrooms regardless of whether they can meet traditional academic standards.[26] (The term inclusion has largely replaced the use of an earlier and similar term, mainstreaming.) As a classroom teacher you will need information and skills specific to teaching learners with special needs who are included in your classes.

Generally speaking, teaching students who have special needs requires more care, better diagnosis, greater skill, more attention to individual needs, and an even greater understanding of the students. The challenges of teaching students with special needs in the regular classroom are great enough that to do it well you need specialized training beyond the general guidelines presented here. At some point in your teacher preparation you should take one or more courses in working with special needs learners in the regular classroom.

When a student with special needs is placed in your classroom, your task is to deal directly with the differences between this student and other students in your classroom. To do this, you should develop an understanding of the general characteristics of different types of special needs learners, identify the student's unique needs relative to your classroom, and design lessons that teach to different needs at the same time, called **multilevel teaching,** or **multitasking,** as exemplified in Figure 2.1. Remember that just because a student has been identified as having one or more special needs does not preclude that person from being gifted or talented.

---

[24]A. Meyer and D. H. Rose, "Universal Design for Individual Differences," *Educational Leadership* 58(3):39–43 (November 2000), p. 40.
[25]See, for example, M. L. Yell, "The Legal Basis of Inclusion," *Educational Leadership* 56(2):70–73 (October 1998). For information about education law as related to special education students, see the website at http://www.access.digex.net/~edlawinc/.
[26]E. Tiegerman-Farber and C. Radziewicz, *Collaborative Decision Making: The Pathway to Inclusion* (Upper Saddle River, NJ: Merrill/Prentice Hall, 1998), p. 12–13.

Congress stipulated in P.L. 94-142 that an Individualized Educational Program (IEP) be devised annually for each special needs child. According to that law, an IEP is developed for each student each year by a team that includes special education teachers, the child's parents or guardians, and the classroom teachers. The IEP contains a statement of the student's present educational levels, the educational goals for the year, specifications for the services to be provided and the extent to which the student should be expected to take part in the regular education program, and the evaluative criteria for the services to be provided. Consultation by special and skilled support personnel is essential in all IEP models. A consultant works directly with teachers or with students and parents. As a classroom teacher, you may play an active role in preparing the specifications for each special needs student assigned to your classroom, and assume a major responsibility for implementing the program.

Guidelines for Working with Special Needs Students in the Regular Classroom

Although the guidelines represented by the paragraphs that follow are important for teaching all students, they are especially important for working with special needs students.

Familiarize yourself with exactly what the special needs of each learner are. Privately ask the special needs student whether there is anything he or she would like for you to know, or anything specific that you can do to facilitate the student's learning.

Adapt and modify materials and procedures to the special needs of each student. For example, a student who has extreme difficulty sitting still for more than a few minutes will need planned changes in learning activities. When establishing student seating arrangements in the classroom, give preference to students according to their special needs. Try to incorporate into lessons activities that engage all learning modalities–visual, auditory, tactile, and kinesthetic. Be flexible in your classroom procedures. For example, allow the use of tape recorders for note taking and test taking when students have trouble with the written language.

Provide high structure and clear expectations by defining the learning objectives in behavioral terms. Teach students the correct procedures for everything. Break complex learning into simpler components, moving from the most concrete to the abstract, rather than the other way around. Check frequently for student understanding of instructions and procedures, and for comprehension of content. Use computers and other self-correcting materials for drill and practice and for provision of immediate and private feedback to the student.

Develop your **withitness** (discussed in Chapters 3 and 4), which is your awareness of everything that is going on in the classroom, at all times, monitoring students for signs of restlessness, confusion, frustration, anxiety, and off-task behaviors. Be ready to reassign individual learners to different activities as the situation warrants. Established classroom learning centers can be a big help.

Have all students maintain assignments for the week or some other period of time in an assignment book or in a folder that is kept in their notebooks. Post assignments in a special place in the classroom and frequently remind students of assignments and deadlines.

Maintain consistency in your expectations and in your responses. Special needs learners, particularly, can become frustrated when they do not understand a teacher's expectations and when they cannot depend on a teacher's reactions.

Plan interesting activities to bridge learning, activities that help the students connect what is being learned with their world. Learning that connects what is being learned with the learner's real world helps to motivate students and to keep them on task.[27]

Plan questions and questioning sequences and write them into your lesson plans. Plan questions that you ask special needs learners so that they are likely to answer them with confidence. Use signals to let students know that you are likely to call on them in class (e.g., prolonged eye contact or mentioning your intention to the student before class begins). After asking a question, give the student adequate time to think and respond. Then, after the student responds, build upon the student's response to indicate that the student's contribution was accepted as being important.

Provide for and teach toward student success. Offer students activities and experiences that ensure each individual student's success and mastery at some level. Use of student portfolios can give evidence of progress and help in building student confidence and self-esteem.

Provide guided or coached practice. Provide time in class for students to work on assignments and projects. During this time, you can monitor the work of each student while looking for misconceptions, thus ensuring that students get started on the right track.

Provide help in the organization of students' learning. For example, give instruction in the organization of notes and notebooks. Have a three-hole punch available in the classroom so students can put papers into their notebooks immediately thus avoiding disorganization and their loss of papers. During class presentations use

---

[27]See, for example, D. Deshler et al., "Making Learning Easier: Connecting New Knowledge to Things Students Already Know," *Teaching Exceptional Children* 33(4):82–85 (March/April 2001.)

an overhead projector with transparencies; students who need more time can then copy material from the transparencies. Ask students to read their notes aloud to each other in dyads (pairs), thereby aiding their recall and understanding, and encouraging them to take notes for meaning rather than for rote learning. Encourage and provide for peer support, peer tutoring or coaching, and cross-age teaching. Ensure that the special needs learner is included in all class activities to the fullest extent possible.

Recognizing and Working with Students of Diversity and Differences

Quickly determine the language and ethnic groups represented by the students in your classroom. A major problem for recent newcomers, as well as some ethnic groups, is learning a second (or third or fourth) language. While in many schools it is not uncommon for more than half the students to come from homes where the spoken language is not English, standard English is a necessity in most communities of this country if a person is to become vocationally successful and enjoy a full life. Learning to communicate reasonably well in English can take an immigrant student at least a year and probably longer; some authorities say three to seven years. By default, then, an increasing percentage of teachers are teachers of English language learning. Helpful to the success of teaching students who are English language learners (ELLs), that is, who have limited proficiency in English language usage, are the demonstration of respect for students' cultural backgrounds, long-term teacher–student cohorts (as in looping, for example), and the use of active and cooperative learning.[28]

There are numerous programs specially designed for English as a second language (ESL) learners. Most use the acronym LEP (limited English proficiency) with five number levels, from LEP 1 that designates non-English-speaking, although the student may understand single sentences and speak simple words or phrases in English, to LEP 5, sometimes designated FEP (fluent English proficiency), for the student who is fully fluent in English, although the student's overall academic achievement may still be less than desired because of language or cultural differences.[29]

Some schools use a "pullout" approach, where part of the student's school time is spent in special bilingual classes and the rest of the time the student is placed in regular classrooms. In some schools, LEP students are placed in academic classrooms that use a simplified or "sheltered" English approach. Regardless of the program, specific techniques recommended for teaching ELL students include:

- Allowing more time for learning activities than one normally would.
- Allowing time for translation by a classroom aide or by a classmate and allowing time for discussion to clarify meaning, encouraging the students to transfer into English what they already know in their native language.
- Avoiding jargon or idioms that might be misunderstood. See the scenario that follows.

A Humorous Scenario Related to Idioms: A Teachable Moment.

While Elina was reciting she had a little difficulty with her throat (due to a cold) and stumbled over some words. The teacher jokingly commented, "That's okay Elina, you must have a horse in your throat." Quickly, Mariya, a recent immigrant from the Ukraine, asked, "How could she have a horse in her throat?" The teacher ignored Mariya's question. Missing this teachable moment, he continued with his planned lesson.

- Dividing complex or extended language discourse into smaller, more manageable units.
- Giving directions in a variety of ways.
- Giving special attention to key words that convey meaning and writing them on the board.
- Maintaining high expectations of each learner.
- Reading written directions aloud and then writing the directions on the board.
- Speaking clearly and naturally but at a slower-than-normal pace.
- Using a variety of examples and observable models.
- Using simplified vocabulary but without talking down to students.[30]

Additional Guidelines for Working with Language-Minority Students

While they are becoming literate in English language usage, LEP students can learn the same curriculum in the various disciplines as native English-speaking students. Although the guidelines presented in the following paragraphs are important for teaching all students, they are

---

[28]See P. Berman et al., *School Reform and Student Diversity, Volume II: Case Studies of Exemplary Practices for LEP Students* (Berkeley, CA: National Center for Research on Cultural Diversity and Second Language Learning, 1995).

[29]D. R. Walling, *English as a Second Language: 25 Questions and Answers,* Fastback 347 (Bloomington, IN: Phi Delta Kappa Educational Foundation, 1993), p. 12–13.

[30]Walling, p. 26.

especially important when working with language-minority students.

Present instruction that is concrete and that includes the most direct learning experiences possible. Use the most concrete (least abstract) forms of instruction.

Build upon (or connect with) what the students already have experienced and know. Building upon what students already know, or think they know, helps them to connect their knowledge and construct their understandings.

Encourage student writing. One way is to use student journals. Two kinds of journals appropriate when working with LEP students are dialogue journals and response journals. *Dialogue journals* are used for students to write anything that is on their minds, usually on the right page. Teachers, parents, and classmates then respond on the left page, thereby "talking with" the journal writers. *Response journals* are used for students to write (record) their responses to what they are reading or studying.

Help students learn the vocabulary. Assist the ELL students in learning two vocabulary sets: the regular English vocabulary needed for learning and the new vocabulary introduced by the subject content. For example, while learning science a student is dealing with both the regular English language vocabulary and the special vocabulary of science.

Involve parents or guardians or older siblings. Students whose primary language is not English may have other differences about which you will also need to become knowledgeable. These differences are related to culture, customs, family life, and expectations. To be most successful in working with language minority students, you should learn as much as possible about each student. To this end it can be valuable to solicit the help of the student's parent, guardian, or even an older sibling. Parents (or guardians) of new immigrant children are usually truly concerned about the education of their children and may be very interested in cooperating with you in any way possible. In a study of schools recognized for their exemplary practices with language-minority students the schools were recognized for being "parent friendly," that is, for welcoming parents and guardians in a variety of innovative ways.[31]

Plan for and use all learning modalities. As with teaching students in general, with language-minority students you need to use multisensory approaches—learning activities that involve students in auditory, visual, tactile, and kinesthetic learning activities.

Use small group cooperative learning. Cooperative learning strategies are particularly effective with language-minority students because they provide opportunities for students to produce language in a setting that is less threatening than is speaking before the entire class.

Use the benefits afforded by modern technology. For example, computer networking allows the language-minority students to write and communicate with peers from around the world as well as to participate in "publishing" their classroom work.

Additional Guidelines for Working with Students of Diverse Backgrounds

To be compatible with, and be able to teach, students who come from backgrounds different from yours, you need to believe that, given adequate support, all students *can* learn regardless of gender, social class, physical characteristics, language, and ethnic or cultural backgrounds. You also need to develop special skills that include those in the following guidelines, each of which is discussed in detail in other chapters. To work successfully and most effectively with students of diverse backgrounds, you should:

• Build the learning around students' individual learning styles. Personalize learning for each student, much like what is by using the IEP with special-needs learners. Involve students in understanding and in making important decisions about their own learning, so that they feel ownership (i.e., a sense of empowerment and connectedness) of that learning. As was said at the beginning of this chapter some schools today report success using personalized learning plans for all students, not only those with special needs.

• Communicate positively with every student and with the student's parents or guardians, learning as much as you can about the student and the student's culture. Involve parents, guardians, and other members of the community in the educational program so that all have a sense of ownership and responsibility and feel positive about the school program.

• Establish and maintain high expectations, although not necessarily the same expectations, for each student. Both you and your students must understand that intelligence is not a fixed entity, but a set of characteristics that, through a feeling of "I can" and with proper coaching, can be developed.

• Teach to individuals by using a variety of strategies to achieve an objective or by using a number of different objectives at the same time (multilevel teaching).

• Use techniques that emphasize collaborative and cooperative learning—that deemphasize competitive learning.

[31]C. Minicucci et al., "School Reform and Student Diversity," *Phi Delta Kappan* 77(1):77–80 (September 1995), p. 78.

Recognizing and Working with Students Who Are Gifted

Historically, educators have used the term *gifted* when referring to a person with identified exceptional ability in one or more academic subjects, and *talented* when referring to a person with exceptional ability in one or more of the visual or performing arts.[32] Today, however, the terms more often are used interchangeably, which is how they are used for this book, that is, as if they are synonymous.

Sometimes, unfortunately, in the regular classroom gifted students are neglected.[33] At least part of the time, it is likely to be because there is no singularly accepted method for identification of these students. In other words, students who are gifted in some way or another may go unidentified as such. For placement in special classes or programs for the gifted and talented, school districts traditionally have used grade point averages and standard intelligence quotient (IQ) scores. On the other hand, because IQ testing measures linguistic and logical/mathematical aspects of giftedness (refer to earlier discussion in this chapter—Learning Capacities: The Theory of Multiple Intelligences), it does not account for others and thus gifted students sometimes are unrecognized; they also are sometimes among the students most at risk of dropping out of school.[34] It is estimated that between 10 and 20 percent of school dropouts are students who are in the range of being intellectually gifted.[35]

To work most effectively with gifted learners, their talents first must be identified. This can be done not only by using tests, rating scales, and auditions but also by observations in the classroom, out of the classroom, and from knowledge about the student's personal life. With those information sources in mind, here is a list of indicators of superior intelligence:[36]

- Ability to assume adult roles and responsibilities at home or at work
- Ability to cope with school while living in poverty

- Ability to cope with school while living with dysfunctional families
- Ability to extrapolate knowledge to different circumstances
- Ability to lead others
- Ability to manipulate a symbol system
- Ability to reason by analogy
- Ability to retrieve and use stored knowledge to solve problems
- Ability to think and act independently
- Ability to think logically
- Creativity and artistic ability
- Strong sense of self, pride, and worth
- Understanding of one's cultural heritage

To assist you in understanding gifted students that may or may not have been identified as being gifted, here are some types of students and the kinds of problems to which they may be prone, that is, personal behaviors that may identify them as being gifted but academically disabled, bored, and alienated.[37]

- *Antisocial* students, alienated by their differences from peers, may become bored and impatient troublemakers.
- *Creative, high achieving* students often feel isolated, weird, and depressed.
- *Divergent thinking* students can develop self-esteem problems when they provide answers that are logical to them but seem unusual and off-the-wall to their peers. They may have only a few peer friends.
- *Perfectionists* may exhibit compulsive behaviors because they feel as though their value comes from their accomplishments. When their accomplishments do not live up to expectations—heir own, their parents', or their teacher's—anxiety and feelings of inadequacy arise. When other students do not live up to the gifted student's high standards, alienation from those students is probable.
- *Sensitive* students who also are gifted may become easily depressed because they are so aware of their surroundings and of their differences.
- *Students with special needs* may be gifted. Attention deficit disorder, dyslexia, hyperactivity, and other learning disorders sometimes mask giftedness.
- *Underachieving* students can also be gifted students but fail in their studies because they learn in ways that are seldom or never challenged by classroom teachers. Although often expected to excel in everything they do, most gifted students can be underachievers in some areas. Having high expectations of themselves, underachievers tend to be highly critical of themselves, develop a low self-esteem, and can become indifferent and even hostile.

---

[32]See the discussion in G. Clark and E. Zimmerman, "Nurturing the Arts in Programs for Gifted and Talented Students," *Phi Delta Kappan* 79(10):747–751 (June 1998).

[33]See, for example, J. F. Feldhusen, "Programs for the Gifted Few or Talent Development for the Many?" *Phi Delta Kappan* 79(10):735–738 (June 1998).

[34]C. Dixon, L. Mains, and M. J. Reeves, *Gifted and At Risk,* Fastback 398 (Bloomington, IN: Phi Delta Kappa Educational Foundation, 1996), p. 7.

[35]S. B. Rimm, "Underachievement Syndrome: A National Epidemic," in N. Colangelo and G. A. Davis (eds.), *Handbook of Gifted Education,* 2d ed. (Needham Heights, MA: Allyn & Bacon, 1997), p. 416.

[36]S. Schwartz, *Strategies for Identifying the Talents of Diverse Students,* ERIC/CUE Digest, Number 122 (New York:ED410323, ERIC Clearinghouse on Urban Education, May 1997).

[37]Adapted from Dixon, Mains, and Reeves, p. 9–12, by permission of the Phi Delta Kappa Educational Foundation.

Curriculum Tracking: Not a Viable Option

All students, not only those who have been identified as gifted, need a challenging academic environment. Although grouping and tracking students into classes based on interest and demonstrated ability is still widely practiced (such as college bound and non-college bound curriculum tracks in high school), an overwhelming abundance of sources in the literature adamantly oppose the homogeneous grouping of students according to ability, or *curriculum tracking,* as it has been known. Grouping and tracking do not seem to increase overall achievement of learning, but they do promote inequity.[38]

Although many, perhaps most, research studies lead one to conclude that tracking as has been traditionally practiced should be discontinued because of its discriminatory and damaging effects on students, many secondary schools continue to use it. Direct examples are counseling students into classes according to evidence of ability and the degree of academic rigor of the program. Tracking also results indirectly by designating certain classes and programs as "academic" or "accelerated" and others as "non-academic" or "standard" and allowing students some degree of latitude to choose, either partly or wholly, from one or the other.

Meaningful Curriculum Options: Multiple Pathways to Success

Because of what is now known about learning and intelligence, the trend today is to assume that each student, to some degree and in some area of learning and doing, has the potential for giftedness, and to provide sufficient curriculum options, or multiple pathways, so each student can reach those potentials. That is the reason why, for example, in a school's mission statement (see Figure 1.1 of Chapter 1) today you will likely find reference to the school's belief that all students can succeed. Clearly, achievement in school increases, students learn more, enjoy learning and remember more of what they have learned when individual learning capacities, styles, and modalities are identified and accommodated.[39]

To provide relevant curriculum options, a trend is to eliminate from the school curriculum what have traditionally been the lower and general curriculum tracks and instead provide curriculum options to try and assure success for all students. Most experts agree that schools should be organized around nontracked, thematic programs of student design to prepare all students for entry ultimately into both post-secondary education and high-skill employment through intellectually rigorous practical education.

While attempting to diminish the discriminatory and damaging effects on students believed to be caused by tracking and homogeneous ability grouping, educators have devised and are refining numerous other seemingly more productive ways of attending to student differences, of providing a more challenging but supportive learning environment, and of stimulating the talents and motivation of each student. Because the advantage gained from utilizing a combination of responsive practices concurrently is generally greater than is the gain from using any singular practice by itself, in many instances in a given school the practices overlap and are used simultaneously. These practices are shown in Figure 2.2, and most are discussed in various places in this book. Check the index for topic locations.

- Advisory programs and adult advocacy relationships for every student
- Allowing a student to attend a high school class while still in middle school or to attend college classes while still in high school
- Allowing a student to skip a traditional grade level, thereby accelerating the time a student passes through the grades
- Community service learning
- Cooperative learning in the classroom
- Curriculum compacting
- Extra effort to provide academic help
- High expectations for all students
- Individualized educational plans and instruction
- Integrating new technologies into the curriculum
- Interdisciplinary teaming and thematic instruction
- Mid-year promotions
- Peer and cross-age teaching
- Personal problems assistance provision on campus
- Problem-centered learning
- Second opportunity recovery strategies
- Specialized schools and flexible block schedules
- Ungraded or multiage grouping
- Within-class and across discipline student-centered projects

Figure 2.2
Multiple pathways to success: Productive ways of attending to student differences, of providing a more challenging learning environment, and of stimulating the talents and motivation of each student.

---

[38]See J. Oakes et al., "Equity Lessons from Detracking Schools," Chap. 3 (pp. 43–72) in A. Hargreaves (ed.), *Rethinking Educational Change With Heart and Mind* (Alexandria, VA: ASCD 1997 Yearbook, Association for Supervision and Curriculum Development, 1997).
[39]Dixon, Mains, and Reeves, p. 21.

Additional Guidelines for Working with Gifted Students

When working in the regular classroom with a student identified as having special gifts and talents, you are advised to:

- Collaborate with students in some planning of their own objectives and activities for learning.
- Emphasize skills in critical thinking, problem solving, and inquiry.
- Identify and showcase the student's special gift or talent.
- Involve the student in selecting and planning activities, encouraging the development of the student's leadership skills.
- Plan assignments and activities that challenge the students to the fullest of their abilities. This does *not* mean overloading them with homework or giving identical assignments to all students. Rather, carefully plan so that the students' time spent on assignments and activities is quality time on meaningful learning.
- Provide in-class seminars for students to discuss topics and problems that they are pursuing individually or as members of a learning team.
- Provide independent and dyad learning opportunities. Gifted and talented students often prefer to work alone or with another gifted student.
- Use *curriculum compacting*, a process that allows a student who already knows the material to pursue enriched or accelerated study.[40] Plan and provide optional and voluntary enrichment activities. Learning centers, special projects, and computer and multimedia activities are excellent tools for provision of enriched learning activities.
- Use preassessments (diagnostic evaluation) for reading level and subject content achievement so that you are better able to prescribe objectives and activities for each student.

Recognizing and Working with Students Who Take More Time but Are Willing to Try

Secondary school students who are slower to learn typically fall into one of two categories: (1) those who try to learn but simply need more time to do it, and (2) those who do not try, referred to variously as underachievers, recalcitrant, or reluctant learners.

Practices that work well with students of one category are often not those that work well with those of the second—making life difficult for a teacher of 30 students, half who try and half who don't.[41] It is worse still for a teacher of 30 students where some try but need time, one or two are academically talented, one or two have special needs, a few are LEP students, and several not only seem unwilling to try but are also disruptive in the classroom.

Remember that just because a student is slow to learn doesn't mean that the student is less intelligent; some students just plain take longer, for any number of reasons. The following guidelines may be helpful when working with a student who is slow but willing to try:

- Adjust the instruction to the student's preferred learning style, which may be different from yours and from other students in the group.
- Be less concerned with the amount of content coverage than with the student's successful understanding of content that is covered.
- Discover something the student does exceptionally well, or a special interest, and try to build on that.
- Emphasize basic communication skills, such as speaking, listening, reading, and writing, to ensure that the student's skills in these areas are sufficient for learning the intended content.
- Help the student learn content in small, sequential steps with frequent checks for comprehension.
- If necessary, help the student to improve his or her reading skills, such as pronunciation and word meanings.
- If using a single textbook, be certain that the reading level is adequate for the student; if it is not, then use other, more appropriate reading materials for that student.
- Maximize the use of in-class, on-task work and cooperative learning, with close monitoring of the student's progress. Avoid relying too much on successful completion of traditional out-of-class assignments unless you can supply coached guidance to the student in the classroom.
- Vary the instructional strategies, using a variety of activities to engage the visual, verbal, tactile, and kinesthetic modalities.
- When appropriate, use frequent positive reinforcement, with the intention of increasing the student's self-esteem.

---

[40]See, for example, J. S. Renzulli and S. M. Reis, "Talent Development Through Curriculum Differentiation," *NASSP (National Association of Secondary School Principals) Bulletin* 82(595:61–64 (February 1998).

[41]R. D. Kellough, "The Humanistic Approach: An Experiment in the Teaching of Biology to Slow Learners in High School-An Experiment in Classroom Experimentation," *Science Education* 54(3):253–262 (1970).

Recognizing and Working with Recalcitrant Learners

For working with recalcitrant learners you can use many of the same guidelines from the preceding list, except that you should understand that the reasons for these students' behaviors may be quite different than those from the other category of slow learners. Slower-learning students who are willing to try may be slow because of their learning style or because of genetic factors, or a combination of those and any number of other reasons. They are simply slower at learning. But they can and will learn. Recalcitrant learners, on the other hand, may be generally quick and bright thinkers but reluctant even to try because of a history of failure, a history of boredom with school, a poor self-concept, severe personal problems that distract from school, or any variety and combination of reasons, many of which are psychological in nature.

Whatever the case, you need to know that a student identified as being a slow or recalcitrant learner might, in fact, be quite gifted or talented in some way, but because of personal problems, may have a history of increasingly poor school attendance, poor attention to schoolwork, poor self-confidence, and an attitude problem. Consider the following guidelines when working with recalcitrant learners:

- As the school year begins, learn as much about each student as you can. Be cautious in how you do it, though, because many of these students will be suspicious of any interest you show in them. Be businesslike, trusting, genuinely interested, and patient. A second caution: although you learn as much as possible about each student, what has happened in the past is history. Use that information not as ammunition, something to be held against the student, but as insight to help you work more productively with the student.
- Avoid lecturing to these students; it won't work.
- Early in the school term, preferably with the help of adult volunteers (e.g., professional community members as mentors has worked well at helping change the student's attitude from rebellion to one of hope, challenge, and success), work out a personalized education program with each student.
- Engage the students in learning by using interactive media, such as the Internet.
- Engage the students in active learning with real-world problem solving and perhaps community service projects.
- Forget about trying to "cover the subject," concentrating instead on student learning of some things well. A good procedure is to use thematic teaching and divide the theme into short segments. Because school attendance for these students is sometimes sporadic, try to individualize their assignments so that they can pick up where they left off and move through the course in an orderly fashion even when they have been absent excessively. Try to assure some degree of success for each student.
- Help students develop their studying and learning skills, such as concentrating, remembering, and comprehension. Mnemonics, for example, is a device these students respond to positively, and are often quick to create their own.
- If using a single textbook, see if the reading level is appropriate; if it is not, then for that student discard the book and select other, more appropriate reading materials.
- Make sure your classroom procedures and rules are understood at the beginning of the school term and be consistent about following them.
- Maximize the use of in-class, on-task work and cooperative learning, with close monitoring of the student's progress. Do not rely on successful completion of traditional out-of-class assignments unless the student gets coached guidance from you before leaving your classroom.
- Use simple language in the classroom. Be concerned less about the words the students use and the way they use them and more about the ideas they are expressing. Let the students use their own idioms without being too hard on grammar and syntax. Always take care, though, to use proper and professional English yourself.
- When appropriate, use frequent positive reinforcement, with the intention of increasing the student's sense of personal worth. When using praise for reinforcement, however, try to praise the deed rather than the student.

TEACHING TOWARD POSITIVE CHARACTER DEVELOPMENT

In what appears to be a cycle, arising in the 1930s, again in the late 1960s, and in the 1990s and continuing today, interest is high in the development of students' values, especially those of honesty, kindness, respect, and responsibility. Today this interest is in what some refer to as *character education*. Whether defined as ethics, citizenship, moral values, or personal development, character education has long been part of public education in this country.[42] Stimulated by a perceived need to

---

[42]See K. Burrett and T. Rusnak, *Integrated Character Education.* Fastback 351 (Bloomington, IN: Phi Delta Kappa Educational Foundation, 1993).

reduce students' antisocial behaviors and to produce more respectful and responsible citizens, many schools and districts recently have or are developing curricula in character education with the ultimate goal of "developing mature adults capable of responsible citizenship and moral action."[43]

You can teach toward positive character development in two general ways: by providing a conducive classroom atmosphere where students actively and positively share in the decision making; and, by being a model that students can proudly emulate. Acquiring knowledge and developing understanding can enhance the learning of attitudes. Nevertheless, changing an attitude is often a long and tedious process, requiring the commitment of the teacher and the school, assistance from the community, and the provision of numerous experiences that will guide students to new convictions. Here are some specific practices, most of which are, as indicated, discussed further in later chapters:

- Build a sense of community, with shared goals, optimism, cooperative efforts, and clearly identified and practiced procedures for reaching those goals.
- Collaboratively plan with students action- and community-oriented projects that relate to curriculum themes; solicit parent/guardian and community members to assist in projects.

- Teach students to negotiate; practice and develop skills in conflict resolution, skills such as empathy, problem solving, impulse control, and anger management.[44]
- Share and highlight examples of class and individual cooperation in serving the classroom, school, and community (discussed throughout the book).
- Make student service projects visible in the school and community[45].
- Promote higher-order thinking about value issues through the development of students' skills in questioning.
- Sensitize students to issues and teach skills of conflict resolution through debate, role play, simulations, and creative drama.

See Figure 2.3 for resources on character education. When compared with traditional instruction, one characteristic of exemplary instruction today is the teacher's encouragement of dialogue among students in the classroom to debate, discuss, and explore their own ideas. Modeling the very behaviors we expect of teachers and students in the classroom is, as promised in the Preface, a constant theme throughout this book. One purpose of Exercise 2.1 is, in a similar fashion, to start that dialogue. Complete that exercise now.

---

[43]Burrett and Rusnak, p. 15.

[44]See D. W. Johnson and R. T. Johnson, *Reducing School Violence Through Conflict Resolution* (Alexandria, VA: Association for Supervision and Curriculum Development, 1995).
[45]See J. Van Til, "Facing Inequality and the End of Work," *Educational Leadership* 54(6):78–81 (March 1997).

- Character Education Institute, 8918 Tesoro Drive, San Antonio, TX 78217 (800) 284-0499.
- Character Education Partnership, 918 16th Street NW, Suite 501, Washington, DC 20006 (800) 988-8081. Website: http://www.characer.org.
- Character Education Resources, PO Box 651, Contoocook, NH 03229.
- Developmental Studies Center, 111 Deerwood Place, San Ramon, CA 94583 (415) 838-7633.
- Ethics Resource Center, 1120 G Street NW, Washington, DC 20005 (202) 434-8465.
- Jefferson Center for Character Education, 202 S. Lake Avenue, Pasadena, CA 91101 (818) 792-8130.
- Josephson Institute of Ethics, 310 Washington Boulevard, Marina Del Rey, CA 90292 (310) 306-1868.
- C. Martin and J. Lehr, *The START Curriculum: An Interactive and Experiential Curriculum for Building Strong Character and Healthy Relationships in Middle and High Schools* (Minneapolis, MN: Educational Media Corporation, 1999). For information via e-mail: emedia@usinternet.com.
- Texas Education Agency, *Building Good Citizens for Texas: Character Education Resource Guide. High School* (Austin, TX: Author, 2000). Available on-line at http://www.tea.state.tx.us.
- Texas Education Agency, *Building Good Citizens for Texas: Character Education Resource Guide. Middle School* (Austin, TX: Author, 2000). Available on-line at http://www.tea.state.tx.us.

Figure 2.3
Selected resources on character education.

FOR YOUR NOTES

EXERCISE 2.1

Reflecting upon My Own Secondary School Experiences

Instructions: The purpose of this exercise is to share with others in your class your reflections on your own secondary school experiences.

1. What secondary schools did you attend? Where? When? Were they public or private?_____

_____

_____

_____

_____

2. What do you remember most from your secondary school experiences? _____

_____

_____

_____

_____

3. What do you remember most about your teachers? _____

_____

_____

_____

_____

4. What do you remember most about the other students? _____

_____

_____

_____

_____

5. What do you remember most about your overall school life?_____

_____

_____

_____

_____

6. What grade (or class) do you specifically recall with fondness? Why?_____

_____

_____

_____

_____

_____

7. What grade (or class) would you particularly like to forget? Why?_____

_____

_____

_____

_____

_____

8. What do you recall about peer and parental pressures? _____

_____

_____

_____

_____

_____

9. What do you recall about your own feelings during those years? _____

_____

_____

_____

_____

_____

10. Is there any other aspect of your life as a secondary school student you wish to share with others? _____

_____

_____

_____

_____

_____

SUMMARY

As a classroom teacher you must acknowledge that students in your classroom have different ways of receiving information and different ways of processing that information—different ways of knowing and of constructing their knowledge. These differences are unique and important, and as you will learn in Part II of this book, are central considerations in curriculum development and instructional practice.

You must try to learn as much as you can about how each student learns and processes information. But because you can never know everything about each student, the more you dialogue with your colleagues, vary your teaching strategies, and assist students in integrating their learning, the more likely you are to reach more students more often. In short, to be an effective classroom teacher you should: (a) learn as much about your students and their preferred styles of learning as you can, (b) develop an eclectic style of teaching that is flexible and adaptable, and (c) help students make bridges or connections between their lives and all that is being learned.

ADDITIONAL EXERCISE

See the companion web site http://www.prenhall.com/ kellough for the following exercise related to the content of this chapter:

• Interviewing a Secondary School Student

QUESTIONS FOR CLASS DISCUSSION

1. Explain why knowledge of learning styles, learning capacities, and teaching styles is or should be important to you.
2. Kelly, a social studies teacher, has a class of 33 eighth graders, who during her lecture, teacher-led discussion, and recitation lessons are restless and inattentive, creating for her a problem in classroom management. At Kelly's invitation, the school psychologist tests the students for learning modality and finds that of the 33 students, 29 are predominately kinesthetic learners. Of what value is this information to Kelly? Describe what, if anything, Kelly should try as a result of this information.
3. What concerns you most about teaching the diversity of students you are likely to have in a classroom? Share those concerns with others in your class. Categorize your group's concerns. By accessing an Internet teacher bulletin board, find out what kinds of problems classroom teachers are currently concerned about. Are block scheduling, thematic instruction, grading, group learning, and classroom management high in frequency of concern? Are the concerns of teachers as expressed on the Internet

similar to yours? As a class, devise a plan and time line for attempting to ameliorate your concerns.
4. Give an example of how and when you would use multi-level instruction. Of what benefit is its use to students? to teachers? What particular skills must a teacher have in order to effectively implement multilevel instruction?
5. Select one of the "Reflective Thoughts" from the opening of Part I (page 2) that is specifically related to the content of this chapter, research it, and write a one-page essay explaining why you agree or disagree with the thought. Share your essay with members of your class for their thoughts.
6. Explain why many educators and researchers discourage the use of curriculum tracking and homogeneous grouping. What strategies are recommended in the place of traditional tracking?
7. Prepare an argument either for or against the following statement and present your argument to your classmates: Since teaching about citizenship, ethics, and moral values is unavoidable, a school should plan and do it well.
8. Describe any prior concepts you held that have changed as a result of your experiences with this chapter. Describe the changes.
9. From your current observations and fieldwork as related to this teacher preparation program, clearly identify one specific example of educational practice that seems contradictory to exemplary practice or theory as presented in this chapter. Present your explanation for the discrepancy.
10. Do you have other questions generated by the content of this chapter? If you do, list them along with ways answers might be found.

FOR FURTHER READING

Alexakos, K. "Inclusive Classrooms." *Science Teacher* 68(3): 40–43 (March 2001).

Allsopp, D. H. "Using Modeling, Manipulatives, and Mnemonics with Eighth-Grade Students." *Teaching Exceptional Children* 32(2):74–81 (November/December 1999).

Bempechat, J. "Learning from Poor and Minority Students Who Succeed in School." *Harvard Education Letter* 15(3):1–3 (May/June 1999).

Brandt, R., and Perkins, D. N. "The Evolving Science of Learning." (Chap. 7, pp. 159 184). In *Education in a New Era*. R. S. Brandt (ed.), Alexandria, VA: ASCD Yearbook, Association for Supervision and Curriculum Development, 2000.

Brisk, M. E., and Harrington, M. M. *Literacy and Bilingualism: A Handbook for ALL Teachers*. Mahwah, NJ: Lawrence Erlbaum, 2000.

Campbell, L., and Campbell, B. *Multiple Intelligences and Student Achievement: Success Stories From Six Schools*. Alexandria, VA: Association for Supervision and Curriculum Development, 1999.

D'Arcangelo, M. "How Does the Brain Develop? A Conversation with Steven Peterson." *Educational Leadership* 58(3):68–71 (November 2000).

Gabriel, A. E. "Brain-Based Learning: The Scent of the Trail." *Clearing House* 72(5):288–290 (May/June 1999).

Gibb, G. S., and Dyches, T. T. *Guide to Writing Quality Individualized Education Programs: What's Best for Students with Disabilities?* Needham Heights, MA: Allyn & Bacon, 2000.

Jenkins, J. M. "Strategies for Personalizing Instruction. Part Two." *International Journal of Educational Reform* 8(1):83–88 (January 1999).

Jensen, E. "Moving with the Brain in Mind." *Educational Leadership* 58(3):34–37 (November 2000).

Kwon, Y-J, and Lawson, A. E. "Linking Brain Growth with the Development of Scientific Reasoning Ability and Conceptual Change during Adolescence." *Journal of Research in Science Teaching* 37(1):44–62 (January 2000).

Lawton, M. "The 'Brain-Based' Ballyhoo." *Harvard Education Letter* 15(4):5–7 (July/August 2000).

Loveless, T. *The Tracking Wars: State Reform Meets School Policy.* Washington, DC: Thomas B. Fordham Foundation, 1999.

Meyer, A., and Rose, D. H. "Universal Design for Individual Differences." *Educational Leadership* 58(3):39–43 (November 2000).

Morgan, R. R., Ponticell, J. A., and Gordon, E. E. *Rethinking Creativity.* Fastback 458. Bloomington, IN: Phi Delta Kappa Educational Foundation, 2000.

Nieto, S. *The Light in Their Eyes: Creating Multicultural Learning Communities.* New York: Teachers College Press, 1999.

O'Brien, T. C. "Parrot Math." *Phi Delta Kappan* 80(6):434–438 (February 1999).

Presseisen, B. Z. (ed.). *Teaching for Intelligence: A Collection of Articles.* Arlington Heights, IL: Skylight, 1999.

Reed, D. F., and Rossi, J. A. "My Three Wishes: Hopes, Aspirations, and Concerns of Middle School Students." *Clearing House* 73(3):141–144 (January/February 2000).

Renzulli, J. S., and Richards, S. "Meeting the Enrichment Needs of Middle School Students." *Principal* 79(4):62–63 (March 2000).

Rieck, W. A., and Wadsworth, D. E. D. "Foreign Exchange: An Inclusion Strategy," *Intervention in School and Clinic* 35(1):22–28 (September 1999).

Sapon-Shevin, M. "Schools Fit for All." *Educational Leadership* 58(4):34–39 (December 2000/January 2001).

Schwartz, W. (ed.). *New Trends in Language Education for Hispanic Students.* ERIC/CUE Digest Number 155. New York: ED442913, ERIC Clearinghouse on Urban Education, 2000.

Silver, H. F., Strong, R. W., and Perini, M. J. *So Each May Learn: Integrating Learning Styles and Multiple Intelligences.* Alexandria, VA: Association for Supervision and Curriculum Development, 2000.

Smith, F. "Just a Matter of Time." *Phi Delta Kappan* 82(8): 572–576 (April 2001).

Stephen, C. *Working with Second Language Learners: Answers to Teachers' Top Ten Questions.* Westport, CT: Heinemann, 2000.

Stodolsky, S. S., and Grossman, P. L. "Changing Students, Changing Teaching." *Teachers College Record* 102(1): 125–172 (February 2000).

Stronge, J. H., and Reed-Victor, E. (eds). *Educating Homeless Students: Promising Practices.* (Larchmont, NY: Eye on Education, 2000).

Wagmeister, J., and Shifrin, B. "Thinking Differently, Learning Differently." *Educational Leadership* 58(3):45–48 (November 2000).

Wallace, M. "Nurturing Nonconformists." *Educational Leadership* 57(4):44–46 (December 1999/January 2000).

II

PLANNING FOR INSTRUCTION

Part II responds to your needs concerning:

- An effective, safe, and supportive classroom environment.
- Collaborative planning.
- Curriculum integration and the interdisciplinary thematic unit.
- Dealing with content and issues that may be controversial.
- Direct and indirect instruction.
- Documents that provide guidance for curriculum planning.

- Domains of learning.
- Goals, objectives, and learning outcomes.
- Levels of curriculum planning.
- National Educational Goals and national curriculum standards.
- Productive ways to start the school term.
- Selected legal guidelines for the classroom teacher.
- Selecting and developing appropriate learning activities.
- Selecting and sequencing content.
- Using textbooks.

A caring and responsive learning environment has as its sole purpose that of helping all students to make the transitions necessary to succeed in school and in life.

As a teacher, you are a professional who deals in matters of human relations and who must exercise professional judgment.

A classroom teacher is responsible for planning at three levels—the year, the units, and the lessons—with critical decisions to be made at each level. Failing to prepare is preparing to fail.

The obsolescence of many past instructional practices has been substantiated repeatedly by those researchers who have made recent studies of exemplary educational practices.

Your challenge is to use performance-based criteria with a teaching style that encourages the development of intrinsic sources of student motivation, and that provides for coincidental learning, which goes beyond what might be considered as predictable, immediately measurable, and minimal expectations.

Teachers must be clear about what it is they expect their students to learn and about the kind of evidence needed to verify their learning. They also need to communicate those things to the students so they are clearly understood.

Curriculum integration refers to a way of thinking, a way of teaching, and a way of planning and organizing the instructional program so the discrete disciplines of subject matter are related to one another in a design that (a) matches the developmental needs of the learners and (b) helps to connect their learning in ways that are meaningful to their current and past experiences.

No matter what else you are prepared to teach, you are primarily a teacher of literacy and of thinking, social, and learning skills.

3

Content and Curriculum

Curriculum is the heart of why we do what we do as teachers and what we
leave as our legacy to the next generation.
—Susan Kovalik 1997

As we move forward in this textbook, we will be discussing the topics of Content and Curriculum within the context of Block Scheduling. Why do we feel this is important? It is because block scheduling works. R.Bruce Williams and Steven E. Dunn have summarized a decade of material on contemporary brain research and argue that block scheduling is compatible with what we know today of how to utilize students' multiple intelligences as well as we know about how students learn best. This chapter examines the weighty issue of content coverage and makes several practical suggestions for using the gift of time that alternative scheduuling provides to delve deeply into content.

DUCK OR COVER?

Perhaps one of the most exciting aspects of moving to, or even considering, block scheduling is that it stimulates dialogue about prioritizing curricular content. As is becoming increasingly clear, it is necessary to balance the massive amounts of content prescribed by fifty states, thirteen of the national subject-area associations, and district mandates with the instructional time available to present it. More and more curriculum is being added, causing many teachers to feel they are drowning in a sea of information (Chapman 1993). Numerous school systems burden teachers with the untenable notion that "covering" vast amounts of material is the only way to prepare students to score well on the standardized tests and entrance examinations that ensure their respective academic futures. A profound realignment of the conventional paradigm is needed—from one in which content is "covered" to one in which students are given the time and tools to draw their own meaning from the material. While teachers may not cover as much content after such an adjustment, the content that is covered is really the students' own material in a way not previously occurring. "By covering less content but learning it better, students in the long run have an overall greater level of mastery" (Wyatt 1996, 17). Students are then better prepared for lifelong learning instead of just for the next big test.

Ultimately, educators are left with three options: increase instructional time, decrease the breadth of the content in favor of more depth, or integrate content area study to address multiple content standards simultaneously.

Multiple class changes per day deeply cut into instructional time, as does time spent reviewing material presented the previous day. Moving to a block schedule can actually provide more time for learning within the confines of the conventional six-and-one-half-hour school day. Extending the school day or school year and eliminating electives from the course offerings are perhaps some of the most controversial ideas for creating more time.

PRIORITIES: QUALITY VERSUS QUANTITY

Robert J. Marzano and John S. Kendall (1998) of the Mid-Continent Regional Educational Laboratory have identified, after an inventory of the 116 documents constructed by thirteen subject-area associations, "200 separate standards that address 3,093 more specific topics, commonly referred to as benchmarks" for grades K through 12. They have extrapolated from this number and the average number of days per year that a student attends school in the United States (180) that conventional instruction in this content would require

twenty-one years of education (eight more than the thirteen years students now attend). In addition, the core curriculum is more demanding than ever. At the same time, mandates have added additional material to be covered: contemporary health topics, conflict management, violence prevention, and other subjects. Teachers are being called upon to make choices in what they teach and how they teach to make the most of the allotted time.

As illustrated in Figure 3.1 "Prioritizing Curriculum in the Block," selective abandonment, jigsawing, graphic organizers, curriculum frameworks, curriculum mapping, and curriculum integration are ways that teachers can confidently prioritize curricular content.

Selective Abandonment

What can a teacher do to help students work smarter, not harder, in the flood of information? One answer, suggested by Arthur Costa (1999), is the *selective abandonment* of portions of content. Carefully and thoughtfully selected content can be cut without negatively impacting student learning. In fact, pruned content often results in fuller student understanding. Selective abandonment, or streamlining the curriculum, calls for serious examination of the curriculum and deciding what to keep and what to leave out.

Marzano and Kendall (1998) suggest that school districts survey local community members and organizations to determine what content standards, and which benchmarks for attaining those standards, are priorities to that particular community or district. They contend that a grassroots local approach to identify standards would be able to do what the subject-matter experts could not: identify a workable set of standards in terms of their practical application. Such an approach would indeed involve the community substantially but may not be palatable to some educational professionals. A more realistic model would be for teachers to take the data derived from the completed surveys and use that to influence team decisions on curriculum and content.

On the other hand, Rettig and Canady (1996) assert that defining curricular priorities is the role and responsibility of the teacher. The expertise of the teacher is needed to discern what is absolutely crucial for the student versus what can be eliminated or lightly acknowledged. Because of the immensity and difficulty of this task, it is most appropriate for departments or teams of teachers to work together. Many perspectives generate a more balanced result than that of only one teacher working on a course alone. The first step for teacher teams in this process is to ask the following questions in relation to potential course material:

- What is the essential concept?
- What content material best facilitates the understanding of what is essential?

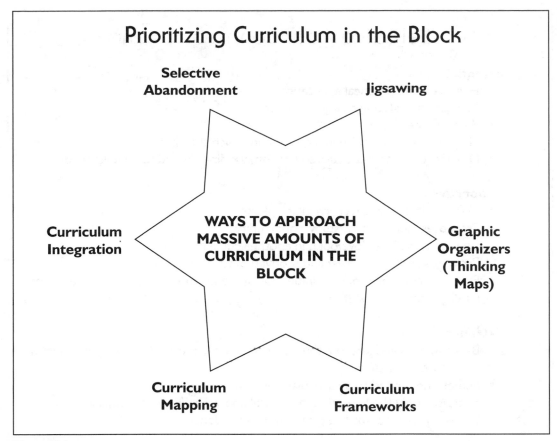

Figure 3.1

- What activities employing what teaching tools are most appropriate?
- What are the essential concepts and standards?

The specific criteria set forth in Figure 3.2 can be used to make decisions about which material to incorporate into lesson and unit plans. Potential topics can be tested to see into which of three categories they might fall: Essential, Supportive, or Extraneous.

Essential

Curriculum items in this category are deemed absolutely necessary by the practitioner(s) for the knowledge base of the student. This category looks to the future. It raises the question of what students will need ten, fifteen, and twenty-five years from now on their journey of lifelong learning. This category also keeps an eye on the standardized tests and includes information that the teacher knows from experience will be included on examinations of this kind.

Supportive

This category includes material that can be covered in passing or touched upon lightly. It may be a simple concept or an event that needs a brief reference and might also include material that could be divided, studied, and shared by student teams in a class "jigsaw" strategy.

Extraneous

Such material is not unimportant; it may actually be useful and helpful. However, when compared with other material, it is not *as* helpful or not *as* useful.

CONTENT DELIVERY STRUCTURES

Many critics of block scheduling are deeply concerned that there is less emphasis on crucial facts and information because in some situations there will be fewer minutes spent in class than in traditional schedules. They would go so far as to talk about the "dumbing down" of curriculum (Rettig and Canady 1996). Precisely the opposite can occur. Although a traditional class may "cover" nine chapters over the course of a semester, static instructional techniques coupled with the brusqueness of the bell schedule may actually cause students to retain only about five chapters worth of meaning because they have not had the time or experiences necessary to make the material part of long-term memory. On the other hand, when only seven chapters are presented using brain-compatible pedagogy, the students may full well be able to grasp and internalize six-and-one-half chapters worth of meaning, resulting in a net gain of a chapter and one half over the traditional schedule. This is, of

Selective Abandonment Criteria

Essential
- Has a real-life practical application
- Fundamental step in a larger process
- Based in the present
- Helps students function in the world in which they live
- District- or system-articulated benchmark directly tied to a vital concept

Supportive
- Collaterally linked to a curricular objective
- Promotes independent study opportunity
- Can be more fully developed in another curricular area
- Provokes student interest and motivation to "learn more"
- Provides additional opportunities for students to develop a wide range of intelligences

Extraneous
- Based in knowledge about theory or the past without practical application in the future or present
- Fun but not linked to a curricular concept
- Exercises only the logical/mathematical and verbal/linguistic intelligences
- Doesn't promote positive group interdependence

Figure 3.2

course, an oversimplification, but it does help make clear that the streamlined curriculum as taught in an extended time format is not a digest or abbreviation and most certainly is not a "dumbing down."

Jigsawing

There are a huge number of cooperative learning strategies, but the focus here is on those that pertain to the issue of curriculum in block scheduling. A commonly used strategy in cooperative learning has been called jigsawing. David Johnson and Roger Johnson (1986) outline this strategy in detail in their book *Circles of Learning*. Material to be studied is divided either among members of a group who then teach it to other group members, or among groups in the class, who then present it to the whole class.

The benefits of the jigsaw technique are several. Most importantly, it can be used in that essential first step of gathering a lot of information and evaluating that information for key insights or critical points. It is only a preliminary step, not a processing or culminating step, which is why it is best used in the gather phase of a Four-Phase lesson plan. The technique allows students to organize the information they reviewed into

words and phrases that make sense to them in order to share the information with other students. Jigsawing is also helpful in reducing the amount of reading or data gathering that might be daunting or overwhelming for some students. The use of expert groups also allows students to have ownership of the information and feel a sense of responsibility to share that information with other students.

Teachers can use jigsawing as a means of...

- introducing students to concepts
- requiring students to become teachers
- teaching students how to read information, synthesize key points, and explain the information to others
- providing students with a learning technique of reading information first for concepts and then returning to it for more details and specifics.

Jigsawing doesn't works for all situations, however, particularly if the information is sequential and each part is necessary to understand the subsequent parts of the material, for instance studying the periodic table in chemistry. As with any cooperative learning strategy, jigsawing requires clear group roles and precise instructions for what the process and the product need to be.

Choosing the material strategically and then passing it out to cooperative learning groups to study and then present to the whole class is one way to get a class familiar with a body of material.

Graphic Organizers

Another commonly used strategy in cooperative learning is the application of graphic organizers. Graphic organizers are visual tools that help students organize and process a great deal of information. They are sometimes called cognitive maps, visual displays, or advance organizers. Graphic organizers can help to make relationships and connections visible or concrete for students. Sometimes they even reveal what students are thinking or even *how* students are thinking. These visual tools can help launch the student into a writing assignment, a project, a debate, a role-play skit, or many other activities. Many consultants and teachers have adapted and named different types of graphic organizers. If you are interested in learning more about visual representations of learning, you may go to the following websites.

http://curry.edschool.virgina.edu/go/edis771/notes/
    graphicorganizers/graphic
http://www.thinkingmaps.com
http://www.graphic.org/goindex.html

(See chapter 4 for a full discussion of the types and uses of graphic organizers.)

Curricular Frameworks

A curricular framework, or curriculum model, is the way a curriculum unit is organized, while instructional strategies (discussed in chapter 4) are ways the material can be presented. The curriculum frameworks are project-oriented curricula, thematic units, performance-based learning, problem-based learning, service learning, and case studies. Brain-compatible learning recognizes that various disciplines relate common information for the brain to recognize and organize. Teachers need to look at the entire course to be taught (the whole semester, trimester, or mini session) and then plan out how and where they can use these curriculum frameworks. Such organizing structures can help to connect several disciplines together. Resultant interconnections can even shorten curriculum time, as similar material is taught only once instead of over and over in different curriculum disciplines. Students are then able to experience relationships and see the real-life connections and applications to material being taught.

The concept of civil rights can encompass:

- The civil rights movement of the 1960s
- African-American history
- Gandhi's nonviolent resistance movement in India

- Thoreau's treatise on civil disobedience
- Protest literature
- Current events issues such as gender-based discrimination
- Recent African struggles
- Songs and art that embody the civil rights theme

In the above example, the disciplines of history, social studies, civics, languages arts, art, and music, are all linked proving a curricular framework is a powerful tool. Such sophisticated teaching takes work as does anything worthwhile. Planning and communicating time for teachers is essential to success. Most block scheduling plans allow for ninety minutes or more of teacher planning per day, far in excess of the measly forty-five to fifty minutes provided for in the traditional structure. The classroom that incorporates interdisciplinary themes and connecting concepts requires a cooperation and connection among teaching staff that the very structure of the classroom and the school day has hindered up until now. Further, rigid, inflexible time schedules and the traditional isolation of teachers, perhaps especially high school teachers, have permitted very few connections among those teaching in similar disciplines, let alone among teachers of totally different disciplines. Block scheduling may catalyze new connections among the staff that will genuinely help to make content material more relevant to how students experience real life.

Many teachers are discovering ways to link disciplines together and save time while enriching the educational experience in the process. It is much more lifelike and brain-compatible to present material in as connected a way as it occurs in everyday life. "Students don't often see the connections among separate and distinct subjects….We need holistic ways to present information and get students involved in learning so they can apply what they've learned to their lives" (Fogarty and Stoehr 1995, 21).

The following six curricular frameworks illustrate some of the ways a unit can be structured to promote meaningful learning:

Project-Oriented Curricula

Projects focus the curriculum and the learning around actually creating and making something to demonstrate the learning. Examples include:

- Social Studies—a project on a continent or a country could call for the creation of a travel brochure.
- Language Arts—a student might construct a model of a house in which a story takes place, making sure that the model accurately reflects the details the author included.
- Algebra—a student could create models of various curves that visually represent their equations.
- Physics—a student could construct various weights and pulleys or electronic circuitry.

Note that all of the above examples involve very hands-on projects that call for authentic demonstration of knowledge and learning. A block format permits time for the teacher to present the material followed by time for the students to work on the projects.

Thematic Units

A rethinking of the common practice of isolating content area curricula is called for. Such isolation is antithetical to how everyone experiences life. There are other ways to organize information than by placing it in discrete categories like language arts, algebra, chemistry, social studies, music, and physical education. A better way, a more brain-compatible way, is to organize curricular concepts around themes or issues such as

LIFE	GLOBAL CHALLENGES
• Birth	• Polluted Environment
• Freedom	• Racism
• Relationships	• Genocide
• Patterns	• Hunger
• Careers	• Shrinking Natural Resources
• Travel	• War
• The Shrinking Globe	• Fragmented Families
• Entertainment	• Forced Migration of Peoples
• Heroes and Heroines	

Figure 3.3 "Circles Make the World Go 'Round" illustrates the way in which the sample lesson plan *Circles and Cycles,* found at the end of this chapter, works into a thematic unit.

If one chose to, the material in every content area could be taught in such a way. In time, with more communication among the teaching staff, teachers will discover more and more opportunities. Ninety minutes of planning time a day (available in the 4 by 4 Plan) or every other day (in a Block 8 Plan) allows for at least occasional meetings among staff who want to explore themes and connecting concepts.

A theme could be developed among various content areas or just within a teacher's own content discipline. It is the intent of thematic units to create themes that will grab the interest of students and teachers. Thematic units encourage teachers to prioritize and order content and precisely define directions for students. Students can do research based on the theme to construct a paper or a cooperative team presentation or project. An extended time format allows the students time to do some of the research within class time, but many students immersed in thematic instruction will continue their process of discovery beyond the class time.

Performance-Based Learning

Performances involve some authentic execution. Musical, dance, and dramatic performances are perhaps obvious, but others can include:

- rewriting and performing a scene with a different spin from a Shakespearean play
- demonstrating a laboratory experiment
- showing a correct wrestling move
- cooking regional or traditional dishes
- acting out a skit in a foreign language

In each of these examples the students demonstrate what they have learned by the act of doing something. An extended time format demands this kind of shift to performance as another way to vary the class time and permits this direct way of embodying what has been learned.

Problem-based Learning

Student meaning making in problem-based learning begins with a very messy problem or issue. Discussion and research are needed in order to grasp what the real problem might be. Then more research is called for before students can come up with some solutions. The challenge for teachers is creating a problem that will genuinely grab the attention of the students in the classroom and calls for awareness of what the lives of the students are really like. A problem in a government course might be: "You are running for political office for a congressional district in the inner city. How will you persuade the legislature to pass your recommended gun control legislation? How will you sell this position to the people you want to vote for you?" An extended time format again permits the students enough class time to do some of the research and group discussion.

Service Learning

Some teachers are linking the curricula to a defined service project that makes a concrete and visible impact in the school or community. Cleaning up a river, turning an unsightly plot of ground into an attractive flower garden, reading to senior citizens, peer teaching, and mentoring younger students are all examples of service projects. It is important for the teacher to make sure that the service project is genuinely connected to curriculum content, standards, and/or benchmarks and also based on real needs. Because many of these service projects are carried out within class time, extended time formats allow for these beautifully. Service learning can have very positive and lasting influences on students' standards of conduct, attitudes, and understanding of course content.

Case Studies

The use of a dramatic and compelling narrative is the kick-off for a particular unit of study. The narrative raises the concept or issue in a way that grabs the emotions of the students. Then through discussion and further research the students come to some resolution or position relative to the concept or issue. Again the case study

Circles Make the World Go 'Round

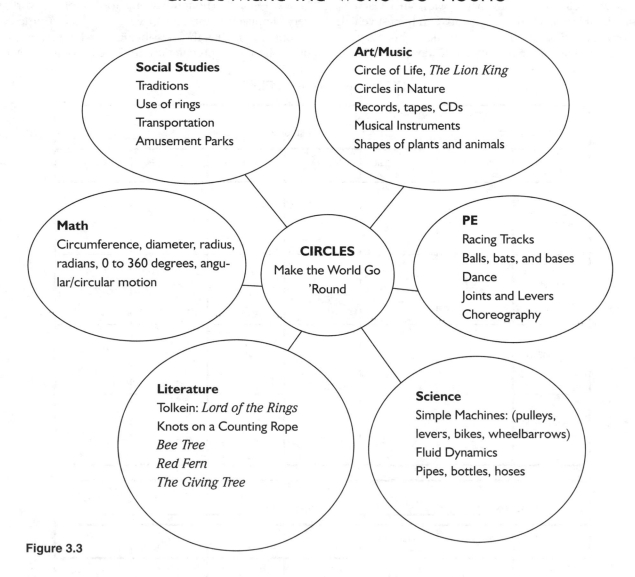

Figure 3.3

could raise an issue as complex and deep as racism or as personal as lying. A math class could use an issue in a case study as a springboard for studying statistics or graphs. A chemistry class could use an issue in a case study to delve into environmental pollution. An extended time format permits the research time and cooperative group dialogue time that is not impossible but much more difficult in more traditional time formats.

Each of the six frameworks discussed provide ingenious ways of hooking the student into participating in the learning experience. Each finds a way to grab the student both in the intellect and in the emotions, at once building upon and sparking student motivation. When these approaches are presented well, the student ends up doing far more work than a teacher ever thought possible. Curricular frameworks can help create a genuine community of learners in the school environment.

Again, the more teacher teams collaborate in talking these through, the more winning insights can be gleaned relative to how such frameworks are carried out in the classroom. The nature of student involvement, the research tasks implied with each model, and finally the demand for teamwork requires more time than forty to fifty minutes.

Curriculum Mapping

Heidi Hayes Jacobs (1997) developed curriculum mapping as a way to help teachers get a hold of what other teachers are doing and to help them grasp what they themselves are doing in the classroom. If one were to imagine a huge matrix, across the top one would lay out the months of the school year or semester and down the left side would be categories such as particular curriculum units, needed skills, projects, guidelines and objectives, etc. (see Figure 3.4). After teachers fill out the matrices, they share their "curriculum maps" with other teachers. "Not only did people find the calendar an honest vehicle for communication about the curriculum, but they reported it was far more efficient than reading through lists of curriculum guidelines from other departments" (Hayes Jacobs 1997, 2). Though it seems too simple to work, its very simplicity is the reason why it works. "Curriculum mapping amplifies the possibilities for long-range planning, short-term preparation, and clear communication"

CURRICULUM MAPPING

Course_____ Instructor_____

	AUGUST	SEPTEMBER	OCTOBER	NOVEMBER	DECEMBER	JANUARY
CONTENT						
SKILLS						
ASSESSMENT						
STANDARDS						

Course_____ Instructor_____

	JANUARY	FEBRUARY	MARCH	APRIL	MAY	JUNE
CONTENT						
SKILLS						
ASSESSMENT						
STANDARDS						

Figure 3.4

(Hayes Jacobs 1997, 5). Software packages such as Lotus notes make such an overview and true networking even more practical and manageable.

Mapping curriculum restores the big picture to a teacher, to a teacher team, or even to a whole district. The big picture is desperately needed in an environment that often focuses on minute details. Mapping curricula can reveal where duplications are occurring in how curriculum is actually taught in the classroom. In this way, it can be a tool to save time by avoiding unnecessary teaching of the same material in different courses or in different grades. While it is best for whole districts to help integrate curriculum by using curriculum mapping, even a single school, a single team, or an individual teacher could make use of this tool (Hayes Jacobs 1997). Curriculum mapping can help give the teacher a sense of control over the content, which is particularly critical when block scheduling is first introduced. Curriculum mapping can be a useful tool to aid the teacher in the transition to the new time organization that block scheduling represents. Finally, curriculum mapping can reveal ways that curriculum can be integrated, thus aiding in the process of making those connections for both teacher and student that can improve the long-term retention of curricular material.

Curriculum Integration

Some ten different models for integrating the curriculum have been identified: fragmented, connected, nested, sequenced, shared, webbed, threaded, integrated, immersed, and networked. Many of these models can be implemented with only two teachers. Obviously, more powerful connections can be made when more than two teachers work together in the process of integration. Figure 3.5 "Toward an Integrated Curriculum" provides definition for these types and examples.

Connections not only make better use of time but foster the kind of learning that sticks with students and enables them to see and make real-life applications. To venture into ways to integrate the curriculum is to question the way in which curricula is organized. "We continue to add things, but we seldomly take things out. How can we possibly teach everything when information today doubles every year and a half? One answer is restructuring schools from the inside out by reviewing the curriculum and setting priorities" (Fogarty and Stoehr 1995, 21).

Brain-Compatible Curriculum

Once the curricular content is identified it must be articulated in terms of brain-compatibility. No matter what group identified the content, Susan Kovalik (1997) asserts that it is a fundamental responsibility of the district to articulate the curriculum in terms of brain-compati-

bility. Brain-compatible curriculum is constructed and expressed in terms of concepts. Once identified at the local level, appropriate concepts must have at their core student success in life instead of student success in later schooling. She further suggests that curriculum is defined as brain-compatible if it...

- is conceptual versus "factoid" based
- has flexibility with direction
- includes the main idea (standard)
- has a rationale for inclusion, including the desired end result
- contains clearly defined concepts, making it clear to the practitioner what is meant and not meant
- includes expected student performance levels (criteria)

ACTIVE INSTRUCTIONAL MATERIAL

A dynamic classroom does not use just one or two types of instructional materials. Instead, it makes use of a variety of instructional materials at one time or another. Luckily, the block class schedule allows time for students to use multiple sources, one of which is the computer. (See Appendix for electronic resources that enhance student learning via the Internet.) Traditional, static educational approaches rely heavily upon students gathering information from printed material and textbooks. Such sources have a clearly delineated beginning, middle, and end, which reinforces a linear way of thinking that may help students be successsful in school. For success in real life however, persons must process information and ideas from several sources. Electronic media offers the advantage of delivering information in a way that is more lifelike and allows students to construct a structure for the information that has personal meaning and that may not always be linear. Resources that allow students to bring their own experiences to bear on information, to discover new understandings, and to construct personal meaning are patently brain-compatible. In addition, electronic resources allow learning to be customized for the learner, which supports brain-comaptible learner-centered education (Tapscott 1999).

Sample Lesson Plan #3 illustrates a way that teachers can move beyond the textbook and the blackboard to illustrate a concept. In addition, it shows how the theme of circles is a magnet for content coverage. As presented here, *Circles That Cycle* is a lesson for elementary students, but teachers at any level can readily create a lesson, or even a unit, on circles (see Figure 3.3 "Circles Make the World Go 'Round" for ideas.) Teachers have a variety of options for developing student skills in measurement, understanding circular motion, and scientific investigation.

TOWARD AN INTEGRATED CURRICULUM

Ten Views for Integrating the Curricula: How Do You See It?

1

Fragmented
Periscope—one direction; one sighting; narrow focus on single discipline

Description
The traditional model of separate and distinct disciplines, which fragments the subject areas.

Example
Teacher applies this view in Math, Science, Social Studies, Language Arts OR Sciences, Humanities, Fine and Practical Arts.

2

Connected
Opera glass—details of one discipline; focus on subtleties and interconnections

Description
Within each subject area, course content is connected topic to topic, concept to concept, one year's work to the next, and relates idea(s) explicitly.

Example
Teacher relates the concept of fractions to decimals, which in turn relates to money, grades, etc.

3

Nested
3-D glasses—multiple dimensions to one scene, topic, or unit

Description
Within each subject area, the teacher targets multiple skills: a social skill, a thinking skill, and a content-specific skill.

Example
Teacher designs the unit on photosynthesis to simultaneously target consensus seeking (social skill), sequencing (thinking skill), and plant life cycle (science content).

4

Sequenced
Eyeglasses—varied internal content framed by broad, related concepts

Description
Topics or units of study are rearranged and sequenced to coincide with one another. Similar ideas are taught in concert while remaining separate subjects.

Example
English teacher presents an historical novel depicting a particular period while the History teacher teaches that same historical period.

5

Shared
Binoculars—two disciplines that share overlapping concepts and skills

Description
Shared planning and teaching take place in two disciplines in which overlapping concepts or ideas emerge as organizing elements.

Example
Science and Math teachers use data collection, charting, and graphing as shared concepts that can be team-taught.

6

Webbed
Telescope—broad view of an entire constellation as one theme, webbed to the various elements

Description
A fertile theme is webbed to curriculum contents and disciplines; subjects use the theme to sift out appropriate concepts, topics, and ideas.

Example
Teacher presents a simple topical theme, such as the circus, and webs it to the subject areas. A conceptual theme, such as conflict, can be webbed for more depth in the theme approach.

7

Threaded
Magnifying glass—big ideas that magnify all content through a metacurricular approach

Description
The metacurricular approach threads thinking skills, social skills, multiple intelligences, technology, and study skills through the various disciplines.

Example
Teaching staff targets prediction in Reading, Math, and Science lab experiments while Social Studies teacher targets forecasting current events, and thus threads the skill (prediction) across disciplines.

8

Integrated
Kaleidoscope—new patterns and designs that use the basic elements of each discipline

Description
This interdisciplinary approach matches subjects for overlaps in topics and concepts with some team teaching in an authentic integrated model.

Example
In Math, Science, Social Studies, Fine Arts, Language Arts, and Practical Arts, teachers look for patterning models and approach content through these patterns.

9

Immersed
Microscope—intensely personal view that allows microscopic explanation as all content is filtered through lens of interest and expertise

Description
The disciplines become part of the learner's lens of expertise; the learner filters all content through this lens and becomes immersed in his or her own experience.

Example
Student or doctoral candidate has an area of expert interest and sees all learning through that lens.

10

Networked
Prism—a view that creates multiple dimensions and directions of focus

Description
Learner filters all learning through the expert's eye and makes internal connections that lead to external networks of experts in related fields.

Example
Architect, while adapting the CAD/CAM technology for design, networks with technical programmers and expands her knowledge base, just as she had traditionally done with interior designers.

© Robin Fogarty, 1991

Figure 3.5

Sample Four-Phase Lesson Plan

CIRCLES THAT CYCLE

Level: Elementary

Curriculum Integration: Math, Science, and Physical Education

Multiple Intelligences

- ☑ Bodily/Kinesthetic
- ☑ Interpersonal
- ☐ Intrapersonal
- ☑ Logical/Mathematical
- ☐ Musical
- ☐ Naturalist
- ☑ Verbal/Linguistic
- ☑ Visual/Spatial

Content Standards

Mathematics

Understands and applies basic and advanced properties of the concepts of measurement

Understands and applies basic and advanced properties of the concepts of geometry

Physical Sciences

Understands motion and the principles that explain it

Knows the relationship between the strength of a force and its effect on an object (e.g., the greater the force, the greater the change in motion; the more massive the object, the smaller the effect of a given force)

Science (Nature)

Understands the nature of scientific inquiry

Physical Education

Uses a variety of basic and advanced movement forms

INQUIRE PHASE
15 MINUTES

Inquire Activity Option A

Objective: Students physically uncover the concepts related to the parts of a circle and the distance across versus the distance around it.

Attend

The teacher asks . . .

- What makes a circle a circle?

- What's the difference between a circle, an oval, and an oblong?
- How can we set up our chairs in a circle? Please do it.

Experience: "Anybody Who"

The teacher . . .

- Arranges chairs in a large circle and instructs students to sit in a chair (no empty chairs should be left in the circle)
- Stands in the center of the circle to begin (the only person without a chair).
- Teaches the phrase: Anybody Who _____.
  Fill in the blank with a characteristic. Potential characteristics can include:
  Behavior: sleeps on his or her stomach, likes to dance, reads comics, and eats ice cream
  Clothing: wears a watch, has on jewelry, wears socks
- Tells students to state a characteristic that applies to some or all of them. If the characteristic fits them, they must quickly move to another chair (at least two chairs away) as you (the teacher) also move to an unoccupied chair.
- Explains that since there is one more person than chairs, one student will be left standing. This person then repeats "Anybody Who" and names another characteristic.

Reflect

The teacher asks . . .

- How many of you ran to a chair following the circumference of our circled chairs? The diameter? The radius?
- What was the quickest way to get to an empty chair?
- What would happen to the game if we made the circle smaller? Bigger?

Inquire Activity Option B

Objective: Students physically demonstrate the meaning of words related to the measurement of a circle.

Attend

While students continue to sit in the circled chairs, the teacher . . .

- Draws a circle on the board or chart paper, assigns students to pairs, and asks them to draw and label as many parts of a circle as they can on a piece of chart paper.
- Directs student pairs to share their labeled circles with other pairs.
- Refers to the circle on the board, asks the groups to indicate the parts of a circle they identified, and writes them on the circle.

- Fills in any parts of the circle the students don't provide, which may include: circumference, radius, diameter, degrees (360, 180, 90), radian, and pi depending on class readiness and level.
- Passes out a piece of paper to each student with five circles drawn on it.
- Completes an observation log while the students perform (see Figure 3.6).

Students . . .

- "Act out" the following by moving around or through the circle of chairs one by one:
  - circumference
  - degree
  - diameter
  - radian
  - radius
- Illustrate the above five words by drawing and labeling each circle on the sheet the teacher passed out.

Reflect

The teacher asks the following questions . . .

- Demonstrating which part of the circle took the most energy? Why?
- Demonstrating which part of the circle took the least energy? Why?
- We used footsteps to measure the length of the parts of a circle. What tool is most appropriately used to do that?

GATHER PHASE
35 MINUTES

Gather Activity

Objective: Students study a multi-speed bike and the gearshift components and label circle parts on the wheel, gearshift wheels, and chain. Students demonstrate how the size of a "circle" effects effort and speed. Students previously volunteered to bring multi-speed bikes with gearshifting capabilities to class. One bike is needed for every four students.

Attend

The teacher . . .

- Asks one student to volunteer to bring a bike to the front of the room.
- Provides students with rulers or tape measure, piece of string, masking tape, chalk, and a large protractor.
- Can model how to use the simple tools or allow students to problem-solve how to use the implements.

Students . . .

- Guided by the teacher, label the parts of a circle on one of the bicycle wheels.

Observation Log

Focus Components	Observation
Parts of a circle	*Audrey, Jose, and Kim remained unsure of how to act out the radius.* *Several other students were unclear regarding the concept of degrees of a circle.* *Design an experience that would mediate these difficulties, decide what phase such an experience would work into.*
Student interaction	*Jamal helped explain the concept of radian to Geoff and the rest of the class by stationing three students at points on the circle.* *Generally students' demonstrations at the end of the line were modeling earlier student representations, which helped the more reluctant and unsure students be confident of their demonstration and set the state for the later phases of the lesson.*
Reasoning	*Most of the students were able to exlain their movements and why they made them. Pam and Lewis were better able to illustrate the concepts on paper using fine motor skills than they were at using the gross motor skills of demonstrating with physical action.*

Figure 3.6

- Measure changes in distance the bike travels as students shift front and back gears.
- Examine their multi-speed bikes in their small groups and observe what happens to the pedal speed, wheel distance, and pedal difficulty during various gear shifting positions.
- Take the bicycles outside to ride them as part of their data gathering.
- Record their observations (see Figure 3.7).
- Work with other groups after completing their observation logs to share and compare their observations.

The teacher . . .

- Leads a class discussion of the students' bicycle observations, clarifying any misunderstandings or misperceptions.

Experience

Students, while still in their small groups . . .

- Demonstrate the impact circle size has on effort and speed. For example: form a crack-the-whip-line to show how slowly the inside person rotates compared to the person who is walking very quickly on the outside.
- Spin with arms extended out compared to spinning with arms folded.

- Jump rope with a large rope compared to a small rope.

Reflect

Teacher asks . . .

- What have you learned about circles you never knew before?
- What is the greatest thing you learned about how bikes work?
- What can you teach your friends about bikes you think they don't understand?
- How can you use your understanding of circles when you play with friends?

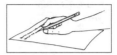

PROCESS PHASE
20 MINUTES

Process Activity

Objective: Students prepare a quiz game on circles.
Students . . .

- As a class, brainstorm four to six categories for a *Jeopardy*-style game, "What's the Question?"

Student Observation Log

Group Members:		Date:	
Gear Shifting	**Pedal Speed** faster/slower	**Wheel Distance** more/less	**Pedaling Difficulty** easier/harder
Front chain on largest sprocket and back chain on largest sprocket			
Front chain on largest sprocket and back chain on smallest sprocket			
Front chain on middle sprocket and back chain on largest sprocket			
Front chain on middle sprocket and back chain on smallest sprocket			
Front chain on smallest sprocket and back chain on largest sprocket			
Front chain on smallest sprocket and back chain on smallest sprocket			
Comments:			

Figure 3.7

Attend

The teacher . . .

- Assigns one student group to each category to prepare at least five answers and their questions for each category
- Monitors groups and facilitates answer and question preparation.

Students play the game by the following rules:

- One group chooses a category.
- Teacher reads the answer.
- Each of the groups has fifteen seconds to write their response to the answer.
- When time is called, students hold up their questions.
- Each group with a correct question gets the points.

Reflect

The teacher asks the following questions . . .

- What did you like most about preparing and playing the game, "What's the Question?"
- How did preparing the answers and questions help clarify the information?
- What can you do to make sure you "know that you know" all that we learned today?
- If you were to tell your family one thing you learned from today's lesson, what would that be? Tell your partner.

APPLY PHASE
20 MINUTES

Apply Activity Option A

Objective: Students participate in a mini field trip to "hunt" for circles on the school grounds.

Attend

The teacher . . .

- Facilitates grouping students into small groups of two or three students to participate in a treasure hunt for circles.
- Asks students to think of all the items that have circular shapes either in the school building or out on the school grounds. Calls on three or four students to share their ideas.

Experience: "Circle Scavenger Hunt"

Students . . .

- Find as many circles as they can and record the ways circles are used on an observation log (see Figure 3.8 "Circle Scavenger Hunt Log").
- Return to class to share the examples they found.

Circle Scavenger Hunt Log

| Names: | | | | Date: | |

For each circle you find, record the following:
1. Describe the circle.
2. Identify where you observed it.
3. Note the parts of the circle that are evident.
4. Explain the function or purpose of the particular circle.
5. List examples of other circles you previously observed elsewhere.

	Describe	Where Observed	Circle Parts	Purpose or Function	Other Examples
Circle #1					
Circle # 2					
Circle # 3					
Circle # 4					
Circle # 5					
Circle # 6					

Figure 3.8

Reflect

The teacher asks the following questions . . .

- What do you see in circles now that you didn't see before? Tell a neighbor.
- What's one thing you understand now that didn't make sense to you earlier?
- What will you do differently now that you understand circles better?

Apply Activity Option B

Objective: Students work together to create a song or design a machine using "circle" concepts.

Attend

Teacher . . .

- Facilitates grouping students into small groups of two or three students to participate in creating a song or

designing a machine to reflect their understanding of circles.

Experience: "Rap up"

Students either . . .

- Make up words about circles that fit a familiar "round" and sing it. (This is more appropriate for younger elementary level students) or
- In small groups, create a machine that uses circles. (This is more appropriate for upper level elementary students.)

Reflect

Students complete a self-assessment of their presentation. See Figure 3.9 "Student Self-Assessment."

Student Self-Assessment

1. Did my song include a mention of each of the circle's five parts we studied today?

YES	NO	MAYBE

2. Did I sing out clearly so the whole class could easily understand what I was saying?

YES	NO	MAYBE

3. Did I work well and cooperatively with the members of my group?

YES	NO	MAYBE

4. Did I make an important contribution to my group's successful performance?

YES	NO	MAYBE

5. Did creating and performing our song help me to remember the parts of a circle?

YES	NO	MAYBE

6. Overall how would you rate your contrubution to the performance?

Excellent	Very Good	Good	Okay	Could Have Done Better

7. Explain the rating you gave yourself.

Figure 3.9

Instruction
The Art and Science of Teaching in the Block

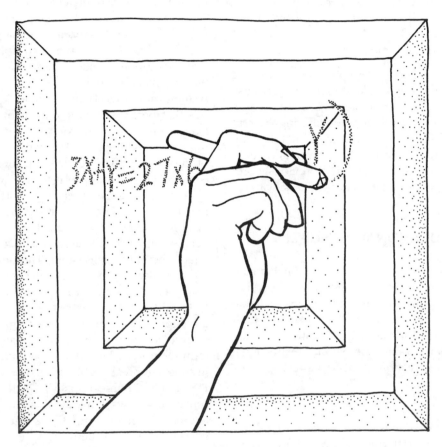

Block scheduling without fundamental changes in instruction is merely longer blocks of the same old stuff. If improved learning is the goal, instructional practices will have to change in order to best take advantage of the opportunity of longer blocks of time.
—Linda Wyatt 1996, 18

OPPORTUNITY FOR GROWTH AND CHANGE

Many teachers accustomed to a forty-five or fifty minute class period are apprehensive about the prospect of filling up twice that amount of time (or more) in an extended time block. Underlying their concern is the question of how to keep students interested and motivated for such an extended period. Both concerns find their answers in brain-compatible pedagogy.

The teacher in the block has the opportunity to orchestrate the curriculum and instruction into events, projects, environments, and graphics that can assist student learning. Such an opportunity calls for sophisticated pedagogy that goes beyond imparting data through lecturing or assigned readings. Instead, it demands strategies that enable information and concepts to be learned through challenges, questions, problems, and situations that encourage students to become interested, research the relevant and appropriate information, process it, and apply it—in other words, learning that is brain compatible. Such a dynamic, interconnected, surprise-filled, challenging environment is more feasible in extended class formats than in shorter bell schedule periods.

Students' brains are far more capable than traditional formats have allowed for; therefore, teachers need to

- Design lessons rich in sensory experiences
- Use the whole body in learning with movement and hands-on experience
- Involve a wide range of emotions and intelligences.

Not only do the above strategies make good use of the additional time, but they also make it much easier to use brain-compatible teaching principles (Fitzgerald 1996). Further, in traditional scheduling, after offering content material teachers would need to wait until the following day for processing and application activities, often needing to review the content-heavy material previously presented before moving on to the higher-order activities.

ENERGIZING EDUCATIONAL PRINCIPLES

Although there may be others, four educational principles (pulsed learning, teaching to long-term memory, beginning-end-middle principle, and varying instructional strategies) help to energize and enhance a teacher's pedagogical repertoire. (See Figure 4.1 "Educational Principles Centered Around Brain-Compatible Instructional Strategies" for a representation of this dynamic.)

Pulsed Learning

Ron Fitzgerald (1996) suggests the concept of *pulsed learning,* which simply stated is that an activity requiring a high degree of concentration needs to be followed by an activity that is more relaxed and allows for the processing of material absorbed in the high-concentration activity. A class period of lecture, video, and a quiz is composed of all high-concentration activities. Figure 4.2 depicts the relative intensity of some activities and how that can help teachers plot a course for learning.

In order to get a handle on high-concentration versus low-concentration activities, teachers can make a list of the kinds of activities and strategies that require a great deal of focus and intense attention (high concentration) and a separate list of the kinds of activities and strategies

that are more relaxed and require less active attention (low concentration). Creating such lists is a great activity for a teacher team to engage in.

Teaching to Long-Term Memory

As discussed in chapter 1, memorization occurs in a part of the brain with limited holding capacity. Unless the information is connected to previously learned information, unless the information is put into some meaningful framework, or unless the information is applied to daily life in some way, then the information stays in short-term memory and gets crowded out with the next deluge of data (Sylwester 1995). Such a simple concept, however, has obvious consequences for how curriculum is taught. This is not to suggest that discrete data and information are unimportant. Rather, it is possible to convey important data and information with concepts, frameworks, and connections in such a way that the brain can retain the information much longer than through rote memorization processes. Brain-compatible instructional methods that best foster long-term memory are most effectively employed in an extended time format.

Most every discipline has core facts and crucial pieces of information that are essential for students to learn. It is part of the teacher's job to know what they are. Reading current material, attending content area classes, and maintaining a dialogue with departmental and grade-level colleagues all help teachers remain abreast of the detailed information attendant to the content area for which they are responsible. The next step is to discern what activity or experience will enable that material to be conveyed in a way that is meaningful and makes sense.

In other words, it is not enough to know what facts are important for the students to grasp. What is needed is for teachers to help content material permeate long-term memory, where it will be readily available for use in some later real-life situation or even in some later test. Figure 4.3 "Brain-Compatible Methods of Content Presentation" shows some actual course content and some alternative (brain-compatible) settings in which to deliver that course content.

The Beginning-End-Middle (BEM) Principle

Fitzgerald (1996) notes that students are most attentive at the beginning and the end of any one learning strategy and least attentive in the middle. He articulated this as the Beginning-End-Middle (BEM) Principle. If a ninety-minute lesson has basically just one learning approach, there will be a rather large "middle" section during which attention dramatically falls off. Therefore, by utilizing more learning strategies or activities, one necessarily decreases the number of less attentive "middles" and increases the number of more attentive "beginnings" and "ends." The BEM principle aligns directly with the Four-Phase Lesson Design

Educational Principles Centered Around Brain-Compatible Instructional Strategies

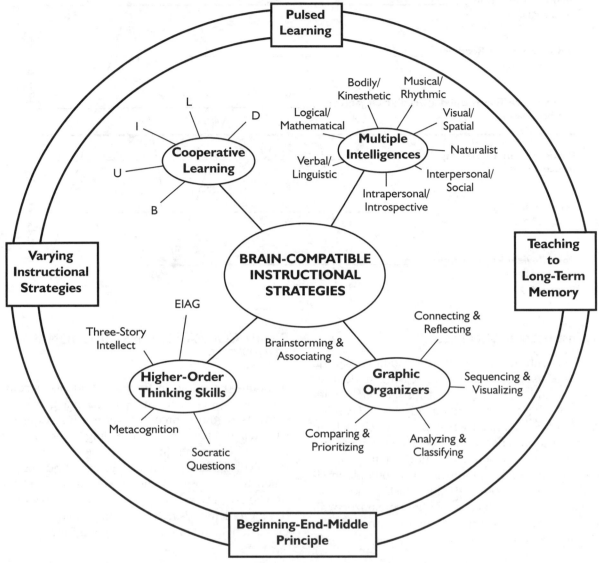

Figure 4.1

promoted throughout this book, which assumes that any one lesson will have a variety of activities interspersed throughout the ninety minutes. If an entire class period is devoted to one activity, energy will inevitably wane (this is especially true of a class period in excess of 100 minutes.) The Four-Phase lesson design builds upon this idea to propose that the activities within the lesson (as well as the lessons within the unit) should be organized to culminate in students working with the material in some authentic and meaningful way. (See chapter 6 for an extensive discussion of constructing brain-compatible lessons for the extended time block.)

There are several concerns that the teacher in extended time formats needs to keep in mind. When it is suggested that several strategies are used to increase the beginnings and ends, the activities still need to be meaningful and connected to the content—not simply activities for activities' sake. A variety of strategies that illuminate the desired curriculum objectives, however, can actually make the content come alive in ways not experienced by students before. Furthermore, diverse strategies can enable the teacher to reach a broader base of students than perhaps have previously been touched.

Pulsed Learning

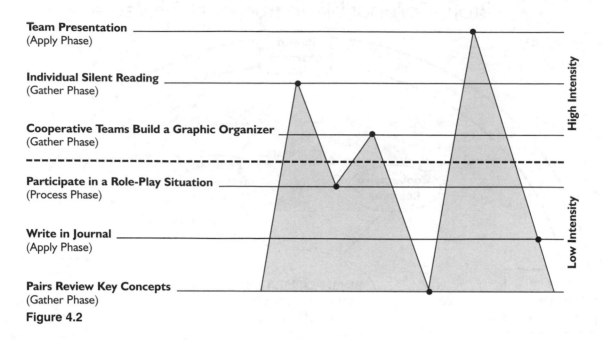

Figure 4.2

Varying Instructional Strategies

What is *done* with the time is more important than the *length* of time itself. The key to increasing student attention is expanding the variety of instructional strategies and approaches (Rettig and Canady 1996). Learning and attention are enhanced when there are shifts from one approach to another within the ninety minute period, or within the fifty minute period for that matter. Blending cooperative learning strategies, multiple intelligence theory, higher-order thinking tasks, and information managing tools such as graphic organizers call forth the very attentiveness and desire to learn from students that teachers want to capture.

BRAIN-COMPATIBLE INSTRUCTIONAL STRATEGIES

In brain-compatible instruction, students become fully involved in their learning. The teacher guides or leads students to the sources of knowledge. Consequently, students and teachers are traveling companions on the journey of learning. In this way, students discover how to solve real-life problems, how to find the answers when the answers are not immediately available, and how to adapt when yesterday's answers no longer fit today's problems. Using brain-compatible learning strategies can help aid in the advance of information from the

Brain-Compatible Methods of Content Presentation

Course Content	Alternative Settings
Vocabulary	Real-life Stories by Students
Historical Dates	Timelines or Museum Trips
Factual Data	Charts or Matrices
Historical Events	Role Playing
General Concepts	Debates or Graphic Organizers
Scientific Concepts	Lab Experiments or Cyber Field Trips

Figure 4.3

short-term working memory system to the long-term memory system, promoting learning for life and not just for a test.

Cooperative Learning Approaches

It is well stated by Robert Sylwester that the central reason for the success of cooperative group activities when used well is that "[s]uch activities . . . place students at the center of the educative process, and thus stimulate learning" (Sylwester 1995, 132). As a consequence, motivation runs high; learning runs deep; and time passes quickly. Ultimately, the skills students gain from working in a cooperative fashion are the very same skills that have become inextricably woven into a great number of the jobs and careers students are in training for today (Fitzgerald 1996). Cooperative skills are becoming as important in the world of work as knowledge and technological skills.

David Johnson, Roger Johnson, and E. J. Holubec (1988) offer five elements of fruitful cooperative learning: positive interdependence, individual accountability, group processing, face-to-face interaction, and collaborative skills. James Bellanca and Robin Fogarty (1991) use the acronym BUILD as the basis of creating cooperative learning lessons:

Bring in higher-order thinking

Unite the teams and the class

Insure individual learning and accountability

Look over, step back, and discuss

Develop social skills

Figure 4.4 "B.U.I.L.D. Cooperative Learning Fundamentals" provides an overview of the cooperative learning process.

Bring in Higher-Order Thinking

Each cooperative learning approach needs to embody some higher-order thinking skill or process. A significant higher-order thinking challenge is one way to make the cooperative experience a richer, more profound one than studying alone. (See the Higher-Order Thinking Skills section of this chapter for elaboration of that concept.)

Unify the Teams and the Class

The use of heterogeneous groups actually helps individuals discover that all the gifts of their fellow members are needed to accomplish the assigned work. Cooperative learning groups

- Have an assigned role for each person
- Learn explicit social skills
- Are given a challenging task demanding the participation of all
- Are given tasks that weave in higher-order thinking

- Are usually heterogeneous in makeup
- Frequently reflect and process how they are learning and how they are working together as a team.

Insure Individual Learning and Accountability

It is the teacher's task to formulate activities in which individual learning and accountability can be guaranteed. Getting an accurate picture of the individual learning removes one common criticism of cooperative learning structures often voiced by parents and students—that one person is too often burdened with all of the work.

Look over, Step Back, and Discuss

An integral part of a lesson is the opportunity to step back and talk about what has just occurred. The key to this is questions that the teacher prepares ahead of time. These questions may focus on the content of the lesson, the methods used in the lesson, or the experience of working as a group. Some students may only make sense of the lesson at this point. The extended class format permits the time to do this job adequately. Even if there are only three or four minutes to do this kind of processing, it is crucial to student learning.

Develop Social Skills

The teacher is called on to teach social skills directly, to provide actual practice time to make the skills automatic and natural, and finally to monitor the ongoing utilization of these skills. It is important to teach social skills in nearly the same way a content discipline is taught throughout the semester. In other words, the teacher cannot assume the students are experienced in the use of social skills on the first day of class. Likewise, the teacher can't teach all of the necessary skills at once. Deciding which skills are most important and focusing on those and phasing others in later is part of the role of the teacher.

Implications for the Extended Time Format

Cooperative learning approaches are crucial for the extended class format because they

- Provide a shift in the intensity of learning activities
- Offer an opportunity for interaction that students appreciate
- Encourage higher-order thinking as content material is worked on and used
- Can help the teacher cover large amounts of material by dividing it among several groups to study and then present to the larger group.

Multiple Intelligences

Multiple intelligence (MI) theory, as pioneered by Howard Gardner (1983), emphasizes the importance of personal meaning-making and problem solving. In the traditional classroom, either out of habit or convention, most of the

B.U.I.L.D. Cooperative Learning Fundamentals

Key Questions	**B** Bring in Higher Order Thinking	**U** Unify the Teams and the Class	**I** Insure Individual Learning and Accountability	**L** Look Over, Step Back, and Discuss	**D** Develop Social Skills
What is the Acronym?					
What Do the Letters Stand For?	Bring in Higher Order Thinking	Unify the Teams and the Class	Insure Individual Learning and Accountability	Look Over, Step Back, and Discuss	Develop Social Skills
What Is Its Function?	To utilize the gifts of the collaborative setting to intensify the cognitive	To create bonding and connections among students in the class and on a team	To make sure that rigorous individual learning is taking place	To reflect on the material learned and the experience of learning / To help the learning and the experience really belong to the learner	To deepen students' abilities to interact so that the learning can be deeper and richer among the team and among the class
What Are Some Ways to Do This In the Classroom?	Teaching Thinking Skills Directly / Graphic Organizers / Fat & Skinny Questions	Assigned Roles / One Set of Materials / Call for One Product From the Team / Team Name, Symbol, Slogan	Random Oral Quizzes / Tests / Conferences / Assigned Section within a Team Project	Reflection Questions / P.M.I. Chart / Team Self-Assessing Checklists	Teaching social skills directly / Team roles of encourager or observer / "That's a good idea because . . ."

Figure 4.4 Adapted from *Blueprints for Thinking in the Cooperative Classroom* by James Bellanca and Robin Fogarty. © 1991 IRI/SkyLight Training and Publishing, Inc. Reprinted with permission of SkyLight Professional Development, Arlington Heights, IL.

activities are based on lecture and computation, which play to only two (verbal/linguistic and logical/mathematical) of the eight intelligences. Conversely, as has been suggested here, brain-compatible instructional strategies such as cooperative learning help develop interpersonal skills (interpersonal intelligence) and at the same time include as many of the other intelligences as possible. (See Figure 4.5 for a list of the types of activities that exercise each intelligence.) Such activities promote cognitive development through intrinsic motivation, which leads to student desire for lifelong learning and inquiry. Perhaps MI theory benefits education the most in that it necessitates the expansion of teaching repertoire, which in turn has positive implications for teaching in the block.

HIGHER-ORDER THINKING SKILLS

Benjamin S. Bloom's *Taxonomy* (1956) proposes a hierarchy of thinking processes that move from the most basic, *knowledge,* through *comprehension, application, analysis,* and *synthesis,* culminating in *evaluation.* The more advanced and intricate thinking processes are therefore referred to as *higher-order thinking skills.* Teachers have been challenged for years to ask students to think in a variety of ways. The highly specialized and technology-driven world in which educators and students alike live demands critical thinking and reasoning as never before. The following approaches can be used to elicit higher-order thinking from students.

The Socratic Method

Socrates applied reasoning to arrive at truth by asking questions. He didn't lecture or provide answers. He used inductive reasoning instead of relying on traditional thinking ("Everybody thinks this way" or "We've always done it like that") or prescribed doctrine ("We think only what we've been told to think" or "I read it somewhere so it must be true").

Socratic irony was his search for truth by assuming he knew nothing about the topic and that he must question everything to arrive finally at truth.

Socrates is famous for creating conceptual conflicts with his questioning techniques. Persons engaged in dialogue with Socrates would then have to revisit what they thought they knew and rethink their position. Teachers can use a similar technique when asking students to actively process new information or learning activities.

By asking questions instead of providing information or lectures, teachers are helping students to think, to discover truth, and to make sense of the topic of the lesson. Socrates was so successful in his approach to learning and discovery that his technique has survived for more than two thousand years.

Metacognition

Metacognition is the key to helping students make sense of the information, thoughts, and feelings they encounter during each learning experience of the unit. As teachers guide students through processing and reflecting on each activity, they help students think about their random, divergent, and disconnected thoughts and transition those thoughts to understand not only what they experienced but what meaning they can derive from the experience.

An important aspect of metacognition is the kind of learning experiences teachers select for their students. Without stimulating, complex, and challenging experiences, metacognitive reflections would be nothing more than students recalling information or the rote memorization of facts and details. Caine and Caine (1997) challenge teachers to design experiences that will facilitate the "ah-ha" moment as well as provide opportunities for frequent meta-questioning throughout the experience.

Students can also learn to ask themselves metacognitive questions as they engage in various learning activities. In this way they become aware of their own learning and thinking processes.

The Three-Story Intellect Model

James Bellanca and Robin Fogarty (1991) have constructed the concept of the three-story intellect based on a quote by Oliver Wendell Holmes. The three stories (floors in a building) refer to levels of understanding and the sequence of the steps in achieving the highest level that would allow one to apply all that has been gathered and processed. The four-phase lesson design examples throughout this book are built upon the three-story intellect but add the *inquire* phase before Bellanca and Fogarty's "first story" of gathering. (See Figure 4.6 "The Three-Story Intellect.")

Experience/Identify/Apply/Generalize

The acronym EIAG is an active processing model developed by H. Stephen Glenn (Glenn and Nelson 1988). This circular model shows that the thinking process is continuous and reflective and that the questions remain linked to the learning activity.

E (experience) refers to questions that ask students to reflect on the experience they have had. Even though teachers design learning activities to be consistent for each student—the same lab experiment, same chapter to study, same novel to read, same homework assignments—the reaction of each student to the learning activity may vary widely. What one student observes, attends to, feels, and thinks about might be something completely different from other students because of the difference in their previous experiences, skill levels, and understanding. Each learning activity, therefore, can be quite different for each student. Questions asking students to reflect on what their

Gardner's Eight Intelligences

Visual/Spatial

Images, graphics, drawings, sketches, maps, charts, doodles, pictures, spatial orientation, puzzles, designs, looks, appeal, mind's eye, imagination, visualization, dreams, nightmares, films, and videos.

Logical/Mathematical

Reasoning, deductive and inductive logic, facts, data, information, spreadsheets, databases, sequencing, ranking, organizing, analyzing, proofs, conclusions, judging, evaluations, and assessments.

Verbal/Linguistic

Words, wordsmiths, speaking, writing, listening, reading, papers, essays, poems, plays, narratives, lyrics, spelling, grammar, foreign languages, memos, bulletins, newsletters, newspapers, E-mail, FAXes, speeches, talks, dialogues, and debates.

Musical/Rhythmic

Music, rhythm, beat, melody, tunes, allegro, pacing, timbre, tenor, soprano, opera, baritone, symphony, choir, chorus, madrigals, rap, rock, rhythm and blues, jazz, classical, folk, ads and jingles.

Bodily/Kinesthetic

Art, activity, action, experiental, hands-on, experiments, try, do, perform, play, drama, sports, throw, toss, catch, jump, twist, twirl, assemble, disassemble, form, re-form, manipulate, touch, feel, immerse, and participate.

Interpersonal/Social

Interact, communicate, converse, share, understand, empathize, sympathize, reach out, care, talk whisper, laugh, cry, shudder, socialize, meet, greet, lead, follow, gangs, clubs, charisma, crowds, gatherings, and twosomes.

Intrapersonal/Introspective

Self, solitude, meditate, think, create, brood, reflect, envision, journal, self-assess, set goals, plot, plan, dream, write, fiction, nonfiction, poetry, affirmations, lyrics, songs, screenplays, commentaries, introspection, and inspection.

Naturalist

Nature, natural, environment, listen, watch, observe, classify, categorize, discern patterns, appreciate, hike, climb, fish, hunt, snorkle, dive, photograph, trees, leaves, animals, living things, flora, fauna, ecosystem, sky, grass, mountains, lakes, and rivers.

Figure 4.5

Adapted from *Problem-Based Learning and Other Curriculum Models for the Multiple Intelligences Classroom* by Robin Fogarty. ©1997 by SkyLight Training and Publishing Inc. Reprinted with permission of SkyLight Professional Development, Arlington Heights, IL.

The Three-Story Intellect

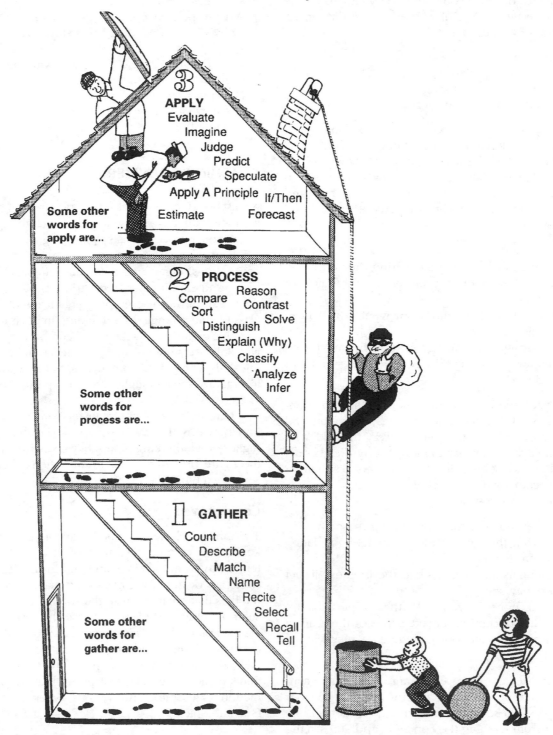

Figure 4.6
From Patterns for *Thinking, Patterns for Transfer* by Robin Fogarty and James Bellanca. ©1993 by IRI/SkyLight Publishing, Inc. Reprinted with permission of SkyLight Professional Development, Arlington Heights, IL.

experiences were provide all students with diverse insights into what others encountered. They can appreciate diverse perspectives as a result of their shared differences.

Examples of **E** questions:

- What just happened?
- What was your experience in the class?
- What did you observe during the activity?
- What was the sequence of events?

I (identify) questions direct students to contemplate four different thinking tasks. This category of questions asks students to describe what their thoughts were, what subsequent feelings, attitudes, or moods they experienced, what changes in their behaviors occurred, and what new discoveries, insights, or perceptions resulted from the experience.

Examples of **I** questions:

- What were you thinking about during the activity?
- How did you feel about the successes and failures of the experience?
- What did you do differently from what you thought you were going to do?
- What new insights did you gain from the activity?
- What changes in perception occurred as a result of the experience?

A (analyze) questions require the students to examine the "whys" of their thoughts, feelings, behaviors, and understandings. Why do they feel the way they do? Why do they think what they are thinking? Why did they act the way they did? Where did their insights come from? What connections did they make?

Examples of **A** questions:

- What influenced your thoughts during the activity?
- How did your thoughts change your feelings during the experience?
- Which thoughts and feelings had the greatest impact on your behaviors?
- What connections did you make that helped you understand the concepts and make sense of the activity?
- How did your perceptions change as a result of the experience?

G (generalize) questions encourage students to consider ways to apply the skills and information to other circumstances. These questions can help students make the transfer from learning the concepts and skills in the classroom to applying these skills and concepts in real-life situations. These questions provide relevancy and demonstrate various contexts of alternative ways to use the classroom skills and concepts.

Examples of **G** questions:

- Where might you be able to apply what you have learned outside this classroom?

- Describe some real-life situations where you have seen these skills used.
- What response would you give to someone who asks, "Why do I have to learn this stuff? Will I ever use it again?"
- What connections did you make with this lesson and some of your past experiences?
- If you were to write a prescription of when and how to use what you have learned from this lesson, what would it be?

GRAPHIC ORGANIZERS

As discussed in the previous chapter, graphic organizers are tools students can use to aid in such thought and organizational processes as synthesizing information, constructing relationships, identifying associations, making connections, organizing data, analyzing and generating ideas, and exploring shared attributes of concepts. Students can further use graphic organizers to order, sort, classify, and arrange their thinking. Implicit in the name "graphic organizers" is the visual component of this tool. Not only are students able to practice numerous thinking skills with graphic organizers, but they are also able to organize their thoughts and to capture their thinking visually.

Figure 4.7 "Graphic Organizers" makes the connection between the use of graphic orgainizers and the higher-order thinking skills they exercise. In addition, the figure provides a visual illustration of each of the seventeen types discussed below.

Concept Web

The inner circle represents the major concept or topic, key theme, or main idea to explore. The lines that extend away from the circle and end in smaller circles are subtopics or minor themes of the main idea. Lines and bubbles that emanate from the subtopic circles are sub-subtopic points. Students can use this graphic organizers to explore shared attributes of a topic or concept and to construct the relationship of subtopics, sub-subtopics, etc., with the topic. For example, in a science class, students explore the details of invertebrates (topic), locomotion (subtopic), and various types of locomotion (sub-subtopic).

Mind Map/Thinking Map

This is similar to a concept web and sunshine wheel in structure. The primary difference is that instead of words captured in circles or bubbles, ideas are represented by pictures or visuals. Students can use this graphic organizer to illustrate ideas visually instead of using words. For example, in an algebra class, students can explore

Bridging Sna

Sequence cha
are used to sh
dents can mak
in a physiolog
an impulse foll
muscle fiber tc
ogy class, stud
quence of came
service advertis

Looks-Sounds

What does it *lo
cal characterist
sound like (its
acoustic charact
it *feel* like (its
tangible or mate
Students can u
shared attributes
does a whale lo
psychology class
like, sound like,

Pie Chart

The pie represent
tire set of data or
the pie represent
whole. Students c
struct relationship
visions, or to show
For example, in a
determine the perc
on offense and def
They can also ider
is spent executing
ning plays.

KWL

This graphic organi
1986 (What do you
want to know? Wh
from the lesson or
organizer to reflect
ciencies, and to ass
ample, in a chemist

• What do students
• What do they *wa
  derstand the table
• What have they *le
  periodic table.

Graphic Organizers

Brainstorming and Associating	Comparing and Prioritizing	Analyzing and Classifying	Sequencing and Visualizing	Connecting and Reflecting
Concept Web	Venn Diagram	Fishbone	Bridging Snapshots	KWL
Mind Map	Analogy/Simile Chart	Matrix	Looks-Sounds-Feels	KDL
Sunshine Wheel	T-Chart	Double T-Chart	Pie Chart	PMI
	Ranking Ladder			Right Angle

Figure 4.7

uses of quadra
sent appropria
class it could
and appropriat

Sunshine Whe

The circle is the
lines extending
sunshine, indica
sult of thinking
graphic organiz
gestions. For ex;
brainstorm idea;
well as possible
other things.

Venn Diagram

In its most frequ
used to show t
characteristics of
be used. In the ar
that are shared or
non-overlapping
listed. Students c;
struct relationship
in a biology class
pared/contrasted.
try/western musi
Four-Phase Lessor
ingbird? students ;
comparing/contras
Mockingbird.

Analogy/Simile C

Unfamiliar concept
familiar and known

Students can use
visually represent tl
disparate entities, c
the other is not. The
derstanding of the
high school science
the function of an e
because (blank).

T-Chart

Information is organ
such as (a) pre- and
and cons, (d) either/c
efits and detriments.
ganizer to synthesiz
example, in a geogr
Poland's political an

- Is the theme within the realm of understanding and experience of the teachers involved?
- Will the theme interest all members of the teaching team?
- Do we have sufficient materials and resources to supply information we might need?
- Does the theme lend itself to active learning experiences?
- Can this theme lead to a unit that is of the proper duration, not too short and not too long?
- Is the theme helpful, worthwhile, and pertinent to the instructional objectives?
- Will the theme be of interest to students, and will it motivate them to do their best?
- Is the theme one with which teachers are not already so familiar that they cannot share in the excitement of the learning?
- Will this theme be of interest to students, and will it motivate them to do their best?

Figure 5.6
Questions to ask when selecting a theme.

teachers and shows the intended length of the unit, when it will start, and in which classes it will be taught.

5. *Develop the scope and sequence for content and instruction.* To develop the unit, follow the six steps for planning and developing a unit of instruction outlined earlier in this chapter. This should be done by each team member as well as by the group during common planning time so members can coordinate dates and activities in logical sequence and depth. This is an organic process and will generate both ideas and anxiety. Under the guidance of the team leader, members should strive to keep this anxiety at a level conducive to learning, experimenting, and arriving at group consensus.

6. *Share goals and objectives.* Each team member should have a copy of the goals and target objectives of every other team member. This helps to refine the unit and lesson plans and to prevent unnecessary overlap and confusion.

7. *Give the unit a name.* The unit has been fashioned and is held together by the theme that is chosen. Giving the theme a name and using that name communicates to the students that this unit of study is integrated, important, and meaningful to school and to life.

8. *Share subject-specific units, lesson plans, and printed and nonprinted materials.* Exchange the finalized unit to obtain one another's comments and suggestions. Keep a copy of each teacher's unit(s) as a resource, and see if you could present a lesson using it as your basis (some modification may be necessary). Lesson planning is the topic that follows.

9. *Field test the unit.* Beginning at the scheduled time and date, present the lessons. Team members may trade classes from time to time. Team teaching may take place if and when two or more classes can be combined for instruction (if a classroom space large enough is available).

10. *Reflect, assess, and perhaps adjust and revise the unit.* During planning time, team members should share and discuss their successes and failures and determine what needs to be changed and how and when that should be done to make the unit successful. Adjustments can be made along the way and revisions for future use can be made after the unit.

The preceding ten steps are not absolutes and should be viewed only as guides. Differing teaching teams and levels of teacher experience and knowledge make the strict adherence to any plan less productive than would be the use of group-generated plans. For instance, some teachers have found that the last point under step 3 could state exactly the opposite; they recommend that the topic for an interdisciplinary unit should be one that a teacher or a teaching team already knows well. In practice, the process that works well—one that results in meaningful learning for the students and in their positive feelings about themselves, about learning, and about school—is the appropriate process.

Developing the Learning Activities: The Heart and Spirit of the ITU

Activities that engage the students in meaningful learning constitute the heart and spirit of the ITU: there are activities that start a unit into motion, that initiate the unit—*initiating activities;* there are the activities that comprise the heart of the unit—*ongoing developmental activities;* and, there are activities that bring the unit to a natural close—*culminating activities.*

The Common Thread

Central to the selection and development of all learning activities for interdisciplinary thematic instruction is a common thread of four tightly interwoven components: (a) the instruction is centered around a big and meaningful idea (theme) rather than on factitious subject areas, (b) the students and the teacher share in the decision making and responsibility for learning, (c) the learning activities are selected so all students are actively engaged in their learning; that is, they are both physically active (hands-on learning) and mentally active (minds-on learning), and (d) there is steady reflection on and frequent sharing of what is being done and what is being learned.

Initiating Activities

An ITU can be initiated in a limitless variety of ways. You must decide which ways are appropriate for your educational goals and objectives, intended time duration, and for your own unique group of students, considering their interests, abilities, and skills. You might start with a current event, a community problem, an artifact, a book, a media presentation, or something interesting found on the Internet.

Ongoing Developmental Activities

Once the ITU has been initiated, students become occupied with a variety of ongoing activities. In working with students to select and plan the ongoing learning activities, you will want to keep in mind the concept represented by the Learning Experiences Ladder (Figure 5.5) as well as the predetermined goals and target objectives.

Culminating Activity

Just as with other types of unit plans, an ITU is brought to close with a culminating activity. Such an activity often includes an exhibition or sharing of the product of the students' study. You could accept the students' suggestions for a culminating activity if it engages them in summarizing what they have learned with others. A culminating activity that brings closure to a unit can give the students an opportunity for synthesis (by assembling, constructing, creating, inventing, producing, or incorporating something) and even an opportunity to present that synthesis to an audience, live or on the World Wide Web. Culminating activities are opportunities for students to proudly demonstrate and share their learning and creativity in different and individual ways.

Examples of actual culminating activities and products of an ITU are endless (see Suggested Readings at the end of this chapter for examples). As just one example, students at King Middle School (Portland, ME) studied the shore life of Maine's Casco Bay for a year. The culminating activity of their study was their writing and publishing of a book that includes student-drawn illustrations and scientific descriptions of the flora and fauna found along the shore. The book is now in the city's libraries where it can be borrowed for use by anybody taking a walk along the shore.

PREPARING LESSON PLANS: RATIONALE AND ASSUMPTIONS

Of all the components of instructional planning perhaps the one that is of utmost concern especially to beginning teachers is that of preparing for class meetings. The process of designing a lesson is important in learning to provide the most efficient use of valuable and limited instructional time and the most effective learning for the students, to meet the unit goals.

Notice the title of this section does not refer to the "*daily* lesson plan," but rather, "the lesson plan." The focus is on how to prepare a lesson plan, and that plan may, in fact, be a daily plan, or it may not. In some instances, a lesson plan may extend for more than one class period or day, perhaps two or three (as, for example, the lesson shown later in this chapter in Figure 5.10). In other instances, the lesson plan is in fact a daily plan and may run for an entire class period. In block scheduling, one lesson plan may run for part of, or for an entire 2-hour block of time. See The Problem of Time later in this chapter.

Effective teachers are always planning for their classes. For the long range, they plan the scope and sequence and develop content. Within this long-range planning, they develop units, and within units, they design the activities to be used and the assessments of learning to be done. They familiarize themselves with books, materials, media, and innovations in their fields of interest. Yet, despite all this planning activity, the lesson plan remains pivotal to the planning process. Let's consider now the rationale, description, and guidelines for writing detailed lesson plans.

Rationale for Preparing Written Plans

First, *carefully prepared and written lesson plans show everyone—first and foremost your students, then your colleagues, your administrator, and, if you are a student teacher, your college or university supervisor—that you are a committed professional.* Sometimes, beginning teachers are concerned with being seen by their students using a written plan in class, thinking it may suggest that the teacher has not mastered the material. On the contrary, a lesson plan is tangible evidence that you are working at your job and demonstrates respect for the students, yourself, and for the profession. A written lesson plan shows that preactive thinking and planning have taken place. There is absolutely no excuse for appearing before a class without evidence of being prepared.

Written and detailed lesson plans provide an important sense of security, which is especially useful to a beginning teacher. Like the rudder of a ship, it helps keep you on course. Without it, you are likely to drift aimlessly. Sometimes a disturbance in the classroom can distract from the lesson, causing the teacher to get "off track" or forget an important part of the lesson. A written and detailed lesson plan provides a road map to guide you and help keep you on track.

Written lesson plans help you to be or become a reflective decision maker. Without a written plan, it is difficult or impossible to analyze how something might have been planned or implemented differently after the lesson has been taught. Written lesson plans serve as resources for the next time you teach the same or a similar lesson and are useful for teacher self-evaluation and for the evaluation of student learning and of the curriculum.

Written lesson plans help you organize material and search for "loopholes," "loose ends," or incomplete content. Careful and thorough planning during the preactive phase of instruction includes anticipation of how the lesson activities will develop as the lesson is being taught. During this anticipation you will actually visualize yourself in the classroom teaching your students, using that visualization to anticipate possible problems.

Written plans help other members of the teaching team understand what you are doing and how you are doing it. This is especially important when implementing an interdisciplinary thematic unit. *Written lesson plans also provide substitute teachers with a guide to follow if you are absent.*

Those reasons clearly express the need to write detailed lesson plans. The list is not exhaustive, however, and you may discover additional reasons why written lesson plans are crucial to effective teaching. In summary, two points must be made: lesson planning is an important and ongoing process; and teachers must take time to plan, reflect, write, test, evaluate, and rewrite their plans to reach optimal performance. In short, preparing written lesson plans is important work.

Assumptions about Lesson Planning

Not all teachers need elaborate written plans for every lesson. Sometimes effective and skilled experienced teachers need only a sketchy outline. Sometimes they may not need written plans at all. Veteran teachers who have taught the topic many times in the past may need only the presence of a class of students to stimulate a pattern of presentation that has often been successful (though frequent use of old patterns may lead one into the rut of unimaginative and uninspiring teaching). You probably do not need to be reminded that the obsolescence of many past classroom practices has been substantiated repeatedly by those researchers who have made serious and recent studies of exemplary educational practices.

Considering the diversity among teachers, their instructional styles, their students, and what research has shown, certain assumptions can be made about lesson planning.

- A plan is more likely to be carefully and thoughtfully plotted during the preactive phase of instruction when the plan is written out.
- Although not all teachers need elaborate written plans for all lessons, all effective teachers do have clearly defined goals and objectives in mind and a planned pattern of instruction for every lesson, whether that plan is written out or not.

- Beginning teachers need to prepare detailed written lesson plans—failing to prepare is preparing to fail.
- Some subject-matter fields, topics, or learning activities require more detailed planning than others do.
- The depth of knowledge a teacher has about a subject or topic influences the amount of planning necessary for the lessons.
- The diversity of students within today's public school classroom necessitates careful and thoughtful consideration about individualizing the instruction—these considerations are best implemented when they have been thoughtfully written into lesson plans.
- The skill a teacher has in remaining calm and in following a trend of thought in the presence of distraction will influence the amount of detail necessary when planning activities and writing the lesson plan.
- There is no particular pattern or format that all teachers need to follow when writing out plans—some teacher-preparation programs have agreed on certain lesson-plan formats for their teacher candidates; you need to know if this is the case for your program.

In summary, well-written lesson plans provide many advantages: they give a teacher an agenda or outline to follow in teaching a lesson; they give a substitute teacher a basis for presenting appropriate lessons to a class—thereby retaining lesson continuity in the regular teacher's absence; they are certainly very useful when a teacher is planning to use the same lesson again in the future; they provide the teacher with something to fall back on in case of a memory lapse, an interruption, or some distraction such as a call from the office or a fire drill; using a written plan demonstrates to students that you care and are working for them; and, above all, they provide beginners security because, with a carefully prepared plan, a beginning teacher can walk into a classroom with the confidence and professional pride gained from having developed a sensible framework for that day's instruction.

Thus, as a beginning teacher, you should make considerably detailed lesson plans. Naturally, this will require a great deal of work for at least the first year or two, but the reward of knowing that you have prepared and presented effective lessons will compensate for that effort. Not only will you discover that student teaching is a demanding experience, you can expect a busy first year of teaching.

A Continual Process

Lesson planning is a continual process even for experienced teachers, for there is always a need to keep materials and plans current and relevant. Because no two classes of students are ever identical, today's lesson plan will need to be tailored to the peculiar needs of each classroom of students. Moreover, because the content of

CLASSROOM VIGNETTE
A Teachable Moment

At Eddy Middle School (Elk Grove, CA), Casey was teaching an eighth-grade humanities block, a two-hour block course that integrates student learning in social studies, reading, and language arts. On this particular day, while Casey and her students were discussing the topic of Manifest Destiny, one of the students raised his hand and when acknowledged by Casey, asked the question, "Why aren't we [referring to the United States] still adding states [i.e., adding territory to the United States]?" Casey immediately replied with "There aren't any more states to add." By responding too quickly, Casey missed one of those "teachable moments," moments when the teacher has the students right where she wants them, where the students are the ones who are thinking and asking questions. What could Casey have done? When was Hawaii added as a state? Why hasn't Puerto Rico become a state? Guam? etc. Aren't those possibilities? Why *aren't* more states or territories being added? What are the political and social ramifications today and how do they differ from those of the 1800s?

instruction and learning will change as each distinct group of students and their needs and interests give input, and as new thematic units are developed, new developments occur, or new theories are introduced, your objectives and the objectives of the students, school, and teaching faculty will change.

For these reasons, lesson plans should be in a constant state of revision—never "set in concrete." Once the basic framework is developed, however, the task of updating and modifying becomes minimal. If your plans are maintained on a computer, making changes from time to time is even easier.

Well Planned but Open to Last-Minute Change

The lesson plan should provide a tentative outline of the time period given for the lesson but should always remain flexible. A carefully worked out plan may have to be set aside because of the unpredictable, serendipitous effect of a "teachable moment" (see the accompanying vignette) or because of unforeseen circumstances, such as a delayed school bus, an impromptu school assembly program, an emergency drill, or the cancellation of school due to inclement weather conditions. Student teachers often are appalled at the frequency of interruptions during a school day and the disruptions to their lesson planning that occur. A daily lesson planned to cover six aspects of a given topic may end with only three of the points having been considered. Although far more frequent than necessary in too many schools these occurrences are natural in a school setting and the teacher and the plans must remain flexible enough to accommodate this reality.

Implementation of Today's Lesson May Necessitate Changes in Tomorrow's Plan

Although you may have your lesson plans completed for several consecutive lessons, as can be inferred by the vignette involving Casey and her students, what actually transpires during the implementation of today's lesson may necessitate last minute adjustments to the lesson you had planned for tomorrow. Consequently, during student teaching in particular it is neither uncommon nor unwanted to have last-minute changes penciled in your lesson plan. If, however, penciled-in modifications are substantial and might be confusing to you during implementation of the lesson, then you should rewrite the lesson plan.

The Problem of Time

A lesson plan should provide enough materials and activities to consume the entire class period or time allotted. As mentioned earlier, you must understand that in your planning for teaching you need to make a conscientious effort to plan for every minute of every class period. The lesson plan, then, is more than a plan for a lesson to be taught; it is a plan that accounts for the entire time that you and your students are together in the classroom. Since planning is a skill that takes years of experience to master, especially when teaching a block of time that may extend for 90 or more minutes and may involve more than one discipline and more than one teacher, as a beginning teacher you should overplan, rather than run the risk of having too few activities to occupy the time the students are in your classroom. One way of assuring that you overplan is to include "if time remains" activities in your lesson plan (see example in Figure 5.7).

LESSON PLAN

Descriptive Course Data

Instructor: Michelle Yendrey   *Course:* Western Civilizations   *Period:* 1
Grade level: 9   *Unit:* History of Religion   *Topic:* Persecution of Christians

Objectives

Upon completion of this lesson students will be able to:
1. Make connections between persecutions today and persecutions that occurred approximately 2,000 years ago.
2. Describe the main teachings of Christianity and how the position of Christianity within the Roman Empire changed over time.
3. Share ideas in a positive and productive manner.

Instructional Components

Activity 1 (Anticipatory Set: 10 minutes) Write on overhead: You have until 8:40 (5 minutes) to write a defense to one of the following statements. (Remember, there are no right or wrong answers. Support your position to the best of your ability.)

• The recent hate crimes in our city can be related to our current unit on the history of religion.
• The recent hate crimes in our city cannot be related to our current unit on the history of religion.

Activity 2 (3–5 minutes) Students will be asked to indicate, by a show of hands, how many chose statement A and how many chose statement B. Some reasons for each will be shared orally and then all papers will be collected.

Activity 3 (3–5 minutes) Return papers of previous assignment. Give students new seat assignments for the activity that follows, and have them assume their new seats.

Activity 4 (15 minutes) The students are now arranged into seven groups. Each group will write a paragraph using the concepts from certain assigned words to answer the essay question(s) at the end of the definition sheet.

   Each group will select a

Task master to keep members of the group on task.
Recorder to write things down.
Spokesperson to present the results.
Timekeeper to keep group alert so task is completed on time.

In addition, some groups will have a

Source master to look up or ask about any questions that arise.

Activity 5 (15–20 minutes) Each group's spokesperson will come to the front of the classroom and present the group's result for activity 4.

Alternate Activity (Plan B: 5–10 minutes) Should the activities run more quickly than anticipated, the students will take out their "Religion Comparison Sheets." With the teacher's direction, the students will fill in the boxes for "similar" and "different" with regard to Christianity and Judaism.

Second Alternate Activity (Plan C: 25–30 minutes) In the unlikely event that timing is really off, each student will be given a blank grid and assigned ten vocabulary words from the definition sheets. Students will be directed to create a crossword puzzle using the definitions as clues and the words as answers. After 15–20 minutes, the crosswords will be collected and distributed to different students to solve. If not completed in class, students will finish and hand them in later along with their essays, for a few points of extra credit. Students will be required to write their names in the appropriate spaces marked "Created By" and "Solved By."

Activity 6 (7–10 minutes) Collect the overhead sheets and pens. Hand out the take-home essay test. Explain and take questions about exactly what is expected from the essay. (This is their first take-home test.)

Materials and Equipment Needed

Overhead projector, transparency sheets (7), and transparency markers (7); 36 copies of the essay question plus directions; 36 copies of the blank grid sheets.

Assessment, Reflection, and Plans for Revision

Figure 5.7
Lesson plan sample with alternative activities.
(*Source:* Courtesy of Michelle Yendrey.)

When a lesson plan does not provide sufficient activity to occupy the entire class period or time that the students are available for the lesson, that is when a beginning teacher often loses control of the class as behavior problems mount. Thus, it is best to prepare more than you likely can accomplish in a given period of time. This is not to imply that you should involve the students in meaningless busy work. Students can be very perceptive when it comes to a teacher who has finished the plan and is attempting to bluff through the minutes that remain before dismissal. And, they are not usually favorably responsive to meaningless busywork.

If you ever do get caught short—as most teachers do at one time or another—one way to avoid embarrassment is to have students work on what is known as an *anchor assignment* (or transitional activity). This is an ongoing assignment, and students understand that whenever they have spare time in class they should be working on it. Example anchor activities include a review of material that has been covered that day or in the past several days, allowing students to work on homework, journal writing, portfolio organization, and long-term project work. Regardless of how you handle time remaining, it works best when you plan for it and write that aspect into your lesson plan. Make sure students understand the purpose and procedures for these anchor assignments.

A Caution about "The Daily Planning Book"

A distinction needs to be made between actual lesson plans and the book for daily planning that many schools require teachers to maintain and even submit to their supervisors a week in advance. Items that a teacher writes into the boxes of a daily planning book (see Figure 5.8) most assuredly are not lesson plans; rather, the pages are a layout by which the teacher writes in the boxes to show what lessons will be taught during the day, week, month, or term. Usually the book provides only a small lined box for time periods for each day of the week. These books are useful for outlining the topics, activities, and assignments projected for the week or term, and supervisors sometimes use them to check the adequacy of teachers' course plans. But they are not lesson plans. Teachers and their supervisors who believe that the notations in the daily planning book are actual lesson plans are fooling themselves. Student teachers should not use these in place of authentic lesson plan formats.

CONSTRUCTING A LESSON PLAN: FORMAT, COMPONENTS, AND SAMPLES

Although it is true that each teacher develops a personal system of lesson planning—the system that works best for that teacher in each unique situation—a beginning teacher needs a more substantial framework from which to work. For that, this section provides a "preferred" lesson plan format (Figure 5.9). Nothing is hallowed about this format, however. Review the preferred format and samples, and unless your program of teacher preparation insists otherwise, use it with your own modifications until you find or develop a better model. All else being equal, however, you are encouraged to begin your teaching following as closely as possible this "preferred" format.

DAILY PLANNING BOOK

Class _____ Lesson _____ Teacher _____

Date	Content	Materials	Procedure	Evaluation
Monday				
Tuesday				
Wednesday				
Thursday				
Friday				

Figure 5.8
A daily planning book.

1. Descriptive Data

Teacher: _____ Class: _____ Date: _____ Grade level: _____

Room number: _____ Period: _____ Unit: _____

Lesson number: _____ Topic: _____

Anticipated noise level (high, moderate, low): _____

2. Goals and Objectives

Instructional goals: _____

_____

_____

Specific objectives:

   Cognitive: _____

   _____

   _____

   Affective: _____

   _____

   _____

   Psychomotor: _____

   _____

   _____

3. Rationale _____

_____

_____

4. Procedure (procedure with modeling examples, transitions, coached practice, and so on)

Content: _____

_____

_____

_____ minutes. Activity 1: Set (introduction) _____

_____

_____

_____ minutes. Activity 2: _____

_____

(continued)

Figure 5.9
Sample of a preferred lesson plan format with seven components. (This sample lesson plan format is placed alone, so if you choose, you may remove it from the book and make copies for use in your teaching.)

_____ minutes. Activity 3 (the exact number of activities in the procedures will vary): _____

_____

_____

_____ minutes. Final activity (lesson conclusion or closure): _____

_____

_____

If time remains: _____

_____

_____

5. Assignments and Reminders of Assignments

_____

_____

_____

Special notes and reminders to myself: _____

_____

_____

_____

6. Materials and Equipment Needed

Audiovisual: _____

_____

Other: _____

_____

7. Assessment, Reflection, and Revision

Assessment of student learning: _____

_____

_____

Reflective thoughts about the lesson: _____

_____

_____

Suggestions for revision: _____

_____

_____

Figure 5.9 *(continued)*

For Guidance, Reflection, and Reference

While student teaching and during your first few years as a beginning teacher, your lesson plans should be printed from a computer or typewritten, or, if that isn't possible, then written out in an intelligible style. If you have a spelling problem, use a spell check and print your plans from the computer. There is good reason to question teachers who say they have no need for a written plan because they have their lessons planned "in their heads." The hours and periods in a school day range from several to many, as are the numbers of students in each class. When multiplied by the number of school days in a week, a semester, or a year, the task of keeping so many things in one's head becomes mind-boggling. Few persons could do that effectively. Until you have considerable experience, you need to prepare and maintain detailed lesson plans for guidance, reflection, and reference.

Basic Elements of a Lesson Plan

The lesson plan format we recommend contains the following basic elements: (1) descriptive course data, (2) goals and objectives, (3) rationale, (4) procedure, (5) assignments and assignment reminders, (6) materials and equipment, and (7) a section for assessment of student learning, reflection on the lesson, and ideas for lesson revision.

Those seven components need not be present in every written lesson plan, nor must they be presented in any particular order. Nor are they inclusive or exclusive. You might choose to include additional components or subsections. Figure 5.10 displays a completed multiple-day lesson that includes the seven components and also incorporates many of the developmentally appropriate learning activities discussed in this book. Following are descriptions of the seven major components of the preferred format, with examples and explanations of why each is important.

FOR YOUR NOTES

1. Descriptive Data

Teacher: _____ Class: _English/Science_   Date: _____ Grade level: _7–12_

Unit: _Investigative Research and Generative Writing_

Lesson Topic: _Writing Response and Peer Assessment via Internet_

Time duration: _several days_

2. Goals and Objectives of Unit

Instructional Goals

2.1. One goal for this lesson is for the students to collaborate and prepare response papers to peers from around the world who have shared the results of their own experimental research findings and research paper about ozone concentrations in the atmosphere.

2.2. The ultimate goal of this unit is for students around the world to prepare and publish for worldwide dissemination a final paper about global ozone levels in the atmosphere.

Objectives

Cognitive:

a. Through cooperative group action, students will conduct experimental research to collect data about the ozone level of air in their environment. (application)

b. In cooperative groups, students will analyze the results of their experiments. (analysis)

c. Students will compile data and infer from their experimental data. (synthesis and evaluation)

d. Through collaborative writing groups, the students will prepare a final paper that summarizes their research study of local atmospheric ozone levels. (evaluation)

e. Through sharing via Internet, students will write response papers to their peers from other locations in the world. (evaluation)

f. From their own collaborative research and worldwide communications with their peers, the students will draw conclusions about global atmospheric ozone levels. (evaluation)

Affective:

a. Students will respond attentively to the response papers of their peers. (attending)

b. Students will willingly cooperate with others during the group activities. (responding)

c. The students will offer opinions about the atmospheric level of ozone. (valuing)

d. The students will form judgments about local, regional, and worldwide ozone levels. (organizing)

e. The students will communicate accurately their findings and attend diligently to the work of their worldwide peers. (internalizing)

Psychomotor:

a. The students will manipulate the computer so that their e-mail communications are transmitted accurately. (manipulating)

b. In a summary, to the study students will describe their feelings about atmospheric ozone concentrations (communicating)

c. The students will ultimately create a proposal for worldwide dissemination. (creating)

3. Rationale

3.1. Important to improvement in one's writing and communication skills are the processes of selecting a topic, decision making, arranging, drafting, proofing, peer review, communicating, revising, editing, rewriting, and publishing the results—processes that are focused on in the writing aspect of this unit.

3.2. Student writers need many readers to respond to their work. Through worldwide communication with peers and dissemination of their final product, this need can be satisfied.

3.3. Students learn best when they are actively pursuing a topic of interest and meaning to them. Resulting from brainstorming potential problems and arriving at their own topic, this unit provides that.

3.4. Real-world problems are interdisciplinary and transcultural; involving writing (English), science, mathematics (e.g., data collecting, graphing, etc.), and intercultural communication, this unit is an interdisciplinary, transcultural unit.

(continued)

Figure 5.10
Lesson plan sample: multiple-day, project-centered, interdisciplinary and transcultural lesson using worldwide communication via the Internet.

4. Procedure

Content

At the start of this unit, collaborative groups were established via Intercultural E-mail Classroom Connections (IECC) (http://www.stolaf.edu/network/iecc) with other classes from schools around the world. These groups of students from around the world conducted several scientific research experiments on the ozone level of their local atmospheric air. To obtain relative measurements of ozone concentrations in the air, students set up experiments that involved stretching rubber bands on a board, then observing the number of days until the bands broke. Students maintained daily journal logs of the temperature, barometric pressure, wind speed/direction, and of the number of days that it took for the bands to break. (The source of information about the science experiment is R. J. Ryder and T. Hughes. *Internet for Educators* [Upper Saddle River, NJ: Prentice Hall, 1997], p. 98.) After compiling their data and preparing single-page summaries of their results via the Internet, students exchanged data with others groups. From data collected worldwide, students wrote a one-page summary as to what conditions may account for the difference in levels of ozone. Following the exchange of students' written responses and their subsequent revisions based on feedback from their worldwide peers, students are now preparing a final summary report about the world's atmospheric ozone level. The intention is to disseminate worldwide (to newspapers and via the Internet) this final report.

Activity 1: Introduction (10 minutes)

Today, in think-share-pairs, you will prepare initial responses to the e-mail responses we have received from other groups from around the world. (Teacher shares the list of places from which e-mail has been received.) Any questions before we get started?

As we discussed earlier, here are the instructions: in your think-share-pairs (each pair is given one response received via e-mail), prepare written responses according to the following outline: (a) note points or information you would like to incorporate in the final paper to be forwarded via Internet, (b) comment on one aspect of the written response you like best, and (c) provide questions to the sender to seek clarification or elaboration. I think you should be able to finish this in about 30 minutes, so let's try for that.

Activity 2: (30 minutes, if needed)

Preparation of dyad responses.

Activity 3: (open)

Let's now hear from each response pair.

Dyad responses are shared with whole class for discussion of inclusion in response paper to be sent via Internet.

Activity 4: (open)

Discussion, conclusion, and preparation of final drafts to be sent to each e-mail correspondent to be done by cooperative groups (the number of groups needed to be decided by the number of e-mail correspondents at this time).

Activity 5: (open)

Later, as students receive e-mail responses from other groups, the responses will be printed and reviewed. The class then responds to each using the same criteria as before and returns this response to the e-mail sender.

Closure

The process continues until all groups (from around the world) have agreed upon and prepared the final report for dissemination.

5. Assignments and Reminders

Remind students of important dates and decisions to be made.

6. Materials and Equipment Needed

School computers with Internet access; printers; copies of e-mail responses.

7. Assessment, Reflection, and Revision

Assessment of student learning for this lesson is formative: journals; daily checklist of student participation in groups; writing drafts.

Reflective thoughts about lesson and suggestions for revision:

Figure 5.10 *(continued)*

Descriptive Data

A lesson plan's descriptive data is demographic and lo-gistical information that identifies details about the class. Anyone reading this information should be able to iden-tify when and where the class meets, who is teaching it, and what is being taught. Although as the teacher you know this information, someone else may not. Members of the teaching team, administrators, and substitute teachers (and, if you are the student teacher, your uni-versity supervisor and cooperating teacher) appreciate this information, especially when asked to fill in for you, even if only for a few minutes during a class session. Most teachers find out which items of descriptive data are most beneficial in their situation and then develop their own identifiers. Remember this: The mark of a well-pre-pared, clearly written lesson plan is the ease with which someone else (such as another member of your teaching team or a substitute teacher) could implement it.

As shown in the sample plans of Figures 5.7 (social studies), 5.10 (English/science), and 5.12 (physical sci-ence), the descriptive data include:

1. *Name of course or class.* These serve as headings for the plan and facilitate orderly filing of plans.
   Social Studies
   Physical Science
   English/Science (integrated block course)
2. *Name of the unit.* Inclusion of this facilitates the or-derly control of the hundreds of lesson plans a teacher constructs. For example:
   Social Studies
       Unit: History of Religion
   Physical Science
       Unit: What's the Matter?
   English/Science
       Unit: Investigative Research and Generative Writing
3. *Topic to be considered within the unit.* This is also useful for control and identification. For example:
   Social Studies
       Unit: History of Religion
       Topic: Persecution of Christians
   Physical Science
       Unit: What's the Matter?
       Topic: Density of Solids
   English/Science
       Unit: Investigative Research and Generative Writing
       Topic: Writing Response and Peer Assessment via the Internet

Anticipated Noise Level

Although not included in the sample lesson plans in this book, the teacher might include in the descriptive data the category of "anticipated classroom noise level," such as "high," "moderate," "low." Its inclusion, or at least considering the idea, is useful during the planning phase of instruction in as far as thinking about how active and noisy the students might be during the lesson, how you might prepare for that, and whether you should warn an administrator and teachers of neighboring classrooms.

Goals and Objectives

The instructional goals are general statements of in-tended accomplishments from that lesson. Teachers and students need to know what the lesson is designed to accomplish. In clear, understandable language, the gen-eral goal statement provides that information. From the sample of Figure 5.10, the goals are:

- To collaborate and prepare response papers to peers from around the world who have shared the results of their own experimental research findings and re-search paper about ozone concentrations in the atmosphere.
- For students worldwide to prepare and publish for worldwide dissemination a final paper about world-wide ozone levels in the atmosphere.

And, from the sample unit of Figure 5.12, goals are to:

- Understand that all matter is made of atoms.
- Develop a positive attitude about physical science.

Because the goals are also included in the unit plan, sometimes a teacher may include only the objectives in the daily lesson plan but not the goals. As a beginning teacher, it usually is a good idea to include both.

SETTING THE LEARNING OBJECTIVES

A crucial step in the development of any lesson plan is that of setting the objectives. It is at this point that many lessons go wrong, and where many beginning teachers have problems.

A Common Error and How to Avoid It

Teachers sometimes confuse "learning activity" (*how* the students will learn it) with the "learning objective" (*what* the student will learn as a result of the learning activity). For example, teachers sometimes mistakenly list what *they* intend to do—such as "lecture on photosynthesis" or "lead a discussion on the causes of the Civil War." They fail to focus on just what the learning objectives in these activities truly are—that is, what the students will be able to do (performance) as a result of the instruc-tional activity. Or, rather than specifying what the stu-dent will be able to do as a result of the learning activi-ties, the teacher mistakenly writes what the students will do in class (the learning activity)—such as "in pairs the students will do the ten problems—as if that were the learning objective. While solving the problems correctly may well be the objective, "doing the ten problems" is not. At the risk of sounding trite or belaboring the point, we emphasize the importance of the teacher being an accurate communicator. If the teacher's stated expectations are fuzzy, the students may never understand them.

When you approach this step in your lesson planning, to avoid error, ask yourself, "What should students learn *as a result* of the activities of this lesson?" Your answer to that question is your objective! Objectives of the lesson are included then as specific statements of performance expectations, detailing precisely what students will be able to do as a result of the instructional activities.

No Need to Include All Domains and Hierarchies in Every Lesson

We have seen beginning teachers worrying needlessly over trying to include objectives from all three domains (cognitive, affective, and psychomotor) in every lesson they write. Please understand that not all three domains are necessarily represented in every lesson plan. As a matter of fact, any given lesson plan may be directed to only one or two, or a few, specific objectives. Over the course of a unit of instruction, however, all domains, and most if not all levels within each, should be addressed.

From the lesson shown in Figure 5.10, sample objectives, and the domain and level (in parentheses) within that domain, are:

- Through cooperative group action, students will conduct experimental research to collect data about the ozone level of air in their environment. (cognitive, application)
- Through the Internet, students will write and share response papers to their peers from other locations in the world. (cognitive, evaluation)
- Students will form judgments about local, regional, and worldwide ozone levels. (affective, organizing)
- Students will create a proposal for worldwide dissemination. (psychomotor, creating)

And, from the lesson illustrated in Figure 5.12, sample objectives are:

- Determine the density of a solid cube. (cognitive, application)
- Communicate the results of their experiments to others in the class. (psychomotor, communicating)

Rationale

The rationale is an explanation of why the lesson is important and why the instructional methods chosen will achieve the objectives. Parents/guardians, students, teachers, administrators, and others have the right to know why specific content is being taught and why the methods employed are being used. Prepare yourself well by setting a goal for yourself of always being prepared with intelligent answers to those two questions.

Teachers become reflective decision makers when they challenge themselves to think about *what* (the content) they are teaching, *how* (the learning activities) they are teaching it, and *why* (the rationale) it must be taught. As illustrated in the sample unit of Figure 5.12, sometimes the rationale is included within the unit introduction and goals, but not in every lesson plan of the unit. Some lessons are carryovers or continuations of a lesson; we see no reason to repeat the rationale for a continuing lesson.

Procedure

The procedure consists of the instructional activities for a scheduled period of time. The substance of the lesson—the information to be presented, obtained, and learned—is the *content*. Appropriate information is selected to meet the learning objectives, the level of competence of the students, and the grade level or course requirements. To be sure your lesson actually covers what it should, you should write down exactly what minimum content you intend to cover. This material may be placed in a separate section or combined with the procedure section. The important thing is to be sure that your information is written down so you can refer to it quickly and easily when you need to.

If, for instance, you intend to conduct the lesson using discussion, you should write out the key discussion questions. Or, if you are going to introduce new material using a ten-minute lecture, then you need to outline the content of that lecture. The word "outline" is not used casually—you need not have pages of notes to sift through; nor should you ever read declarative statements to your students. You should be familiar enough with the content so that an outline (in as much detail as you believe necessary) will be sufficient to carry on the lesson as in the following example of a content outline:

Causes of the Civil War
  A. Primary causes
    1. Economics
    2. Abolitionist pressure
    3. Slavery
    4. etc.
  B. Secondary causes
    1. North–South friction
    2. Southern economic dependence
    3. etc.

The procedure or procedures to be used, sometimes referred to as the *instructional components,* comprise the *procedure* component of the lesson plan. It is the section that outlines what you and your students will do during the lesson. Appropriate instructional activities are chosen to meet the objectives, to match the students' learning styles and special needs, and to assure that all students have an equal opportunity to learn. Ordinarily, you should plan this section of your lesson as an organized entity having a beginning (called the introduction or set), a middle, and an end (called the closure) to be completed during the lesson. This structure is not always needed because some lessons are simply parts of units or long-term plans and merely carry on activities spelled out in those long-term plans. Still, most lessons need to include in the procedure: (a) an *introduction,* the process used to prepare the students mentally for the lesson, sometimes referred to as the set, or initiating activity; (b) *lesson development,* the detailing of *activities* that occur between the beginning and the end of the lesson, including the transitions that connect activities; (c) plans for *practice,* or, sometimes referred to as the follow up (i.e., ways that you intend having students interacting in the classroom) such as individual practice, in dyads, or small groups—receiving guidance or coaching from each other and from you; (d) the *lesson conclusion* (closure)—the planned process of bringing the lesson to an end, thereby providing students with a sense of completeness and, with effective teaching, accomplishment and comprehension by helping students to synthesize the information learned from the lesson; (e) a *timetable* that serves simply as a planning and implementation guide; (f) a plan for what to do if you finish the lesson and time remains; and (g) *assignments,* that is, what students are instructed to do as follow up to the lesson, either as homework or as in-class work, providing students an opportunity to practice and enhance what is being learned. Let's now consider some of those elements in detail.

Introduction to the Lesson

Like any good performance, a lesson needs an effective beginning. In many respects the introduction sets the tone for the rest of the lesson by alerting the students that the business of learning is to begin. The introduction should be an attention-getter. If it is exciting, interesting, or innovative, it can create a favorable mood for the lesson. In any case, a thoughtful introduction serves as a solid indicator that you are well prepared. Although it is difficult to develop an exciting introduction to every lesson taught each day, there are always a variety of options available by which to spice up the launching of a lesson. You might, for instance, begin the lesson by briefly reviewing the pre-

vious lesson, thereby helping students connect the learning. Another possibility is to review vocabulary words from previous lessons and to introduce new ones. Still another possibility is to use the key point of the day's lesson as an introduction and then again as the conclusion. Sometimes teachers begin a lesson by demonstrating a discrepant event (i.e., an event that is contrary to what one might expect), sometimes called a "hook." Yet another possibility is to begin the lesson with a writing activity on some controversial aspect of the ensuing lesson. Sample introductions are:

For U.S. history, study of westward expansion:

- The teacher asks, "Who has lived somewhere other than *(name of your state)?"* After students show hands and answer, the teacher asks individuals why they moved to *(name of your state).* The teacher then asks students to recall why the first European settlers came to the United States, then moves into the next activity.

For science, study of the science process skill of predicting:

- The teacher takes a glass filled to the brim with colored water (colored so it is more visible) and asks students to discuss and predict (in dyads) how many pennies can be added to the glass before any water spills over the rim of the glass.

In short, you can use the introduction of the lesson to review past learning, tie the new lesson to the previous lesson, introduce new material, point out the objectives of the new lesson, help students connect their learning with other disciplines or with real life or, by showing what will be learned and why the learning is important, inducing in students motivation and a mindset favorable to the new lesson.

Lesson Development

The developmental activities that comprise the bulk of the plan are the specifics by which you intend to achieve your lesson objectives. They include activities that present information, demonstrate skills, provide reinforcement of previously learned material, and provide other opportunities to develop understanding and skill. Furthermore, by actions and words, during lesson development the teacher models the behaviors expected of the students. Students need such modeling. By effective modeling, the teacher can exemplify the anticipated learning outcomes. Activities of this section of the lesson plan should be described in some detail so you will know exactly what it is you plan to do and, during the intensity of the class meeting, you do not forget important details and content. It is for this reason you should consider, for example, noting answers (if known) to questions you intend to ask and solutions (if known) to problems you intend to have students solve.

Lesson Conclusion

Having a concise closure to the lesson is as important as having a strong introduction. The concluding activity should summarize and bind together what has ensued in the developmental stage and should reinforce the principal points of the lesson. One way to accomplish these ends is to restate the key points of the lesson. Another is to briefly outline the major points. Still another is to review the major concept. Sometimes the closure is not only a review of what was learned but also the summarizing of a question left unanswered that signals a change in your plan of activities for the next day. In other words, it becomes a *transitional closure.*

Timetable

To estimate, during the preactive phase of instruction, the time factors in any lesson can be very difficult, especially for the beginning teacher. A good procedure is to gauge the amount of time needed for each learning activity and note that alongside the activity and strategy in your plan, as shown in the preferred sample lesson plan format. Placing too much faith in your time estimate may be foolish—an estimate is more for your guidance during the preactive phase of instruction than for anything else. Beginning teachers frequently find that their planned discussions and presentations do not last as long as was expected. As we said earlier in this chapter (see The Problem of Time), to avoid being embarrassed by running out of material, you can purposefully overplan and you can plan in your lesson an "if time remains" section. Another important reason for including a time plan in your lesson is to be able to give information to students about how much time they have for a particular activity, such as a quiz or a group activity.

Assignments

When an assignment is to be given, the assignment should be noted in your lesson plan. When to present an assignment to the students is optional, but it should never be yelled as an afterthought as the students are exiting the classroom at the end of the period. Whether they are to be begun and completed during class time or done outside of class, assignments should be written on the writing board, in a special place on the bulletin board, on the school website, in the course syllabus, in each student's assignment log maintained in a binder, or on a special handout. Take extra care to be sure that assignment specifications are clear to the students. Many teachers give assignments to their students on a weekly or other periodic basis. When given on a periodic basis, rather than daily, assignments should still show in your daily lesson plans so to remind yourself to remind students of them.

Once assignment specifications and due dates are given, it is a good idea not to make major modifications to them, and it is especially important to not change assignment specifications several days after an assignment has been given. Last-minute changes in assignment specifications can be very frustrating to students who have already begun or completed the assignment; it shows little respect to those students.

Understand the difference between assignments and procedures. An assignment tells students *what* is to be done; procedures explain *how* to do it. Although an assignment may include procedures, spelling out procedures alone is not the same thing as giving an academic assignment. When students are given an assignment, they need to understand the reasons for doing it as well as have some notion of ways the assignment might be done.

Allowing time in class for students to begin work on homework assignments and long-term projects is highly recommended; it provides an opportunity for the teacher to give individual attention to students. Being able to coach students is the reason for in-class time to begin assignments. The benefits of *coached practice* include being able to: (a) monitor student work so a student doesn't go too far in a wrong direction, (b) help students to reflect on their thinking, (c) assess the progress of individual students, (d) provide for peer tutoring, and (e) discover or create a "teachable moment." For the latter, for example, while observing and monitoring student practice the teacher might discover a commonly shared student misconception. The teacher then stops and discusses that and attempts to clarify the misconception or, collaboratively with students, plans a subsequent lesson focusing on the common misconception.

Special Notes and Reminders

It is useful to have in the lesson plan format a regular place for special notes and reminders, perhaps (as our preferred format shows) in the same location as assignments. In that special section that can be referred to quickly you can place reminders concerning such things as announcements to be made, school programs, assignment due dates, and makeup work or special tasks for certain students.

Materials and Equipment to Be Used

Materials of instruction include books, media, handouts, and other supplies necessary to accomplish the lesson's learning objectives. You must be *certain* that the proper and necessary materials and equipment are available for the lesson; to be certain requires planning. Teachers who, for one reason or another, have to busy themselves during class time looking for materials or equipment that should have been readied before class began are likely to experience classroom control problems. Plus, if it happens very often, it demonstrates incompetency, and the teacher loses credibility with the students. Teachers want students to be prepared; students expect competent teachers to be prepared.

Assessment, Reflection, and Revision

Details of how you will assess how well students *are learning* (formative assessment) and how well they *have learned* (summative assessment) should be included in your lesson plan. This does not mean to imply that both types of assessment will be found in every daily plan. Comprehension checks for formative assessment can be in the form of questions you ask and that the students ask during the lesson (in the procedural section), as well as various kinds of checklists.

For summative assessment, teachers typically use review questions at the end of a lesson (as a closure) or the beginning of the next lesson (as a review or transfer introduction), independent practice or summary activities at the completion of a lesson, and tests.

In most lesson plan formats, for the reflective phase of instruction there is a section reserved for the teacher to make notes or reflective comments about the lesson. Many student teachers seem to prefer to write their reflections at the end or on the reverse page of their lesson plans. As well as useful to yourself, reflections about the lesson are useful for those who are supervising you if you are a student teacher or a teacher being mentored or considered for tenure. Sample reflective questions you might ask yourself are shown in Figure 5.11.

Writing and later reading your reflections can provide not only ideas that may be useful if you plan to use the lesson again at some later date, but offer cathar-

- What is my overall feeling about today's lesson—good, fair, or bad? What made me feel this way?
- Did students seem to enjoy the lesson? What makes me think so?
- Did the objectives seem to be met? What evidence do I have?
- What aspects of the lesson went well? What makes me believe so?
- Were I to repeat the lesson, what changes might I make?
- Which students seemed to do well? Which ones should I give more attention to? Why and how?
- To what extent was this lesson individualized according to student learning styles, abilities, interests, talents, and needs? Could I do more in this regard? If so, what? If not, then why not?
- Did the students seem to have sufficient time to think and apply? Why or why not?
- Would I have been proud had the school district superintendent been present to observe this lesson? Why or why not?

Figure 5.11
Questions for self-reflection for the reflective phase of instruction.

sis, easing the tension caused from teaching. To continue working effectively at a challenging task (i.e., to prevent intellectual downshifting, or reverting to earlier learned, lower cognitive level behaviors) requires significant amounts of reflection.

If you have reviewed the sample lesson plan formats, proceed now to Exercise 5.3, where you will analyze a lesson that failed; then, as instructed by your course instructor, do Exercises 5.4 and 5.5.

FOR YOUR NOTES

UNIT PLAN SAMPLE WITH A DAILY LESSON

Course _Ninth-Grade Physical Science_

Teacher _____   **Duration of Unit** _Ten days_

Unit Title _What's the Matter?_

Purpose of the Unit

This unit is designed to develop students' understanding of the concept of matter. At the completion of the unit, students should have a clearer understanding of matter and its properties, of the basic units of matter, and of the source of matter.

Rationale of the Unit

This unit topic is important for building a foundation of knowledge for subsequent courses in science. This can increase students' chances of success in those courses, and thereby improve their self-confidence and self-esteem. A basic understanding of matter and its properties is important because of daily decisions that affect the manipulation of matter. It is more likely that students will make correct and safe decisions when they understand what matter is, how it changes form, and how its properties determine its use.

Goals of the Unit

The goals of this unit are for students to:

1. Understand that all matter is made of atoms.
2. Understand that matter stays constant and that it is neither created nor destroyed.
3. Develop certain basic physical science laboratory skills.
4. Develop a positive attitude about physical science.
5. Look forward to taking other science courses.
6. Understand how science is relevant to their daily lives.

Instructional Objectives of the Unit

Upon completion of this unit of study, students should be able to:

1. List at least ten examples of matter.
2. List the four states of matter, with one example of each.
3. Calculate the density of an object when given its mass and volume.
4. Describe the properties of solids, liquids, and gases.
5. Demonstrate an understanding that matter is made of elements and that elements are made of atoms.
6. Identify and explain one way that knowledge of matter is important to their daily lives.
7. Demonstrate increased self-confidence in pursuing laboratory investigations in physical science.
8. Demonstrate skill in communicating within the cooperative learning group.
9. Demonstrate skill in working with the triple-beam balance.

Unit Overview

Throughout this unit, students will be developing a visual learning map of matter. Information for the map will be derived from laboratory work, class discussions, lectures, student readings, and research. The overall instructional model is that of concept attainment. Important to this is an assessment of students' concepts about matter at the beginning of the unit. The preassessment and the continuing assessment of their concepts will center on the following:

1. What is matter, and what are its properties? Students will develop the concept of matter by discovering the properties that all matter contains (that is, it has mass and takes up space).
2. Students will continue to build upon their understanding of the concept of matter by organizing matter into its four major states (that is, solid, liquid, gas, plasma). The concept development will be used to define the attributes of each state of matter, and students will gather information by participating in laboratory activities and class discussions.
3. What are some of the physical properties of matter that make certain kinds of matter unique? Students will experiment with properties of matter such as elasticity, brittleness, and density. Laboratory activities will allow students to contribute their observations and information to the further development of their concept of matter. Density activities enable students to practice their lab and math skills.

(continued)

Figure 5.12
Sample integrated unit plan with one daily lesson.
(*Source:* Courtesy of Will Hightower.)

4. What are the basic units of matter, and where did matter come from? Students will continue to develop their concept of matter by working on this understanding of mixtures, compounds, elements, and atoms.

Assessment of Student Achievement

For this unit, assessment of student achievement will be both formative and summative. Formative evaluation will be done daily by checklists of student behavior, knowledge, and skills. Summative evaluation will be based on the following criteria:

1. Student participation as evidenced by completion of daily homework, class work, laboratory activities, and class discussions and by the information on the student behavior checklists.
2. Weekly quizzes on content.
3. Unit test.

Lesson Number _____   **Duration of Lesson** *1–2 hours*_____

Unit Title *What's the Matter?*_____   **Teacher** _____

Lesson Title *Mission Impossible*_____   **Lesson Topic** *Density of Solids*_____

Objectives of the Lesson

Upon completion of this lesson, students should be able to:

1. Determine the density of a solid cube.
2. Based on data gathered in class, develop their own definition of density.
3. Prepare and interpret graphs of data.
4. Communicate the results of their experiments to others in the class.

Materials Needed

1. Two large boxes of cereal and two snack-size boxes of the same cereal.
2. Four brownies (two whole and two cut in halves).
3. Four sandboxes (two large plastic boxes and two small boxes, each filled with sand).
4. Two triple-beam balances.
5. Several rulers.
6. Six hand-held calculators.
7. Eighteen colored pencils (six sets with three different colors per set).
8. Copies of lab instructions (one copy for each student).

Instructional Procedure with Approximate Time Line

ANTICIPATORY SET (10–15 MINUTES)
Begin class by brainstorming to find what students already know about density. Place the word on the board or overhead, and ask students if they have heard of it. Write down their definitions and examples. Hold up a large box of cereal in one hand and the snack-size box in the other. Ask students which is more dense. Allow them time to explain their responses. Then tell them that by the end of this lesson they will know the answer to the question and that they will develop their own definition of density.

LABORATORY INVESTIGATION (30–60 MINUTES)
Students are divided into teams of four students of mixed abilities. Each member has a role:

1. *Measure master:* In charge of the group's ruler and ruler measurements.
2. *Mass master:* In charge of the group's weighings.
3. *Engineer:* In charge of the group's calculator and calculations.
4. *Graph master:* In charge of plotting the group's data on the graph paper.

Each team has eight minutes before switching stations. Each team completes three stations and then meets to make their graphs and to discuss results.

Station 1: **Cereal Box Density.** Students calculate the density of a large and a small box of cereal to determine if a larger and heavier object is more dense. The masses versus the volumes of the two boxes are plotted on graph paper using one of the pencil colors.

Figure 5.12 *(continued)*

INSTRUCTIONS

1. The density of any object is determined by dividing its mass by its volume. Density in grams is divided by volume in cubic centimeters. Example: 20 g/10 cm^3 = 2 g/cm^3.
2. Measure the volume of the small cereal box (length × width × height), and use the balance to determine its mass in grams. The engineer can do the calculations on the calculator. The graph master should graph the results of each trial and connect two points with a straight line.
3. Repeat the procedure using the large box of cereal.
4. The engineer computes the density of both cereal boxes with the calculator and records the results on the proper blank below the graph.

(continued)

Figure 5.12 *(continued)*

a. Density of large box of cereal _____

b. Density of small box of cereal _____

c. Density of large brownie _____

d. Density of small brownie _____

e. Density of large sandbox _____

f. Density of small sandbox _____

Station 2: **Brownie Density.** Students calculate the density of a full-size brownie and a half-size brownie. Results are plotted on the same graph as in Station 1, but with the second color.

INSTRUCTIONS

1. The density of any object is determined by dividing its mass by its volume. Density in grams is divided by volume in cubic centimeters. Example: 20 g/10 cm^3 = 2 g/cm^3.
2. Measure the volume of a small brownie (length × width × height), and use the balance to determine its mass in grams. The engineer can do the calculations on the calculator. The graph master should graph the results of each trial and connect two points with a straight line.
3. Repeat the procedure using the large brownie.
4. The engineer computes the density of both brownies and records the results on the proper blank.

Station 3: **Sandbox Density.** Students calculate the density of a large and a small box filled with sand. Results are plotted on the graph, but with the third color.

INSTRUCTIONS

1. The density of any object is determined by dividing its mass by its volume. Density in grams is divided by volume in cubic centimeters. Example: 20 g/10 cm^3 = 2 g/cm^3.
2. Measure the volume of the small sandbox (length × width × height), and use the balance to determine its mass in grams. The engineer can do the calculations on the calculator. The graph master should graph the results of each trial and connect two points with a straight line.
3. Repeat the procedure using the large sandbox.
4. The engineer computes the density of both boxes and records the results on the proper blank.

Lab Worksheet. Teams return to their seats to do the graphing, analyze the results, and answer the following questions from their lab sheets:

1. Is a larger, heavier object more dense than its smaller counterpart? Explain your evidence.
2. What is your definition of density?
3. Which is more dense, a pound of feathers or a pound of gold? Explain your answer.

LESSON CLOSURE (10 MINUTES OR MORE)
When all teams are finished, teams should display their graphs and share and discuss the results.

Concepts
1. Density is one of the properties of matter.
2. Mass and volume are related.
3. Density is determined by dividing mass by volume.

Extension Activities
1. Use a density graph to calculate the mass and volume of a smaller brownie.
2. Explore the story of Archimedes and the king's crown.

Evaluation, Reflection, and Revision of Lesson
Upon completion of this lesson and of the unit, revision in this lesson may be made on the basis of teacher observations and student achievement.

Figure 5.12 *(continued)*

EXERCISE 5.3

Analysis of a Lesson That Failed

Instructions: The planning and structure of a lesson are often predictors of the success of its implementation. The purpose of this exercise is to read the following synopsis of the implementation of a lesson, answer the discussion questions individually, and use your responses as a basis for class discussion in small groups about lesson.

The Setting: Junior high life science class; 1:12–2:07 P.M., spring semester.

Synopsis of Events

1:12	Bell rings.
1:12–1:21	Teacher directs students to read from their text, while he takes attendance.
1:21–1:31	Teacher distributes a ditto to each student; students are now to label the parts of a flower shown on the handout.
1:31–1:37	Silent reading and labeling of ditto.
1:37–1:39	Teacher verbally gives instructions for working on a real flower (e.g., by comparing it with the drawing on the handout). Students may use the microscopes if they want.
1:39–1:45	Teacher walks around room, giving each student a real flower.
1:45–2:05	Chaos erupts. There is much confusion with students wandering around, throwing flower parts at each other. Teacher begins writing referrals and sends two students to the office for their misbehavior. Teacher is flustered, directs students to spend remainder of period quietly reading from their texts. Two more referrals are written.
2:05–2:07	A few students begin meandering toward the exit.
2:07	End of period (much to the delight of the teacher).

Questions for Class Discussion

1. Do you think the teacher had a lesson plan? If so, what (if any) were its good points? Its problems? _____

   _____

   _____

   _____

2. If you believed that the teacher had a lesson plan, do you believe the teacher had a written and detailed lesson plan? Explain. What is your evidence? _____

   _____

   _____

   _____

3. How might the lesson have been prepared and implemented to avoid the chaos? _____

   _____

   _____

   _____

4. Was the format of the lesson traditional? Explain. _____

_____

_____

_____

5. Have you experienced a class such as this? Explain. _____

_____

_____

_____

6. Which teacher behaviors were probable causes of much of the chaos?

_____

_____

_____

7. What teacher behaviors could have prevented the chaos and made the lesson more effective?

_____

_____

_____

8. Within the 55-minute class period, students were expected to operate rather high on the Learning Experiences Ladder (see Figure 5.5). Consider this analysis: nine minutes of silent reading; ten minutes of listening; six minutes of silent reading and labeling; two minutes of listening; six minutes of action (the only direct experience); and an additional 22 minutes of silent reading. In all, there were approximately 49 minutes (89 percent of the class time) of abstract verbal and visual symbolization. Is that a problem? _____

_____

_____

_____

9. What have you learned from this exercise? _____

_____

_____

_____

EXERCISE 5.4A
Preparing a Lesson Plan

Instructions: Use the model lesson format or an alternative format that is approved by your instructor to prepare a _____-minute lesson plan (length to be decided in your class) for a grade and course of your choice. After completing your lesson plan, evaluate it yourself, modify it, and then have your modified version evaluated by at least three peers, using Exercise 5.4b for the evaluation, before turning it in for your instructor's evaluation. This exercise may be connected with Exercise 5.5.

EXERCISE 5.4B
Self and Peer Assessment of My Lesson Plan

Instructions: You may duplicate blank copies of this form for evaluation of the lesson you developed for Exercise 5.4a. Have your lesson plan evaluated by two of your peers and yourself. For each of the items below, evaluators should check either "yes" or "no," and write instructive comments. Compare the results of your self-evaluation with the other evaluations.

	No	*Yes*	*Comments*
1. Are descriptive data adequately provided?	____	____	_____
2. Are the goals clearly stated?	____	____	_____
3. Are the objectives specific and measureable?	____	____	_____
4. Are objectives correctly classified?	____	____	_____
5. Are objectives only low-order or is higher-order thinking expected?	____	____	_____
6. Is the rationale clear and justifiable?	____	____	_____
7. Is the plan's content appropriate?	____	____	_____
8. Is the content likely to contribute to achievement of the objectives?	____	____	_____
9. Given the time frame and other logistical considerations, is the plan workable?	____	____	_____
10. Will the opening (set) likely engage the students?	____	____	_____

	No	Yes	Comments
11. Is there a preassessment strategy?	___	___	_____
12. Is there a proper mix of learning activities for the time frame of the lesson?	___	___	_____
13. Are the activities developmentally appropriate for the intended students?	___	___	_____
14. Are transitions planned?	___	___	_____
15. If relevant, are key questions written out and key ideas noted in the plan?	___	___	_____
16. Does the plan indicate how coached practice will be provided for each student?	___	___	_____
17. Is adequate closure provided in the plan?	___	___	_____
18. Are materials and equipment needed identified, and are they appropriate?	___	___	_____
19. Is there a planned formative assessment, formal or informal?	___	___	_____
20. Is there a planned summative assessment?	___	___	_____
21. Is the lesson coordinated in any way with other aspects of the curriculum?	___	___	_____
22. Is the lesson likely to provide a sense of meaning for the students by helping to bridge their learning?	___	___	_____
23. Is an adequate amount of time allotted to address the information presented?	___	___	_____
24. Is a thoughtfully prepared and relevant student assignment planned?	___	___	_____
25. Could a substitute who is knowledgeable follow the plan?	___	___	_____

Additional comments:

EXERCISE 5.5

Preparing an Instructional Unit: Bringing It All Together

Instructions. The purpose of this exercise is threefold: (1) to give you experience in preparing an instructional unit, (2) to assist you in preparing an instructional unit that you can use in your teaching, and (3) to start your collection of instructional units that you may be able to use later in your teaching. This assignment that will take several hours to complete, and you will need to read ahead in this book. Our advice, therefore, is to start the assignment early, with a due date much later in the course. Your course instructor may have specific guidelines for your completion of this exercise; what follows is the essence of what you are to do.

First, with help from your instructor divide your class into three teams, each with a different assignment pertaining to this exercise. The units completed by these teams are to be shared with all members of the class for feedback and possible use later.

Team 1

Members of this team, individually or in dyads, will develop standard teaching units, perhaps with different grade levels, grades 6–12, in mind. Using a format that is practical, *each member or pair of this team* will develop a minimum two-week (10-day) unit for a particular grade level, subject, and topic. Regardless of format chosen, each unit plan should include the following elements:

1. Identification of (a) grade level, (b) subject, (c) topic, and (d) time duration.

2. Statement of rationale and general goals.

3. Separate listing of instructional objectives for each daily lesson. Wherever possible, the unit should include objectives from all three domains—cognitive, affective, and psychomotor.

4. List of materials and resources needed and where they can be obtained (if you have that information). These should also be listed for each daily lesson.

5. Ten consecutive daily lesson plans (see Exercise 5.4A).

6. List of all items that will be used to assess student learning *during* and *at completion* of the unit of study.

7. Statement of how the unit will attend to the diversity of students one is likely to find; such as pertaining to students' reading levels, socioethnic backgrounds, and special needs.

Team 2

Following the steps of Exercise 8.1 (Chapter 8), *each member* of this team will develop a self-instructional module.

Team 3

In collaboration, members of this team will develop interdisciplinary thematic units. Depending upon the number of students in your class, Team 3 may actually comprise several teams, with each team developing an ITU. Each team should be comprised of no less than two members (e.g., a math specialist and a science specialist) and no more than four (e.g., history/social studies, English/language arts/reading, mathematics, and science).

SUMMARY

You have learned of the importance of learning modalities and instructional modes. You have learned about the importance of providing an accepting and supportive learning environment, as well as about teacher behaviors that are necessary to facilitate student learning beyond that of procedural knowledge.

With this chapter you continued building your knowledge base about why planning is important and how units with lessons are useful pedagogical tools. Developing units of instruction that integrate student learning and provide a sense of meaning for the students requires coordination throughout the curriculum. Hence, for students, learning is a process of discovering how information, knowledge, and ideas are interrelated so they can make sense out of self, of school, and of life. Preparing chunks of information into units and units into lessons helps students to process and understand knowledge. You have developed your first unit of instruction and are well on your way to becoming a competent planner of instruction.

You have been guided through the processes necessary to prepare yourself to teach in a classroom. Later, after you have studied Part III on specific instructional strategies, aids, media, and resources to supplement your instruction, you may choose to revisit this chapter and make revisions to your completed unit and lessons. In Part III your attention is directed to the selection and implementation of specific strategies, aids, and resources from which you may select to facilitate students learning of particular skills and content, beginning with the use of questioning.

ADDITIONAL EXERCISES

See the companion website http://www.prenhall.com/kellough for the following exercises related to the content of this chapter:

- Methods of Instruction
- Generating Ideas for Interdisciplinary Units
- Initiating an ITU with a Question Map
- Integrating the Topic
- Planning Culminating Activities
- Putting Objectives, Resources, and Learning Activities Together for a Teaching Plan

QUESTIONS FOR CLASS DISCUSSION

1. In subject field discussion groups, list and describe specific considerations you should give to student safety (a topic that this book cannot adequately otherwise address) when preparing instructional plans. Share your lists with other groups.
2. Explain the importance of the notion that all teachers are teachers of literacy and of thinking, social, and learning skills. Do you agree or disagree with the notion? Why?
3. Give several reasons why both a student teacher and a first-year teacher need to prepare detailed lesson plans. Describe when, if ever, the teacher can or should divert from the written lesson plan.
4. Divide your class into grade level (middle school or high school) and subject area groups. Have each group devise two separate lesson plans to teach the same topic to the same group of students (identified), but one plan uses direct instruction while the other uses indirect. Have groups share the outcomes of this activity with one another.
5. Explain why, when taught by access strategies, students learn less content but learn it more effectively? For a teacher using access strategies, could this be a problem? Explain.
6. Select one of the Reflective Thoughts from the opening of Part II (page 70) that is specifically related to the content of this chapter, research it, and write a one-page essay explaining why you agree or disagree with the thought. Share your essay with members of your class for their thoughts.
7. Describe observable behaviors that would enable you to tell whether a student is learning to think critically. Describe where, specifically, in a unit plan, one would expect to find these observable behaviors.
8. Describe any prior concepts you held that changed as a result of your experiences with this chapter. Describe the changes.
9. From your current observations and field work as related to this teacher preparation program, clearly identify one specific example of educational practice that seems contradictory to exemplary practice or theory as presented in this chapter. Present your explanation for the discrepancy.
10. Do you have questions generated by the content of this chapter? If you do, list them along with ways answers might be found.

FOR FURTHER READING

Bergstrom, J. M., and O'Brien, L. A. "Themes of Discovery." *Educational Leadership* 58(7):29–33 (April 2001).

Charischak, I. "In the Spirit of Eratosthenes: Measuring the Circumference of the Earth." *Learning and Leading with Technology* 25(6):42–47 (March 1998).

Erlandson, C., and McVittie, J. "Student Voices on Integrative Curriculum." *Middle School Journal* 33(2):28–36 (November 2001).

Johnson, A. "Fiber Meets Fibonacci: The Shape of Things to Come." *Mathematics Teaching in the Middle School* 4(4):256–262 (January 1999).

Kirkwood, T. F. "Integrating an Interdisciplinary Unit in Middle School: A School—University Partnership." *Clearing House* 72(3):160–163 (January/February 1999).

Michael, J. "Lewis Latimer: African American Inventor, Poet and Activist." OAH *Magazine of History* 12(2):25–30 (Winter 1998).

Richburg, R. W., and Nelson, B. J. "Integrating Content Standards and Higher-Order Thinking: A Geography Lesson Plan." *Social Studies* 89(2):85–90 (March/April 1998).

Roberts, P. L., and Kellough, R. D. *A Guide for Developing an Interdisciplinary Thematic Unit*. 2d. Ed. Upper Saddle River, NJ: Prentice Hall, 2000.

Roblyer, M. D. *Integrating Technology across the Curriculum: A Database of Strategies and Lesson Plans*. Upper Saddle River, NJ: Merrill/Prentice Hall, 1999.

Rubink, W. L., and Taube, S. R. "Mathematical Connections from Biology: 'Killer' Bees Come to Life in the Classroom." *Mathematics Teaching in the Middle School* 4(6):350–356 (March 1999).

Shiman, D. "Human Rights and Foreign Policy: A Lesson Plan." *Social Education* 63(1):58–60 (January/February 1999).

Smith, C. "Addressing Standards through Curriculum Integration." *Middle School Journal*. 33(2):5–6 (November 2001).

Smulyan, S., Goldstein, C., and Gerhard, J. "The Stocking Story: You Be the Historian." *OAH Magazine of History* 12(2):31–35 (Winter 1998).

Smulyan, S., Kosty, C., and Brennan, S. "The Vindex Special: Learning about Technology through Advertising." *OAH Magazine of History* 12(2):36–39 (Winter 1998).

Totten, S. "Using Reader-Response Theory to Study Poetry about the Holocaust with High School Students." *Social Studies* 89(1):30–34 (January/February 1998).

Wasley, P. "Teaching Worth Celebrating." *Educational Leadership* 56(8):8–13 (May 1999).

Weilbacher, G. "Is Curriculum Integration an Endangered Species?" *Middle School Journal* 33(2):18–27 (November 2001).

CHAPTER 6

Four-Phase Lesson and Unit Design

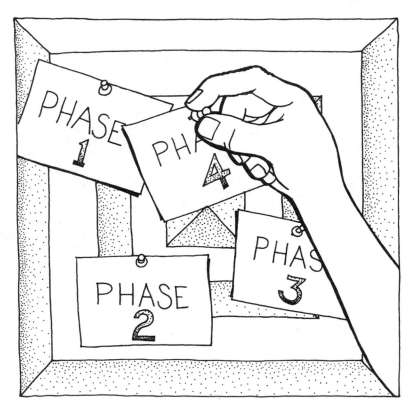

Whereas short lectures and memorization play a part, much more learning takes place when learners are constantly immersed in complex experience; when they process, analyze, and examine this experience for meaning and understanding; and when they constantly relate what they have learned to their own central purposes. When teachers assist students in engaging their own purposes, teachers may find that skill development, with its emphasis on practice, rehearsal, and refinement, becomes more effective. The challenge, therefore, is to fit skills and content to the learner, rather than fit the learner to the curriculum.
—Renate and Geoffrey Caine 1997, 18–19

INQUIRING—GATHERING— PROCESSING—APPLYING

The challenge of lesson and unit design is to package curriculum and instruction in a way that both engages students in significant curriculum and stimulates high-level thinking skills. Information and concepts are crucial to student understanding, but just as crucial is the ability to think and to manipulate the information and concepts in ways that demonstrate that the students know how to use and apply the sum of their experience to new situations.

The four-phase lesson and unit design mirrors both the processing model (see Figure 6.1) and the natural progression of the learning process (see Figure 6.2) and is thus both brain-compatible and well-suited to teaching in the block.

Many of the prevailing lesson plan models are not brain-compatible and do not necessarily work well as the organizational structure of a lesson in an extended time format because they:

- Promote one major activity during a lesson rather than several "pulsed activities"
- Do not incorporate brain-compatible activities
- Do not recommend/accommodate mediation, metacognition, or processing
- Reinforce the outmoded concept that the teacher's principle function is to disseminate information
- Lack real problem-solving focus

On the other hand, the four-phase lesson design begins with the *inquire* phase in which questions are posed that the study of the particular curriculum lesson or unit can answer. It is in the first phase that the teacher discovers what prior knowledge is present and hears the questions students would like to see answered throughout the study of the unit. Beginning connections are established here that help the class see the applicability of whatever the content area is. It is in this phase that the teacher helps to generate the kind of interest that can catalyze enough motivation to begin the serious study of the curriculum content.

The remaining three phases are built on Bellanca and Fogarty's (1991) work on the Three-Story Intellect as described in *Blueprints for Thinking in the Cooperative Classroom*. In the *gather* phase, information is presented; data and concepts are researched and amassed; material is observed and described; and stories are summarized or narrated (Bellanca and Fogarty 1991, 88).

In the *process* phase, the gathered information is analyzed, compared, prioritized, and categorized in ways that make sense for the student. It is in this phase that students begin to internalize the material of the curriculum unit (Bellanca and Fogarty 1991, 90).

In the *apply* phase, the internalized information is used to create a product, is built upon to figure out the next steps, is used to imagine a different outcome, and is applied to something concrete and real in the students' lives (Bellanca and Fogarty 1991, 92).

The dimensions of inquiring, gathering, processing, and applying may not flow precisely from one to the other. For example, the gathering and processing may go back and forth for awhile before actually moving on to the applying. What is crucial is for all four phases to be included, even as they spiral back on themselves, and for the lesson and unit to culminate with the student applying the knowledge gained in the other three phases in an authentic activity or experience. It is the *apply* phase that helps students discern why all the effort of learning and studying is going on. When the application phase is shortchanged or skipped altogether, motivation is squelched. The four phases work together to create informed students who can utilize the material learned.

In addition to the four phases, Figure 6.3 includes space to write in the particular lesson focus, the two or three multiple intelligences to target that day, and the specific thinking skill and specific social skill targeted that day. The last line is for the lesson wrap-up, which could simply be concluding remarks by the teacher such as "Tomorrow we'll explore how the information you gathered today has implications for playing sports." Or, "As you can see, the insights we reflected on today reveal that the character in this play is very much like some of your friends."

Each phase is described below in terms of

- The relative potential student benefits
- The teacher's role
- Brain-compatibility

(See Figure 6.4)

THE INQUIRE PHASE

Brain research suggests students must bring previously formed patterns from long-term memory to working memory so the brain can connect new information with stored schemas as well as modify and expand them.

In the Inquire Phase Students Benefit from

- Constructing meaning of lesson content from their past experiences and stored information, knowledge, and understanding
- Identifying what they know about the lesson content, what they want to know about the subject, and eventually what they actually learned

The Processing Model and the Four-Phase
Lesson Design

What?	Inquire Phase	• What do students know about the lesson content? • What experiences have students had? • What do others know? • What would students like to know?
So what?	Gather Phase	• So what else do students need to know? • So what are the important ideas, knowledge, and skills needed? • So what do students need to do to understand the information or improve their skills?
Now what?	Process Phase	• Now what can students do to remember this information. • Now what activities will clarify the concepts and ensure student learning and understanding • Now what can the students do with the information that will help them know it?
What else?	Apply Phase	• What else can students do with the information and skills? • What else is related to what students are learning or experiencing in their daily lives? • What else is done with this knowledge that the student can try?

Figure 6.1

Natural Learning Progression

Identify past, related student experiences and their impact on student knowledge and perception of the topic at hand.

Provide new insights and information, complex interrelated concepts, extensive concepts, and an opportunity to understand relationships and make multiple appropriate connections.

Engage students to act on the information, to reinforce concepts through involvement in various problem-solving, to participate in complex tasks that require open-ended strategies, etc.

Consider various ways the concepts, information, and skills can be applied in settings that are new and dynamic.

Figure 6.2

- Participating in "communities of practice"—the learning theory that states that everyone learns as part of a group, that the collective knowledge of the group elevates each member's understanding and learning—to identify the collective knowledge, skills, and expertise of the learning group through discussions and sharing
- Demonstrating or sharing what they know or think they know about the lesson content so the teacher can identify strengths and weaknesses of the group and adjust activities and time accordingly
- Gauging their level of motivation and emotional involvement in the lesson content

The Teacher's Role in the Inquire Phase: Consultant

The role of the teacher varies within each phase and among the phases. There isn't one role that fits with each phase perfectly. All four roles can be used during each phase or combined in a variety of configurations for each phase. Teachers can select the roles they feel are most appropriate for the learning experience of students. Descriptions of the teacher's role in each phase are generalizations.

The teacher acts as a consultant by assessing what the students know, what they misunderstand, what they have experienced, and what they need to improve their understanding and develop appropriate skills.

Brain-Compatibility in the Inquire Phase

The activities in this phase are brain compatible because they

- Draw on what the students know and have experienced
- Call upon the emotions that are linked with the knowledge

- Elicit input from peers and cooperative groups
- Help students assess themselves and others
- Begin the connection-making process with new information and skills
- Do not require a prescribed set of responses or outcomes

THE GATHER PHASE

In the Gather Phase Students Benefit from

- Thinking through concepts to arrive at an understanding that they construct instead of being supplied information without having to think about the basis or genesis of the information
- Beginning to connect new ideas and understandings to those they previously learned
- Beginning to organize, classifying, and categorizing new information and concepts
- Beginning to identify patterns and relationships among new concepts and skills
- Participating in group investigations
- Collecting information by various means that accommodate each student's unique learning style and multiple intelligences

The Teacher's Role in the Gather Phase: Presenter

As a presenter, the teacher can prepare mini-lectures, model recommended learning and thinking strategies and behaviors, present students with experiences that can teach or reinforce content, require students to present their data and/or their processes, invite experts to share their insights, and develop opportunities for students to learn from a variety of sources, including

Lesson Plan

Lesson Topic:
Content Area(s):

Lesson Benchmarks/Goals	Focused Multiple Intelligences	Assessment Methods

Inquire Phase _____ Minutes	**Gather Phase** _____ Minutes	**Process Phase** _____ Minutes	**Apply Phase** _____ Minutes
Attend:	Attend:	Attend:	Attend:
Experience:	Experience:	Experience:	Experience:
Reflect:	Reflect:	Reflect:	Reflect:

Wrap-Up

Figure 6.3

Four Phases for Lesson and Unit Planning

	Inquiring	Gathering	Processing	Applying
Function	• Raises questions the unit will answer • Discovers prior knowledge	• Information is presented • Data and concepts are amassed • Material is observed and described	• Gathered information is analyzed, compared, prioritized and categorized	• Now understood information is used to create a product or applied to something concrete in the student's life
Student Benefit(s)	• Teacher checks what they want to get out of the lesson • Student's own knowledge is affirmed	• The students collect information by various means that accomodate each student's unique multiple intelligences	• Organizing, classifying, and categorizing new information and concepts • Making connections with prior material and experiences	• Explores ways to apply the data & concepts in ways that connect with the student's real life
Teacher's Role	• Teachers assess what the students know • Teachers assess the content and skills the students need to grasp	• Prepare mini-lectures • Model learning and thinking strategies • Invite experts • Develop learning opportunities	• Organizes individual and group activities to help construct the meaning of the information	• Enables the students to express their knowledge in various ways • Catalyzes applications beyond those in one content area
Brain Compatibility	• Draws on what the students know and have experienced • Calls upon the emotions to generate involvement	• Requires the students to become immersed in data gathering • Offers interaction with peers	• Asks students to create the meaning and significance • Students teach each other and help to clarify the data	• Encourages transfer and application of material learned • Occasions reflecting on the learning process

Figure 6.4

technology, resource materials like books, magazines, television, the Internet, and their peers, and any other appropriate sources.

Brain-Compatibility in the Gather Phase

The activities in this phase are brain compatible because they

- Require students to become immersed in information gathering or data collecting
- Ask students to think through the information to identify processes and to make meaning
- Offer students an opportunity to interact regularly with peers, teachers, and others who can answer questions, share information, and reinforce understanding
- Allow students a chance to learn in their preferred way without prescribing one technique or strategy
- Assist students in looking for patterns and recognizing appropriate examples
- Do not require a prescribed set of procedures for making sense of the information, so students can start with wholes and look for parts or study parts to construct wholes.

THE PROCESS PHASE

In the Process Phase Students Benefit from

- Rehearsing skills in a context that is familiar and relevant
- Exploring concepts through a variety of processes, with a particular focus on the multiple intelligences
- Practicing concepts in new and challenging ways that may differ from earlier models
- Observing others as they practice to develop competencies and compare their own processes with those of others
- Receiving immediate and appropriate feedback
- Engaging in a variety of different ways of teaching and helping others understand and learn

The Teacher's Role in the Process Phase: Facilitator

The facilitator's role is to guide learning and to help students acquire knowledge and skills. The facilitator utilizes the constructivist approach to learning by designing cooperative learning activities, group discussions, and individual reflection time. The constructivist model of learning relies on the group, the group process, and individual involvement for constructing meaning from experiences and prior knowledge. The facilitator

- Organizes group activities where the synergy of group interaction discovers and constructs meaning and learning from experiences

- Leads processing and open discussions with the group(s) as they explore their understandings from experiences
- Asks participants to personally reflect on each experience

Brain-Compatibility in the Process Phase

The activities in this phase are brain compatible because they

- Require students to challenge themselves
- Ask students to think through the information again and again
- Offer students an opportunity to teach others, to clarify both understandings and misunderstandings
- Allow students a chance to learn in their preferred way without prescribing one technique or strategy
- Assist students in giving and receiving feedback
- Allow students to deviate from a prescribed set of procedures to follow the process where it takes them

THE APPLY PHASE

In the Apply Phase Students Benefit from

- Looking for other curricular connections with the skills, knowledge, and concepts they learned
- Exploring ways to apply the lesson material that are different from what was used in the lesson
- Choosing various ways to express their understanding or demonstrate individual competence
- Evaluating the effectiveness of the learning and the validity of the information or skills they have acquired
- Taking the homework assignments and looking for ways to scaffold the learning
- Engaging others to explore and compare their understanding

The Teacher's Role in the Apply Phase: Mediator

The mediator's role is to guide, realign, and focus students' thinking and attention through learning experiences. The mediator uses metacognition activities, diagnostic/prescriptive assessments, and techniques that occasion transfer. The mediator

- Guides the direction of the reflective or introspective thinking of students
- Identifies problems or concerns of students, helps them realize their particular challenges, and assists and encourages them to modify their understandings and behaviors
- Focuses students' attention on key ideas, main themes, or critical issues. They do this by eliminating distracters such as side issues or extraneous information

- Explores with students the personal meaning and the various applications of each experience or episode.
- Encourages students to transfer their new knowledge to broader applications

When fulfilling the role of mediator, teachers need to

- Label and draw attention to their instructional strategies and behaviors
- Think "out loud" as they perform cognitive functions like problem-solving, making conceptual or informational connections, recognizing patterns, or identifying relationships
- Discuss how their experiences lead to new understandings or insights and that they occurred through self reflection, introspection, and personal evaluation
- Provide feedback to the group
- Reveal their own strengths and challenges
- Explore other applications of what has been learned by teaching students how to transfer their understanding to related disciplines and concepts
- Encourage students to do the same things modeled by the teacher

Whichever role teachers assume throughout the course of a lesson, they select the teaching strategies that will help them accomplish the role and facilitate student learning. Appropriate instructional strategies keep students focused and engaged in making meaning of the learning experiences.

Brain-Compatibility in the Apply Phase

The activities in this phase are brain compatible because they

- Require students to look for ways the information, concepts, and/or skills can be transferred to activities outside the classroom
- Ask students to search for curriculum connections, allowing the brain to make numerous links
- Offer students an opportunity to scaffold learning by engaging in homework activities that require them to extend concepts or create guidelines
- Allow students a chance to demonstrate, in a variety of ways, their understanding of the lesson content
- Assist students in reflecting on their own learning processes
- Allow students to become independent in designing additional learning activities

ATTEND–EXPERIENCE–REFLECT

Three components, attend, experience, and reflect, are central to each of the four phases and are discussed below. When beginning to design a lesson plan teachers may consult Figure 6.5 "Ways to Experience Learning," which shows where within the four-phase lesson (and where within each phase's attend-experience-reflect circuit) each activity can most effectively be used.

Attend

In the attend component teachers help students understand and appreciate what they are learning and experiencing by guiding them through each learning activity. Students learn how to think about information, how to filter out unimportant or irrelevant details, how to organize their thoughts, how to make sense of new experiences, and how to connect new information with what they already know or understand. Teachers help students focus their concentration and raise their level of consciousness or mindfulness by asking discerning questions and by assigning students specific cognitive tasks.

The purpose of the attend section within each phase is for students to begin to make meaning of each learning experience or new information. During every experience students should focus on the meaning of the experience by reflecting on or thinking about particular aspects of the experience as they occur. Thinking during the experience is as important as the experience itself. And helping students filter out extraneous information or helping them focus their attention is itself an important learning process.

Experience

Learning is ultimately active and experiential; therefore, the learning activities, instructional strategies, and experiences presented to students in the experience section will affect students' perception, thought processes, and ability to process the activity's content.

Reflect

Reflection, as used here, is a thinking process in which teachers lead students through intrapersonal reflections and group discussions to assist students in a meaning-making process. Reflecting on a learning experience requires students to revisit the thinking they were encouraged to attend to throughout the learning activity. Reflection gives students a chance to process and discuss what they have just learned or experienced. As students encounter new information, they need time to make sense of it and to connect what they have learned with other things they already know or understand. When students share their perceptions and understandings, they offer insights to each other. Such social interaction reinforces what the students learned or challenges what they think they learned. As students verbalize or write down what they understand, they are forming an observable expression of their comprehension for themselves, their

Ways to Experience Learning				
	Inquire	**Gather**	**Process**	**Apply**
Analyzing			A, E, R	
Assessing		E, R		
Clarifying	A, E			
Classifying		R	E, R	
Comparing			R	A, E, R
Composing				E
Critiquing			E, R	
Diagramming		R	E, R	
Dialoguing	A, E, R	A, E, R	A, E, R	A, E, R
Discovering			E	
Dramatizing				E
Evaluate		R, E		
Exploring		E		
Graphing		R	E	
Identifying	A, E			E
Labeling	A, E			
Listing	A, E			
Logging		E		
Observing	A, E, R	E		
Painting				E
Paraphrasing			R	E
Questioning	E			
Ranking			E	
Reading		A, E		
Reflecting	R	R	R	R
Relating				
Reporting			R	E
Self-Assessing	A, R	A, R	A, R	A, R
Studying		A, E, R		
Surveying				E
Telling/Retelling				E, R
Uncovering	E			

A = during the ATTEND part of the activity
E = during the EXPERIENCE part of the activity
R = during the REFLECT part of the activity

Figure 6.5

classmates, and/or the teacher depending upon the reflection activity. They are able to consider again and again what they just experienced. Revisiting the learning activity assists students in creating meaning from the information and consequently strengthening brain connections with prior knowledge and experience.

As students share their perceptions, understandings, and insights, they reinforce learning or challenge the thinking. As students express what they think they understand, they are required to express their comprehension of the material and to consider again and again what they just experienced. Revisiting the learning activity assists students in formulating the meaning of the information and in strengthening connections with patterns they have already established.

Internal Structure

Inherent in the four phases is the idea that at least four different activities are included in each lesson. However, teachers may include additional activities in selected phases, or even revisit that phase at a later time in the lesson, depending on the desired emphasis or the needs of the students. By engaging in at least four different activities students

- Participate in four Beginning-End-Middle (BEM) cycles
- Cycle through at least four attend-experience-reflect sequences
- Benefit from pulsed learning
- Interact with the information in four different ways, allowing different learning styles and intelligences to be used
- Stay on task within the recommended "age plus or minus two minutes" time frame
- Receive feedback at least four different times from the teacher, from peers, or through self-evaluation
- Take time to build understanding through the use of multiple examples or experiences
- Engage in metacognition and processing of the lesson at least four times throughout the lesson

INTEGRATED ASSESSMENT

The attend and reflect sections of the attend-experience-reflect sequence of each phase of the lesson plan are ideal for integrating assessment and learning. During the attend activities, students can focus on the requirements of a job well done illustrated by a criterion-based rubric. Keeping the requirements in mind as a standard, students can monitor themselves during each learning experience. The reflect strategies can serve as the checkpoint for students to reflect on how their performance compares with the rubric. The continual evaluation helps students determine how closely their behavior approximates the

ideal standard. The extended-time format provides teachers with the opportunity to engage regularly in the attend and reflect activities critical for integrating authentic assessment tools into a teaching design.

UNIT DESIGN

A unit is a division of information for study supported by state and/or national benchmarks and standards. Standards that are knowledge related, that support understanding of major concepts, and that provide required skill development form the underpinnings for the teaching unit. Units can be centered around

- Themes (human rights or life)
- Concepts (gravity or democracy)
- Issues (women's suffrage or religious differences that lead to political and social crises)
- Skills (short story writing or the use of a protractor or other measurement device)
- Problems to solve (any shortage or scarcity or pollution)
- Knowledge to relate (historical events and their contemporary counterparts)

Units follow a developmental process to ensure the acquisition of both skills and understanding. Figure 6.6 provides an outline for teachers to construct four-phase unit plans of their own. In addition to the four phases, the blank "Unit Plan" page includes space to note the unit standards and curriculum goals, the particular multiple intelligences to be stressed overall, and the assessment tools and methods for the unit. The wrap-up could include remarks by the teacher concerning how the unit will connect to the next one; a mention of how this unit has implications for other content disciplines; or a comment on what he or she is particularly pleased with in terms of the class work on the unit.

THE LESSON/UNIT DYNAMIC

Units need to be composed of an adequate number of lessons to ensure that objectives of the unit are met. The unit follows the same cycle as the lesson (inquire-gather-process-apply). It is important to remember that while each lesson within the unit has four phases the lessons themselves may be concentrated in one phase more than the others. Figure 6.7 "Emphasis at Each Phase of the Unit" illustrates the lesson emphasis at each phase of the unit.

In addition, enough time needs to be allocated for student understanding and skill acquisition and for student demonstration of understanding and skills. Units may last for one week or for three to four weeks. The number of lessons could then range from five lessons in

Unit Plan

Unit Topic:
Content Area:

Unit Content Standards/Goals	Focused Multiple Intelligences	Assessment Methods

Inquire Phase
____ Class Meetings

Gather Phase
____ Class Meetings

Process Phase
____ Class Meetings

Apply Phase
____ Class Meetings

Wrap-Up

Figure 6.6

Emphasis at Each Phase of the Unit				
Inquire Phase		Gather Phase	Process Phase	Apply Phase
Inquire Phase	Gather Phase		Process Phase	Apply Phase
Inquire Phase	Gather Phase	Process Phase		Apply Phase
Inquire Phase	Gather Phase	Process Phase	Apply Phase	

Figure 6.7

a one-week unit up to twenty lessons in a four-week unit on a 4 by 4 Block schedule. In a Block 8 schedule, the number of lessons stays the same, but the weeks to cover the units are doubled.

The school year can be separated into the following timeframes:

36 weeks = Year-long course; from 12 to 18 units
18 weeks = Semester or ½-year course; from 6 to 9 units
12 weeks = Trimester or ⅓-year course; from 3 to 6 units
3 week = mini-course; 1 or 2 units

If a month-long unit in traditional schedules has now become just two weeks in a 4 by 4, for example, these four phases can be laid out over the two weeks.

Day One: The Inquiry Phase
Days Two through Five: The Gather Phase, pulling together all the necessary information on the unit at hand
Days Six through Eight: The Process Phase, spent using various methods and working with the material gathered in the previous phase
Days Nine and Ten: The Apply Phase, in which the material is applied, expanded on, or something new is created from it.

Such a plan calls for a whole new form of information delivery. It absolutely necessitates using the students to prepare and deliver some of that information and demands the teacher become a facilitator in addition to being the instructor.

The four-phase unit format that encourages meaning making for each successive experience throughout the unit mirrors the cycle followed in lesson design. Each lesson of the unit is an experience, and the progression of experiences throughout the unit helps students in their individual meaning making of the unit goals and objectives.

The unit format, the lesson design, and the teaching strategies used throughout the unit are based on brain research and proven instructional techniques for facilitating learning. There are four fundamental strategies that serve as the basis for each unit of instruction: co-

operative learning, multiple intelligences, higher-order thinking skills, and graphic organizers.

Before designing the content flow and sequence of the unit, teachers can ask themselves these essential questions:

- What are the key concepts students need to learn during this unit?
- What skills ("know how") do the students need to demonstrate and represent their understanding of the concepts?
- What are some individual and general applications ("know why") of the key concepts?
- What experiences will provide students with not only emotional connections to the concepts but also the invaluable insights into the meaning and applications of the concepts?

After the framework for the unit has been set (see Figure 6.8), the teacher then determines the delivery structure. In the case of the biology unit example, thematic instruction is used in the inquire phase, problem-based instruction and case studies in the gather phase, performance learning in the process phase, and both project and service learning in the apply phase. The lessons are then "hung from" the scaffold of the delivery structure.

Inquire Phase

The purpose of the first phase of the unit is to investigate what students know about the unit concepts and what skills they possess and to identify the goals and objectives of the unit. In addition, during the first phase the teacher along with students may decide how to assess changes in student "know how" and "know why."

Gather Phase

The goal of the gather phase of the unit is to obtain information that introduces students to new ideas, concepts, or skills. Teachers can also select activities that help students understand why they each have diverse associations or different understandings regarding the new information and skills. Students can also be assisted

Unit Plan

Unit Topic: *Cardiovascular system*
Content Area: *Biology*

Unit Content Standards/Goals	Focused Multiple Intelligences	Assessment Methods
Understands the major systems of the human body	*Logical/Mathematical* *Bodily/Kinesthetic* *Visual/Spatial* *Verbal/Linguistic*	*Project rubric* *Quiz* *Self-evaluation* *Peer performance evaluation*

Inquire Phase _1_ Class Meeting(s)	**Gather Phase** _3_ Class Meeting(s)	**Process Phase** _2_ Class Meeting(s)	**Apply Phase** _2_ Class Meeting(s)
Video excerpt "Incredible Journey" *Discussion* *Web graphic organizer on definition of systems* *Small group study of paragraphs on social, biological, ecological, and solar systems* *Fishbone graphic organizer on traits of systems* *KWL on cardiovascular system*	*Describe projects* • *design a video presentation for PBS on how to keep your CV system healthy* • *sculpt a detailed model of the CV system* • *create a brochure containing guidelines for person recovering from heart attacks* *Create project plans* *Share info sources* *Submit project plan*	*Each team creates a matrix, fishbone, or concept web on info gathered* *Debate:* • *Exercise has/has no effect* • *Tension has/has no effect* • *Unhealthy diet has/has no effect* *Quiz on important facts and details* *Give time to work on projects*	*Finish projects* *Present projects* *Self-evaluation in journal* *Peer performance evaluation checklist*

Wrap-Up

Show how this unit provides a bridge between what was studied up until now and future work.

Figure 6.8

in linking the new information with their past experiences and connecting their new knowledge with insights and concepts they have stored in long-term memory. During this phase, teachers can select examples that place the new information and skills into context for the students. Context provides students with an understanding of how useful and practical the new information and skills can be.

Process Phase

Processing the new knowledge and skills that students have acquired during the gather phase occurs through a variety of activities. Students can participate in practice drills, in peer tutoring, in preparing charts and graphs, or in any number of student performances that will reinforce their understandings, clarify any misunderstandings they might have, and possibly add new understandings or insights related to the unit concepts.

Apply Phase

During this last phase of the unit, the focus of the learning activities is on relating the new knowledge and skills to real-life settings. Relevance and application are the primary goals of this phase. In order for students to transfer unit concepts to other courses they are taking

and to other real-life experiences, students can be asked to look for examples of who, how, and when they have seen others use the skills and knowledge presented during the unit. They can be asked to make connections to activities with which they are already engaged. Further, they can share with each other the insights they have gained as they have reflected on the unit concepts and how they can be applied to their lives.

FUNCTION FOLLOWS FORM

The four-phase plan presented here is important for teachers to follow because it reminds them of the various components of the learning process and of the reason for using the strategies they use. It can help them provide diversity in learning opportunities for students. The design can help teachers remember to include successful strategies and techniques they used to use but discarded, lost, or forgot over time. In addition, it helps teachers think about and evaluate the effectiveness of their instructional strategies. The lesson design also helps students recognize a process they can use when designing their own learning experiences.

III

STRATEGIES, AIDS, MEDIA, AND RESOURCES FOR EFFECTIVE INSTRUCTION

Part III responds to your needs concerning:

- Assuring equality in the classroom
- Developing ideas for lessons and projects
- Employing service learning
- Ensuring academic success for each student
- Helping students develop a repertoire of skills for life-long learning
- Individualizing (personalizing) student learning

- Making homework and assignments
- Preparing and implementing a lesson for feedback
- Resources for free and inexpensive instructional materials
- Teaching for thinking
- Teaching toward mastery
- Using electronic media and the Internet
- Using games and simulations

- Using inquiry and discovery learning
- Using learning centers, lectures, and demonstrations
- Using peer teaching and small group and cooperative learning
- Using project-based learning and student exhibitions and presentations

- Using questioning and discussions
- Using student writing and journals
- Using the writing board, the bulletin board, guest speakers, and field trips

Reflective Thoughts

Your goals should include helping students learn how to solve problems, to make decisions, to think creatively and critically, and to feel good about themselves and their learning. To do this, you will:

1. *Involve students in direct experiences, both hands-on and minds-on, so they use more of their sensory modalities, and develop their learning capacities. When all the senses are engaged, learning is the most effective and longest lasting.*
2. *Use questioning in a way designed to guide students to higher levels of thinking and doing.*
3. *Share in the responsibility for teaching reading, writing, thinking, and study skills.*

Today's teenagers are used to multimillion-dollar productions on television, compact discs, arcade games, and the movie screen. When they come to school, into a classroom and are subjected each day to something short of a high-budget production, it is little wonder that they sometimes react in a less than highly motivated fashion. No doubt, today's youth are

growing up in a highly stimulated instant-action society, a society that has learned to expect instant headache relief, instant meals, instant gratification, and perhaps, in the minds of many youth, instant high-paying employment for jobs that entail more fun than hard work. In light of this cultural phenomenon, we, the authors of this book, are on your side: the classroom teacher is on the firing line each day and is expected to perform—perhaps instantly and entertainingly, but most certainly in a highly competent and professional manner—in situations that are far from ideal.

Experiences afforded by inquiry help students understand the importance of suspending judgment and also the tentativeness of answers and solutions. With those understandings, students eventually are better able to deal with life's ambiguities.

Teaching all students how to access Internet sites is an important addition to their repertoire of skills for lifelong learning.

7

Questioning for Teaching and Learning

A strategy of fundamental importance to any mode of instruction is questioning. You will use questioning for so many purposes that you must be skilled in its use to teach effectively. Because it is so important, and because it is so frequently used and abused, this chapter is devoted to assisting you in the development of your skills in using questioning.

Specifically, upon completion of this chapter you should be able to:

1. Contrast the levels of questioning and compare those with levels of thinking and doing.

2. Demonstrate developing skill in the use of questioning for teaching and learning.
3. Demonstrate understanding of the types of cognitive questions.
4. Describe ways of helping students to develop their metacognitive skills.
5. Explain the value and use of students' questions.
6. Identify categories of purposes for which questioning can be used as an instructional strategy.

PURPOSES FOR USING QUESTIONING

You will adapt the type and form of each question to the purpose for which it is asked. The purposes that questions can serve can be separated into five categories, as follows.

1. *To politely give instructions.* An example is, "Mariya, would you please turn out the lights so we can show the slides?" Although they probably should avoid doing so, teachers sometimes also use rhetorical questions for the purpose of regaining student attention and maintaining classroom control, for example, "Marcello, would you please attend to your work?" Rhetorical questions can sometimes backfire on the teacher. In this case, Marcello might say "No;" then the teacher would have a problem that could perhaps have been avoided had the teacher been more direct and simply told Marcello to attend to his work, rather than asking him if he would. Consider the scenario.

CLASSROOM SCENARIO
A Student Responds to the Teacher's Rhetorical Question

At the completion of the class opener, Jennifer, a high school mathematics teacher, asked, "Shall we check our homework problems now?" One of the students in the class, Mario, answered "No." Ignoring Mario's response Jennifer continued with her planned lesson.

What are your thoughts about this scenario? Should Jennifer have acted differently? Explain why or why not.

---

2. *To review and remind students of classroom procedures.* For example, if students continue to talk when they shouldn't, you can stop the lesson and ask, "Class, I think we need to review the procedure we agreed on for when someone else is talking. Who can tell me what is the procedure that we agreed upon?"

3. *To gather information.* Examples are: "How many of you have finished the assignment?" or, to find out whether a student knows something, "Charlie, can you please explain for us the difference between a synonym and antonym?"

4. *To discover student knowledge, interests, or experiences.* Examples might be: "How many of you think you know the process by which water in our city is made potable?" or "How many of you have visited the local water treatment plant?"

5. *To guide student thinking and learning.* It is this category of questioning that is the focus for your learning in this chapter. In teaching, questions in this category are used to:

- *Develop appreciation.* For example, "Do you now understand the ecological relationship between that particular root fungus, voles, and the survival of the large conifers of the forests of the Pacific Northwest?"
- *Develop student thinking.* For example, "What do you suppose the effects to the ecology are when standing water is sprayed with an insecticide that is designed to kill all mosquito larvae?"
- *Diagnose learning difficulty.* For example, "What part of the formula don't you understand, Sarah?"
- *Emphasize major points.* For example, "If no one has ever been to the sun, how can we be confident that we know of what it is made?"
- *Encourage students.* For example, "OK, so you didn't remember the formula for glucose. What really impressed me in your essay is what you did understand about photosynthesis. Do you know specifically what part impressed me?"
- *Establish rapport.* For example, "We have a problem here, but I think we can solve it if we put our heads together. What do you think ought to be our first step?"
- *Evaluate learning.* For example, "Siobhan, what is the effect when two rough surfaces are rubbed together?"
- *Give practice in expression.* For example, "Yvonne, would you please share with us the examples of shadowing that you found?"
- *Help students in their metacognition.* For example, "Yes, something did go wrong in the experiment. Do you still think your original hypothesis is correct? If not, then where was the error in your thinking? Or if you still think your hypothesis is correct, then where might the error have been in the design of your experiment? How might we find out?"
- *Help students interpret materials.* For example, "Something seems to be wrong with this compass. How do you suppose we can find out what is wrong with it? For example, if the needle is marked N and S in reverse, how can we find out if that is the problem?"
- *Help students organize materials.* For example, "If you really want to carry out your proposed experiment, then we are going to need certain materials. We are going to have to deal with some strategic questions here, such as, what do you think we will need, where can we find those things, who will be responsible for getting them, and how will we store and arrange them once we are ready to start the investigation?"
- *Provide drill and practice.* For example, "Team A has prepared some questions that they would like to use as practice questions for our unit exam, and they are suggesting that we use them to play the game of Jeopardy on Friday. Is everyone in agreement with their idea?"

- *Provide review.* For example, "Today, in your groups, you are going to study the unit review questions. After each group has studied and prepared its answers to these written questions, your group will pick another group and ask them your set of review questions. Each group has a different set of questions. Members of Team A are going to keep score, and the group that has the highest score from this review session will receive free pizza at tomorrow's lunch. Ready?"
- *Show agreement or disagreement.* For example, "Some scientists fear that the Antarctic ice shelf is breaking up and melting and that there will be worldwide flooding. With evidence that you have collected from recent articles, do you agree with this conclusion? Explain why or why not."
- *Show relationships, such as cause and effect.* For example, "What do you suppose would be the global effect if just one inch of the total Antarctic ice shelf were to melt rather suddenly?"
- *Build the curriculum.* It is the students' questions that provide the basis for the learning that occurs in an effective program that is inquiry based and project centered. More on this subject follows in Chapters 8 and 9.

Questions to Avoid Asking

Before going further, while it is important to avoid asking rhetorical questions, questions for which you do not want a response, you should also avoid asking questions that call for little or no student thinking, such as those that can be answered with a simple yes or no or some other sort of alternative answer response. Unless followed up with questions calling for clarification, questions that call for simple responses have little or no learning and diagnostic value; they encourage guessing and inappropriate student responses that can cause classroom control problems for the teacher.

It is even more important to avoid using questions that embarrass a student, punish a student, or in any way deny the student's dignity. Questions that embarrass or punish tend to damage the student's developing self-esteem and serve no meaningful academic or instructional purpose. Questioning is an important instructional tool that should be used by the teacher only for academic reasons. Although it is not always possible to predict when a student might be embarrassed by a question, a teacher should *never* deliberately ask questions for the purpose of embarrassment or punishment. For example, avoid asking a student a content question when you know the student was not paying attention and/or does not know the answer. When done deliberately to punish or embarrass, that teacher's action borders on abuse!

TYPES OF COGNITIVE QUESTIONS: A GLOSSARY

Let us now define, describe, and provide examples for each of the *types* of cognitive (or mental) questions that you will use in teaching. Please note that although we refer to these in the traditional fashion as cognitive questions, any question type could relate to any of the three domains of learning (cognitive, affective, or psychomotor). In the section that follows, your attention is focused on the levels of cognitive questions.

Clarifying Question

The clarifying question is used to gain more information from a student to help the teacher better understand a student's ideas, feelings, and thought processes. Often, asking a student to elaborate on an initial response will lead the student to think more deeply, restructure his or her thinking, and while doing so, discover a fallacy in the original response. Examples of clarifying questions are "What I hear you saying is that you would rather work alone than in your group. Is that correct?" "So, Denise, you think the poem is a sad one, is that right?" There is a strong positive correlation between student learning and development of metacognitive skills (i.e., their thinking about thinking) and the teacher's use of questions that ask for clarification.[1] In addition, by seeking clarification, you are likely to be demonstrating an interest in the student and her or his thinking.

Convergent-Thinking Question

Convergent thinking questions, also called *narrow questions* are low-order thinking questions that have a single correct answer (such as recall questions, discussed further in the next section). Examples of convergent questions are "What is geophagy?" "If the circumference of a circle is 31 meters, what is its radius?" "What engineering feat allowed Xerxes to invade Greece in 481 B.C.E.?" When using questions of this type, try to come back with follow-up questions so the student answering can demonstrate thinking beyond rote memory.

Cueing Question

If you ask a question to which, after sufficient **wait time** (longer than two seconds; see discussion on wait time in section Implementing Questioning), no students respond or to which their inadequate responses indicate they need more information, then you can ask

[1]A. L. Costa, *The School as a Home for the Mind* (Palatine, IL: Skylight Publishing, 1991), p. 63.

a question that cues the answer or response you are seeking.[2] In essence, you are going backward in your questioning sequence, to cue the students. For example, as an introduction to a lesson on the study of prefixes, a teacher asks her students, "How many legs each do crayfish, lobsters, and shrimp have?" and there is no accurate response. She might then cue the answer with the following information and question, "The class to which those animals belong is class Decapoda. Does that give you a clue about the number of legs they have?" If that clue is not enough, and after allowing sufficient time for students to think, then she might ask, "What is a decathlon?" or "What is the decimal system?" or "What is a decimeter?" or "What is a decibel?" or "What is a decade?" or "What is the Decalogue?" and so on.

When questioning students over reading material, you can use the Question Answer Relationship (QAR) strategy.[3] QAR involves asking a question and, if a student is unable to respond, providing one of three types of cues. "Right there" is used for questions for which the answer can be found explicitly stated in the sentence or paragraph. "Search and think" means the answer is not directly stated and therefore must be inferred. "On your own" is used for critical thinking questions for which the answers are neither explicit nor inferred in the text.[4]

Divergent-Thinking Question

Divergent-thinking questions (also known as *broad, reflective,* or *thought questions*) are open-ended (i.e., usually having no singularly correct answer), high-order thinking questions (requiring analysis, synthesis, or evaluation), which require students to think creatively, to leave the comfortable confines of the known and reach out into the unknown. Examples of questions that require divergent thinking are "Do you believe Mark Twain was a racist?" and "What measures could be taken to improve the post-lunchtime trash problem on our campus?"

Evaluative Question

Whether convergent or divergent, some questions require students to place a value on something or to take a stance on some issue; these are referred to as *evaluative questions.* If the teacher and the students all agree on certain

premises, then the evaluative question would also be a convergent question. If original assumptions differ, then the response to the evaluative question would be more subjective, and therefore that evaluative question would be divergent. Examples of evaluative questions are "Should the United States allow clear-cutting in its national forests?" and "Should the Electoral College be abolished?"

Focus Question

This is any question that is designed to focus student thinking. For example, the first question of the preceding paragraph is a focus question when the teacher asking it is attempting to focus student attention on the economic issues involved in clear-cutting.

Probing Question

Similar to a clarifying question, the probing question requires student thinking to go beyond superficial first-answer or single-word responses. Examples of probing questions are "Why, Eloy, do you think it to be the case that every citizen has the right to have a gun?" and "Could you give an example?"

Socratic Questioning

In the fifth century B.C.E., the great Athenian teacher Socrates used the art of questioning so successfully that to this day we still hear of the Socratic method.[5] What, exactly, is the Socratic method? Socrates' strategy was to ask his students a series of leading questions that gradually snarled them up to the point where they had to look carefully at their own ideas and to think rigorously for themselves. Today that strategy is referred to as the Socratic approach or method.

Socratic discussions were informal dialogues taking place in a natural, pleasant environment. Although Socrates sometimes had to go to considerable lengths to ignite his students' intrinsic interest, their response was natural and spontaneous. In his dialogues, Socrates tried to aid students in developing ideas. He did not impose his own notions on the students. Rather, he encouraged them to develop their own conclusions and draw their own inferences. Of course, Socrates may have had preconceived notions about what the final learning should be and carefully aimed his questions so that the students

[2]Studies in wait time began with the classic study of M. B. Rowe, "Wait Time and Reward As Instructional Variables, Their Influence On Language, Logic and Fate Control: Part I. Wait Time," *Journal of Research in Science Teaching* 11(2):81–94 (1974).

[3]See, for example, M. E. McIntosh and R. J. Draper, "Using the Question-Answer Relationship Strategy to Improve Students' Reading of Mathematics Texts," *Clearing House* 69(3):154–162 (January/February 1996).

[4]J. S. Choate and T. A. Rakes, *Inclusive Instruction for Struggling Readers,* (Bloomington, IN: Fastback 434, Phi Delta Kappa Educational Foundation, 1998), p. 27.

[5]See, for example, V. C. Polite and A. H. Adams, *Improving Critical Thinking through Socratic Seminars.* Spotlight on Student Success, no. 110 (Philadelphia, PA: Mid-Atlantic Laboratory for Student Success, 1996); S. Schoeman, "Using the Socratic Method in Secondary Teaching," *NASSP Bulletin* 81(587):19–21 (March 1997); and M. L. Tanner and L. Casados, "Promoting and Studying Discussions in Math Classes," *Journal of Adolescent & Adult Literacy* 41(5):342–350 (February 1998).

would arrive at the desired conclusions. Still, his questions were open-ended, causing divergent rather than convergent thinking. The students were free to go mentally wherever the facts and their thinking led them.

Throughout history, teachers have tried to adapt the methods of Socrates to the classroom. In some situations, they have been quite successful and are a major mode of instruction. However, we must remember that Socrates used this method in the context of a one-to-one relationship between the student and himself. Some teachers have adapted it for whole-class direct instruction by asking questions first of one student and then of another, moving slowly about the class. This technique may work, but it is difficult because the essence of the Socratic technique is to build question on question in a logical fashion so that each question leads the student a step further toward the understanding sought. When you spread the questions around the classroom, you may find it difficult to build up the desired sequence and to keep all the students involved in the discussion. Sometimes you may be able to use the Socratic method by directing all the questions at one student—at least for several minutes—while the other students look on and listen in. That is how Socrates did it. When the topic is interesting enough, this technique can be quite successful and even exciting, but in the long run, the Socratic method works best when the teacher is working in one-on-one coaching situations or with small groups of students, rather than in whole-class direct instruction.

In using Socratic questioning, the focus is on the questions, not answers, and thinking is valued as the quintessential activity.[6] In essence, to conduct Socratic questioning, with the student or class, identify a problem (either student- or teacher-posed) and then ask the students a series of probing questions designed to cause them to examine critically the problem and potential solutions to it. The main thrust of the questioning and the key questions must be planned in advance so that the questioning will proceed logically. To think of quality probing questions on the spur of the moment is too difficult. It is the Socratic method that you will be using in a micro peer teaching exercise later in this chapter (Exercise 6.5).

LEVELS OF COGNITIVE QUESTIONS AND STUDENT THINKING

Questions posed by you are cues to your students to the level of thinking expected of them, ranging from the lowest level of mental operation, requiring simple recall

of knowledge (convergent thinking), to the highest, requiring divergent thought and application of that thought. It is important that you are aware of the levels of thinking, that you understand the importance of attending to student thinking from low to higher levels of operation, and that you understand that what may be a matter of simple recall of information for one student, may for another require a higher-order mental activity, such as figuring something out by deduction.

You should structure and sequence your questions (and assist students in developing their own skill in structuring and sequencing their questions) in a way that is designed to guide students to higher levels of thinking. For example, when students respond to questions in complete sentences that provide supportive evidence for their ideas, it is fairly safe to assume that their thinking is at a higher level than were the response an imprecise and nondescriptive single-word answer.

To help your understanding, three levels of questioning and thinking are described as follows.[7] You should recognize the similarity between these three levels of questions and the six levels of thinking and doing from Bloom's taxonomy of cognitive objectives (Chapter 5). For your daily use of questioning it is just as useful but more practical to think and behave in terms of these three levels, rather than of six.

1. *Lowest level: Gathering and recalling information.* At this level questions are designed to solicit from students concepts, information, feelings, or experiences that were gained in the past and stored in memory. Sample key words and desired behaviors are *complete, count, define, describe, identify, list, match, name, observe, recall, recite,* and *select.*

Thinking involves receiving data through the senses, followed by the processing of those data. Inputting without processing is brain-dysfunctional. Information that has not been processed is stored only in short-term memory.

2. *Intermediate level: Processing information.* At this level questions are designed to draw relationships of cause and effect, to synthesize, analyze, summarize, compare, contrast, or classify data. Sample key words and desired behaviors are *analyze, classify, compare, contrast, distinguish, explain, group, infer, make an analogy, organize, plan,* and *synthesize.*

Thinking and questioning that involve processing of information can be conscious or unconscious. When students observe the teacher thinking aloud, and when

[6]B. R. Brogan, and W. A. Brogan, "The Socratic Questioner: Teaching and Learning in the Dialogical Classroom," *Educational Forum* 59(3):288–296 (Spring 1995).

[7]This three-tiered model of thinking has been described variously by others. For example, in E. Eisner, *The Educational Imagination* (Upper Saddle River, NJ: Prentice Hall, 1979), the levels are referred to as "descriptive," "interpretive," and "evaluative." For a comparison of thinking models, see Costa, 1991, p. 44.

they are urged to think aloud, to think about their thinking, and to analyze it as it occurs, they are in the process of developing their intellectual skills.

At the processing level, this internal analysis of new data may challenge a learner's preconceptions (and misconceptions) about a phenomenon. The learner's brain will naturally resist this challenge to existing beliefs. The greater the mental challenge, the greater the brain's effort to draw upon data already in storage. With increasing data, the mind will gradually examine existing concepts and ultimately, as necessary, develop new mental concepts.

If there is a match between new input and existing mental concepts, no problem exists. Piaget called this process *assimilation*.[8] If, however, in processing new data there is no match with existing mental concepts, then the situation is what Piaget called *cognitive disequilibrium*. The brain is uncomfortable with disequilibrium and will drive the learner to search for an explanation for the discrepancy. Piaget called this process *accommodation*. However, although learning is enhanced by challenge, in situations that are threatening the brain is less flexible in accommodating new ideas. That is why each student must feel welcomed in the classroom, and learners must perceive the classroom environment as challenging but nonthreatening, an environment of *relaxed alertness*.[9]

Questions and experiences must be designed to elicit more than merely recall memory responses (assimilation). Many teachers find it useful to use discrepant events to introduce concepts. *Discrepant events* are phenomena that cause cognitive disequilibrium, thus stimulating higher-level mental functioning. However, merely exposing students to a discrepant event will not in itself cause them to develop new conceptual understandings. It simply stirs the mind into processing, without which mental development does not occur (see Figure 7.1).

3. *Highest level: Applying and evaluating in new situations*. Questions at the highest level encourage learners to think intuitively, creatively, and hypothetically, to use their imagination, to expose a value system, or to

---

Balloon Will Not Pop

Practice this first. Partially blow up a balloon and then tie it off. Take a large but sharp sewing needle and slowly push it into the balloon. Because the needle immediately plugs the hole, the balloon remains filled. Sure, you say, students have seen this done by magicians or birthday party clowns. But wait. Now for the real discrepant event: slowly remove the needle, and Voila! The balloon does not collapse. The balloon material expands to plug the hole. Make several holes. Take a long needle (as used in doll making) and push it through the balloon and out through the other side, keeping the needle in both holes. The balloon stays filled. (Hint: push the needle into the thickest portion of the balloon, opposite the opening.) If students believe you are using a fake balloon, take the same needle and quickly puncture the balloon, popping it.

Figure 7.1
Example of a discrepant event demonstration.

---

make a judgment. Sample key words and desired behaviors are *apply, build, evaluate, extrapolate, forecast, generalize, hypothesize, imagine, judge, predict,* and *speculate*.

You must use questions at the level best suited for the purpose, use questions of a variety of different levels, and structure questions in a way intended to move student thinking to higher levels. When teachers use higher-level questions, their students tend to score higher on tests of critical thinking and on standardized tests of achievement.[10]

With the use of questions as a strategy to move student thinking to higher levels, the teacher is facilitating the students' intellectual development. Developing your skill in using questioning requires attention to detail and practice. The guidelines that follow will provide that detail and some practice, but first, do Exercise 7.1 to check your understanding of the levels of questions.

---

[8]See, for example, J. Piaget, *The Development of Thought: Elaboration of Cognitive Structures* (New York: Viking, 1977).
[9]R. N. Caine and G. Caine, *Education on the Edge of Possibility* (Alexandria, VA: Association for Supervision and Curriculum Development, 1997), p. 107.

---

[10]See, for example, B. Newton, "Theoretical Basis for Higher Cognitive Questioning—An Avenue to Critical Thinking," *Education* 98(3):286–290 (March-April 1978); and D. Redfield and E. Rousseau, "A Meta-Analysis of Experimental Research on Teacher Questioning Behavior," *Review of Educational Research* 51(2):237–245 (Summer 1981).

EXERCISE 7.1
Identifying the Cognitive Levels of Questions—
A Self-Check Exercise

Instructions: The purpose of this exercise is to test your understanding and recognition of the levels of questions. Mark each of the following questions with a:

- 1, if it is at the lowest level of mental operation, gathering and recalling data.
- 2, if it is at a middle level, processing data.
- 3, if it is at the highest level, applying or evaluating data in a new situation.

Check your answers against the key that follows. Resolve problems by discussing them with your classmates and instructor.

_____ 1. Do you recall the differences between an Asian elephant and an African elephant?

_____ 2. How are the natural habitats of the Asian and African elephants similar? How are they different?

_____ 3. Which of the elephants do you think is the more interesting?

_____ 4. For what do you think the elephant uses its tusks?

_____ 5. Do all elephants have tusks?

_____ 6. Did the trick ending make the story more interesting for you?

_____ 7. How might these evergreen needles be grouped?

_____ 8. How do these two types of pine needles differ?

_____ 9. For how many years was the Soviet Union a communist-dominated nation?

_____ 10. How many republics do you believe will be in the new Commonwealth of Independent States (the former Soviet Union) by the year 2010?

_____ 11. Why do you think the city decided to move the zoo?

_____ 12. How would the park be different today had the zoo been left there?

_____ 13. How do zoos today differ from those of the mid-nineteenth century?

_____ 14. Should a teacher be entitled to unemployment benefits during the summer or when school is not in session?

_____ 15. If $4X + 40 = 44$, what is X?

_____ 16. What happens when I spin this egg?

_____ 17. How does this poem make you feel?

_____ 18. What will happen when we mix equal amounts of the red and yellow solutions?

_____ 19. What is the capital of West Virginia?

_____ 20. What will be the long-term global effects if the rain forests continue to be removed at the present rate?

Answer Key

1. = 1 (recall)	11. = 2 (explain cause and effect)
2. = 2 (compare)	12. = 3 (speculate)
3. = 3 (judge)	13. = 2 (contrast)
4. = 3 (imagine)	14. = 3 (judge)
5. = 3 (extrapolate)	15. = 1 (recall of how to work the problem)
6. = 3 (evaluate)	16. = 1 (observe)
7. = 2 (classify)	17. = 1 (describe)
8. = 2 (contrast)	18. = 3 (hypothesize)
9. = 1 (recall)	19. = 1 (recall)
10. = 3 (predict)	20. = 3 (speculate or generalize)

GUIDELINES FOR USING QUESTIONING

As emphasized in several ways throughout this book, your goals are to help your students learn how to solve problems, to make decisions and value judgments, to think creatively and critically, and to feel good about themselves, their schools, and their learning—rather than simply to fill their minds with bits and pieces of information that will likely last only a brief time in the students' short-term memory. How you construct your questions and how you implement your questioning strategy is important to the realization of these goals.

Preparing Questions

When preparing questions, consider the following guidelines.

Key cognitive questions should be planned, thoughtfully worded, and written into your lesson plan. Thoughtful preparation of questions helps to assure that they are clear and specific, not ambiguous, that the vocabulary is appropriate, and that each question matches its purpose. Incorporate questions into your lessons as instructional devices, welcomed pauses, attention grab-bers, and as checks for student comprehension. Thoughtful teachers even plan questions that they intend to ask specific students, targeting questions to the readiness level, interest, or learning profile of a student.

Match questions with their target purposes. Carefully planned questions allow them to be sequenced and worded to match the levels of cognitive thinking expected of students. To help students in developing their thinking skills, you need to demonstrate how to do this. To demonstrate, you must use terminology that is specific and that provides students with examples of experiences consonant with the meanings of the cognitive words. You should demonstrate this every day so students learn the cognitive terminology. As stated by Brooks and Brooks, "framing tasks around cognitive activities such as analysis, interpretation, and prediction—and explicitly using those terms with students—fosters the construction of new understandings."[11] See the three examples in Figure 7.2.

---

[11]J. G. Brooks and M. G. Brooks, *In Search of Understanding: The Case for Constructivist Classrooms* (Alexandria, VA: Association for Supervision and Curriculum Development, 1993), p. 105.

Instead of	Say
How else might it be done?	How could you *apply*...?
Are you going to get quiet?	If we are going to hear what Joan has to say, what do you need to do?
How do you know that is so?	What evidence do you have?

Figure 7.2
Examples of questions that use appropriate cognitive terminology.

Implementing Questioning

Careful preparation of questions is one part of the skill in questioning. Implementation is the other part. Here are guidelines for effective implementation.

Ask your well-worded question before *calling on a student for a response.* A common error made is when the teacher first calls on a student and then asks the question, such as "Sean, would you please tell us what you believe the author meant by the title 'we are one'?" Although probably not intended by the teacher, as soon as the teacher called on Sean, that signaled to the rest of the class that they were released from having to pay further attention and to think about the question. The preferred strategy is to phrase the question, allow time for all students to think, and then call on Sean and other students for their interpretations of the author's meaning of the title.

Avoid bombarding students with too much teacher talk. Sometimes teachers talk too much. This could be especially true for teachers who are nervous, as might be the case for many during the initial weeks of their student teaching. Knowing the guidelines presented here will help you avoid that syndrome. Remind yourself to be quiet after you ask a question that you have carefully formulated. Sometimes, due to lack of confidence, and especially when a question hasn't been carefully planned, the teacher asks the question and then, with a slight change in wording, asks it again, or asks several questions, one after another. That is too much verbiage. It's called "machine gun questioning" and only confuses students, allowing too little time for them to think.

After asking a question, provide students with adequate time to think. The pause after asking a question is called *wait time* (or *think time*). Knowing the subject better than the students know it and having given prior thought to the subject, too many teachers fail to allow students sufficient time to think after asking a question. In addition, by the time they have reached middle school, students have learned pretty well how to play

the "game"—that is, they know that if they remain silent long enough the teacher will probably answer his or her own question. After asking a well-worded question you should remain quiet for awhile, allowing students time to think and to respond. If you wait long enough, they usually will. You may need to rehearse your students on this procedure.

After asking a question, how long should you wait before you do something? You should wait at least two seconds, and perhaps as long as seven or sometimes even longer (when it appears it is needed because students are still thinking).[12] Stop reading now and look at your watch or a clock to get a feeling for how long two seconds is. Then, observe how long seven seconds is. Did seven seconds seem a long time? Because most of us are not used to silence in the classroom, two seconds of silence can seem quite long, while seven seconds may seem eternal. If, for some reason, students have not responded after a period of two to seven seconds of wait time, then you can ask the question again (but don't reword an already carefully worded question, or else students are likely to think it is a new question). Pause for several seconds; then if you still haven't received a response you can call on a student, then another, if necessary, after sufficient wait time. Soon you will get a response that can be built upon. Avoid answering your own question!

Now, to better understand the art of questioning, the importance of well-worded questions and well-prepared and clear instructions, and of allowing students time to think, do Exercise 7.2.

---

[12]See, for example, the work of K. G. Tobin, "The Effects of Teacher Wait Time on Discourse Characteristics in Mathematics and Language Arts Classes," *American Educational Research Journal* 23(2):191–200 (Summer 1986), and K. G. Tobin, "The Role of Wait Time in Higher Cognitive Level Learning," *Review of Educational Research* 57(1):69–95 (Spring 1987).

EXERCISE 7.2

Think Time and the Art of Questioning: An In-Class Exercise

Instructions: The purpose of this exercise is to further your understanding of the art and power of questioning, the importance of well-worded questions with well-prepared and clear instructions, and the need to give students time to think.

1. Roleplay simulation: From your class ask for three volunteers. One volunteer will read the lines of Estella, a second will read the one line of the student, while the third volunteer uses a stop watch to direct Estella and the student to speak their lines at the designated times. The rest of your class can pretend to be students in Estella's English class.

1:00: *Estella:* "Think of a man whom you admire, perhaps a father figure, and write a three-sentence paragraph describing that person." Students begin their writing.

1:00:05: *Estella:* "Only three sentences about someone you look up to. It might be your father, uncle, anyone."

1:00:07: *Student:* "Does it have to be about a man?"
Estella: "No, it can be a man or a woman, but someone you truly admire."

1:01: Estella works the rows, seeing that students are on task.

1:01:10: *Estella:* "Three sentences are all you need to write."

1:01:15: *Estella:* "Think of someone you really look up to, and write three sentences in a paragraph that describes that person."

1:01:30: *Estella:* "Someone you would like to be like."

1:02: Estella continues walking around helping students who are having difficulty. All students are on task.

1:04: *Estella:* "Now I want you to exchange papers with the person behind or beside you, read that person's description of the person they admire, and describe a setting that you see their person in. Write a paragraph that describes that setting."

1:04–1:05: Students exchange papers; teacher walks around seeing that everyone has received another student's paper.

1:05: *Estella:* "Where do you see that person being? Below the paragraph I want you to write a new paragraph describing where you see this person, perhaps in an easy chair watching a ball game, on a porch, in a car, or in the kitchen cooking."

1:05:10: *Estella:* "Describe a scene you see this person in."

1:05:15: *Estella:* "After you read the description I want you to create a setting for the person described."

1:05:18: Students seem confused either about what they are reading (e.g., asking the writer what a word is or means) or what they are supposed to do.

1:05:19: *Estella:* "Anything is fine. Use your imagination to describe the setting."

1:05:22: *Estella:* "Describe a setting for this person."

1:09: *Estella:* "Now I want you to exchange papers with yet someone else, and after reading the previous two paragraphs written by two other students, write a third paragraph describing a problem you think this admired person has."

2. After the roleplay simulation, hold a whole-class discussion or small group discussions and use the following as a springboard for your discussion: Describe what you believe are the good points and weak points of this portion of Estella's lesson and her implementation of it.

Practice gender equity. To practice gender equity, here are four rules to follow when using questioning: (a) Avoid going to a boy to bail out a girl who fails to answer a question, (b) avoid going to a boy to improve upon a girl's answer. (For the first, without seeming to badger, try to give the student clues until she can answer with success. For the second, hold and demonstrate high expectations for all students.), (c) allow equal wait time regardless of student gender, and (d) call on boys and girls equally.

Practice calling on all students. Related to the last rule of the preceding paragraph, you must call on not just the bright or the slow, not just the boys or the girls, not only those in the front or middle of the room, but all of them. To do these things takes concentrated effort on your part, but it is important. To ensure that students are called on equally, some teachers have in hand laminated copies of their seating charts, perhaps on bright, neon-colored clipboards (gives students a visual focus), and, with a wax pencil or water soluble marker, make a mark next to the name of the student each time he or she is called on. With the seating chart laminated, and using erasable markers, the marks can be erased at the end of the day and the seating chart used over and over.

Give the same minimum amount of wait time (think time) to all students. This, too, will require concentrated effort on your part, but is important to do. A teacher who waits for less time when calling on a slow student or students of one gender, is showing a prejudice or a lack of confidence in certain students, both of which are detrimental when a teacher is striving to establish for all students a positive, equal, and safe environment for classroom learning. Show confidence in all students, and never discriminate by expecting less or more from some than from others. Although some students may take longer to respond, it is not necessarily because they are not thinking or have less ability. There may be cultural differences to think about, in that some cultures simply allow more wait time than others. The important point here is to individualize to allow students who need more time to have it. Variation in wait time allowed should not be used to single out some students and to lead to lower expectations but rather to allow for higher expectations.

Require students to raise their hands and be called on. When you ask questions, instead of allowing students to randomly shout out their answers, require them to raise their hands and to be called on before they respond. Establish that procedure and stick with it. This helps to assure both that you call on all students equally, fairly distributing your interactions with the students, and that girls are not interacted with less because boys tend to be more vociferous. Even in college classrooms, male students tend to be more vocal than are female students

and, when allowed by the instructor, tend to outtalk and to interrupt their female peers. Even in same-gender classrooms, some students tend to be more vocal while others are less so and, when allowed by the instructor, tend to monopolize and control the flow of the verbal interactions. Regardless of grade level, every teacher has the responsibility to guarantee a nonbiased classroom and an equal distribution of interaction time in the classroom. That is impossible to do if students are allowed to speak out at will.

Another important reason for this advice is to aid students in learning to control their impulsivity. Controlling one's impulsivity is one of the characteristics of intelligent behavior. One of your many instructional responsibilities is to help students develop this skill.

Actively involve as many students as possible in the questioning-answering discussion session. The traditional method of the teacher asking a question and then calling on a student to respond is essentially a one-on-one interaction. Many students, those not called on, are likely to view that as their opportunity to disengage in the lesson at hand. Even though you call on one student, you don't want the other students to mentally disengage. There are many effective ways to keep all engaged. Consider the following.

To keep all students mentally engaged, you will want to call on students who are sitting quietly and have not raised their hands as well as those who have, but avoid badgering or humiliating an unwilling participant. When a student has no response, you might suggest he or she think about it and you will come back to the student to assure the student eventually understands or has an answer to the original question.

By dividing a single question into several parts, the number of students involved can be increased. For example, "What are the causes of the Civil War? Who can give one reason?" followed then by "Who can give another?" Or, you can involve several students in answering a single question. For example, ask one student for an answer to the question "What was the first battle of the Civil War?", a second to read the text aloud to verify the student's answer, and sometimes a third to explore the reason or thinking that makes it the accepted answer.

Carefully gauge your responses to students' responses to your questions. The way you respond to students' answers influences students' subsequent participation. Responses by the teacher that encourage student participation include probing for elaboration, discussing student answers, requesting justification, asking how answers were arrived at, and providing positive reinforcement.

Use strong praise sparingly. Although a teacher's use of strong praise is sometimes okay, when you want students to think divergently and creatively, you should be stingy with use of strong praise to student responses. Strong praise from a teacher tends to terminate divergent and creative thinking. Strong praise can also cause children to become dependent on external sources of praise—to become "praise junkies."

One of your goals is to help students find intrinsic sources for motivation, that is, an inner drive of intent or desire that causes them to want to learn. Use of strong praise tends to build conformity, causing students to depend on outside forces—that is, the giver of praise—for their worth rather than upon themselves. An example of a strong praise response is "That's right! Very good." On the other hand, passive acceptance responses, such as "Okay, that seems to be one possibility," keep the door open for further thinking, particularly for higher level, divergent thinking.

Another example of a passive acceptance response is one used in brainstorming sessions, when the teacher says, "After asking the question and giving you time to think about it, I will hear your ideas and record them on the board." Only after all student responses have been heard and recorded does the class begin its consideration of each. That kind of nonjudgmental acceptance of all ideas in the classroom will generate a great deal of expression of high-level thought.

QUESTIONS FROM STUDENTS: THE QUESTION-DRIVEN CLASSROOM AND CURRICULUM

Student questions can and should be used as springboards for further questioning, discussions, and investigations. Indeed, in a constructivist learning environment, student questions often drive content. Students should be encouraged to ask questions that challenge the textbook, the process, or other persons' statements, and they should be encouraged to seek the supporting evidence behind a statement.

Being able to ask questions may be more important than having right answers. Knowledge is derived from asking questions. Being able to recognize problems and to formulate questions is a skill and the key to problem solving and critical thinking skill development. You have a responsibility to encourage students to formulate questions and to help them word their questions in such a way that tentative answers can be sought. That is the process necessary to build a base of knowledge that can be drawn upon whenever necessary to link, interpret, and explain new information in new situations.

Questioning: The Cornerstone of Critical Thinking, Real-World Problem Solving, and Meaningful Learning

With real-world problem solving, there are usually no absolute right answers. Rather than "correct" answers, some are better than others. The student with a problem needs to learn how to: (1) recognize the problem, (2) formulate a question about that problem (e.g., Should I date this person or not? Should I take this after-school job or not? Should I smoke or not? To which colleges should I apply?), (3) collect data, and (4) arrive at a temporarily acceptable answer to the problem, while realizing that at some later time, new data may dictate a review of the former conclusion. For example, if a biochemist believes she has discovered a new enzyme, there is no textbook or teacher or any other outside authoritative source to which she may refer to inquire if she is correct. Rather, on the basis of her self-confidence in problem identification, asking questions, collecting enough data, and arriving at a tentative conclusion based on those data, she assumes that for now her conclusion is safe.

Encourage students to ask questions about content and process. As emphasized in *Tried and True,* question asking often indicates that the inquirer is curious, puzzled, and uncertain; it is a sign of being engaged in thinking. And, yet, in too many classrooms too few students ask questions.[13] Students should be encouraged to ask questions. From students, there is no such thing as a "dumb" question. Sometimes students, like everyone else, ask questions that could just as easily have been looked up or are irrelevant or show lack of thought or sensitivity. Those questions can consume precious class time. For a teacher, they can be frustrating. A teacher's initial reaction may be to quickly and mistakenly brush off that type of question with sarcasm, while assuming that the student is too lazy to look up an answer. In such instances, you are advised to think before responding and to respond kindly and professionally, although in the busy life of a classroom teacher, that may not always be so easy to remember to do. However, be assured, there is a reason for a student's question. Perhaps the student is signaling a need for recognition or simply demanding attention.

---

[13] United States Department of Education, *Tried and True: Tested Ideas for Teaching and Learning from the Regional Educational Laboratories* (Washington, DC: Office of Educational Research and Improvement, U.S. Department of Education, 1997), p. 53.

In large schools, it is sometimes easy for a student to feel alone and insignificant (although this seems less the case with schools that use a school-within-a-school plan and where teachers and students work together in interdisciplinary teams, or, as in looping, where one cadre of teachers remains with the same cohort of students for two or more years). When a student makes an effort to interact with you, that can be a positive sign, so gauge carefully your responses to those efforts. If a student's question is really off track, off the wall, out of order, and out of context with the content of the lesson, consider this as a possible response: "That is an interesting question (or comment) and I would very much like to talk with you more about it. Could we meet at lunch time or before or after school or at some other time that is mutually convenient?"

Avoid bluffing an answer to a question for which you do not have an answer. Nothing will cause you to lose credibility with students any faster than faking an answer. There is nothing wrong with admitting that you do not know. It helps students realize that you are human. It helps them maintain an adequate self-esteem, realizing that they are okay. What *is* important is that you know where and how to find possible answers and that you help students develop that same knowledge and those same process skills.

Now, to reinforce your understanding, do Exercises 7.3–7.7.

FOR YOUR NOTES

EXERCISE 7.3
Examining Course Materials for Level of Questioning

Instructions: It is the purpose of this exercise for you to examine course materials for the levels of questions presented to students. For a subject and grade level you intend to teach, examine a textbook (or other instructional material) for the questions posed to the students, perhaps at the ends of the chapters. Also examine workbooks, examinations, instructional packages, and any other printed or electronic material used by students. Complete the exercise that follows; then share your findings with your classmates.

1. Materials examined (include date of publication and target students): _____

_____

2. Questions at the recall (lowest) level:_____

_____

_____

_____

_____

3. Questions at the processing (intermediate) level: _____

_____

_____

_____

_____

4. Questions at the application (highest) level: _____

_____

_____

_____

_____

5. Approximate percentages of questions at each level:_____

   a. Recall = _____%

   b. Processing = _____%

   c. Application = _____%

6. Did you find evidence of question-level sequencing? If so, describe it.

_____

_____

_____

_____

7. After sharing and discussing your results with your classmates, what do you conclude from this exercise?

_____

_____

_____

_____

8. When using instructional materials that you believe have a disproportionately high percentage of questions at the input (or recall) level, in addition to the two examples provided, what should or could you do?

Example 1: Have students scan chapter subheadings and develop higher-level cognitive questions based on the subheadings, which they would then answer through their reading.

Example 2: Require students to defend their answers to low-level cognitive chapter review and end-of-chapter questions with textual information and experience.

_____

_____

_____

_____

_____

_____

_____

_____

_____

_____

_____

_____

_____

_____

EXERCISE 7.4

Observing the Cognitive Levels of Classroom Verbal Interaction

Instructions: The purpose of this exercise is to develop your skill in recognizing the levels of classroom questions. Arrange to visit a secondary school classroom. On the lines provided here, tally each time you hear a question (or statement) from the teacher that causes students to gather or recall information, to process information, or to apply or evaluate data. In the left column, you may want to write additional key words to assist your memory. After your observation, compare and discuss the results of this exercise with your colleagues.

School and class visited: _____

Date of observation: _____

Level	*Tallies of Level of Question or Statement*
Recall level (key words: *complete, count, define, describe,* and so on)	1. _____
Processing level (key words: *analyze, classify, compare,* and so on)	2. _____
Application level (key words: *apply, build, evaluate,* and so on)	3. _____

FOR YOUR NOTES

EXERCISE 7.5

Practice in Raising Questions to Higher Levels

Instructions: The purpose of this exercise is to further develop your skill in raising questions from one level to the next higher level. Complete the blank lines with questions at the appropriate levels (for the last series, create your own recall question and then vary it for the higher levels). Share and discuss your responses with your classmates.

Recall Level	*Processing Level*	*Application Level*
1. How many of you read a newspaper today?	1. Why did you read a newspaper today?	1. What do you think would happen if nobody ever read a newspaper again?
2. What was today's newspaper headline?	2. Why was that so important to be a headline?	2. Do you think that news items will be in tomorrow's paper?
3. Who is the vice-president of the United States today?	3. How does the work he has done compare with that done by the previous vice-president?	3. _____
4. How many presidents has the United States had?	4. _____	4. _____
5. _____	5. _____	5. _____

FOR YOUR NOTES

EXERCISE 7.6
Creating Cognitive Questions

Instructions: The purpose of this exercise is to provide practice in writing cognitive questions. Read the following example of verse. Then, from that verse, compose three questions about it that would cause students to identify, list, and recall; three that would cause students to analyze, compare, and explain; and three that would cause students to predict, apply, and hypothesize. Share and check questions with your peers.

We Are One

Truth, love, peace, and beauty,
We have sought apart
    but will find within, as our
Moods—explored, shared,
    questioned, and accepted—
Together become one and all.

Through life my friends
We can travel together,
for we now know
each could go it alone.

To assimilate our efforts into one,
While growing in accepting,
and trusting, and sharing the
    individuality of the other,
Is truly to enjoy our greatest gift—
Feeling—knowing love and compassion.

Through life my friends
We are together,
for we must know
we are one.

—R. D. Kellough

Recall Questions

1. (to *identify*) _____

   _____

   _____

2. (to *list*) _____

   _____

   _____

3. (to *recall*) _____

_____

_____

Processing Questions

1. (to *analyze*) _____

_____

_____

_____

2. (to *compare*) _____

_____

_____

_____

3. (to *explain*) _____

_____

_____

_____

Application Questions

1. (to *predict*) _____

_____

_____

_____

2. (to *apply*) _____

_____

_____

_____

3. (to *hypothesize*) _____

_____

_____

_____

_____

EXERCISE 7.7

A Cooperative Learning and Micro Peer Teaching Exercise in the Use of Questioning—Micro Peer Teaching I

Instructions: The purpose of this exercise is to practice preparing and asking questions that are designed to lead student thinking from the lowest level to the highest. Before class, prepare a five-minute lesson for posing questions that will guide the learner from lowest to highest levels of thinking. Teaching will be one-on-one, in groups of four, with each member of the group assuming a particular role—teacher, student, judge, or recorder. Each of the four members of your group will assume each of those roles once for five minutes. (If there are only three members in a group, the roles of judge and recorder can be combined during each five-minute lesson; or, if there are five members in the group, one member can sit out each round, or two can work together as judge.) Each member of the group should have his or her own tally sheet.

Suggested Lesson Topics

- Teaching styles
- Characteristics of youngsters of a particular age
- Learning styles of students
- Evaluation of learning achievement
- A skill or hobby
- Teaching competencies
- A particular teaching strategy
- Student teaching and what it will really be like

Each of your group members should keep the following role descriptions in mind:

- *Teacher (sender).* Pose recall (input), processing, and application (output) questions related to one of the topics above or to any topic you choose.
- *Student (receiver).* Respond to the questions of the teacher.
- *Judge.* Identify the level of each question or statement used by the teacher *and* the level of the student's response.
- *Recorder.* Tally the number of each level of question or statement used by the teacher (S = sender) as indicated by the judge; also tally the level of student responses (R = receiver). Record any problems encountered by your group.

TALLY SHEET

	Minute	Input	Processing	Output
Sender _____	1 S			
Receiver _____	R			
	2 S			
	R			
	3 S			
	R			
	4 S			
	R			
	5 S			
	R			

TALLY SHEET

	Minute	Input	Processing	Output
Sender _____	1 S			
Receiver _____	R			
	2 S			
	R			
	3 S			
	R			
	4 S			
	R			
	5 S			
	R			

SUMMARY

This chapter presented a great deal of information about one teaching strategy, which will be perhaps the most important one in your teaching repertoire. Questioning is the cornerstone to meaningful learning, thinking, communication, and real-world problem-solving. The art of its use is something you will continue to develop throughout your teaching career.

In the next two chapters, your attention is directed to how teachers group students and to the selection and implementation of specific instructional strategies to facilitate students' meaningful learning of skills and content of the curriculum.

ADDITIONAL EXERCISE

See the companion website http://www.prenhall.com/kellough for the following exercise related to the content of this chapter:

• Observe a Television Quiz Show to Tabulate and Analyze the Levels of Questions and Levels of Thinking Expected of its Contestants.

QUESTIONS FOR CLASS DISCUSSION

1. Have you ever noticed that some teachers seem to anticipate a lower level response to their questions from particular students? Discuss your answer with your peers.
2. Should a teacher verbally respond to every student's verbal comment or inquiry? Explain why or why not. If not, on what basis does the teacher decide when and how to respond?
3. Describe when, if ever, and how, strong praise could be used by a teacher. Explain the difference, if any, between strong praise and positive reinforcement.
4. Explain why it is important to wait after asking students a content question? How long should you wait? What should you do if after waiting a certain amount of time there is no student response?
5. To what extent should (or can) a classroom teacher allow student questions to determine content studied? To what extent should students' initial interest, or lack of interest, in a topic determine whether the topic gets taught?
6. Explain the meaning of the following statement: We should look not for what students can reiterate but for what they can demonstrate and produce. Explain why you agree or disagree with the concept.
7. Select one of the Reflective Thoughts from the opening of Part III (page 220) that is specifically related to the content of this chapter, research it, and write a one-page essay explaining why you agree or disagree with the thought. Share your essay with members of your class for their thoughts.
8. Describe any prior concepts you held that changed as a result of your experiences with this chapter. Describe the changes.
9. From your current observations and field work as related to this teacher preparation program, clearly identify one specific example of educational practice that seems contradictory to exemplary practice or theory as presented in this chapter. Present your explanation for the discrepancy.
10. Do you have questions generated by the content of this chapter? If you do, list them along with ways answers might be found.

FOR FURTHER READING

Brualdi, A. C. *Classroom Questions.* ERIC/AE Digest 422407 (Washington, DC: ERIC Clearinghouse on Assessment and Evaluation, 1998).

Cardellichio, T., and Field, W. "Seven Strategies That Encourage Neural Branching." *Educational Leadership* 54(6):33–36 (March 1997).

Chappell, M. F., and Thompson, D. "Modifying Our Questions To Assess Students' Thinking." *Mathematics Teaching in the Middle School* 4(7):470–474 (April 1999).

Cuccio-Schirripa, S. and Steiner, H. E. "Enhancement and Analysis of Science Question Level for Middle School Students." *Journal of Research in Science Teaching* 37(2): 210–224 (February 2000).

Good, T. L., and Brophy, J. E. *Looking in Classrooms.* 8th ed. Chap. 9. New York: Addison Wesley Longman, 2000.

Harpaz, Y., and Lefstein, A. "Communities of Thinking." *Educational Leadership* 58(3):54–57 (November 2000).

Latham, A. "Asking Students the Right Questions." *Educational Leadership* 54(6):84–85 (March 1997).

Martinello, M. L. "Learning to Question for Inquiry." *Educational Forum* 62(2):164–171 (Winter 1998).

Marzano, R. J., Pickering, D. J., and Pollock, J. E. *Classroom Instruction that Works: Research-Based Strategies for Increasing Student Achievement.* Chap. 10, "Cues, Questions, and Advance Organizers," pp. 111–120. Alexandria, VA: Association for Supervision and Curriculum Development, 2001.

Ochoa-Becker, A. S. "Decision Making in Middle School Social Studies: An Imperative for Youth and Democracy." *Clearing House* 72(6):337–340 (July 1999).

Ostergard, S. A. "Asking Good Questions in Mathematics Class: How Long Does It Take to Learn How?" *Clearing House* 71(1):48–50 (September/October 1997).

Owens, V. *Chemistry Quickies.* Waynesboro, VA: Eschar, 1998.

Traver, R. "What Is a Good Guiding Question?" *Educational Leadership* 55(6):70–73 (March 1998).

8

Grouping and Assignments for Positive Interaction and Quality Learning

Rather than diluting standards and expectations, believing in the learning potential of every student, exemplary schools and teachers are those who are able to effectively modify the key variables of time, methodology, and grouping, to help individual students achieve mastery of the curriculum. Throughout the book we talk of ways of varying the methodology. In this chapter we focus on ways of grouping students to enhance positive interaction and quality learning.

In the most effective instructional environments, during any given week or even day of school, a secondary school student might experience a succession of group settings. Ways of grouping learners for instruction is the initial topic of this chapter, from individualized instruction to working with dyads, small groups, and large groups. You also will learn how to ensure equality in the classroom, how to use assignments and homework, and how to coordinate various forms of independent and small-group project-based study.

Specifically, upon completion of this chapter you should be able to:

1. Describe the meaning of *mastery learning* and its implications for secondary school teaching.
2. Explain the advantages and disadvantages of various ways of grouping students for quality learning.
3. Explain how the teacher can personalize the instruction to ensure success for each student.
4. Demonstrate an understanding of the meaning and importance of classroom equity and how it can be achieved.
5. Demonstrate a theoretical and practical understanding of how to effectively use each of these instructional strategies: assignments, homework, written and oral reports, cooperative learning, learning centers, problem-based learning, and student-centered projects.

MASTERY LEARNING AND PERSONALIZED INSTRUCTION

Learning is an individual or personal experience. Yet as a classroom teacher you will be expected to work effectively with students on other than an individual basis—often 30 or more at a time. Much has been written on the importance of individualizing the instruction for learners. Virtually all the research concerning better instructional practice emphasizes greater individualization, or personalization, of instruction.[1] We know of the individuality of the learning experience. And we know that while some students are primarily verbal learners, many more are primarily visual, tactile, or kinesthetic learners. As the teacher, though, you find yourself in the difficult position of simultaneously "treating" many separate and individual learners with individual learning capacities, styles, and preferences.

In lieu of traditional academic tracking, to individualize the learning, schools use exploratory programs, cooperative learning groups, project-based learning, and independent study to respond to the variety of individual student competencies, interests, needs, and abilities. They also use non-conventional scheduling so that teaching teams can vary the length of time in periods and also vary the size of instructional groups and the learning strategies within a given time period.

Common sense tells us that student achievement in learning is related to both the quality of attention and the length of time given to learning tasks. In 1968, Benjamin Bloom, building upon a model developed earlier by John Carroll, developed the concept of individualized instruction called **mastery learning,** saying that students need sufficient time on task (i.e., engaged time) to master content before moving on to new content.[2] From that concept Fred Keller developed an instructional plan called the *Personalized System of Instruction* (PSI), or the *Keller Plan,* which by the early 1970s enjoyed popularity and success, especially at many two-year colleges. PSI involves the student's learning from printed modules of instruction (which, today, would likely be presented as computer software programs), which allow the student greater control over the learning pace.[3] The instruction is mastery oriented; that is, the student demonstrates mastery of the content of one module before proceeding to the next.

Today's Emphasis: Quality Learning for All Students

Emphasis today is on mastery of content, or quality learning, rather than coverage of content, or quantity of learning. Because of that emphasis and research that indicates that quality learning programs positively affect achievement, the importance of the concept of mastery learning has resurfaced. For example, in today's efforts to restructure schools, two approaches—*Results-Driven Education* (RDE), also known as *Outcome-Based Education* (OBE), and the *Coalition of Essential Schools* (CES), utilize a goal-driven curriculum model with instruction that focuses on the construction of individual knowledge through mastery and assessment of student learning against the anticipated outcomes.[4]

In some instances, unfortunately, attention may only be on the mastery of minimum competencies; thus, students are not encouraged to work and learn to the maximum of their talents and abilities. By mastery of content, we mean that the student demonstrates his or her use of what has been learned. In some schools using the mastery approach, the final demonstration by a student is what is known as graduation by exhibition. However, the more recent trend toward graduation by standardized achievement testing may, if it continues, put a damper on the "graduation by exhibition" aspect of a mastery approach.

---

[1] J. M. Carroll, "The Copernican Plan Evaluated," *Phi Delta Kappan* 76(2):105–113 (October 1994).

[2] See B. Bloom, *Human Characteristics and School Learning* (New York: McGraw-Hill, 1987), and J. Carroll, "A Model of School Learning," *Teachers College Record* 64(8):723–733 (May 1963).
[3] See, for example, I. R. Hambleton, W. H. Foster, and J. T. E. Richardson, "Improving Student Learning Using the Personalized System of Instruction," *Higher Education* 35(2):187–203 (March 1998).
[4] Information about CES, such as a directory of participating schools, can be obtained from http://www.essentialschools.org.

Assumptions about Mastery, or Quality, Learning

Today's concept of mastery, or quality, learning is based on six assumptions:

1. Mastery learning can ensure that students experience success at each level of the instructional process—experiencing success at each level provides incentive and motivation for further learning.
2. Mastery of content, or quality learning, is possible for all students.
3. Although all students can achieve mastery, to master a particular content some students may require more time than others—the teacher and the school must provide for this difference in time need to complete a task successfully.
4. For quality learning to occur, it is the instruction that must be modified and adapted, not the students—tracking and ability grouping do not fit with the concept of mastery learning.
5. Most learning is sequential and logical.
6. Most desired learning outcomes can be specified in terms of observable and measurable performance.[5]

Components of Any Mastery Learning Model

Any instructional model designed to teach toward mastery (quality) learning will contain the following components: (a) clearly defined instructional objectives; (b) a preassessment of the learner's present knowledge; (c) an instructional component, with choices and options for students; (d) practice, reinforcement, frequent comprehension checks (both diagnostic and formative assessment), and corrective instruction at each step to keep the learner on track; and (e) a postassessment to determine the extent of student mastery of the objectives.

Strategies for Personalizing the Instruction

You can immediately provide personalized instruction by: (a) starting study of a topic from where the students are in terms of what they know (or think they know) and what they want to know about the topic (see "think-pair-share" discussed in section titled Learning in Pairs that follows), (b) providing students with choices from a rich variety of pathways and hands-on experiences to learn more about the topic, (c) providing multiple instructional approaches (i.e., using multilevel instruction in a variety of settings, from learning alone to whole-class instruction), and (d) empowering students with responsibility for decision making, reflection, and self-assessment.

LEARNING ALONE

While some students learn well in pairs (dyads), and others learn well with their peers in groups—collaboratively, cooperatively, or competitively—or collaboratively with adults, and others learn well in combinations of these patterns, researchers tell us that more than ten percent of students learn best alone. Learning-alone students often are gifted, nonconforming, able to work at their own pace successfully, comfortable using media, or seemingly underachieving but potentially able students for whom unconventional instructional strategies, such as *contract learning packages* (i.e., agreements between the teacher and individual students to proceed with tasks appropriate to their readiness, interests, or learning profiles in a sequence and at a pace each student selects) or multisensory instructional packages, encourage academic success.[6]

The Self-Instructional Module

One technique that can be used to ensure mastery of learning, and that can be connected to the use of contract learning packages, is the self-instructional module (SIM), which is a learning package (written, recorded, or on computer disk) specifically designed for an individual student. It uses small sequential steps, with frequent practice and immediate learning feedback to the student. It is designed to teach a relatively small amount of material, at the mastery level, requiring a brief amount of learning time (about 30 minutes for middle school students; up to an hour for high school students). The SIM can be designed to teach any topic, at any level of student maturity and skill, in any subject, for any domain or combination of domains of learning. Exercise 8.1 is an actual self-instructional module that is designed to guide you through completion of your first SIM.

As instructed by your course instructor, do Exercise 8.1.

---

[5]See J. Battistini, *From Theory to Practice: Classroom Application of Outcome-Based Education* (Bloomington, IN: ERIC Clearinghouse on Reading, English, and Communication, 1995), and L. Horton, *Mastery Learning,* Fastback 154 (Bloomington, IN: Phi Delta Kappa Educational Foundation, 1981).

[6]R. Dunn, *Strategies for Diverse Learners,* Fastback 384 (Bloomington, IN: Phi Delta Kappa Educational Foundation, 1995), p. 15.

EXERCISE 8.1

*Preparing a Self-Instructional Module**

Instructions: The purpose of this exercise is to guide you through the process of preparing a self-instructional module for use in your own teaching. The exercise continues for several pages; it is important that you follow it step-by-step, beginning with the following boxed-in "cover page."

Self-Instructional Module Number: 1
Instructor's Name: Professor Richard D. Kellough
School: California State University, Sacramento
Course: Methods of Teaching
Intended Students: Students in Teacher Preparation
Topic: How to Write a Self-Instructional Module
Estimated Working Time: Ten hours

For the challenge of today's classroom . . .

The Self-Instructional Module

You are about to embark upon creating and writing a perfect lesson plan. The result of your hard work will be an instructional module in which you will take a lot of pride. More important, you will have learned a technique of teaching that ensures learning takes place. For what more could you ask?

*Copyright 1991 by Richard D. Kellough.

Let us get to the essence of what this self-instructional module (SIM) is: This SIM is about how to write an SIM. The general objective is to guide you gently through the process of preparing and writing your first SIM. Let's begin the experience with background about the history of the SIM.

A History

Research evidence indicates that student achievement in learning is related to time and to the *quality of attention* being given to the learning task. You knew that already! In 1968, Benjamin Bloom developed a concept of individualized instruction called mastery learning, based on the idea that students need sufficient time on task to master content before moving on to new content. Did you know that? _____. (Please read along with a pencil, and fill in the blanks as you go.)

Although Bloom is usually given credit for the concept of mastery learning, the idea did not originate with him. He reinforced and made popular a model developed earlier by John Carroll. In 1968, Fred Keller developed a similar model called the Keller Plan, or the Personalized System of Instruction (PSI). The PSI quickly became a popular teaching technique in the community and four-year colleges. In about 1972, enter Johnson and Johnson (not of the Band-Aid family, but Rita and Stuart Johnson), who developed their model of mastery learning and called it the Self-Instructional Package (SIP). Since 1972, I (Richard D. Kellough) have been developing my version, the Self-Instructional Module, which you are now experiencing. As you will learn, *frequent comprehension checks and corrective instructions* are important to the effectiveness of the SIM.

One other thing. There are several devices available to individualize instruction, but the SIM has the flexibility to be adaptable for use at all grade levels, from kindergarten through college. I believe the following to be the reasons for the popularity of this strategy:

- The SIM allows the teacher to *create an experience that ensures learning.* Creating makes you feel good; when your students learn, you feel good—two reasons for the SIM's popularity.
- The SIM is truly *individualized,* because it is a package written for an individual student, with that student in mind as it is being written.
- Although it takes time to prepare, the SIM *requires little financial expenditure,* a fact important to today's teacher.
- Once you have prepared your first SIM, it is possible that you will see that you have begun a series. Subsequent packages are easier to do, and you may see the value in having a series available.
- With today's emphasis on the *basics,* the SIM is particularly helpful for use in remediation.
- When you finish your SIM, you will have collected the content that could be used for a computer program.
- With today's *large and mixed-ability classes,* teachers need help! Here is time- and cost-effective help!
- With emphasis today on competency-based instruction, the SIM makes sense.

How are we doing so far? _____ Are your interests and curiosity aroused?

_____ Do you have questions? _____ If so, write them down, then continue.

Questions: _____

_____

_____

_____

What Is the Self-Instructional Module and Why Use It?

The SIM is a learning package designed for an individual student; it is self-instructional (i.e., if you, the teacher, drop dead—heaven forbid—the student can continue to learn), and *it requires about 15 to 50 minutes of learning time.* The final package can be recorded on tape, video, or computer disc, or it can be written in booklet form, or it can exist in any combination of these.

Here are ways that teachers have found the SIM to be useful:

- As an *enrichment* activity for an accelerated student.
- As a strategy for make-up for a student who has been absent.
- As a strategy for a student in need of *remediation.*
- As a strategy for introducing basic information to an entire class, freeing the teacher to work with individual students, making the act of teaching more *time-efficient,* a particularly significant value of the SIM.
- As a learning experience especially coordinated with manipulatives, perhaps in connection with a science experiment, library work, a computer, a tape recording, a videotape, a videodisc, or hands-on materials for an activity, or any combination of these.

One other point before we stop and check your comprehension: *The single most important characteristic of the SIM is that it uses small, sequential steps followed by immediate and corrective feedback to the learner.* In that respect, the SIM resembles programmed instruction.

   Stop the action!

Let's check your learning with the review questions and instructions that follow.

Comprehension Check 1

Answer the following three questions, then check your responses by reviewing Feedback Check 1. If you answer all three questions correctly, continue the package; otherwise, back up and review.

---

1. How would you define a SIM? _____

_____

_____

2. What is the single most important characteristic of the SIM? _____

_____

3. What is one way that the SIM could be used in your own teaching, a way that currently stands out in your thinking? _____

_____

_____

Feedback Check 1

1. Although we will continue development of the definition, at this point it should resemble this: The SIM is an individualization of learning—teaching strategy that teaches toward mastery learning of one relatively small bit of content by building upon small, sequential steps and providing corrective feedback throughout.
2. Referring to the small, sequential steps, followed by immediate and corrective feedback.
3. Your answer is probably related to one of those listed earlier but it could differ.

How Does the SIM Differ from Other Kinds of Learning Packages?

Another characteristic of the SIM is the *amount of learning contained in one package.* Each SIM is designed to teach a relatively small amount of material, but to do it well. *This is a major difference in the SIM from other types of learning activity packages.*

And, in case you have been wondering about what the SIM can be designed to teach, I want to emphasize that it *can be designed:*

- For any topic,
  - At any grade level,
    - In any discipline,
      - For cognitive understanding,
        - For psychomotor development, and
          - For affective learning.

That probably brings to your mind all sorts of thoughts and questions. Hold them for a moment, and let's do another comprehension check.

 Stop the action and check your learning.

Comprehension Check 2

Answer the following two questions, then check your responses in the feedback box that follows.

1. How does the SIM differ from other self-contained learning packages?

_____

_____

_____

2. Although teachers frequently emphasize learning that falls within the cognitive domain, is it possible for the SIM to be written to include learning in the psychomotor and affective domains? Yes or no? _____

Feedback Check 2

1. Length of learning time is shorter for the SIM, and it is written with an individual student in mind. It is written to teach one thing well, to one student.
2. The SIM *can* be written for any domain, although evaluation is trickier for the affective and for the highest-level psychomotor.

Perhaps we should now say a word about what we mean when we use the expression *teach one thing well*—that is, to explain what is meant by mastery learning. Theoretically, if the package is being used by an individual student, performance level expectation is 100 percent. In reality, performance level will most likely be between 85 and 95 percent, particularly if you are using the SIM for a group of students rather than an individual. That 5–15 percent difference allows for human errors that can occur in writing and in reading.

Now that you have learned what the SIM is—and how this learning strategy differs from other learning activity packages—it is time to concentrate on development of your SIM. Please continue.

SIM Development

How Do I Develop a SIM?

As with any good lesson plan, it takes time to develop an effective SIM. Indeed, preparation of your first SIM will test your imagination and writing skills! Nevertheless, it will be time well spent; you will be proud of your product. *It is important that you continue following this package, step-by-step; do not skip parts, or I will assume no responsibility for your final product! Understand?* _____ Development of your SIM emphasizes the importance of

- Writing the learning objectives clearly, precisely, and in behavioral terms.
- Planning the learning activities in small, sequential steps.
- Providing frequent practice and learning comprehension checks.
- Providing immediate feedback, corrective instruction, and assurance to the learner.
- Preparing evaluative questions that measure against the learning objectives.

As you embark on preparing what may be the perfect lesson plan, keep in mind the following two points:

1. Prepare your first SIM so that it will take no more than

---

30 minutes for middle school students
    50 to 60 minutes for high school students

☞

2. Use a *conversational tone* in your writing. Write in the first person, as though you are talking directly to the student for whom it is intended. For example, when speaking of the learning objectives, use **You will be able to** rather than *The student will be able to*. Keep in mind that you are communicating with one person rather than with an entire class (even though you may be preparing your package for entire class use). It helps to pretend that you are in a one-on-one situation tutoring the student at the writing board.

 Stop the action, and again check your learning.

Comprehension Check 3

Answer the following two questions, then check your responses in Feedback Check 3.

---

1. What maximum learning-time duration is recommended?_____

2. What major item of importance has been recommended for you to keep in mind as you write

   your SIM? _____

   _____

   _____

Feedback Check 3

1. Approximately 30 to 60 minutes, depending upon the grade and achievement level.
2. Write in the first person, as if you are speaking directly with the student.

Now that we have emphasized the *length of learning time* and *the personalization of your writing,* here are other important reminders.

1. Make your SIM attractive and stimulating. Consider using cartoons, puns, graphics, scratch-and-sniff stickers, and interesting manipulatives. Use your creative imagination! Use both cerebral hemispheres!

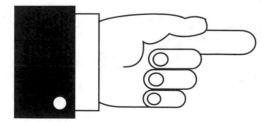

Add sketches, diagrams, modules, pictures, magazine clippings, humor, and a conversational tone, as students appreciate a departure from the usual textbooks and worksheets.

2. Use colleagues as resource persons, brainstorming ideas as you proceed through each step of package production.

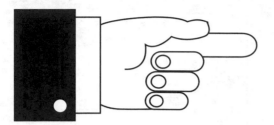

During production, use your best cooperative learning skills.

3. The package should not be read (or heard) like a lecture. It *must* involve small, sequential steps with frequent practice and corrective feedback instruction (as modeled in this package).

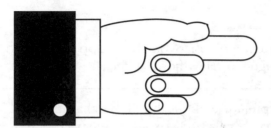

". . . and with the course material broken down into small, self-instructional units, students can move through at individual rates."

4. The package should contain a variety of activities, preferably involving all four learning modalities—*visual, auditory, tactile, and kinesthetic.*

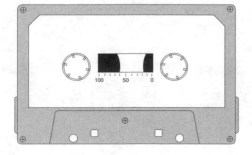

5. Vary margins, indentations, and fonts

so the final package does not have the usual textbook or worksheet appearance with which students are so familiar. Build into your package the "Hawthorne Effect."

Note about the cosmetics of your SIM: My own prejudice about the SIM is that it should be spread out more than the usual textbook page or worksheet. Use double-spaced lines, varied margins, and so on. Make cosmetic improvements after finishing your final draft. Write, review, sleep on it, write more, revise, add that final touch. This package that you are using has been "toned down" and modified for practical inclusion in this textbook.

6. Your SIM does not have to fit the common 8 1/2" × 11" size. You are encouraged to be creative in the design of your SIM's shape, size, and format.
7. Like all lesson plans, the SIM is subject to revision and improvement after use. *Write, review, sleep on it, write more, revise, test, revise. . . .*

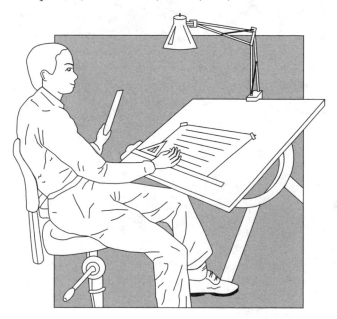

Perhaps before proceeding, it would be useful to review the preceding points. Remember, too, the well-written package *will ensure learning*. Your first SIM will take several hours to produce, but it will be worth it!

Proceed with the steps that follow.

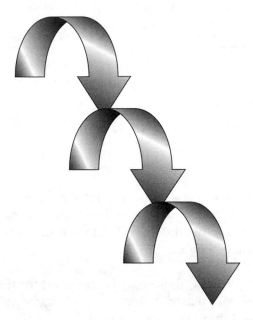

STEPS FOR DEVELOPING YOUR SIM

Instructions: It is important that you proceed through the following package development step-by-step.

One thing you will notice is that immediately after writing your learning objectives you prepare the evaluative test items; both steps precede the preparation of the learning activities. That is not the usual order followed by a teacher when preparing lessons, but it does help to ensure that test items match objectives. Now, here we go! *Step-by-step,* please.

Note: From here on, write on separate paper for draft planning.

Step 1. Prepare the cover page. It should include the following items:

- Instructor's name (that is you)
  - School (yours)
    - Class or intended students (whom it's for)
      - Topic (specific but not wordy)
        - Estimated working time

For a sample, refer to the beginning of this package. You can vary the design of the cover page according to your needs.

☞

Step 2. Prepare the instructional objectives. For now, these should be written in specific behavioral terms. Later, when writing these into your package introduction, you can phrase them in more general terms.

Recommended is the inclusion of at least one attitudinal (affective) objective, such as "Upon completion of this package, you will tell me your feelings about this kind of learning."

Step 3. **Comprehension Check 4**

Share with your colleagues what you have accomplished (with steps 1 and 2) to solicit their valuable feedback and input.

Step 4. Depending on feedback (from step 3), *modify items 1 and 2,* if necessary. For example, after listing the learning instructions, you may find that you really have more than one package in preparation, and within the list of objectives you may find a natural cut-off between packages 1 and 2. You may discover that you have a *series* of modules begun.

Step 5. Prepare the pretest. If the learner does well on the pretest, there may be no need for the student to continue the package. Some packages (like this one) may not include a pretest, though most will. And if this is your first SIM writing experience, I think you *should* include a pretest.

Suggestion: The pretest need not be as long as the posttest but should include a limited sample of questions to determine whether the student already knows the material and need not continue with the package. A pretest also serves to set the student mentally for the SIM.

Step 6. Prepare the posttest. The pretest and posttest could be identical, but usually the pretest is shorter. It is important that both pretest and posttest items actually test against the objectives (of step 2). Try to keep the items objective (e.g., multiple-choice type), avoiding as much as possible the use of subjective test items (e.g., essay type), but do include at least one item measuring an affective objective (see boxed item in step 2).

Important reminder: If your package is well written, the student should *achieve 85–100 percent on the posttest.*

Step 7. **Comprehension Check 5**

Share with colleagues your pretest and posttest items (providing a copy of your objectives) for suggested improvement changes before continuing to the next step.

Use the following space to write notes to yourself about ideas you are having and regarding any materials you may need to complete your package.

Dear Self—

Good work so far! Before continuing, take a break.

It is time to stop working for a while . . .   . . . and go play!

Step 8. Okay, enough play, it is time to prepare the text of your SIM. This is the "meat" of your package, what goes between the pretest and the posttest. It is the INSTRUCTION. *Reminder:* For the SIM to be self-instructional, the learner should be able to work through the package with little or no help from you.

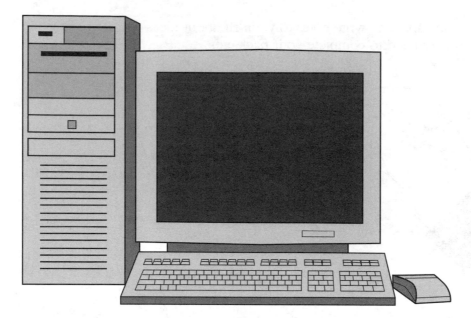

An important ingredient in your package is the *directions*. The package should be self-directed and self-paced. Therefore, each step of the package should be clear to the learner, making you, the instructor, literally unnecessary. *Everything needed by the learner to complete the package should be provided with the package.*

Use small, sequential steps with frequent practice cycles, followed by comprehension checks and corrective feedback. Make it fun and interesting with a variety of activities for the student, activities that provide for learning in several ways, from writing to reading, from viewing a videotape to drawing, from listening to a tape recording to doing a hands-on activity. And be certain the activities correlate with the learning objectives. The learning cycles should lead to satisfaction of the stated objectives, and the posttest items *must* measure against those objectives.

Step 9. **Comprehension Check 6**

Test your package. Try it out on your colleagues as they look for content errors, spelling and grammar errors, clarity, as well as offer suggestions for improvement. Duplicate and use the SIM Assessment Form provided at the end of this exercise.

Stop the Action!
Congratulations on the development of your first SIM!
However, two additional steps need your consideration.

Step 10. Revise if necessary. Make appropriate changes to your SIM as a result of the feedback from your colleagues. Then you are ready to give your SIM its first real test—try it out on the student for whom it is intended.

Step 11. Further revisions. This comes later, after you have used it with the student for whom it was originally intended. Like any other well-prepared lesson or unit plan, it should always be subject to revision and to improvement, never "set in concrete."

SIM ASSESSMENT FORM

1. Module identification

   Author: _____

   _____

   _____

   Title of SIM: _____

   _____

   _____

2. Module Objectives: Do they tell the student

   a. What the student will be able to do? _____

   _____

   _____

   _____

   _____

   b. How the student will demonstrate this new knowledge or skill?_____

   _____

   _____

   _____

   _____

   Is there a clear statement (overview or introduction) of the importance, telling the learner
   what will be learned by completing the module?_____

   _____

   _____

   _____

   _____

   _____

3. Pretest

   _____

   _____

   _____

   _____

   _____

   _____

4. Activities (practice cycles)

   Are small, sequential steps used? _____

   _____

   _____

   _____

   Are there frequent practice cycles, with comprehension checks and corrective feedback to the learner? _____

   _____

   _____

   _____

   _____

5. Posttest: Does it test against the objectives? _____

   _____

   _____

   _____

   _____

6. Is there clarity and continuity of expression? _____

   _____

   _____

   _____

   _____

7. Is the module informative, attractive, and enjoyable? _____

   _____

   _____

   _____

   _____

8. Additional comments useful to the author of this module: _____

   _____

   _____

   _____

   _____

LEARNING IN PAIRS

It is sometimes advantageous to pair students (dyads) for learning. Four types of dyads are described as follows.

Peer Tutoring, Mentoring, and Cross-Age Coaching. Peer tutoring, mentoring, or peer-assisted learning (PAL) is a strategy whereby one classmate tutors another. It is useful, for example, when one student helps another who has limited English proficiency or when a student skilled in math helps another who is less skilled. It has been demonstrated repeatedly that peer tutoring is a significant strategy for promoting active learning.[7]

Cross-age coaching is a strategy whereby one student coaches another from a different, and sometimes lower, grade level. This is similar to peer tutoring, except that the coach is from a different age level than the student being coached.[8] Many schools have service learning projects that involve older students mentoring younger children.

Paired Team Learning. Paired team learning is a strategy whereby students study and learn in teams of two. Students identified as gifted work and learn especially well when paired. Specific uses for paired team learning include drill partners, book report pairs, elaboration pairs, summary pairs, homework partners,[9] and project assignment pairs.

Think-Pair-Share. Think-pair-share is a strategy where students, in pairs, examine a new concept or topic about to be studied. After the students of each dyad discuss what they already know or think they know about the concept, they present their perceptions to the whole group. This is an excellent technique for discovering student's prior misconceptions (also called naïve theories) about a topic to be studied. Introducing a writing step, the modification called *think-write-pair-share,* is when the dyad thinks and writes their ideas or conclusions before sharing with the larger group.

The Learning Center

Another significantly beneficial way of pairing students for instruction (as well as of individualizing the instruction and learning alone and integrating the learning) is by using the learning center (LC) or learning station. [*Note:* Whereas each *learning center* is distinct and unrelated to others, *learning stations* are sequenced or in some way linked to one another.] The LC is a special place in the classroom where one student (or two, if student interaction is necessary or preferred at the center) can quietly work and learn at the student's own pace more about a special topic or to improve specific skills. All materials needed are provided at that center, including clear instructions for operation of the center. Whereas the LC used to be thought of as belonging to the domain of elementary school teachers with self-contained classrooms, now, with block scheduling and longer class periods, the LC has special relevance for all teachers, regardless of grade level. In the words of a teacher of French and Spanish at Bailey Middle School (Austin, TX):

> As other teachers in our district have begun to use center techniques, I hear comments such as, "The students are so excited," and "There was none of the chaos I was afraid of." In using centers as a teaching tool, I have found that students are eager to participate in all class work and excited about speaking a new language both inside and outside the classroom.[10]

The value of learning centers as instructional devices undoubtedly lies in the following facts. LCs can provide instructional diversity. While working at a center, the student is giving time and quality attention to the learning task (learning toward mastery) and is likely to be engaging her or his most effective learning modality, or integrating several modalities or all of them. To adapt instruction to students' individual needs and preferences it is possible to design a learning environment that includes several learning centers, each of which uses a different medium and modality or focuses on a special aspect of the curriculum. Students then rotate through the various learning centers according to their needs and preferences.[11]

Learning centers are of three types. In the *direct-learning center,* performance expectations for cognitive learning are quite specific and the focus is on mastery of content. In the *open-learning center,* the goal is to provide opportunity for exploration, enrichment, motivation, and creative discovery. In the *skill center,* as in a direct-learning center, performance expectations are quite specific, but the focus is on the development of a particular skill or process.

---

[7]See, for example, E. S. Foster-Harrison, *Peer Tutoring for K–12 Success,* Fastback 415 (Bloomington, IN: Phi Delta Kappa Educational Foundation, 1997), and A. W. Longwill and H. L. Kleinert, "The Unexpected Benefits of High School Peer Tutoring," *Teaching Exceptional Children* 30(4):60–65 (March/April 1998).
[8]See, for example, C. Fischer, "An Effective (and Affordable) Intervention Model for At-Risk High School Readers," *Journal of Adolescent & Adult Literacy* 43(4):326–335 (December 1999/January 2000); J. Wagmeister and B. Shifrin, "Thinking Differently, Learning Differently," *Educational Leadership* 58(3):45–48 (November 2000); and T. G. Jones et al., "Show-and-Tell Physics," *Science Teacher* (63(8):24–27 (November 1996).
[9]See, for example, C. Kaplan, "Homework Partners," *Mathematics Teaching in the Middle School* 2(3):168–169 (January 1997).

[10]L. Voelzel, "Making Foreign Language Instruction the Center of Attention," *Middle Ground* 4(2):44–46 (October 2000).
[11]A. A. Glatthorn, *Developing A Quality Curriculum* (Alexandria, VA: Association for Supervision and Curriculum Development, 1994), p. 105.

Although in all instances the primary reason for using a learning center is to individualize—that is, to provide collections of materials and activities adjusted to the various readiness levels, interests, and learning profiles of students—there are additional reasons. Other reasons to use a LC are to provide (a) a mechanism for learning that crosses discipline boundaries; (b) a special place for a student with special needs; (c) opportunities for creative work, enrichment experiences, and multisensory experiences; and (d) an opportunity to learn from learning packages that utilize special equipment or media of which only one or a limited supply may be available for use in your classroom (e.g., science materials, a microscope, a computer, a laser videodisc player, or some combination of these).

To construct a LC you can be as elaborate and as creative as your time, imagination, and resources allow. Students can even help you plan and set up learning centers, which will relieve some of the burden from your busy schedule. The following paragraphs present guidelines for setting up and using this valuable instructional tool.

The center should be designed with a theme in mind, preferably one that integrates the student's learning by providing activities that cross discipline boundaries. Decide the purpose of the center and give the center a name, such as "The Center for the Study of Wetlands," or "A Walking Tour of Florence," or "Traveling to Quebec City," or "Structure and Function," or "Patterns in Nature," or "The United Nations," or "Patterns of Discrimination," or "Editing a Video," or "The Center for World Wide Communication," or "Sound Mixing," and so on. The purpose of the center should be clearly understood by the students. Learning centers should always be used for educational purposes, *never* for punishment.

The center should be designed so as to be attractive, purposeful, and uncluttered, and should be identified with an attractive sign. Learning centers should be activity-oriented (i.e., dependent on the student's manipulation of materials, not just paper-and-pencil tasks).

Topics for the center should be related to the instructional program—for review and reinforcement, remediation, or enrichment. The center should be self-directing (i.e., specific instructional objectives and procedures for using the center should be clearly posted and understandable to the student user). An audio- or videocassette or a computer program is sometimes used for this purpose. The center should also be self-correcting (i.e., student users should be able to tell by the way they have completed the task whether or not they have done it correctly and have learned).

The center should contain a variety of activities geared to the varying abilities and interest levels of the students. A choice of two or more activities at a center is one way to provide for this.

Materials to be used at the center should be maintained at the center, with descriptions for use provided to the students. Materials should be safe for student use, and you or another adult should easily supervise the center. Some centers may become more or less permanent centers, that is, remain for the school term or longer, whereas other centers may change according to what is being studied at the time.

LEARNING IN SMALL GROUPS

Small groups are those involving three to five students, in either a teacher- or a student-directed setting. Using small groups for instruction, including the cooperative learning group (CLG), enhances the opportunities for students to assume greater control over their own learning, sometimes referred to as *empowerment*.

Purposes for Using Small Groups

Small groups can be formed to serve a number of purposes. They might be useful for a specific learning activity (e.g., reciprocal reading groups, where students take turns asking questions, summarizing, making predictions about, and clarifying a story). Or they might be formed to complete an activity that requires materials that are of short supply, to complete a science experiment or a project, only lasting as long as the project does. Teachers have various rationales for assigning students to groups. Groups can be formed by grouping students according to: (a) personality type (e.g., sometimes a teacher may want to team less-assertive students together in order to give them the opportunity for greater management of their own learning), (b) social pattern (e.g., sometimes it may be necessary to break up a group of rowdy friends, or it may be desirable to broaden the association among students), (c) common interest, (d) learning styles (e.g., forming groups of either mixed styles or of styles in common), or (e) according to their abilities in a particular skill or their knowledge in a particular area. One specific type of small group instruction is the cooperative learning group.

COOPERATIVE LEARNING

Lev Vygotsky (1896–1934) studied the importance of a learner's social interactions in learning situations. Vygotsky argued that learning is most effective when learners cooperate with one another in a supportive learning environment under the careful guidance of a teacher. Cooperative learning, group problem solving, problem-based learning, and cross-age tutoring are instructional strategies used by teachers that have grown in popularity as a result of research evolving from the work of Vygotsky.

The Cooperative Learning Group (CLG)

The *cooperative learning group* is a heterogeneous group (i.e., mixed according to one or more criteria, such as ability or skill level, ethnicity, learning style, learning capacity, gender, and language proficiency) of three to five students who work together in a teacher- or student-directed setting, emphasizing support for one another. Often times, a CLG consists of four students of mixed ability, learning styles, gender, and ethnicity, with each member of the group assuming a particular role. Teachers usually change the membership of each group several to many times during the year.

The Theory and Use of Cooperative Learning

The theory of cooperative learning is that when small groups of students of mixed backgrounds and capabilities work together toward a common goal, members of the group increase their friendship and respect for one another. As a consequence, each individual's self-esteem is enhanced, students are more motivated to participate in higher order thinking, and academic achievement is accomplished.[12]

There are several techniques for using cooperative learning. Of special interest to teachers are general methods of cooperative learning, such as: "student team—achievement division" (STAD) where the teacher presents a lesson, students work together in teams to help each other learn the material, individuals take quizzes and team rewards are earned based on the individual scores on the quizzes; "teams-games-tournaments" (TGT) where tournaments (rather than quizzes) are held in which students compete against others of similar academic achievements and then winners contribute toward their team's score; group investigations.[13] Yet the primary purpose of each is for the groups to learn—which means, of course, that individuals within a group must learn. Group achievement in learning, then, is dependent upon the learning of individuals within the group. Rather than competing for rewards for achievement, members of the group cooperate by helping one another learn, so that the group reward will be a good one.

Roles within the Cooperative Learning Group

It is advisable to assign roles (specific functions) to each member of the CLG.

[12]See, for example R. E. Slavin, "Cooperative Learning in Middle and Secondary Schools", *Clearing House* 69(4):200–204 (March/April 1996).
[13]For details about these CLG strategies and others, see R. E. Slavin, *Student Team Learning: A Practical Guide for Cooperative Learning*, 3rd ed. (Washington, DC: National Education Association, 1991); E. Coelho, *Learning Together in the Multicultural Classroom* (Portsmouth, NH: Heinemann, 1994); and Y. Sharan and S. Sharan, *Expanding Cooperative Learning through Group Investigation* (New York: Teachers College Press, 1992).

These roles should be rotated, either during the activity or from one time to the next. Although titles may vary, five typical roles are

- *Group facilitator*—role is to keep the group on task.
- *Materials manager*—role is to obtain, maintain, and return materials needed for the group to function.
- *Recorder*—role is to record all group activities and processes, and perhaps to periodically assess how the group is doing.
- *Reporter*—role is to report group processes and accomplishments to the teacher and/or to the entire class. When using groups of four members, the roles of recorder and reporter can easily be combined.
- *Thinking monitor*—role is to identify and record the sequence and processes of the group's thinking. This role encourages metacognition and the development of thinking skills.

It is important that students understand and perform their individual roles, and that each member of the CLG performs her or his tasks as expected. No student should be allowed to ride on the coattails of the group. To give significance to and to reinforce the importance of each role, and to be able to readily recognize the role any student is playing during CLG activity, one teacher made a trip to an office supplier and had permanent badges made for the various CLG roles. During CLGs, then, each student attaches the appropriate badge to her or his clothing.

What Students and the Teacher Do When Using Cooperative Learning Groups

Actually, for learning by CLGs to work, each member of the CLG must understand and assume two roles or responsibilities—the role he or she is assigned as a member of the group, and that of seeing that all others in the group are performing their roles. Sometimes this requires interpersonal skills that students have yet to learn or to learn well. This is where the teacher must assume some responsibility, too. Simply placing students into CLGs and expecting each member and each group to function and to learn the expected outcomes may not work. In other words, skills of cooperation must be taught, and if all your students have not yet learned the skills of cooperation, then you will have to teach them. This doesn't mean that if a group is not functioning you immediately break up the group and reassign members to new groups. Part of group learning is learning the process of how to work out conflict. For a group to work out a conflict may require your assistance. With your guidance the group should be able to discover what the problem is that is causing the conflict, then identify some options and mediate at least a temporary solution. If a particular skill is needed, then with your guidance students identify and learn that skill.

When to Use Cooperative Learning Groups

CLGs can be used for problem solving, investigations, opinion surveys, experiments, review, project work, test making, or almost any other instructional purpose. Just as you would for small group work in general, you can use CLGs for most any purpose at any time, but as with any other type of instructional strategy, it should not be overused.

Outcomes of Using Cooperative Learning Groups

When the process is well-planned and managed, the outcomes of cooperative learning include: (a) improved communication and relationships of acceptance among students of differences, (b) quality learning with fewer off-task behaviors, and (c) increased academic achievement. For example, for the latter, students who practice in cooperative groups demonstrate greater long-term memory of problem-solving strategies in mathematics.[14] In the words of Good and Brophy,

> Cooperative learning arrangements promote friendships and prosocial interaction among students who differ in achievement, sex, race, or ethnicity, and they promote the acceptance of mainstreamed handicapped students by their nonhandicapped classmates. Cooperative methods also frequently have positive effects, and rarely have negative effects, on affective outcomes such as self-esteem, academic self-confidence, liking for the class, liking and feeling liked by classmates, and various measures of empathy and social cooperation.[15]

Cooperative Group Learning, Assessment, and Grading

Normally, the CLG is rewarded on the basis of group achievement, though individual members within the group can later be rewarded for individual contributions (see Figure 8.1). Because of peer pressure, when using CLGs you must be cautious about using group grading.[16] Some teachers give bonus points to all members of a group to add to their individual scores when everyone in the group has reached preset criteria. In

establishing preset standards, the standards can be different for individuals within a group, depending on each member's ability and past performance. It is important that each member of a group feel rewarded and successful. For determination of students' report card grades, individual student achievement is measured later through individual results on tests and other sources of data.

Why Some Teachers Have Difficulty Using CLGs

Sometimes, when they think they are using CLGs, teachers have difficulty and either give up trying to use the strategy or simply tell students to divide into groups for an activity and call it cooperative learning.[17] As emphasized earlier, for the strategy to work, each student must be given training in and have acquired basic skills in interaction and group processing and must realize that individual achievement rests with that of their group. And, as true for any other strategy, the use of CLGs must not be overused—teachers must vary their strategies.

For the use of CLGs to work well, advanced planning and effective management are a must. Students must be instructed in the necessary skills for group learning. Each student must be assigned a responsible role within the group and be held accountable for fulfilling that responsibility. And, when a CLG activity is in process, groups must be continually monitored by the teacher for possible breakdown of this process within a group. In other words, while students are working in groups the teacher must exercise his or her skills of withitness. When a potential breakdown is noticed, the teacher quickly intervenes to help the group get back on track.

LEARNING IN LARGE GROUPS

Large groups are those that involve more than five students, usually the entire class. Most often, they are teacher-directed. Student presentations and whole-class discussions are two techniques that involve the use of large groups.

Student Presentations

Students should be encouraged to be presenters for discussion of the ideas, opinions, and knowledge obtained from their own independent and small-group study. Several techniques encourage the development of certain

---

[14]See, for example, P. E. Duren and A. Cherrington, "The Effects of Cooperative Group Work versus Independent Practice on the Learning of Some Problem-Solving Strategies," *School Science and Mathematics* 92(2):80–83 (February 1992).

[15]T. L. Good and J. E. Brophy, *Looking in Classrooms,* 8th ed. (New York: Addison Wesley Longman, 2000), p. 291.

[16]See S. Kagan, "Group Grades Miss the Mark," *Educational Leadership* 52(8):68–71 (May 1995), and D. W. Johnson and R. T. Johnson, "The Role of Cooperative Learning in Assessing and Communicating Student Learning," Chap. 4 in T. R. Guskey (ed.), *Communicating Student Learning,* ASCD Yearbook (Alexandria, VA: Association for Supervision and Curriculum Development, 1996).

[17]See, for example, C. A. Tomlinson et al., "Use of Cooperative Learning at the Middle Level: Insights from a National Survey," *Research in Middle Level Education Quarterly* 20(4):37–55 (Summer 1997).

	9–10	8	7	1–6
Goals	Consistently and actively helps identify group goals; works effectively to meet goals.	Consistently communicates commitment to group goals; carries out assigned roles.	Sporadically communicates commitment to group goals; carries out assigned role.	Rarely, if ever, works toward group goals or may work against them.
Interpersonal Skills	Cooperates with group members by encouraging, compromising, and/or taking a leadership role without dominating; shows sensitivity to feelings and knowledge of others.	Cooperates with group members by encouraging, compromising, and/or taking a leadership role.	Participates with group but has own agenda; may not be willing to compromise or to make significant contributions.	May discourage others, harass group members, or encourage off-task behavior. Makes significant changes to others' work without their knowledge or permission.
Quality Producer	Contributes significant information, ideas, time, and/or talent to produce a quality product.	Contributes information, ideas, time, and/or talent to produce a quality product.	Contributes some ideas, though not significant; may be more supportive than contributive; shows willingness to complete assignment but has no desire to go beyond average expectations.	Does little or no work toward the completion of group product; shows little or no interest in contributing to the task; produces work that fails to meet minimum standards for quality.
Participation	Attends daily; consistently and actively utilizes class time by working on the task.	Attends consistently; sends in work to group if absent; utilizes class time by working on the task.	Attends sporadically; absences or tardies may hinder group involvement; may send in work when absent; utilizes some time; may be off task by talking to others, interrupting other groups, or watching others do the majority of the work.	Frequent absences or tardies hinder group involvement; fails to send in work when absent; wastes class time by talking, doing other work, or avoiding tasks; group has asked that member be reproved by teacher or removed from the group.
Commitment	Consistently contributes time out of class to produce a quality product; attends all group meetings as evidenced by the group meeting log.	Contributes time out of class to produce a quality product; attends a majority of group meetings as evidenced by the group meeting log.	Willing to work toward completion of task during class time; attends some of the group meetings; may arrive late or leave early; may keep inconsistent meeting log.	Rarely, if ever, attends group meetings outside of class or may attend and hinder progress of the group; fails to keep meeting log.

Figure 8.1

Sample scoring rubric for assessing individual students in cooperative learning group project.

(*Source:* Courtesy of Susan Abbott and Pam Benedetti, Elk Grove School District, Elk Grove, CA.) Explanation for use: Possible score = 50. Scorer marks a relevant square in each of the six categories (horizontal rows), and student's score for that category is the small number in the top right corner within that square.

skills, such as studying and organizing material, discovery, discussion, rebuttal, listening, analysis, suspending judgment, and critical thinking. Possible forms of discussions involving student presentations are described in the following paragraphs.

• *Debate.* The debate is an arrangement in which oral presentations are made by members of two opposing teams, on topics preassigned and researched. The speeches are followed by rebuttals from each team.[18]
• *Jury Trial.* The jury trial is a discussion approach in which the class simulates a courtroom, with class members playing various roles of judge, attorneys, jury members, bailiff, and court recorder.[19]
• *Panel.* The panel is a setting in which four to six students, with one designated as the chairperson or moderator, discuss a topic about which they have studied, followed by a question-and-answer period involving the entire class. The panel usually begins with each panel member giving a brief opening statement.
• *Research Report.* One or two students or a small group of students gives a report on a topic that they investigated, followed by questions and discussions by the entire class.
• *Roundtable.* The roundtable is a small group of three to five students, who sit around a table and discuss

among themselves (and perhaps with the rest of the class listening and perhaps later asking questions) a problem or issue that they have studied. One member of the panel may serve as moderator.

• *Symposium.* Similar to a roundtable discussion but more formal, the symposium is an arrangement in which each student participant presents an explanation of his or her position on a preassigned topic researched by the student. Again, one student should serve as moderator. After the presentations, questions are accepted from the rest of the class.

To use these techniques effectively, students may need to be coached by you—individually, in small groups, or in whole-class sessions—on how and where to gather information; how to listen, take notes, select major points, organize material, and present a position succinctly and convincingly (see Figure 8.2); and how to play roles; and, how to engage in dialogue and debate with one another.

Whole-Class Discussion

Direct, whole-class discussion is a teaching technique used frequently by most or all teachers. On this topic, you should consider yourself an expert. Having been a student in formal learning for at least 15 years, you are undoubtedly knowledgeable about the advantages and disadvantages of whole-class discussions, as least from your personal vantagepoint. So, explore your knowledge and share your experiences by responding to Exercise 8.2. Then do Exercise 8.3, where guidelines for using whole-class discussion will be generated.

---

[18]See, for example, M. Koenig, "Debating Real-World Issues," *Science Scope* 24(5):19–23 (February 2001).

[19]See, for example, M. A. Jones, "Use of a Classroom Jury Trial to Enhance Students' Perceptions of Science as Part of Their Lives," *Journal of Chemical Education* 74(5):537 (May 1997).

PRESENTATION SCORING RUBRIC

5. Presentation was excellent. Project clearly understood and delivery organized.
   • Made eye contact throughout presentation.
   • Spoke loud enough for all to hear.
   • Spoke clearly.
   • Spoke for time allotted.
   • Stood straight and confidently.
   • Covered at least five pieces of important information.
   • Introduced project.
   • All members spoke.
4. Presentation was well thought out and planned.
   • Made eye contact throughout most of presentation.
   • Spoke loud enough and clearly most of the time.
   • Spoke nearly for time allotted.
   • Covered at least four pieces of important information.
   • Introduced project.
   • All members spoke.

3. Adequate presentation. Mostly organized.
   • Made eye contact at times.
   • Some of audience could hear the presentation.
   • Audience could understand most of what was said.
   • Spoke for about half of time allotted.
   • At least half of team spoke.
   • Covered at least three pieces of important information.
   • Project was vaguely introduced.
2–1. Underprepared presentation. Disorganized and incomplete information.
   • No eye contact during presentation.
   • Most of audience were unable to hear presentation.
   • Information presented was unclear.
   • Spoke for only brief time.
   • Covered less than three pieces of information.
   • Project was not introduced or only vaguely introduced.

Figure 8.2
Sample scoring rubric for group or individual presentation.

EXERCISE 8.2

Whole-Class Discussion as a Teaching Strategy: What Do I Already Know?

Instructions: The purpose of this exercise is to explore your knowledge and share your experiences about whole-class discussion. Answer the following questions, and then share your responses with your class, perhaps in discussion groups organized by subject field or grade level.

1. Your grade-level interest or subject field: _____

2. For what reasons would you hold a whole-class discussion? _____

   _____

   _____

   _____

   _____

3. Assuming that your classroom has movable seats, how would you arrange them? _____

   _____

   _____

   _____

   _____

4. What would you do if the seats were not movable? _____

   _____

   _____

   _____

   _____

5. What rules would you establish before starting the discussion? _____

   _____

   _____

   _____

   _____

6. Should student participation be forced? Why or why not? If so, how? _____

   _____

   _____

   _____

   _____

7. How would you discourage a few students from dominating the discussion? _____

_____

_____

_____

_____

8. What preparation should be expected of the students and teacher before beginning the discussion? _____

_____

_____

_____

9. How would you handle digression from the topic? _____

_____

_____

_____

10. Should students be discussion leaders? Why or why not? If so, what training, if any, should they receive, and how? _____

_____

_____

_____

_____

11. What teacher roles are options during a class discussion? _____

_____

_____

_____

_____

12. When is each of these roles most appropriate? _____

_____

_____

_____

_____

13. When, if ever, is it appropriate to hold a class meeting for discussing class procedures, not subject matter? _____

_____

_____

_____

_____

_____

14. Can brainstorming be a form of whole-class discussion? Why or why not? _____

_____

_____

_____

_____

_____

15. What follow-up activities would be appropriate after a whole-class discussion? On what basis would you decide to use each? _____

_____

_____

_____

_____

_____

16. What sorts of activities should precede a class discussion? _____

_____

_____

_____

_____

_____

17. Should a discussion be given a set length? Why or why not? If so, how long? How is the length to be decided? _____

_____

_____

_____

_____

_____

18. Should students be graded for their participation in class discussion? Why or why not? If so, how? On what basis? By whom? _____

_____

_____

_____

_____

_____

19. For effective discussions, 10 to 12 feet is the maximum recommended distance between participants. During a teacher-led discussion, what can a teacher do to keep within this limit? _____

_____

_____

_____

_____

_____

20. Are there any pitfalls or other points of importance that a teacher should be aware of when planning and implementing a whole-class discussion? If so, explain them and how to guard against them. _____

_____

_____

_____

_____

_____

EXERCISE 8.3

Whole-Class Discussion as a Teaching Strategy: Building upon What I Already Know

Instructions: The purpose of this exercise is to generate guidelines for using whole-class discussion as an instructional strategy. Share your responses to Exercise 8.2 with your colleagues. Then individually answer the first two questions below. Next, as a group, use all three questions to guide you as you generate a list of five general guidelines for the use of whole-class discussion as a strategy in teaching. Share your group's guidelines with the entire class. Then, as a class, derive a final list of general guidelines.

1. How effective was your small-group discussion in sharing Exercise 8.2? _____

_____

_____

_____

_____

_____

2. What allowed for or inhibited the effectiveness of that small-group discussion? _____

_____

_____

_____

_____

_____

_____

3. How effective is this small-group discussion? Why? _____

_____

_____

_____

_____

_____

_____

_____

_____

General Guidelines Generated from Small-Group Discussion

1. _____
   _____

2. _____
   _____

3. _____
   _____

4. _____
   _____

5. _____
   _____

General Guidelines: Final List Derived from Whole Class

_____
_____
_____
_____
_____
_____
_____
_____
_____
_____
_____
_____
_____
_____
_____
_____
_____
_____

EQUALITY IN THE CLASSROOM

Especially when conducting direct whole-group discussions, it is easy for a teacher to fall into the trap of interacting with only "the stars," or only those in the front of the room or on one side, or only the most vocal and assertive. You must exercise caution and avoid falling into that trap. To ensure a psychologically safe and effective environment for learning for every person in your classroom, you must attend to all students and try to involve all students equally in all class activities. You must avoid any biased expectations about certain students, and you must avoid discriminating against students according to their gender or some other personal characteristic.

You must avoid the unintentional tendency of teachers of *both* sexes to discriminate on the basis of gender. For example, teachers, along with the rest of society, tend to have lower expectations for girls than for boys in mathematics and science. They tend to call on and encourage boys more than girls. They often let boys interrupt girls but praise girls for being polite and waiting their turn. To avoid such discrimination may take special effort on your part, no matter how aware of the problem you may be. Some researchers believe the problem is so insidious that separate courses about it are needed in teacher training.[20]

To guarantee equity in interaction with students, many teachers have found it helpful to ask someone secretly to tally classroom interactions between the teacher and students during a class discussion. After an analysis of the results, the teacher arrives at decisions about his or her own attending and facilitating behaviors. Such an analysis is the purpose of Exercise 8.4. You are welcome to make blank copies and share them with your teaching colleagues.

In addition to the variables mentioned at the beginning of Exercise 8.4, the exercise can be modified to include responses and their frequencies according to other teacher–student interactions, such as calling on all students equally for responses to your questions, calling on students equally to assist you with classroom helping jobs, chastising students for their inappropriate behavior, or asking questions to assume classroom leadership roles.

Ensuring Equity

In addition to the advice given in Chapter 7 about using questioning, there are many other ways of assuring that students are treated fairly in the classroom, including the following:

- Encourage students to demonstrate an appreciation for one another by applauding all individual and group presentations.
- Have and maintain high expectations, although not necessarily identical expectations, for all students.
- Insist on politeness in the classroom. For example, a student can be shown appreciation—such as with a sincere "thank you," or "I appreciate your contribution," or with whole-class applause, or with a genuine smile—for her or his contribution to the learning process.
- Insist students be allowed to finish what they are saying, without being interrupted by others. Be certain that you model this behavior yourself.
- During whole-class instruction, insist that students raise their hands and be called on by you before they are allowed to speak.
- Keep a stopwatch handy to unobtrusively control the wait time given for each student. Although at first this idea may sound impractical, it works.
- Use a seating chart attached to a clipboard and next to each student's name, make a tally for each interaction you have with a student. This also is a good way to maintain records to reward students for their contributions to class discussion. Again, it is workable at any grade level. The seating chart can be laminated so it can be used day after day simply by erasing the marks of the previous day.

Now, do Exercise 8.4, through which you will examine a teacher's behavior with students according to gender or some other personal characteristic.

---

[20]See, for example, S. Zaher, "Gender and Curriculum in the School Room," *Education Canada* 36(1):26–29 (Spring 1996), and S. M. Bailey, "Shortchanging Girls and Boys," *Educational Leadership* 53(8):75–79 (May 1996). For information on identifying equity problems and developing programs to help schools achieve academic excellence for all students, contact EQUITY 2000, 1233 20th St. NW, Washington, DC 20056-2304; (202) 822–5930.

FOR YOUR NOTES

EXERCISE 8.4

Teacher Interaction with Students According to Student Gender

---

Instructions: The purpose of this exercise is to provide a tool for the analysis of your own interactions with students according to gender. To become accustomed to the exercise, you should do a trial run in one of your university classes, then use it during your student teaching, and again during your first years of teaching. The exercise can be modified to include: (1) the amount of time given for each interaction, (2) the response time given by the teacher according to student gender, and (3) other student characteristics, such as ethnicity.

Prior to class, select a student (this will be you during the trial run recommended above) or an outside observer, such as a colleague, to do the tallying and calculations as follows. Ask the person to tally secretly the interactions between you and the students by placing a mark after the name of each student (or on the student's position on a seating chart) with whom you have verbal interaction. If a student does the tallying, she should not be counted in any of the calculations.

Exact time at start: _____

Exact time at end: _____

Total time in minutes: _____

Total in class today = _____	Girls = _____	Boys = _____
	% Girls = _____	% Boys = _____

Tally of Interactions

With girls	With boys

Total Interactions = _____

% with girls = _____   % with boys = _____

Teacher Reflections and Conclusions: _____

_____

_____

_____

_____

FOR YOUR NOTES

LEARNING FROM ASSIGNMENTS AND HOMEWORK

An *assignment* is a statement of *what* the student is to accomplish and is tied to a specific instructional objective. Assignments, whether completed at home or at school, can ease student learning in many ways, but when poorly planned they can discourage the student and upset an entire family. *Homework* is any out-of-class task that a student is assigned as an extension of classroom learning. Like all else that you do as a teacher, it is your professional responsibility to think about and plan carefully any and all homework assignments you give to students. Consider how you would feel were you given the assignment and about how much out-of-class time you expect the assignment to take. The time a student needs to complete assignments beyond school time will vary according to grade level, subject, school policy, and, of course, the student. Very generally, students of middle level grades may spend about an hour or so while those in high school may have two or more hours of homework each school night.

Purposes for Assignments

Purposes for giving homework assignments can be any of the following: to constructively extend the time that students are engaged in learning, to help students develop personal learning, to help students develop their research skills, to help students develop their study skills, to help students organize their learning, to individualize the learning, to involve parents and guardians in their children's learning, to provide a mechanism by which students receive constructive feedback, to provide students with the opportunity to review and practice what has been learned, to reinforce classroom experiences, and to teach new content.

Guidelines for Using Assignments

To use assignments, consider the guidelines in the following paragraphs. While an assignment is a statement of *what* the student is to accomplish, procedures are statements of *how* to do something. Although students may need some procedural guidelines, especially with respect to your expectations on an assignment, generally, you will want to avoid supplying too much detail on how to accomplish an assignment.

Plan early and thoughtfully the types of assignments you will give (e.g., daily and long-range; minor and major; in class, at home, or both; individual, paired, or group[21]), and prepare assignment specifications. As-

signments must correlate with specific instructional objectives and should *never* be given as busy work or as punishment. For each assignment, let students know what the objectives are; for example, whether the assignment is to prepare the student for what is to come in class, to practice what has been learned in class, or to extend the learning of class activities.

Use caution in giving assignments that could be controversial or that could pose a hazard to the safety of students. In such cases (especially if you are new to the community), before giving the assignment it is probably a good idea to talk it over with members of your teaching team, the departmental chair, or an administrator. Also, for a particular assignment, you may need to have parental or guardian permission and even support for students to do it or be prepared to give an alternate assignment for some students.

Provide differentiated, tiered, or optional assignments—assignment variations given to students or selected by them on the basis of their interests and learning capacities.[22] Students can select or be assigned different activities to accomplish the same objective, such as read and discuss, or they can participate with others in a more direct learning experience. After their study, as a portion of the assignment, students share what they have learned. This is an example of using multilevel teaching.

Teachers have found it beneficial to prepare individualized study guides with questions to be answered and activities to be done by the student while reading textbook chapters as homework. One advantage of a study guide is that it can make the reading more than a visual experience. A study guide can help to organize student learning by accenting instructional objectives, emphasizing important points to be learned, providing a guide for studying for tests, and encouraging the student to read the homework assignment.

Beginning teachers need to understand that not only can homework help students learn factual information, develop study skills, and involve parents or guardians in their child's education, but it can also overwhelm students and cause them to dislike learning, encourage them to take shortcuts such as copying others' work, and prevent them from participating in extracurricular activities. Teachers sometimes underestimate just how long it will take a student to complete a homework assignment. With these facts in mind, during your preactive phase of instruction and decision making, think carefully about all homework assignments before giving them to the students.

---

[21]See, for example, C. Kaplan, "Homework Partners," *Mathematics Teaching in the Middle School* 2(3):168–169 (January 1997).

[22]See, for example, M. H. Sullivan and P. V. Sequeira, "The Impact of Purposeful Homework on Learning," *Clearing House* 69(6):346–348 (July/August 1996).

Some students find homework and assignments very difficult, especially those who have limited English proficiency, or special needs, and those who have little to no support from home. As an aide to these students in particular and to any student in general, many teachers use student volunteers who serve as homework helpers to assist other students both during class and after school by exchanging telephone numbers. In some schools, teachers also use upper grade students and even paid college students and adults as mentors.

As a general rule, homework assignments should stimulate thinking by arousing a student's curiosity, raising questions for further study, and encouraging and supporting the self-discipline required for independent study.

Determine the resources that students will need to complete assignments, and check the availability of these resources. This is important; students can't be expected to use that which is unavailable to them. Many will not use that which is not readily available.

Avoid yelling out assignments as students are leaving your classroom. When giving assignments in class, you should write them on a special place on the writing board or give a copy to each student, or require that each student write the assignment into his or her assignment folder, or include them in the course syllabus or on the school's website, taking extra care to be sure assignment specifications are clear to students and allow time for students to ask questions about an assignment. It's important that your procedure for giving and collecting assignments be consistent throughout the school year.

Students should be given sufficient time to complete their assignments. In other words, avoid announcing an assignment that is due the very next day. As a general rule, all assignments should be given much longer than the day before they are due. Try to avoid changing assignment specifications after they are given. Especially avoid changing them at the last minute. Changing specifications at the last minute can be very frustrating to students who have already completed the assignment, and it shows little respect for those students.

Allow time in class for students to begin work on homework assignments, so you can give them individual attention (guided or coached practice). Your ability to coach students is *the reason* for in-class time to begin work on assignments. As you have learned, many secondary schools have extended the length of class periods to allow more in-class time for teacher guidance on assignments. As said in earlier chapters, the benefits of this coached practice include being able to: (a) monitor student work so that a student does not go too far in a wrong direction, (b) help students reflect on their thinking, (c) assess the progress of individual students, and (d) discover or create a "teachable moment." For example, while monitoring students doing their work, you might discover a commonly shared student misconception. Then, taking advantage of this teachable moment, you stop and talk about that and attempt to clarify the misconception.

Timely, constructive, and corrective feedback from the teacher on the homework—and grading of homework—increases the positive contributions of homework.[23] If the assignment is important for students to do, then you must give your full and immediate attention to the product of their efforts. Read almost everything that students write. Students are much more willing to do homework when they believe it is useful, when it is treated as an integral part of instruction, when it is read and evaluated by the teacher, and when it counts as part of the grade. See "How to Avoid . . ." that follows.

Provide feedback about each student's work, and be positive and constructive in your comments. Always think about the written comments that you make as to be relatively certain they will convey your intended message to the student. When writing comments on student papers, consider using a color other than red, such as green or blue. Although to you this may sound unimportant, to many people, red brings with it a host of negative connotations (e.g., blood, hurt, danger, stop), and students often perceive it as punitive.

Most routine homework assignments should not be graded for accuracy, only for completion. Rather than giving a percentage or numerical grade, with its negative connotations, teachers often prefer to mark assignment papers with constructive and reinforcing comments and symbols they have created for this purpose.

Regardless of grade level or subject taught, you must give attention to the development of students' reading, listening, speaking, and writing skills. Attention to these skills must also be obvious in your assignment specifications and your assignment grading policy. Reading is crucial to the development of a person's ability to write. For example, to foster high-order thinking, students in any subject can and should be encouraged to write (in their journals, as discussed in Chapter 5 and later in this chapter) their thoughts and feelings about the material they have read.

Opportunities for Recovery

The concept of mastery (quality) learning would seem to us to necessitate a policy whereby students are able to revise and resubmit assignments for reassessment and grading. Although it is important to encourage good initial efforts by students, sometimes, for a multitude of reasons, a student's first effort is inadequate or is lacking entirely. Perhaps the student is absent from school without legitimate excuse, or the student does poorly on an assignment

[23]H. J. Walberg, "Productive Teaching and Instruction: Assessing the Knowledge Base," *Phi Delta Kappan* 71(6):472 (February 1990).

or fails to turn in an assignment on time, or at all. Although accepting late work from students is extra work for the teacher, and although allowing the resubmission of a marked or tentative-graded paper increases the amount of paperwork, many teachers report that it is worthwhile to give students opportunity for recovery and a day or so to make corrections and resubmit an assignment for an improved score. However, out of regard for students who do well from the start, you are advised against allowing a resubmitted paper to receive an *A* grade (unless, of course, it was an *A* paper originally).

Talent Development secondary schools provide recovery methods that encourage students by recognizing both achievement and improvement on report cards and by providing students with second opportunities for success on assignments, although at some cost to encourage a good first effort. For example, although the school's policy is that a student automatically fails a course when the student accumulates five or more absences per quarter, each absence can be nullified if the student accumulates perfect school attendance for five consecutive days.[24]

Students sometimes have legitimate reasons for not completing an assignment by the due date. (Consider the classroom vignette Late Homework Paper from an At-Risk Student.) It is our opinion that the teacher should listen and exercise professional judgment in each instance. As often said, there is nothing democratic about treating unequals as equals. The provision of recovery options seems a sensible and scholastic tactic.

CLASSROOM VIGNETTE
Late Homework Paper from an At-Risk Student

An eleventh-grade student turned in an English class assignment several days late, and the paper was accepted by the teacher without penalty although the teacher's policy was that late papers would be severely penalized. During the week that the assignment was due, the student had suffered a miscarriage. In this instance her teacher accepted the paper late sans penalty because the student carried a great deal of psychological baggage, and the teacher felt that turning in the paper at all was a positive act; if the paper had not been accepted, or had been accepted only with severe penalty to her grade, then, in the teacher's opinion, the student would have simply quit trying and probably dropped out of school altogether.

How to Avoid Having So Many Papers to Grade That Time for Effective Planning Is Restricted

A waterloo for some beginning teachers is that of being buried beneath mounds of homework to be read and marked, leaving less and less time for effective planning. To keep this from happening to you, consider the following suggestions. Although in our opinion the teacher should read almost everything that students write, papers can be read with varying degrees of intensity and scrutiny, depending on the purpose of the assignment. For assignments that are designed for learning, understanding, and practice, you can allow students to check the work themselves using either self-checking or peer-checking. During the self- or peer-checking, you can walk around the room, monitor the activity, and record whether a student did the assignment or not, or, after the checking, you can collect the papers and do your recording. Besides reducing the amount of paperwork for you, student self- or peer-checking provides other advantages: (a) it allows students to see and understand their errors, (b) it encourages productive peer dialogue, and (c) it helps them develop self-assessment techniques and standards. If the purpose of the assignment is to assess mastery competence, then the papers should be read, marked, and graded only by you.

Caution about Using Peer-Checking*

Peer-checking can, however, be a problem. During peer-checking of student work, students may spend more time watching the person checking their paper than accurately checking the one given to them. And this strategy does not necessarily allow the student to see or understand his or her mistakes.

Of even greater concern is the matter of privacy. When Student A becomes knowledgeable of the academic success or failure of Student B, Student A, the "checker," could cause emotional or social embarrassment to Student B. Peer-checking of papers should perhaps be done only for the editing of classmates' drafts of stories or research projects, making suggestions about content and grammar, but not assigning a grade or marking answers right or wrong. To protect students' privacy rights, like the public posting of grades, the use of peers grading each other's papers also should be avoided. Harassment and embarrassment have no place in a classroom; they do not provide a safe learning environment.

[24]V. LaPoint et al., *Report 1: The Talent Development High School-Essential Components* [On-line]. Available (Downloaded June 19, 1998): http://www.csos.jhu.edu/crespar/Reports/Entire%20Reports/report01 entire.html. P. 6.

* Regarding this caution, you and your students should know that on February 19, 2002, the U.S. Supreme Court ruled unanimously that students may grade each other's work in class without violating federal privacy law.

After reading the novel *Lord of the Flies,* students are required to make a culminating presentation that is focused on representing various themes and events as depicted in the novel. Students may choose from the following:

1. Story in a shoebox — A representation of major events in the novel through the presentation of various symbolic objects (e.g., glasses, shell, cap).
2. Poster board presentation — A poster board designed with at least five different events depicted and titled appropriately. May use miniature drawings or graphics.
3. Sketching/drawing — A collection of detailed drawings depicting at least five major events in the novel.
4. Model — A model depicting the island or any part of the island that serves as the setting of the novel.
5. Play or skit — A play or skit performed by the student(s) in class with a script for the teacher to follow. Must involve at least one major event in the novel and five to ten minutes of acting.

Figure 8.3
Sample choices for culminating presentation in English class.

PROJECT-CENTERED LEARNING: GUIDING LEARNING FROM INDEPENDENT AND GROUP INVESTIGATIONS, PAPERS, AND ORAL REPORTS

For the most meaningful student learning to occur, independent study, individual writing, student-centered projects, and oral reports should be major features of your instruction. There will be times when the students are interested in an in-depth inquiry of a topic and will want to pursue a particular topic for study. This undertaking of a learning project can be flexible—an individual student, a team of two, a small group of three or four students, or the entire class can do the investigation. The project is a relatively long-term investigative study from which students produce something called the *culminating presentation*. It is a way for students to apply what they are learning. The culminating presentation is usually an oral and written report accompanied by a hands-on item of some kind (e.g., a display, play or skit, book, song or poem, multimedia presentation, diorama, poster, maps, charts, and so on.). See the sample in Figure 8.3.

Values and Purposes of Project-Centered Learning

The values and purposes of encouraging project-centered learning are to:

- Develop individual skills in cooperation and social-interaction.
- Develop student skills in writing, communication, and in higher-level thinking and doing.
- Foster student engagement, independent learning, and thinking skills.
- Optimize personal meaning of the learning to each student by considering, valuing, and accommodating individual interests, learning styles, learning capacities, and life experiences.
- Provide the opportunity for each student to become especially knowledgeable and experienced in one area of subject content or in one process skill, thus adding to the student's knowledge and experience base and sense of importance and self-worth.
- Provide the opportunity for students to become intrinsically motivated to learn because they are working on topics of personal meaning, with outcomes and time-lines that are relatively open ended.
- Provide an opportunity for students to make decisions about their own learning and to develop their skills in managing time and materials.
- Provide an opportunity for students to make some sort of a real contribution.

As has been demonstrated time and again, when students choose their own projects, integrating knowledge as the need arises, motivation and learning follow naturally.[25]

Guidelines for Guiding Students in Project-Centered Learning

In collaboration with the teacher, students select a topic for the project. What you can do is to stimulate ideas and provide anchor studies. You can stimulate ideas by providing lists of things students might do, by mentioning each time an idea comes up in class that this would be a good idea for an independent, small group, or class project, by having former students tell about their projects, by showing the results of other students' projects (anchor studies), by suggesting Internet resources and readings that are likely to give students ideas, and by using class discussions to brainstorm ideas.

Sometimes a teacher will write the general problem or topic in the center of a graphic web and ask the students to brainstorm some questions. The questions will lead to ways for students to investigate, draw sketches, construct models, record findings, predict items, compare and con-

---

[25]See, for example, M. Tassinari, "Hands-On Projects Take Students Beyond the Book," *Social Studies Review* 34(3):16–20 (Spring 1996).

trast, and discuss understandings. In essence, brainstorming such as this is the technique often used by teachers in collaboration with students for the selection of an interdisciplinary thematic unit of study.

Allow students to individually choose whether they will work alone, in pairs, or in small groups. If they choose to work in groups, then help them delineate job descriptions for each member of the group. For project work, groups of four or fewer students usually work better than groups of more than four. Even if the project is one the whole class is pursuing, the project should be broken down into parts with individuals or small groups of students undertaking independent study of these parts.

You can keep track of the students' progress by reviewing weekly updates of their work. Set deadlines with the groups. Meet with groups daily to discuss any questions or problems they have. Based on their investigations, the students will prepare and present their findings in culminating presentations.

Provide coaching and guidance. Work with each student or student team in topic selection, as well as in the processes of written and oral reporting. Allow students to develop their own procedures, but guide their preparation of work outlines and preliminary drafts, giving them constructive feedback and encouragement along the way. Aid students in their identification of potential resources and in the techniques of research. Your coordination with the library and other resource centers is central to the success of project-centered teaching. Frequent drafts and progress reports from the students are a must. With each of these stages, provide students with constructive feedback and encouragement. Provide written guidelines and negotiate time lines for the outlines, drafts, and the completed project.

Promote sharing. Insist that students share both the progress and the results of their study with the rest of the class. The amount of time allowed for this sharing will, of course, depend upon many variables. The value of this type of instructional strategy comes not only from individual contributions but also from the learning that results from the experience and the communication of that experience with others. For project work and student sharing of the outcomes of a study, consider having your students use the KWHLS strategy, a modified version of the KWL strategy. With KWHLS, the student identifies what she already knows about the topic of study, What she wants to learn, How the student plans to learn it, what she Learned from the study, and how the student will Share with others what she has learned from the study.

Without careful planning, and unless students are given steady guidance, project-based teaching can be a frustrating experience, for both the teacher and the students, and especially for a beginning teacher who is inexperienced in such an undertaking. Students should do

projects because they want to and because the project seems meaningful. Therefore, students with guidance from you should decide *what* project to do and *how* to do it. Your role is to advise and guide students so they experience success. If the teacher lays out a project in too much detail, that project is a procedure rather than a student-centered project. There must be a balance between structure and opportunities for student choices and decision making. Without frequent progress reporting by the student and guidance and reinforcement from the teacher, a student can get frustrated and quickly lose interest in the project.

Writing Should Be a Required Component of Project-Centered Learning

Provide options but insist that writing be a part of each student's work. Research examining the links among writing, thinking, and learning has helped emphasize the importance of writing. Writing is a complex, intellectual behavior and process that helps the learner create and record his understanding—that is, to construct meaning.

When teachers use project-centered teaching, a paper and an oral presentation are almost automatically required of all students. It is recommended that you use the *I-Search paper* instead of the traditional research paper. Under your careful guidance, the student: (a) lists things that she would like to know, and from the list selects one which becomes the research topic; (b) conducts the study while maintaining a log of activities and findings, which, in fact, becomes a process journal; (c) prepares a booklet that presents the student's findings, and which consists of paragraphs and visual representations; (d) prepares a summary of the findings including the significance of the study and the student's personal feelings; and (e) shares the project as a final oral report with the teacher and classmates.

Assess the Final Product

The final product of the project, including papers, oral reports, and presentations should be graded. The method of determining the grade should be clear to students from the beginning, as well as the weight of the project grade toward the term grade. Provide students with clear descriptions (rubrics) of how evaluation and grading will be done. Evaluation should include meeting deadlines for drafts and progress reports. The final grade for the study should be based on four criteria: (a) how well it was organized, including meeting draft deadlines; (b) the quality and quantity of both content and procedural knowledge gained from the experience; (c) the quality of the student's sharing of that learning experience with the rest of the class; and (d) the quality of the student's final written or oral report. For oral presentations, a sample scoring rubric and a checklist are shown in Figure 8.1.

WRITING ACROSS THE CURRICULUM

Because writing is a discrete representation of thinking, every teacher should consider himself or herself to be a teacher of writing. In exemplary schools, student writing is encouraged in all subjects across the curriculum.

Kinds of Writing

A student should experience a variety of kinds of writing rather than the same form, class after class, year after year. Perhaps most important is that writing should be emphasized as a process that illustrates one's thinking, rather than solely as a product completed as an assignment. Writing and thinking develop best when a student experiences, during any school day, various forms of writing to express their ideas, such as the following.

Autobiographical incident. The writer narrates a specific event in his or her life and states or implies the significance of the event.

Evaluation. The writer presents a judgment on the worth of an item—book, movie, artwork, consumer product—and supports this with reasons and evidence.

Eyewitness account. The writer tells about a person, group, or event that was objectively observed from the outside.

First-hand biographical sketch. Through incident and description, the writer characterizes a person he or she knows well.

Interpretation. The writer conjectures about the causes and effects of a specific event.

Problem solving. The writer describes and analyzes a specific problem and then proposes and argues for a solution.

Report of information. The writer collects data from observation and research and chooses material that best represents a phenomenon or concept.

Story. Using dialogue and description, the writer shows conflict between characters or between a character and the environment.

Student Journal

Many teachers across the curriculum have their students maintain journals in which the students keep a log of their activities, findings, and thoughts (i.e., *process journal,* as discussed previously) and write their thoughts about what it is they are studying (*response journal*). Actually, commonly used are two types of response journals: dialogue journals and reading-response journals. *Dialogue journals* are used for students to write anything that is on their minds, usually on the right side of a page, while peers, teachers, and parents or guardians respond on left side of a page, thereby "talking with" the

journal writer. *Response journals* are used for students to write (and perhaps draw—a "visual learning log") their reactions to what is being studied.

Purpose and Assessment of Student Journal Writing

Normally, academic journals are *not* the personal diaries of the writer's recollection of daily events and the writer's thoughts about the events. Rather, the purpose of journal writing is to encourage students to write, to think about their writing, to record their creative thoughts about *what they are learning,* and to share their written thoughts with an audience—all of which help in the development of their thinking skills, in their learning, and in their development as writers. Students are encouraged to write about experiences, both in school and out, that are related to the topics being studied. They should be encouraged to record their feelings about what and how they are learning.

Journal writing provides practice in expression and should not be graded by the teacher. Negative comments and evaluations from the teacher will discourage creative and spontaneous expression by students. Teachers should read the journal writing and then offer constructive and positive feedback, but teachers should avoid negative comments or grading the journals. For grading purposes, most teachers simply record whether or not a student does, in fact, maintain the required journal.

The National Council of Teachers of English (NCTE) has developed guidelines for journal writing. Your school English/language arts department will likely have a copy of these guidelines, or you can contact NCTE directly via the Internet http://www.ncte.org.

A COLLECTION OF MORE THAN 100 ANNOTATED MOTIVATIONAL TEACHING STRATEGIES WITH IDEAS FOR LESSONS, INTERDISCIPLINARY TEACHING, TRANSCULTURAL STUDIES, AND STUDENT PROJECTS

Today's teenagers are used to multimillion-dollar productions on television, videodiscs, arcade games, and the movie screen. When they come to school, into a classroom and are subjected each day to something short of a high-budget production, it is little wonder that they sometimes react in a less than highly motivated fashion. No doubt, today's youth are growing up in a highly stimulated instant-action society, a society that has learned to expect instant communications, instant information retrieval, instant headache relief, instant meals, instant gratification, and perhaps, in the minds of many young people, instant high-paying employment for jobs that entail more fun than hard work. In light of this cultural phenomenon, we are on your side: the classroom teacher is on the firing line each day and is expected to perform—perhaps instantly and entertainingly, but most certainly in a highly competent and professional manner—in situations that are far from ideal. In any case, you must gain your students' attention before you can teach them.

In this final section of the chapter, you will find an annotated list of ideas, many of which have been offered over recent years by classroom teachers. (See also Figure 8.4 at the conclusion of this chapter.) Although the ideas are organized according to discipline, and some may be more appropriate for one group of students than another, you may profit from reading all entries for each field. Although a particular entry might be identified as specific to one discipline, it might also be useful in others (many of them can be used in interdisciplinary teaching—for example number one can clearly be combined with mathematics and science, as well as art), or it might stimulate a creative thought for your own stock of motivational techniques, such as an idea for a way to utilize the theory of multiple learning capacities, or to emphasize the multicultural aspect of a lesson in math, or social studies, or whatever the central discipline or theme of a lesson or unit of instruction.

The Visual and Performing Arts

1. As part of a unit combining design or creativity with science, have students construct, design, and decorate their own kite. When the projects are complete, designate a time to fly them.

2. Use lyrics from popular music to influence classwork, such as by putting the lyrics into pictures.

3. Utilize the outdoors or another environment for a free drawing experience.

4. Invite a local artist who has created a community mural to speak to the class about the mural. Plan and create a class mural, perhaps on a large sheet of plywood or some other location approved by the school administration.

5. Use a mandala to demonstrate the importance of individual experience, as in interpreting paintings and in interpreting poetry.

6. Collect books/magazines/posters/films/videos/computer software programs and so forth that show different kinds of masks people around the world wear. Ask students to identify the similarities and differences in the masks. Have them research the meanings that mask characters have in various cultures. Have students design and create their own masks to illustrate their own personalities, cultures, and so forth.

7. As part of a unit on the creative process, have each student draw or sketch on a piece of paper, then pass it on to the next person, and that person will make additions to the drawing. Instructions could include "improve the drawing," "make the drawing ugly," and "add what you think would be necessary to complete the composition."

8. Imagine that you're a bird flying over the largest city you have visited. What do you see, hear, smell, feel, and taste? Draw a "sensory" map.

9. Assign a different color to each student. Have them arrange themselves into warm and cool colors and explain their decisions (why blue is cool, etc.). Discuss people's emotional responses to each of the colors.

10. Watch videos of dances from various countries and cultures. Have students identify similarities and differences. Have students research meanings and occasions of particular dances.

11. Have students discover ways in which music, art, and dance are used around them and in their community.

12. Find a popular song that students like. Transpose the melody into unfamiliar keys for each instrument. This makes the student want to learn the song, but in the process the student will have to become more familiar with his or her instrument.

13. Set aside one weekend morning a month and hold small, informal recitals (workshops) allowing students to participate/observe the performance situation(s) among their peers and themselves. (Students might be told previously about these "special days" and encouraged to prepare a selection of their own choosing.)

14. Play a rhythm game, one such as the "Dutch Shoe Game," to get students to cooperate, work together, and enjoy themselves using rhythm. Participants sit in a circle, and as the song is sung, each person passes one of his or her shoes to the person on the right in rhythm to the music. Shoes continue to be passed as long as verses are sung. Those with poor rhythm will end up with a pile of shoes in front of them!

15. Choose a rhythmical, humorous poem or verse to conduct. The students read the poem in chorus, while the teacher stands before them and conducts the poem as if it were a musical work. Students must be sensitive to the intonation, speed, inflection, mood, and dynamics that the teacher wants them to convey in their reading.

16. Start a Retired Senior Citizens Volunteer Program (RSCVP) with senior citizens presenting folk art workshops with students, and where the students and seniors then work together to create artworks for the school. For example, students at one school make tray favors, napkin rings, place mats, door decorations, and cards and treat cups for the residents of the local Veterans home.

Family and Consumer Economics, Foods, and Textiles

17. Often the foods we like originated from another part of our country or the world. Have the students identify such foods and from where they came—foods such as spaghetti, enchiladas, fajitas, wontons, tacos, quiche, croissants, teriyaki, fried rice, pizza, hot dogs, hamburgers, noodles, tomatoes, chocolate, potatoes, hoagy, chop suey, ice cream cones, submarines, and poor boys. Have them list the names and origins, and put pictures of the food in place on a large world map.

18. Take still photos of class members at special events such as dinners, fashion shows, field trips, and special projects. Build a scrapbook or bulletin board with these and display on campus.

19. Plan thematic units on cultural foods, using the traditions, costumes, and music of a particular culture. Have the students decorate the room. Invite the principal and perhaps community representatives for a meal and visit.

20. Have students plan and create a bulletin board displaying pictures of 100-calorie portions of basic nutritional foods and popular fad foods that contain only empty calories. The display can motivate a discussion on foods with calories and nutrients versus foods with empty calories.

21. Pin the names of different garments on the backs of students. The students are then to sort themselves into different wash loads.

22. For a clothing unit, hold an "idea day." Ask each student to bring in an idea of something that can be done to give clothes a new look, a fun touch, or an extended wearing life. Ideas they may come up with include appliqués, embroidery, tie-dye, batik, colorful patches, and restyling old clothes into current or creative fashions.

23. Have the students write, practice, and present skits, for videotape presentation, on consumer fraud.

24. Once a month have students plan a menu, prepare the food, and serve it to invited senior citizens from the community.

25. Organize a program with senior citizens and students working together on a community garden.

26. Plan a program at a senior citizens center whereby students and seniors work together on planning and decorating the center for special occasions and holidays.

27. With your students, plan a community service program. For example, at Discovery Middle School (Vancouver, WA), students provide childcare, cross-age tutoring, and companionship to preschool, elementary, and elderly clients at off-campus locations.

English, Languages, and the Language Arts

28. Organize a letter writing activity between senior citizens and your students.

29. For a unit on the Renaissance, creation of a wall-to-wall mural depicting a village of the times may be a total team project. Some students can research customs, costumes, and architecture. Others may paint or draw.

30. On a U.S. road map, have students find the names of places that sound "foreign," and categorize the names according to nationality or culture.

31. To enhance understanding of parts of speech, set up this problem: Provide several boxes containing different parts of speech. Each student is to form one sentence from the fragments chosen from each box, being allowed to discard only at a penalty. The students then nonverbally make trades with other students to make coherent and perhaps meaningfully amusing sentences. A student may trade a noun for a verb but will have to keep in mind what parts of speech are essential for a sentence. Results may be read aloud as a culmination to this activity.

32. Have students match American English and British English words (or any other combination of languages), such as cookies and biscuits; hood and bonnet; canned meat and tinned meat; elevator and lift; flashlight and torch; subway and tube; garbage collector and dustman; undershirt and vest; sweater and jumper; gasoline and petrol. Or, have students compare pronunciations and spellings.

33. English words derive from many other languages. Have students research and list some, such as ketchup (Malay), alcohol (Arabic), kindergarten (German), menu (French), shampoo (Hindi), bonanza (Spanish), piano (Italian), kosher (Yiddish), and smorgasbord (Swedish).

34. Try this for an exercise in objective versus subjective writing: After a lesson on descriptive writing, bring to the class a nondescript object, such as a potato, and place it before the class. Ask them to write a paragraph either describing the potato in detail (i.e., its color, size, markings, and other characteristics) or describing how the potato feels about them.

35. Read to the class a story without an ending, then ask the students (as individuals or in think-write-share-pairs) to create and write their own endings or conclusions, which they will share with the rest of the class.

36. Ask students to create in groups of no more than three students each an advertisement using a propaganda device of their choice. Video record their presentations.

37. Ask students to (individually or in dyads) create and design an invention and then to write a "patent description" for the invention.

38. Using think-write-pair-share, have students write a physical description of some well-known (but unnamed) public figure, such as a movie star, politician, athlete, or musician. Other class members may enjoy trying to identify the "mystery" personality from the written description.

39. A bulletin board may be designated for current events and news in the world of writers. Included may be new books and recording releases as well as reviews. News of poets and authors (student authors and poets, too) may also be displayed.

40. Everyone has heard of or experienced stereotyping. For example, girls are not as athletic as boys, boys are insensitive, women are better cooks than men, men are more mechanical. Ask students to list some stereotypes they have heard, and examples they find in newspapers, magazines, movies, and television. Have students discuss these questions: How do you suppose these stereotypes came to be? Does stereotyping have any useful value? Is it sometimes harmful?

41. Remove the text from a Sunday newspaper comic strip and have the students work in pairs to create a story line; or, give each pair a picture from a magazine and have the pair create a story about the picture.

42. Use newspaper want ads to locate jobs as a base for completing job application forms and creating letters of inquiry. Use videotape equipment to record employer–employee role-play situations, interviews for jobs, or child–parent situations to develop language and listening skills.

43. Have students choose a short story from a text and write it into a play and perform the play for parents.

44. When beginning a poetry unit, ask students to bring in the words to their favorite songs. Show how these fit into the genre of poetry.

45. Have students look for commercial examples of advertisements that might be classed as "ecopornographic," i.e., ads that push a product that is potentially damaging to our environment; or have students analyze advertisements for the emotions they appeal to, techniques used, and their integrity. Try the same thing with radio, teen magazines, the Internet, and other media.

46. Change the environment by moving to an outdoor location, and ask students to write poetry to see if the change in surroundings stimulates or discourages their creativeness. Discuss the results. For example, take your class to a large supermarket to write, or to a lake, or into a forest, or to the school athletic stadium.

47. To introduce the concept of interpretations, use your state's seal to start the study. Have students analyze the seal for its history and the meaning of its various symbols.

48. When learning a second language, provide puppets in native costume for students to use while practicing dialogue.

49. Use the Internet to establish communication with students from another area of the country or world; establish a web page for your school.

50. Use drama to build a student's language arts and thinking skills. Have students write dialogue, set scenes, and communicate emotions through expressive language and mime.

51. Establish a community-service learning literacy project. For example, students from Greenville High School (Greenville, TN) serve as mentors to local elementary school students to help the students develop their reading and comprehension skills, and students from Urbana High School (Urbana, IL) are trained to give one-on-one tutoring in reading to students from a local elementary school.

Mathematics

52. Collaboratively plan with students a simulation where members role-play the solar system. Students calculate their weights, set up a proportion system, find a large field, and on the final day actually simulate the solar system, using their own bodies to represent the sun, planets, and moons. Arrange to have the event photographed.

53. Encourage students to look for evidence of the Fibonacci number series (i.e., 1, 1, 2, 3, 5, 8, 13, 21, etc.) outside of mathematics, such as in nature and in manufactured objects. Here are examples of where evidence may be found: piano keyboard, petals on flowers, spermatogenesis and oogenesis. Perhaps your students might like to organize a Fibonacci Club and through the Internet establish communication with other clubs around the world.[26]

54. Have students research the history of cost of a first-class U.S. postage stamp, and ask them to devise ways of predicting its cost by the year they graduate, or are grandparents, or some other target year.

55. Give students a list of the frequencies of each of the 88 keys and strings of a piano (a local music store can provide the information). Challenge students to derive an equation to express the relation between key position and frequency. After they have done this, research and tell them about the Bösendorfer piano (Germany) with its nine extra keys at the lower end of the keyboard. See if students can predict the frequencies of those extra keys.

---

[26]For further information about Fibonacci numbers see C. Andreasen, "Fibonacci and Pascal Together Again: Pattern Exploration in the Fibonacci Sequence," *Mathematics Teacher* 91(3):250–253 (March 1998); T. H. Garland and C. V. Kahn, *Math and Music: Harmonious Connections* (Palo Alto, CA: Dale Seymour, 1995); A. Johnson, "Fiber Meets Fibonacci; The Shape of Things to Come," *Mathematics Teacher* 4(4):256–262 (January 1999); R. Lewand, "Fibonacci Melodies," *Humanistic Mathematics Network Journal,* (14):36–39 (November 1996); J. L. Morgan and J. L. Ginther, "The Magic of Mathematics," *Mathematics Teacher* 87(3):150–153 (March 1994); B. Rulf, "A Geometric Puzzle That Leads to Fibonacci Sequences," *Mathematics Teacher* 91(1):21–23 (January 1998); D. L. Shaw and L. Aspinwall, "The Recurring Fibonacci Sequence: Using a Pose-and-Probe Rubric," *Mathematics Teacher* 92(3):192–196 (March 1999); and M. J. Zerger, "The Dating Game," *Mathematics Teacher* 91(2):172–174 (February 1998).

56. Using a light sensor to measure the intensity of a light source from various distances, have students graph the data points and then, with their scientific calculators, find the relevant equation.

57. Establish a service-learning project at your school.

58. Eighth-grade students at George Washington Middle School (Alexandria, VA) participate in a parachute creation contest. Using plastic from trash bags, string, and a paperclip as the skydiver, the challenge is to design a parachute with the least surface area and longest hang time.[27]

Physical Education

59. Have students choose individually (or in dyads) a famous athlete they most (or least) admire. A short report will be written about the athlete. The student will then discuss the attributes and/or characteristics that they admire (or dislike) in the athlete, and how they feel they can emulate (or avoid) those qualities. After all pairs of students have made their presentations, as a class, devise two lists, one of common attributes admired, the other of qualities to avoid.

60. Have students in cooperative learning groups make up an exercise routine to their favorite music recording, then share it with the class and discuss how they arrived at decisions along the way.

61. Have the class divide into groups. Given the basic nonlocomotor skills, have each group come up with a "people machine." Each student within the group is hooked up to another demonstrating a nonlocomotor skill and adding some sort of noise to it. Have a contest for the most creative people machine.

62. Give students a chance to design a balance-beam routine that has two passes on the beam and that must include: front-support mount, forward roll, leap, low or high turn, visit, chassé, and cross-support dismount. These routines will be posted to show the variety of ways the different maneuvers can be put together.

63. Divide the class into groups. Have them create a new game or activity for the class, using only the equipment they are given. Let the class play their newly created games.

64. Have the students plan ways of educating the school and local community about general nutrition and exercise.

Science

65. Have students create and test their own microscopes using bamboo rods with a drop of water in each end.

66. Have students use the petals of flowers to create litmus indicators.

67. Use cassette-tape recorders to record sounds of the environment. Compare and write about day and night sounds.

68. On the first day of a life science class, give each student one live guppy in a test tube and one live cactus plant in a three-inch pot. Tell the students that the minimum they each need to pass the course is to bring their pet plant and fish back to you during the final week of school, alive.

69. Plan a yearlong project where each student, or small group of students, must develop knowledge and understanding of some specific piece of technology. Each project culmination presentation must have five components: visual, oral, written, artistic, and creative.

70. If you are a life science teacher, make sure your classroom looks like a place for studying life rather than a place of death.

71. Students of one urban school used landlord–tenant situations to develop a simulation of predator–prey relationships.

72. With each student playing the role of a cell part, have students set up and perform a role-play simulation of cells.

73. Divide your class into groups, and ask each group to create an environment for an imaginary animal using discarded items from the environment. By asking questions, each group will try and learn about other groups' "mystery" animals.

74. Have each student, or student pair, "adopt" a chemical element. The student then researches that element and becomes the class expert whenever that particular substance comes up in discussion. There could be a special bulletin board for putting up questions on interesting or little-known facts about the elements.

75. Milk can be precipitated, separated, and the solid product dried to form a very hard substance that was, in the days before plastic, used to make buttons. Let students make their own buttons from milk.

76. As a class or interdisciplinary team project, obtain permission and "adopt" a wetlands area near the school.

77. Have students research the composition and development of familiar objects. For example, the ordinary pencil is made of cedar wood from the forests of the Pacific Northwest. The graphite is often from Montana or Mexico and is reinforced with clays from Georgia and Kentucky. The eraser is made from soybean oil, latex from trees in South America, and reinforced with pumice from California or New Mexico, and sulfur, calcium, and barium. The metal band is aluminum or brass, made from copper and zinc, mined in no fewer than 13 states and nine provinces of Canada. The paint to color the wood and the lacquer to make it shine are made from a

[27]L. Mann, "Recalculating Middle School Math," *Education Update* 42(1):2–3, 8 (January 2000).

variety of different minerals and metals, as is the glue that holds the wood together.

78. Have students locate and design large posters to hang on the classroom walls that show the meaning of words used in science that are not typical of their meaning in everyday language usage—the word "theory" for example.

79. To bridge cross-cultural differences, have students design large posters to hang on the classroom walls showing potential differences in perceptions or views according to ethnoscience and formal science.

80. With your students, plan a community service project. For example, students from classes at Hollidaysburg Area Senior High School (Hollidaysburg, PA) joined to renovate a local cemetery.

81. Sometimes projects become ongoing, permanent endeavors with many spin-off projects of shorter duration. For example, what began as a science classroom project at W. H. English Middle School (Scottsburg, IN) has become the largest animal refuge shelter in the Midwest. While nursing animals back to health, the students study them and learn about environmental policies. Over the years, students in the program have shared their work by making presentations in ten states and as guests of the International Animal Rights Convention in Russia.[28]

Social Sciences

82. Organize an Intergenerational Advocacy program, in which students and senior citizens work together to make a better society for both groups.[29] For example, at Burns Middle School (Owensboro, KY) students work in collaboration with a retired senior volunteer program to develop their understanding of personal and social responsibilities.

83. Initiate a service-learning project where, for an extended period of time, students work directly with community organizations and agencies. For example, at John Ford Middle School (St. Matthews, SC) students incorporate The Constitutional Right Foundation "City Youth" program into the curriculum, helping to make decisions about areas of the community that need improvement.

84. Develop a yearlong three-stage project. During the first, stage students individually research the question "Who Am I?"; during the second stage, "Who Are They?"; and in the third stage, "Who Are We?" Multimedia presentations should be part of the culminating presentations.

85. During their study of Ancient Egypt, have students create and build their own model pyramids.

86. Let students devise ways they would improve their living environment, beginning with the classroom, then moving out to the school, home, community, and global.

87. Start a pictorial essay on the development and/or changes of a given area in your community, such as a major corner or block adjacent to the school. This is a study project that could continue for years and that has many social, political, and economic implications.

88. Start a folk hero study. Each year ask, "What prominent human being who has lived during (a particular period of time) do you most (and/or least) admire?" Collect individual responses to the question, tally, and discuss. After you have done this for several years you may wish to share with your class (for discussion purposes) the results of your surveys from previous years.

89. Start a sister school program. Establish a class relationship with another, similar class from another school from around the country or the world, perhaps via the Internet.

90. Role-play a simulated family movement to the West in the 1800s. What items would they take? What would they throw out of the wagon to lighten the load?

91. Have students collect music, art, or athletic records from a particular period of history. Have them compare with today and predict the future.

92. Using play money, establish a capitalistic economic system within your classroom. Salaries may be paid for attendance and bonus income for work well done, taxes may be collected for poor work, and a welfare section established in a corner of the room.

93. Divide your class into small groups and ask that each group make predictions as to what world governments, world geography, world social issues, or some other related topic will be like some time in the future. Let each group give its report, followed by debate and discussion. Plant the predictions in some secret location on the school grounds for a future discovery.

94. As the opener to a unit on the U.S. Constitution, have students design their own classroom "bill of rights."

95. One day, organize your students in class as if your class were a socialist society; the next day treat them as if they were a fascist society; on another day as a communist society; etc. At the end of the simulation, have students discuss and compare their feelings about each day.

96. Using Legos™ as construction blocks and assigned roles, have students simulate the building of the Great Wall of China or the Great Pyramids of Egypt.

---

[28]J. Arnold, "High Expectations For All: Perspective and Practice," *Middle School Journal* 28(3):52 (January 1997).

[29]See, for example: R. Cuevas, "I Can Help," and G. R. Hopkins, "How Important Are Intergenerational Programs in Today's Schools?" both in *Phi Delta Kappan* 82(4):316 and 317–319, respectively, (December 2000). Additional information about intergenerational programs can be obtained from the Center for Intergenerational Learning, Temple University, 1601 N. Broad St., Room 206, Philadelphia, PA 19122 (http://www.temple.edu/cil/).

97. At Indian Trail Junior High School (Addison, IL) all eighth graders and teachers from not only social studies but various other content areas, including English, mathematics, physical education, and science, work together on a "real world" problem-based project titled the Inspector Red Ribbon Unit, which focuses on a social problem that has truly occurred too many times—the prom night automobile accident. During the study, under guidance from teachers of the various classes, students interview witnesses, visit and assess the scene of the accident, review medical reports, and make their recommendations in a press conference.[30]

98. Establish a caring and anti-violence program. For example, at Lynn High School (Haven, FL) students work as tutors/mentors with elementary school children to help boost confidence and self-esteem among both groups of students.

99. Students at Northern Wayne Vocational-Technical School (Wayne, WV) study castles and build model castles that are shared with students at Wayne High School who are in an interdisciplinary thematic unit of study about the history and literature of medieval Europe.

100. At Davis Senior High School (Davis, CA), students in U.S. History are given this assignment for an activity titled "Creating a Candidate." The assignment is done in pairs. Research electronic and print media about the progressive movement in early California history. Determine relevant issues a candidate for governor of the state in 1910 would need to address. Create a fictitious candidate. Your exhibition must include: (a) an election poster, (b) a slogan, (c) a theme song that you must sing, and (d) a five-minute platform speech addressing the issues, your solutions, and the position of your opponents.

Vocational-Career Education

101. At Bell County High School (Pineville, KY), students operate an on-campus bank where the students can actually make deposits, earn interest, and borrow money.

102. At North Penn High School (Lansdale, PA), students designed and built equipment for the school's child development playground.

---

[30]K. Rasmussen, "Using Real-Life Problems to Make Real-World Connections," *ASCD Curriculum Update* (Summer 1997), p. 2.

All subjects, lessons, units, and project ideas
- *Columbia Education Center Lesson Plans* http://www.col-ed.org/cur/
- *Global Schoolhouse* http://www.gsh.org
- *Intercultural E-Mail Classroom Connections*, http://www.iecc.org/.
- *Teachers Net Lesson Exchange* http://www.teachers.net/lessons

Art
- *Eyes on Art* http://www.kn.pacbell.com/wired/art/art.html
- *Kinder Art* http://www.bconnex.net/~jarea/lessons.htm
- *World Wide Arts Resources* http://wwar.com/

Dance
- *CyberDance* http://www.cyberdance.org
- *Dance links* http://www.SapphireSwan.com/dance/

Drama and film
- *Performing Arts Resources,* http://www.educationindex.com/theater/
- *Screensite* http://www.tcf.ua.edu/screensite

Environmental issues
- *Environmental links* http://www.nceet.snre.umich.edu/
- *North American Association for Environmental Education* http://www.naaee.org
- *World Bank's site* http://www.worldbank.org/depweb
- *World Resources* http://www.wri.org

History/social studies
- *Amigo! Mexico Web Center* http://www.mexonline.com/
- *FedWorld* http://www.fedworld.gov
- *Historical Text Archive* http://historicaltextarchive.com
- *The History Net* http://www.thehistorynet.com
- *History/social studies resources* http://www.execpc.com/~dboals/boals.html.
- *Houghton Mifflin Social Studies Center* http://www.eduplace.com/ss/

- *The Library in the Sky* http://www.nwrel.org/sky/Classroom/Social_Studies/History/History.html
- *Links to lesson plans,* unit plans, thematic units, and resources http://www.csun.edu/~hcedu013/index.html
- *The Presidents of the United States* http://www.netcolony.com/news/presidents/
- *Scrolls from the Dead Sea* http://sunsite.unc.edu/expo/deadsea.scrolls.exhibit/intro.html
- *Social Sciences Research Network On-line* http://www.ssrn.com/index.html
- *U.S. History, From Revolution to Reconstruction* http://grid.let.rug.nl/~welling/usa/usa.html
- *Women's History* http://frank.mtsu.edu/~kmiddlet/history/women.html

Language and literacy
- *ESL/EFL links* http://www.pacificnet.net/~sperling/eslcafe.html
- *Foreign language links* http://polyglot.lss.wisc.edu/lss/lang/langlink.html
- *Language and Literacy Project* http://www.uis.edu/~cook/langlit/index.html
- *Literature and humanities links* http://galaxy.einet.net/galaxy/Humanities/Literature.html

Mathematics
- *Math Archieves* http://archives.math.utk.edu/
- The *Math Forum* http://mathforum.org
- *Mathematics Lesson Plans* http://www.col-ed.org/cur/math.html#math3
- *MathSource* http://mathsource.wri.com/
- *More math project ideas* http://www.luc.edu/schools/education/csimath/zmathed.htm
- *PBS Mathline* http://www.pbs.org/learn/mathline/
- *Plane Math* http://www.planemath.com/
- *Show-Me Project* http://www.showmecenter.missouri.edu

Music
- *Music Education Resource Links* http://www.isd77.k12.mn.us/resources/staffpages/shirk/k12.music.html

Science
- *BioRap* http://www.biorap.org.
- *Chemistry tutorial* http://dbhs.wvusd.k12.ca.us/ChemTeamIndex.html
- *Earthshots* www.usgs.gov/Earthshots
- *Mandel's* http://www.pacificnet.net/~mandel/Science.html
- *NASA Spacelink* http://spacelink.nasa.gov/index.html
- *Science and Mathematics Education Resources*
- *Stanford Solar Center* http://solar-center.stanford.edu
- *Weather Underground* http://groundhog.sprl.umich.edu/
- *Windows to the Universe Project* http://www.windows.umich.edu

Figure 8.4
Internet sites for teaching ideas.

SUMMARY

This chapter has continued the development of your repertoire of teaching strategies. As you know, young people can be quite peer-conscious, can have relatively short attention spans for experiences in which they are uninterested, and prefer active experiences that engage many or all of their senses. Most are intensely curious about things of interest to them. Cooperative learning, student-centered projects, and teaching strategies that emphasize shared discovery and inquiry (discussed in the next chapter) within a psychologically safe environment encourage the most positive aspects of thinking and learning. Central to your strategy selection should

be those strategies that encourage students to become independent thinkers and skilled learners who can help in the planning, structuring, regulating, and assessing of their own learning and learning activities.

ADDITIONAL EXERCISES

See the companion website http://www.prenhall.com/kellough for the following exercises related to the content of this chapter:

- A Reflection on My Past Involvement with Student-Centered Instructional Activities
- Practical Ways for Individualizing the Instruction

QUESTIONS FOR CLASS DISCUSSION

1. Describe research that you can find on the use of cooperation (cooperative learning groups) vs. competition (competitive learning groups) in teaching. Explain why you would or would not use cooperative learning groups as they were discussed in this chapter.

2. Do you have concerns about using project-based teaching and not being able to cover all the content you believe you should be covering? Think back to your own schooling. What do you really remember? Most likely you remember projects, yours and other students' presentations, the lengthy research you did, and your extra effort for the artwork to accompany your presentation. Maybe you remember a compliment by a teacher or a pat on the back by peers. Most likely you do not remember the massive amount of content that was covered. Discuss your feelings about this with your classmates. Share common experiences and common concerns.

3. It is an aphorism that to learn something well students need time to practice it. There is a difference, however, between solitary practice and coached practice. Describe the difference and conditions where you would use each.

4. Divide into teams of four, and have each team develop one learning center. Set up and share the LCs in your classroom.

5. Explain how a teacher can tell when he or she is truly using cooperative learning groups for instruction as opposed to traditional small group learning.

6. When a student is said to be on task, does that necessarily imply that the student is mentally engaged? Is it possible for a student to be mentally engaged although not on task? Explain your answers.

7. Select one of the Reflective Thoughts from the opening of Part III (page 220) that is specifically related to the content of this chapter, research it, and write a one-page essay explaining why you agree or disagree with the thought. Share your essay with members of your class for their thoughts.

8. Describe any prior concepts you held that changed as a result of your experiences with this chapter. Describe the changes.

9. From your current observations and field work as related to this teacher preparation program, clearly identify one specific example of educational practice that seems contradictory to exemplary practice or theory as presented in this chapter. Present your explanation for the discrepancy.

10. Do you have questions generated by the content of this chapter? If you do, list them along with ways answers might be found.

FOR FURTHER READING

Albrecht, B., and Firedrake, G. "The Hands-On and Far-Out Physics Team: It Starts Out Walking." *Learning and Leading with Technology* 25(6):36–40 (March 1998).

Barak, M., and Raz, E. "Hot-Air Balloons: Project-Centered Study as a Bridge between Science and Technology Education." *Science Education* 84(1):27–42 (January 2000).

Bevilacqua, M. "Collaborative Learning in the Secondary English Class." Clearing House 73(3): 132–133 (January/February 2000).

Bowen, C. W. "A Quantitative Literature Review of Cooperative Learning Effects on High School and College Chemistry Achievement." *Journal of Chemical Education* 77(1):16–19 (January 2000).

Bower, B., and Lobdell, J. "History Alive! Six Powerful Constructivist Strategies." *Social Education* 62(1):50–53 (January 1998).

Carter, C. S., Cohen, S., Keyes, M., Kusimo, P. S., and Lunsford, C. *Uncommon Knowledge: Projects That Help Middle-School-Age Youth Discover the Science and Mathematics in Everyday Life.* Volume Two: Hands-On Math Projects. Charleston, WV: ED439002, ERIC Clearinghouse on Rural Education and Small Schools, 2000.

Crocco, M. S. "Putting the Actors Back on Stage: Oral History in the Secondary School Classroom." *Social Studies* 89(1): 19–24 (January/February 1998).

Downs, A. "Successful School Reform Efforts Share Common Features." *Harvard Education Letter* 16(2):1–5 (March/April 2000).

Fuchs, L. S., Fuchs, D., and Kazdan, S. "Effects of Peer-Assisted Learning Strategies on High School Students with Serious Reading Problems," *Remedial and Special Education* 20(5):309–318 (September/October 1999).

Gardiner, S. "Cybercheating: A New Twist on an Old Problem." *Phi Delta Kappan* 83(2):172–174 (October 2001).

Glazer, N. T., and Williams, S. "Averting the Homework Crisis." *Educational Leadership* 43–45 (April 2001).

Holt, P. W. "The Oregon Trail: Wyoming Students Construct a CD-ROM." *Social Education* 62(1):41–45 (January 1998).

Kesson, K., and Oyler, C. "Integrated Curriculum and Service Learning: Linking School-Based Knowledge and Social Action." *English Education* 31(2):135–149 (January 1999).

Larson, B. E. "Influences on Social Studies Teachers' Use of Classroom Discussion." *Clearing House* 73(3):174–181 (January/February 2000).

Leinhardt, G., Stainton, C., and Bausmith, J. M. "Constructing Maps Collaboratively." *Journal of Geography* 97(1):19–30 (January/February 1998).

Leloup, J. W., and Ponterio, R. "Cooperative Learning Activities for the Foreign Language Classroom." *Language Learning and Technology* 3(2):3–5 (January 2000).

Marzano, R. J., Pickering, D. J., and Pollock, J. E. *Classroom Instruction that Works.* Chap. 7, "Cooperative Learning." Alexandria, VA: Association for Supervision and Curriculum Development, 2001. pp. 84–91.

McClure, L. J. "Wimpy Boys and Macho Girls: Gender Equity at the Crossroads." *English Journal* 88(3):78–82 (January 1999).

Mewborn, D. S. "Creating a Gender Equitable School Environment." *International Journal of Leadership in Education* 2(2):103–115 (April–June 1999).

Murphey, C. E. "Using the Five Themes of Geography to Explore a School Site." *Social Studies Review* 37(2):49–52 (Spring/Summer 1998).

Ngeow, K. Y. *Enhancing Student Thinking through Collaborative Learning*. Bloomington, IN: ED422586 98, ERIC Clearinghouse on Reading, English, and Communication, 1998.

Oden, D. "Constructing a Prehistoric Adventure." *Science Teacher* 65(4):38–41 (April 1998).

Randall, V. "Cooperative Learning: Abused and Overused?" *Gifted Child Today Magazine* 22(2):14–16 (March/April 1999).

Rieck, W. A., and Wadsworth, D. E. D. "Foreign Exchange: An Inclusion Strategy," *Intervention in School and Clinic* 35(1):22–28 (September 1999).

Rillero, P., Gonzalez-Jensen, M., and Moy, T. "Moon Watch: A Parental-Involvement Homework Activity." *Science Activities* 36(4):11–15 (Winter 2000).

Sadker, D. "Gender Equity: Still Knocking at the Classroom Door." *Educational Leadership* 56(7):22–26 (April 1999).

Schlenker, R. M., Cullen, D., and Schlenker, K. R. "Using Acid–Base Reagent Problems as a High School Science Research Activity." *Science Activities* 35(4):19–23 (Winter 1999).

Simonson, M., and Schlosser, C. "The DaVinci Project: Multimedia in Art and Chemistry." *TechTrends* 43(3):19–22 (April/May 1998).

Smith, F. "Just a Matter of Time." *Phi Delta Kappan* 82(8):572–576 (April 2001).

Stearns, C. J. "A Middle School Venture into Cooperative Learning: Successes and Dilemmas." *Theory into Practice* 38(2):100–104 (Spring 1999).

Tomlinson, C. A. *The Differentiated Classroom*. Alexandria, VA: Association for Supervision and Curriculum Development, 1999.

Townsend, J. S. "Silent Voices: What Happens to Quiet Students During Classroom Discussions?" *English Journal* 87(2):72–80 (February 1998).

Walters, L. S. "Putting Cooperative Learning to the Test." *Harvard Education Letter* 16(3):1–5 (May/June 2000).

Weinman, J., and Haag, P. "Gender Equity in Cyberspace." *Educational Leadership* 56(5):44–49 (February 1999).

Wiest, L. R. "Mathematics That Whets the Appetite: Student-Posed Problems." *Mathematics Teaching in the Middle School* 5(5):286–291 (January 2000).

Zinn, B., Gnut, S., and Kafkafi, U. "First-Rate Crops from Second-Rate Water: Classroom Activities Model a Real-World Problem." *Science Activities* 35(4):27–30 (Winter 1999).

Using Teacher Talk, Demonstrations, Thinking, Inquiry, and Games

Perhaps no other strategy is used more by teachers than is teacher talk, so this chapter begins with a presentation of guidelines for using that vital and significant instructional strategy. A strategy related to teacher talk is the demonstration, which is addressed later in the chapter, followed by guidelines for other important strategies; namely, for thinking, inquiry and discovery, and games.

Specifically, upon your completion of this chapter you should be able to:

1. Present an effective demonstration.
2. Demonstrate how and when to use student inquiry.

3. Demonstrate how to help students learn to think and behave intelligently.
4. Demonstrate an understanding of the relationship between thinking, problem solving, discovery, and inquiry.
5. Demonstrate ways of integrating strategies for integrated learning.
6. Demonstrate when and how to use teacher talk for instruction.
7. Demonstrate your knowledge of advantages and disadvantages of each of seven categories of games for learning.

TEACHING VIGNETTE
A Precious Moment in Teaching with Advice to Beginning Teachers

We share with you this teaching vignette that we believe to be both humorous and indicative of creative thinking.

While teaching a high school history class, the teacher began her lesson with the question, "What comes to mind when you hear the words 'Puritan' and 'Pilgrim'?" Without hesitation, a rather quiet student voice from somewhere near the rear of the room replied, "Cooking oil and John Wayne." To us, that represented one of those rare and precious moments in teaching, reaffirming our belief that every teacher is well advised to maintain throughout his or her teaching career a journal in which such intrinsically rewarding moments can be recorded so as to be reviewed and enjoyed again years later.

TEACHER TALK: FORMAL AND INFORMAL

Teacher talk encompasses both lecturing *to* students and talking *with* students. A lecture is considered formal teacher talk, whereas a discussion with students is considered informal teacher talk.

Cautions in Using Teacher Talk

Whether your talk is formal or informal, there are certain cautions that you need to be mindful of. Perhaps the most important is that of *talking too much*. If a teacher talks too much, the significance of the teacher's words may be lost because some students will tune the teacher out.

Another caution is to avoid *talking too fast*. Students can hear faster than they can understand what they hear. It is a good idea to remind yourself to talk slowly and to check frequently for student comprehension of what you are talking about. It is also important to remember that your one brain is communicating with many student brains, each of which responds to sensory input (auditory in this instance) at different rates. Because of this, you will need to pause to let words sink in and you will need to pause during transitions from one point or activity to the next.

A third caution is to be sure you are being *heard and understood*. Sometimes teachers talk in too low a pitch or use words that are not understood by many of the students, or both. You should vary the pitch of your voice, and you should stop and help students with their understanding of vocabulary that may be new to them.

A fourth caution is to remember that just *because students have heard something before does not necessarily mean that they understand it or learned it*. From our earlier discussions of learning experiences (such as The Learning Experiences Ladder in Chapter 6), remember that although verbal communication is an important form of communication, because of its reliance on the use of abstract symbolization it is not a very reliable

form of communication. Teacher talk relies on words and on skill in listening, a skill that is not mastered by many teenagers (or for that matter, even many adults). For that and other reasons, to ensure student understanding, it is good to reinforce your teacher talk with either direct or simulated learning experiences.

A related caution is to *resist believing that students have attained a skill or have learned something that was taught previously by you or by another teacher*. During any discussion (formal or informal), rather than assuming that your students know something, you should ensure they know it. For example, if the discussion and a student activity involve a particular thinking skill, then you will want to make sure students know how to use that skill (thinking skills are discussed later in this chapter).

Still another problem is *talking in monotone*. Students need teachers whose voices exude enthusiasm and excitement (although not to be overdone) about the subject and about teaching and learning. Such enthusiasm and excitement for learning is contagious. A voice that demonstrates genuine enthusiasm for teaching and learning is more likely to motivate students to learn.

A final caution is *just because your speaking channel is engaged doesn't mean that you should disengage your sensory input channels*. While an exemplary teacher is talking she is still seeing and listening and capable of changing her physical location in the classroom, without missing a beat in her talk. This is another time when the exemplary teachers' skills of withitness and overlapping are put into play.

Keep those cautions in mind as you study the general principles and specific guidelines for the productive and effective use of teacher-talk.

Teacher Talk: General Guidelines

Certain general guidelines should be followed whether your talk is formal or informal. First, begin the talk with an advance organizer. Advance organizers are introductions that mentally prepare students for a study by helping them make connections with material already learned or experienced—a *comparative organizer*—or by providing students with a conceptual arrangement of what is to be learned—an *expository organizer*.[1] The value of using advance organizers is well documented by research.[2] An advance organizer can be a brief introduction or statement about the main idea you intend to convey and how it is related to other aspects of the students' learning (an expository organizer), or it can be a presentation of a discrepancy to arouse curiosity (a comparative organizer, in this instance causing students to compare what they have observed with what they already knew or thought they knew). Preparing an organizer helps you plan and organize the sequence of ideas, and its presentation helps students organize their own learning and become motivated about it. An advance organizer can also make their learning meaningful by providing important connections between what they already know and what is being learned.

Second, *your talk should be planned so that it has a beginning and an end, with a logical order between*. During your talk, you should reinforce your words with visuals (discussed in the specific guidelines that follow). These visuals may include writing unfamiliar terms on the board (helping students learn new vocabulary), visual organizers, and prepared graphs, charts, photographs, and various audiovisuals.

Third, *pacing is important*. Your talk should move briskly, but not too fast. The ability to pace the instruction is a difficult skill for many beginning teachers (the tendency among many beginning teachers is to talk too fast and too much), but one that will improve with experience. Until you have developed your skill in pacing lessons, you probably will need to constantly remind yourself to slow down during lessons and to provide silent pauses (allowing for think-time) and frequent checks for student comprehension. Specifically, your talk should:

- be brisk, though not too fast, but with occasional slowdowns to change the pace and to check for student comprehension. Allow students time to think, ask questions, and to make notes.[3]
- have a time plan. A talk planned for ten minutes, if interesting to students, will probably take longer. If not interesting to them, it will probably take less time.
- always be planned with careful consideration to the characteristics of the students. For example, if you

have a fairly high percentage of LEP students or of students with special needs, then your teacher talk may be less brisk, sprinkled with even more visuals and repeated statements, and frequent checks for student comprehension.

Fourth, *encourage student participation*. Their active participation enhances their learning. This encouragement can be planned as questions that you ask, as time allowed for students to comment and ask questions, or as some sort of a visual and conceptual outline that students complete during the talk.

Fifth, *plan a clear ending (closure)*. Be sure your talk has a clear ending, followed by another activity (during the same or next class period) that will help secure the learning. As for all lessons, you want to strive for planning a clear and mesmerizing beginning, an involving lesson body, and a firm and meaningful closure.

Teacher Talk: Specific Guidelines

Specific guidelines for using teacher talk are presented in the following paragraphs.

Understand the various purposes for using teacher talk. Teacher talk, formal or informal, can be useful to discuss the progress of a unit of study, explain an inquiry, introduce a unit of study, present a problem, promote student inquiry or critical thinking, provide a transition from one unit of study to the next, provide information otherwise unobtainable to students, share the teacher's experiences, share the teacher's thinking, summarize a problem, summarize a unit of study, and teach a thinking skill by modeling that skill.

Clarify the objectives of the talk. Your talk should center around one idea. The learning objectives, which should not be too numerous for one talk, should be clearly understood by the students.

Choose between informal and formal talk. Although an occasional, formal "cutting edge" lecture may be appropriate for some classes, spontaneous, interactive, informal talks of 5 to 12 minutes are preferred. You should *never* give long lectures with no teacher–student interaction. Remember, though a formal period-long noninteractive lecture, common in some college teaching, is developmentally inappropriate when teaching most groups of teenagers. (Some experts believe that its appropriateness is questionable for learning even at the college level.) On the other hand, to arouse student interest and to provide new information in relatively small and intellectually digestible chunks, the lecture may be appropriate. If, during your student teaching, you have doubt or questions about your selection and use of a particular instructional strategy, discuss it with your cooperating teacher, your university supervisor, or both. When you have doubt about the appropriateness of a particular strategy, trust your intuition—without some modification, the strategy probably is inappropriate.

[1]D. P. Ausubel, *The Psychology of Meaningful Learning* (New York: Grune & Stratton, 1963).

[2]T. L. Good and J. E. Brophy, *Looking in Classrooms*, 8th ed. (New York: Addison Wesley Longman, 2000), pp. 252–253.

[3]For additional resource information about student note taking, see "Research and Theory on Note Taking," in R. J. Marzano et al., *Classroom Instruction that Works* (Alexandria, VA: Association for Supervision and Curriculum Development, 2001). pp. 43–48.

Remember also, today's youth are of the "media, or light, generation," and are used to video interactions as well as "commercial breaks"—for many lessons, especially those that are teacher-centered, after about ten minutes student attention is likely to stray. For that eventuality you need elements planned to recapture student attention. These planned elements can include: analogies to help connect the topic to students' experiences; verbal cues, such as voice inflections; pauses to allow information to sink in; humor; visual cues, such as the use of slides, overhead transparencies, charts, board drawings, excerpts from videodisks, real objects (realia), or body gestures; and, sensory cues, such as eye contact and proximity (as in moving around the room, or casually and gently touching a student on the shoulder without interrupting your talk).

Vary strategies and activities frequently. Perhaps most useful as a strategy for recapturing student attention is to change to an entirely different strategy or learning modality. For example, from teacher talk (a teacher-centered strategy) you would change to a student activity (a student-centered strategy). Notice that changing from a lecture (mostly teacher talk) to a teacher-led discussion (mostly more teacher talk) would not be changing to an entirely different modality. Figure 9.1 provides a comparison of different changes.

As a generalization, when using teacher-centered direct instruction, with most classes you will want to change the learning activities about every 10 to 15 minutes. (That is one reason that in the sample lesson plan format of Chapter 5, you find space for at least four activities, including the introduction and closure.) This means that in a 50- or 60-minute time block (the length of traditional class periods), for example, you should probably plan three or four *sequenced* learning activities, with some that are teacher-centered and many others that are more student-centered. In a 90-minute block, plan five or six learning activities.

In exemplary classrooms, rather than using teacher-centered direct instruction, teachers often have several activities *concurrently* being performed by individuals, dyads, and small groups of students (that is, the teachers use multitasking or multilevel instruction). Multilevel instruction is particularly important for use during long block periods, called macroperiods (discussed in Chapter 1). Macroperiods provide more time for student inquiry and for interactive and interdisciplinary thematic instruction that might otherwise be difficult or impossible to accomplish in shorter class periods.

Prepare and use notes as a guide for your talk. Planning your talk and preparing notes to be used during formal and informal teacher talk is important—just as important as implementing the talk with visuals. There is absolutely nothing wrong with using notes during your teaching. You can carry them on a clipboard, perhaps a brightly colored one that gives students a visual

focus, as you move around the room. Your notes for a formal talk can first be prepared in narrative form; for class use, though, they should be reduced to an outline form. *Talks to students should always be from an outline, never read from prose.* The only time that a teacher's reading from prose aloud to students is appropriate is when reading a brief, published article (such as in science or social studies) or portions of a story or poem (such as in reading/English/language arts).

In your outline, use color coding with abbreviated visual cues to yourself. You will eventually develop your own coding system—though keep whatever coding system you use simple lest you forget what the codes are for. Consider these examples of coding: where transition of ideas occur and you want to allow silent moments for ideas to sink in, mark *P* for *pause, T* for a *transition,* and *S* for moments of *silence;* where a slide or other visual aid will be used, mark *AV* for *audiovisual;* where you intend to stop and ask a question, mark *TQ* for *teacher question,* and mark *SQ* or *?* where you want to stop and allow time for *student questions;* where you plan to have a discussion, mark *D;* mark *SG* where you plan *small-group work* and *L* where you plan to switch to a *laboratory* investigation; and for *reviews* and *comprehension checks,* mark *R* and *CS.*

Share your note organization with your students. Sharing with them how you organize for your work (your teaching) is important modeling for them for the organization of their learning. Teach the students how to take notes and what kinds of things they should write down. Use colored chalk or markers to outline and highlight your talk; encourage your students to use colored pencils for notetaking, so their notes can be color-coded to match your writing board notes.

Rehearse your talk. Using your lesson plan as your guide, rehearse your talk using a camcorder or an audiorecorder, or rehearse it while talking into a mirror or to a roommate. (For example, when we see professors walking across the campus mumbling to themselves, we like to think that they are rehearsing their lecture.) You may want to include a time plan for each subtopic to allow you to gauge your timing during implementation of the talk.

Avoid racing through the talk solely to complete it by a certain time. It is more important that students understand some of what you say than that you cover it all and they understand none of it. If you do not finish, continue it later.

Augment your talk with multisensory stimulation and allow for think-time. Your presentation should not rely too much on verbal communication. When using visuals, such as video excerpts or overhead transparencies, do not think that you must be constantly talking; after clearly explaining the purpose of a visual, give students sufficient time to look at it, think about it, and ask questions about it. The visual is new to the students, so give them time to take it in.

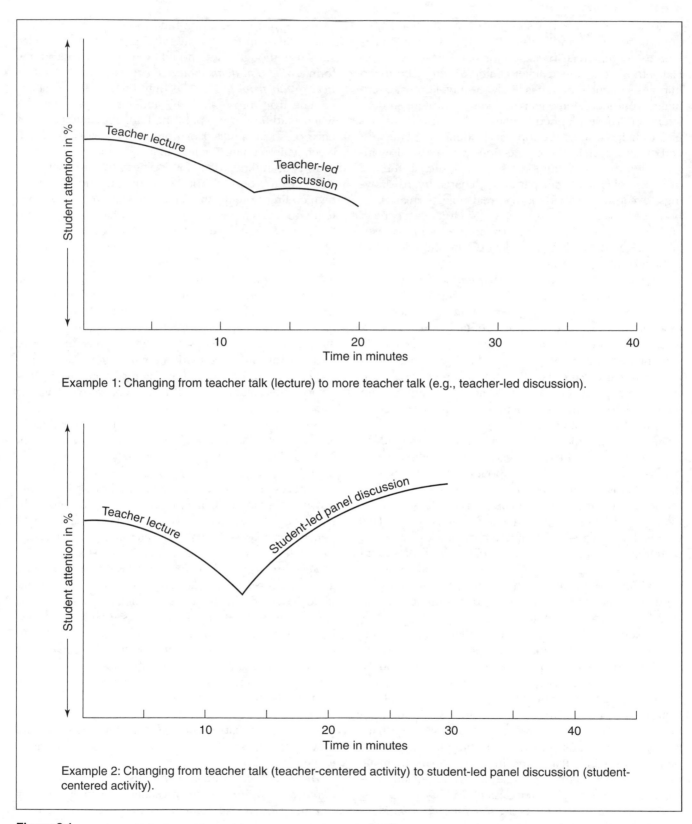

Example 1: Changing from teacher talk (lecture) to more teacher talk (e.g., teacher-led discussion).

Example 2: Changing from teacher talk (teacher-centered activity) to student-led panel discussion (student-centered activity).

Figure 9.1
Comparison of recapturing student attention by changing the instructional strategy.

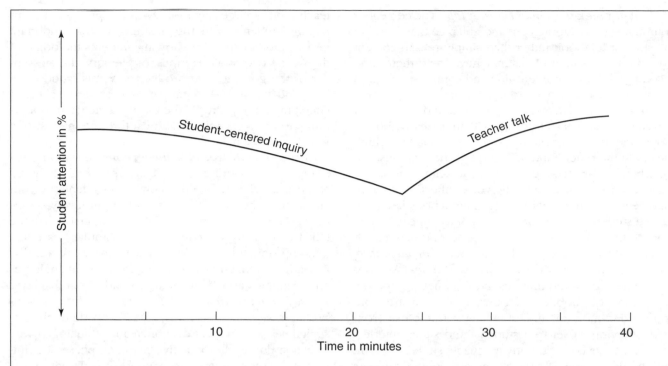

Example 3: Changing from inquiry (student-centered) to teacher talk, fueled by student questions from inquiry.

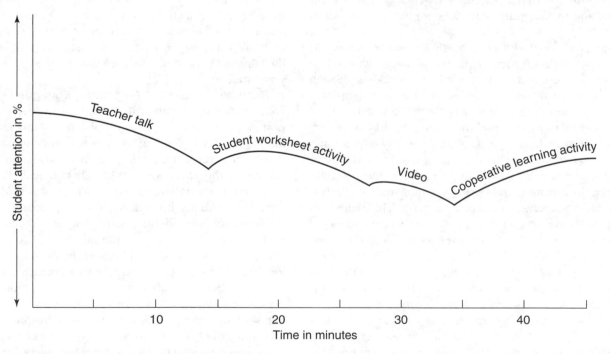

Example 4: Changing from teacher talk (teacher-centered activity) to cooperative learning activity (student-centered activity).

Figure 9.1 *(continued)*

Carefully plan the content of your talk. The content of your talk should supplement and enhance that found in the student textbook rather than simply rehash content from the textbook. Students may never read their book if you tell them in an interesting and condensed fashion everything that they need to know from it.

Monitor your delivery. Your voice should be pleasant and interesting to listen to rather than a steady, boring monotone or a constantly shrieking, irritating, high pitch. On the other hand, it is good to show enthusiasm for what you are talking about, for teaching and learning. Occasionally use dramatic voice inflections to emphasize important points and meaningful body language to give students a visual focus. So not to appear phony, practice these skills so they become second nature.

As is always the case when teaching, *avoid standing in the same spot for long periods of time.* (We consider standing for ten minutes in the same spot to be a long time.) Be mobile! Even during direct instruction, you need to monitor student behavior and to use proximity (moving closer to a student) and signal interference (e.g., eye contact, body language, smile or frown, thumbs up or down) as a means of keeping students focused. It is especially during extended periods of direct instruction that a beginning teacher's skills in with-itness and overlapping behaviors are likely to be put to the test.

View the vocabulary of the talk as an opportunity to help students with their word morphology. Words you use should be easily understood by the students, though you should still model professionalism and help students develop their vocabulary—both the vocabulary of your special discipline and the more general vocabulary of the English language. During your lesson planning, predict when you are likely to use a word that is new to most students, and plan to stop to ask a student to help explain its meaning and perhaps demonstrate its derivation. Help students with word meaning. This helps students with their remembering. Remember, regardless of subject or grade level, *all teachers are language arts teachers.* Knowledge of word morphology is an important component of skilled reading and includes the ability to generate new words from prefixes, roots, and suffixes. For some students, nearly every subject in the curriculum is like a foreign language. That is certainly true for some LEP students, for whom teacher talk, especially formal teacher talk, should be used sparingly, if at all. Every teacher has the responsibility of helping students learn how to learn, and that includes helping students develop their word comprehension skills, reading skills, thinking and memory skills, and their motivation for learning.

For example, if introducing to students the word *hermaphrodite,* the biology teacher has the opportunity to teach a bit of Greek mythology in the process of helping the students with the meaning of that important term in biology through showing students the origin of the word's two roots (Hermes, or Mercury, the messenger of the gods, and Aphrodite, or Venus, goddess of love and beauty). And taking time to teach a bit of Greek mythology affords the biology teacher an opportunity to cross disciplines and capture the interest of a few more students.

Give thoughtful and intelligent consideration to student diversity. During the preactive phase of planning, while preparing your talk, consider students in your classroom who are culturally and linguistically different and those who have special needs. Personalize the talk for them by choosing your vocabulary carefully and appropriately, speaking slowly and methodically, repeating often, and by planning meaningful analogies and examples and relevant audio and visual displays.

Use familiar examples and analogies to help students make relevant connections (bridges). Although this sometimes takes a great deal of creative thinking as well as action during the preactive planning phase, it is important that you attempt to connect the talk with ideas and events with which the students are already familiar. The most effective talk is one that makes frequent and meaningful connections between what students already know and what they are learning, which bridges what they are learning with what they have experienced in their lives. Of course, this means you need to "know" your students.

Establish eye contact frequently. Your primary eye contact should be with your students—always! That important point cannot be overemphasized. Only momentarily should you look at your notes, your visuals, the projection screen, the writing board, and other adults or objects in the classroom. Although you will probably raise your eyebrows when you read this, it is true and it is important that with practice you can learn to scan a classroom of 30 students, establishing eye contact with each student about once a minute. To "establish" eye contact means that the student is aware that you are looking at him or her. Frequent eye contact can have two major benefits. First, as you "read" a student's body posture and facial expressions, you obtain clues about that student's attentiveness and comprehension. Second, eye contact helps to establish rapport between you and a student. A look with a smile from the teacher to a student can say so much! Be alert, though, for students who are from cultures where eye contact is infrequent or unwanted and could have negative consequences. In other words, don't push it!

Frequent eye contact is easier when using an overhead projector than when using the writing board. When using a writing board, you have to turn at least

CLASSROOM SCENARIO
Chemistry Students Write and Stage a One-act Play

For the purpose of motivating more of his students to enjoy and learn chemistry, and perhaps also to find regeneration in his interest in teaching, Robert, a high school chemistry teacher with 11 years experience, decided that this year he would try some teaching strategies that were new to his teaching of chemistry. Early in the year, in preparation for a unit on the study of oxygen and other gases, he told the 28 students in one of his chemistry classes that, if they were interested, he would like for them to plan, write, and stage a one-act play about the life of Joseph Priestley, the theologian and scientist, who in 1774, discovered what he called "dephlogisticated air," later named *oxygen* by Lavoisier. Furthermore the students would be given one week to plan. The play would be presented and videotaped in class. The students accepted Robert's idea with enthusiasm and immediately went about the task of organizing and putting their ideas into motion. They took on the challenging task with such vigor and seriousness that they asked Robert for an additional three days to prepare. Sean, a bright eleventh-grade student who was really more interested in theatre than science, was selected by the students to play the role of Priestley and also to be the producer. Other students played lesser rolls. Students with special interest in writing wrote the play. Others with interest in art and stagecraft assumed the task of designing and preparing the set, while another assumed the role of sound stage manager. The resulting 60-minute presentation was more successful than Robert, and perhaps the students, could ever have anticipated, so much so that the school principal requested the students put on the play two more times, once for the entire student body, a second time for the school's parent–teacher–student organization, both times resulting in standing ovations.

During the performance before the PTO, the student production was simultaneously recorded by the local cable television network and later played several times over the community cable channel. Robert later said that during this experience the students learned far more content than they ever would have via his traditional approach to the topic, plus these students were highly motivated in chemistry for the entire rest of the year. Sean went on to attend the University of California where he graduated with honors with a degree in theatre and a minor in chemistry.

partially away from your audience, and you may also have to pace back and forth from the board to the students in order to retain that important proximity to them.

Remember our discussions in Chapters 3 and 4 about "overlapping" as an important teaching skill? Well, this is one of those times when its importance really comes into play. While lecturing on a topic, you must remain aware and attentive to everything that is happening in the classroom (i.e., to student behavior as well as to the content of your lecture). No one ever said that good teaching is easy, or if they did, they didn't know what they were talking about. But don't dismay; with the knowledge of the preceding guidelines and with practice, experience, and intelligent reflection, you will develop the necessary skills.

Now do Exercise 9.1.

EXERCISE 9.1

The Lecture—Summary Review and Practice

Instructions: The purpose of this exercise is to provide a summary review to check your comprehension of this important, often used, and sometimes abused teaching strategy. Answer each of the following questions, and then share your responses with your classmates.

1. Describe how the lecture differs from informal teacher talk. _____

    _____

    _____

    _____

2. Although sometimes a useful strategy, lecturing should be used sparingly in high school teaching and even more sparingly in middle school teaching. Why is it less useful than some other teaching strategies? _____

    _____

    _____

    _____

    _____

3. Specifically, when might you use a lecture? _____

    _____

    _____

    _____

4. What can a lecturer to do arouse and maintain student interest in the lecture? _____

    _____

    _____

    _____

5. Identify principles that should be kept in mind when a teacher is planning a lecture. _____

    _____

    _____

    _____

    _____

6. Identify at least five things you can do to assure that your lecture is successful. _____

_____

_____

_____

_____

7. Thinking back to classes given by the best lecturers in your college experience, what did that professor do that made his or her lectures better than average? _____

_____

_____

_____

_____

8. Thinking of a lecture or informal talk given by one of your current professors or colleagues, what aids did the lecturer use to spice up the lecture? What devices might have been used that were not? If you were the lecturer, would you have performed differently? If so, explain how.

_____

_____

_____

_____

9. For a specific topic at a grade level and in your subject field, prepare a major instructional objective. Identify the major points that you would try to make and how you would try to get those points across in a lecture designed to support that objective.

Field: _____   Grade level: _____

Topic: _____   Major objective: _____

Major points: _____

_____

_____

Methods of achieving: _____

_____

_____

Estimate of amount of time needed to present this lecture: _____

10. Now implement the lecture of the previous item (number 9) to a group of peers and obtain their feedback, using the criteria of item 8 for that feedback. If the equipment is available, you may wish to videorecord your lecture so you can watch it and evaluate it yourself. After implementing the lecture and obtaining evaluative feedback from your peers, prepare a self-evaluation of this experience, again using the criteria of item 8. Share this self-evaluation with your course instructor. Use separate paper for the self-evaluation.

DEMONSTRATION

Most students like demonstrations because the demonstrator is actively engaged in a learning activity rather than merely verbalizing about it. Demonstrations can be used in teaching any subject and for a variety of purposes. The teacher demonstrates role-playing in preparation for a social studies simulation. A teacher demonstrates steps in solving a mathematics problem. A language arts/English teacher demonstrates clustering to students ready for a creative writing assignment. A foreign language teacher demonstrates proper social greetings in the target language. A science teacher demonstrates the effect of combining an acid and a base to form saltwater. The physical education teacher demonstrates the proper way to serve in volleyball.

Purposes of Demonstrations

A demonstration can be designed to serve any of the following purposes: to assist in recognizing a solution to an existing problem; to bring an unusual closure to a lesson or unit of study; to demonstrate a thinking skill; to model a skill used in conflict resolution; to establish problem recognition; to give students an opportunity for vicarious participation in active learning; to illustrate a particular point of content; to introduce a lesson or unit of study in a way that grabs the students' attention; to reduce potential safety hazards (where the teacher demonstrates with materials that are too dangerous for students to handle); to review; to save time and resources (as opposed to the entire class doing that which is being demonstrated); and to set up a discrepancy recognition.

Guidelines for Using Demonstrations

When planning a demonstration, you should consider the following guidelines.

Decide the most effective way to conduct the demonstration. It might be a verbal or a silent demonstration, by a student or by the teacher, by the teacher with a student helper, to the entire class or to small groups, or by some combination of these such as first by the teacher followed then by a repeat of the demonstration by a student or a succession of students.

Be sure that the demonstration is visible to all students. Some classrooms, where demonstrations are frequent and where financial resources have been made available, use mirrors that have been installed overhead or video cameras that are connected to large-screen television monitors.

Practice with the materials and procedure before demonstrating to the students. During your practice, try to prepare for anything that could go wrong during the real demonstration; if you don't, as "Murphy's Law" states, if anything can go wrong, it probably will. Then, if something does go wrong during the live demonstration, use that as an opportunity for a teachable moment; engage the students in working with you to try to figure out what went wrong, or if that isn't feasible, then go to Plan B.

Consider your pacing of the demonstration, allowing for enough student wait, see, and think time. At the start of the demonstration, explain its purpose and the learning objectives. Remember this adage: tell them what you are going to do, show them, and then help them understand what they saw. As with any lesson, plan your closure and allow time for questions and discussion. During the demonstration, as in other types of teacher talk, use frequent stops to check for student understanding.

Consider using special lighting to highlight the demonstration. For example, a slide projector can be used as a spotlight.

Be sure that the demonstration table and area are free of unnecessary objects that could distract, be in the way, or pose a safety hazard. With potentially hazardous demonstrations, such as might occur in physical education, science, or vocational classes, you must *model* proper safety precautions. Wear safety goggles, have fire-safety equipment at hand, and position a protective transparent shield between the demonstration table and nearby students.

TEACHING THINKING FOR INTELLIGENT BEHAVIOR

Pulling together what has been learned about learning and brain functioning, teachers are encouraged to integrate explicit thinking instruction into daily lessons. In other words, teachers should help students develop their thinking skills. In teaching for thinking, we are interested not only in what students know but also in how students behave when they don't know. Gathering evidence of the performance and growth of intelligent behavior requires observing students as they try to solve the day-to-day academic and real-life problems they encounter. By collecting anecdotes and examples of written, oral, and visual expressions, we can see students' increasingly voluntary and spontaneous performance of intelligent behaviors.

Characteristics of Intelligent Behavior

Characteristics of intelligent behavior that you should model, teach for, and observe developing in your students, as identified by Costa,[4] are described in the following paragraphs.

Persistence. Persistence is sticking to a task until it is completed. Consider the following examples.

- *Clara Barton.* Nearly single-handedly and against formidable odds, Clara Barton persevered to form the American Red Cross in 1882.
- *Rachel Carson.* Refusing to be intimidated by the chemical industry, powerful politicians, and the media, Carson was persistent in her pursuit to educate society about the ill effects of pesticides on humans and the natural world and refused to accept the premise that damage to nature was the inevitable cost of technological and scientific progress. Her book *Silent Spring,* published in 1963, was the seed for the beginning of the development of today's more responsible ecological attitude.
- *Amelia Earhart.* Born in 1898, Earhart demonstrated from the time she was a young girl that she was creative, curious, and persistent. Learning to fly in 1920, just eight years later she became the first woman to fly the Atlantic Ocean, thereby paving the way for other women to become active in aviation.
- *Thomas Edison.* Persistent in his efforts to invent the electric light bulb, Edison and his associates tried approximately 3,000 filaments before finding one that worked.
- *Wilma Rudolf.* As the result of childhood diseases, Wilma Rudolf, at the age of ten, could not walk without the aid of leg braces. Just ten years later, at the age of 20, she was declared to be the fastest running woman in the world, having won three gold medals in the 1960 World Olympics.
- *Babe Ruth.* For years Ruth owned not only the highest number of home runs in professional baseball but also the highest number of strikeouts.
- *Margaret Sanger.* Born in 1883, Sanger persevered in her belief in a woman's right to control her own fertility. Nearly single-handedly and against formidable odds she founded the birth-control movement in the United States, beginning in 1914 with her founding of the National Birth Control League. In 1953 she was named the first president of the International Planned Parenthood Federation.

Managing impulsivity. When students develop impulse control, they think before acting. Impulsive behavior can worsen conflict and inhibit effective problem solving.[5] Students can be taught to think before shouting out an answer, before beginning a project or task, and before arriving at conclusions with insufficient data. One of several reasons that teachers should usually insist on a show of student hands before a student is acknowledged to respond or question is to help students develop control over the impulsive behavior of shouting out in class.[6]

Listening with understanding and empathy. Some psychologists believe that the ability to listen to others, to empathize with and to understand their point of view, is one of the highest forms of intelligent behavior. Empathic behavior is considered an important skill for conflict resolution. Piaget refers to this behavior as *overcoming egocentrism.* In class meetings, brainstorming sessions, think tanks, town meetings, advisory councils, board meetings, and legislative bodies, people from various walks of life convene to share their thinking, to explore their ideas, and to broaden their perspectives by listening to the ideas and reactions of others.

Thinking interdependently. Real-world problem solving has become so complex that seldom can any person go it alone. Not all students come to school knowing how to work effectively in groups. They may exhibit competitiveness, narrow-mindedness, egocentrism, ethnocentrism, or criticism of others' values, emotions, and beliefs. Listening, consensus seeking, giving up an idea to work on someone else's, empathy, compassion, group leadership, cooperative learning, knowing how to support group efforts, altruism—those are behaviors indicative of intelligent human beings, and they can be learned by students at school and in the classroom.

Thinking flexibly. Sometimes referred to as *lateral thinking,* flexibility in thinking is the ability to approach a problem from a new angle, using a novel approach. With modeling by the teacher, students can develop this behavior as they learn to consider alternative points of view and to deal with several sources of information simultaneously.

---

[4]A. L. Costa, *The School as a Home for the Mind* (Palatine, IL: Skylight Publishing, 1991), pp. 20–31. See also D. Shein, "Intelligent Behavior, Art Costa, and the Role of the Library Media Specialist," *School Library Media Activities Monthly* 15(5):28–30 (January 1999). Costa has expanded the list to include "thinking and communicating with clarity and precision" and "remaining open to continuous learning." See A. L. Costa and B. Kallick, *Discovering and Exploring Habits of Mind,* Book 1 of *Habits of Mind: A Developmental Series* (Alexandria, VA: Association for Supervision and Curriculum Development, 2000). See also Armstrong's 12 qualities of genius—curiosity, playfulness, imagination, creativity, wonderment, wisdom, inventivenss, vitality, sensitivity, flexibility, humor, and joy—in T. Armstrong, *Awakening Genius in the Classroom* (Alexandria, VA: Association for Supervision and Curriculum Development, 1998), pp. 2–15.

[5]See, for example, M. Goos and P. Galbraith, "Do It This Way! Metacognitive Strategies in Collaborative Mathematics Problem Solving," *Educational Studies in Mathematics* 30(3):229–260 (April 1996).
[6]For further reading about the relation of impulse control to intelligence, see D. Goleman, *Emotional Intelligence: Why It Can Matter More Than IQ* (New York: Bantam Books, 1995); R. Brandt, "On Teaching Brains to Think: A Conversation with Robert Sylwester," *Educational Leadership* 57(7):72–75 (April 2000), p. 73; and D. Harrington-Lueker, "Emotional Intelligence," *High Strides* 9(4):1, 4–5 (March/April 1997).

Metacognition. Learning to plan, monitor, assess, and reflect on one's own thinking is another characteristic of intelligent behavior. Cooperative learning groups, journals, portfolio conferences, self-assessment, and thinking aloud in dyads, are strategies that can be used to help students develop this intelligent behavior. Thinking aloud is good modeling for your students, helping them to develop their own cognitive skills of thinking, learning, and reasoning.[7]

Striving for accuracy and communicating with precision. Teachers can observe students growing in this behavior when students take time to check over their work, review the procedures, refuse to draw conclusions with only limited data, and use concise and descriptive language.

Sense of humor. The positive effects of humor on the body's physiological functions are well established: a drop in the pulse rate, an increase of oxygen in the blood, the activation of antibodies that fight against harmful microorganisms, and the release of gamma interferon, a hormone that fights viruses and regulates cell growth. Humor liberates creativity and provides high-level thinking skills, such as anticipation, finding novel relationships, and visual imagery. The acquisition of a sense of humor follows a developmental sequence similar to that described by Piaget[8] and Kohlberg.[9] Initially, young children and immature youth may find humor in all the wrong things—human frailty, ethnic humor, sacrilegious riddles, ribald profanities. Later, creative youth thrive on finding incongruity and will demonstrate a whimsical frame of mind during problem solving.

Questioning and problem posing. Youth are usually full of questions, and, unless discouraged, they do ask them. We want students to be alert to, and recognize, discrepancies and phenomena in their environment and to freely inquire about their causes. In exemplary educational programs, students are encouraged to ask questions (see Chapter 7) and then from those questions to develop a problem-solving strategy to investigate their questions.

Drawing on knowledge and applying it to new situations. A major goal of formal education is for students to apply school-learned knowledge to real-life situations. To develop skills in drawing on past knowledge and applying that knowledge to new situations, students must be given the opportunity to practice doing that very thing. Problem recognition, problem solving, and project-based learning are ways of providing that opportunity.

Taking risks: venture forth and explore ideas beyond the usual zone of comfort. Such exploration, of course, must be done with thoughtfulness; it must not be done in ways that could put the student at risk psychologically or physically. Using the analogy of a turtle going nowhere until it sticks its neck out, teachers should model this behavior and provide opportunities for students to develop this intelligent behavior by using techniques such as brainstorming strategies, divergent-thinking questioning, think-pair-share, cooperative learning, inquiry, and project-based learning.

Using all the senses. As often as is appropriate and feasible, students should be encouraged to learn to use and develop all their sensory input channels to learn (i.e., verbal, visual, tactile, and kinesthetic).

Ingenuity, originality, insightfulness = Creativity. All students must be encouraged to do, and discouraged from saying "I can't." Students must be taught in such a way as to encourage intrinsic motivation rather than reliance on extrinsic sources. Teachers must be able to offer criticism so the student understands that the criticism is not a criticism of self. In exemplary programs, students learn the value of feedback. They learn the value of their own intuition, of guessing—they learn "I can."

Wonderment, inquisitiveness, curiosity, and the enjoyment of problem solving: A sense of efficacy as a thinker. Young children express wonderment, an expression that should never be stifled. Through effective teaching, adolescents can recapture that sense of wonderment as they are guided by an effective teacher into a feeling of "I can," and express a feeling of "I enjoy."

We should strive to help our own students develop these characteristics of intelligent behavior. In Chapter 3 you learned of specific teacher behaviors that facilitate this development. Now, let's review additional research findings that offer important considerations in the facilitation of student learning and intelligent behaving.

Direct Teaching for Thinking and Intelligent Behavior

The curriculum of any school includes the development of skills that are used in thinking, skills such as *classifying, comparing and contrasting, concluding, generalizing, inferring,* and others (see Figure 9.3). Because the academic achievement of students increases when they are taught thinking skills directly, many researchers and educators concur that direct instruction should be given to all students on how to think and to behave intelligently.[10] Several research perspectives have influenced today's interest in the direct teaching of thinking. The

---

[7]See, for example, J. W. Astington, "Theory of Mind Goes to School," *Educational Leadership* 56(3):46–48 (November 1998).

[8]J. Piaget, *The Psychology of Intelligence* (Totowa, NJ: Littlefield Adams, 1972).

[9]I. Kohlberg, *The Meaning and Measurement of Moral Development* (Worcester, MA: Clark University Press, 1981).

[10]See, for example, A. Whimbey, "Test Results From Teaching Thinking," in A. L. Costa (ed.) *Developing Minds: A Resource Book for Teaching Thinking* (Alexandria, VA: Association for Supervision and Curriculum Development, 1985), pp. 269–271.

Table 9.1 Levels of Inquiry[*]

	Level I (not true inquiry)	Level II	Level III
Problem Identification	By teacher or textbook	By teacher or textbook	By student
Process of Solving the Problem	Decided by teacher or text	Decided by student	Decided by student
Identification of Tentative Solution	Resolved by student	Resolved by student	Resolved by student

[*]The Levels of inquiry are adapted from "the three different levels of openness and permissiveness . . . for laboratory enquiry" by Joseph J. Schwab, *The Teaching of Science as Enquiry* (Cambridge, MA: Harvard University Press, 1962), p. 55.

cognitive view of intelligence asserts that intellectual ability is not fixed but can be developed. The *constructivist approach to learning* maintains that learners actively and independently construct knowledge by creating and coordinating relationships in their mental repertoire. The *social psychology view of classroom experience* focuses on the learner as an individual who is a member of various peer groups and a society. The *perspective of information processing* deals with the acquisition, elaboration, and management of information.[11]

Rather than assuming students have developed thinking skills, teachers should devote classroom time to teaching them directly. When teaching a thinking skill directly, the subject content becomes the vehicle for thinking. For example, a social studies lesson can teach students how to distinguish fact and opinion; a language arts lesson instructs students how to compare and analyze; a science lesson can teach students how to set up a problem for their inquiry.

Inquiry teaching and discovery learning are both useful tools for learning and for teaching thinking skills. For further insight and additional strategies, as well as for the many programs concerned with teaching thinking, see the resources in this chapter's footnotes and the list of readings at the end of the chapter.

INQUIRY TEACHING AND DISCOVERY LEARNING

Intrinsic to the effectiveness of both inquiry and discovery is the assumption that students would rather actively seek knowledge than receive it through traditional expository (i.e., information delivery) methods such as lectures, demonstrations, and textbook reading. Although inquiry and discovery are important teaching tools, there is sometimes confusion about exactly what inquiry teaching is and how it differs from discovery learning. The distinction should become clear as you study the following descriptions of these two important tools for teaching and learning.

Problem Solving

Perhaps a major reason why inquiry and discovery are sometimes confused is that in both, students are actively engaged in problem solving. Problem solving is the ability to define or describe a problem, determine the desired outcome, select possible solutions, choose strategics, test trial solutions, evaluate outcomes, and revise these steps where necessary.[12]

Inquiry vs. Discovery

Problem solving is *not* a teaching strategy but a high-order intellectual behavior that facilitates learning. What a teacher can and should do is provide opportunities for students to identify and tentatively solve problems. Experiences in inquiry and discovery can provide those opportunities. With the processes involved in inquiry and discovery, teachers can help students develop the skills necessary for effective problem solving. Two major differences between discovery and inquiry are (1) who identifies the problem and (2) the percentage of decisions that are made by the students. Table 9.1 shows three levels of inquiry, each level defined according to what the student does and decides.

It should be evident from Table 9.1 that what is called *Level I inquiry* is actually traditional, didactic, "cookbook" teaching, where both the problem and the process for resolving it are defined for the student. The student then works through the process to its inevitable resolution. If the process is well designed, the result is inevitable, because the student "discovers" what was intended by the writers of the program. This level is also called *guided inquiry* or *discovery*, because the students are carefully guided through the investigation to (the predicable) "discovery."

Level I is in reality a strategy within the *delivery mode*, the advantages of which were described in Chapter 6. Because Level I "inquiry" is highly manageable and the learning outcome is predictable; it is probably best for teaching basic concepts and principles. Students who never experience learning beyond Level I are missing an opportunity to engage their highest mental operations, and they seldom (or never) get

---

[11]B. Z. Presseisen, *Implementing Thinking in the School's Curriculum,* unpublished paper presented at the Third Annual Meeting of the International Association for Cognitive Education, Riverside, CA, on February 9, 1992.

[12]A. L. Costa (ed.), *Developing Minds: A Resource for Teaching Thinking* (Alexandria, VA: Association for Supervision and Curriculum Development, 1985), p. 312.

REAL-LIFE SCENARIO
Problem Solving and Decision Making in the Real World is an Integrated and Interdisciplinary Inquiry Activity

On any given day or specified time period, teachers and students can look at a problem or subject of study from the point of view of many separate disciplines. Such an interdisciplinary approach to some matter of concern has been adopted not only by educators but by other professionals as well. It is the mode of meaningful learning and real-life problem solving.

For example, consider the fact-finding and decision-making approach of public officials in the State of Colorado when confronted with the task of making decisions about projects proposed for watersheds in their state. While gathering information, the officials brought in Dave Rosgen, a state hydrologist. Rosgen led the officials into the field to demonstrate specific ways by which he helped control erosion and rehabilitate damaged streams. He took the officials to Wolf Creek, where they donned high waders. Rosgen led the group down the creek to examine various features of that complex natural stream. He pointed out evidence of the creek's past meanders, patterns that he had incorporated into his rehabilitation projects. In addition to listening to this scientist's point of view, the public officials listened to other experts to consider related economic and political issues before making final decisions about projects that had been proposed for watersheds in that state.

During interdisciplinary thematic units, students study a topic and its underlying ideas as well as related knowledge from various disciplines on an ongoing basis. The teacher, sometimes with the help of students and other teachers and adults, introduces experiences designed to ideas and skills from various disciplines, just as Rosgen introduced information from hydrology, to develop literacy skills through the unit. For instance, the teacher might stimulate communication skills through creative writing and other projects. Throughout the unit, the students are guided in exploring ideas related to different disciplines to integrate their knowledge.

---

to experience more motivating, real-life problem solving. Furthermore, those students may come away with the false notion that problem solving is a linear process, which it is not. As illustrated in Figure 9.2, true inquiry is cyclical rather than linear. For that reason, Level I is *not* true inquiry, because it is a linear process. Real-world problem solving is a cyclical rather than linear process. One enters the cycle whenever a discrepancy or problem is observed and recognized, and that can occur at any point in the cycle.

True Inquiry

By the time students are in middle school, they should be provided experiences for true inquiry, which begins with *Level II*, where students actually decide and design processes for their inquiry. In true inquiry there is an emphasis on the tentative nature of conclusions, which makes the activity more like real-life problem solving, where decisions are always subject to revision if and when new data so prescribe.

At *Level III* inquiry students recognize and identify the problem as well as decide the processes and reach a conclusion. In *project-centered teaching*, as has been discussed and described throughout this book, students are usually engaged at this level of inquiry. By the time students are in middle grades, Level III inquiry should be a major strategy for instruction, which is often the case in schools that use cross-age teaching and interdisciplinary thematic instruction. But, it is not easy; like most good teaching practices it is a lot of work. But also like good teaching, the intrinsic rewards make the effort worthwhile. As exclaimed by one teacher using interdisciplinary thematic instruction with student-centered inquiry, "I've never worked harder in my life, but I've never had this much fun, either."

The Critical Thinking Skills of Discovery and Inquiry

In true inquiry, students generate ideas and then design ways to test those ideas. The various processes used represent the many critical thinking skills. Some of those skills are concerned with generating and organizing data; others are concerned with building and using ideas. Figure 9.3 provides four main categories of these

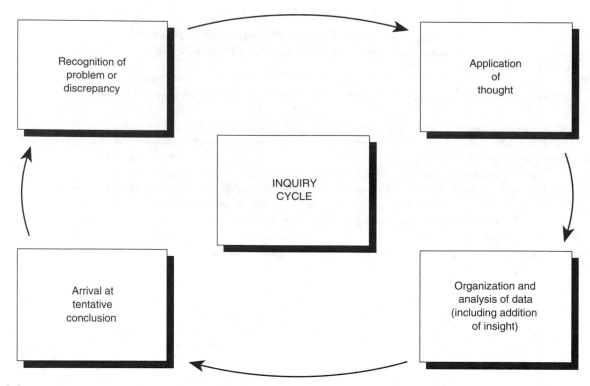

Figure 9.2
The inquiry cycle.

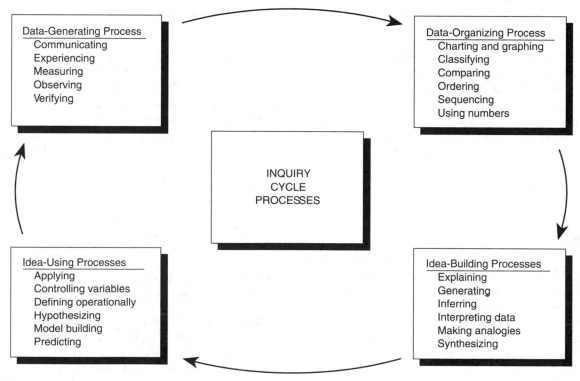

Figure 9.3
Inquiry cycle processes.

thinking processes and illustrates the place of each within the inquiry cycle.

Some processes in the cycle are discovery processes, and others are inquiry processes. Inquiry processes include the more complex mental operations (including all of those in the idea-using category). Project-centered teaching provides an avenue for doing that, as does problem-centered teaching.

Inquiry learning is a higher-level mental operation that introduces the concept of the discrepant event, something that establishes cognitive disequilibrium (using the element of surprise to challenge their prior notions) to help students develop skills in observing and being alert for discrepancies. Such a strategy provides opportunities for students to investigate their own ideas about explanations. Inquiry, like discovery, depends upon skill in problem solving; the difference between the two is in the amount of decision-making responsibility given to students. Experiences afforded by inquiry help students understand the importance of suspending judgment and also the tentativeness of answers and solutions. With those understandings, students eventually are better able to deal with life's ambiguities. When students are not provided these important educational experiences their education is incomplete.

One of the most effective ways of stimulating inquiry is to use materials that provoke students' interest. These materials should be presented in a nonthreatening, noncompetitive context, so students think and hypothesize freely. The teacher's role is to encourage students to form as many hypotheses as possible and then support their hypotheses with reasons. After the students suggest several ideas, the teacher should begin to move on to higher-order, more abstract questions that involve the development of generalizations and evaluations. True inquiry problems have a special advantage in that they can be used with almost any group of students. Members of a group approach the problem as an adventure in thinking and apply it to whatever background they can muster. Background experience may enrich a student's approach to the problem, but is not crucial to the use or understanding of the evidence presented to him or her. Locating a Colony, Figure 9.4, is a Level II inquiry. As a class, do the inquiry now.

INTEGRATING STRATEGIES FOR INTEGRATED LEARNING

In today's exemplary classrooms, instructional strategies are combined to establish the most effective teaching-learning experience. For example, in an integrated language arts program, teachers are interested in their students' speaking, reading, listening, thinking, study, and writing skills. These skills (and not textbooks)

form a holistic process that is the primary aspect of integrated language arts.

In the area of speaking skills, oral discourse (discussion) in the classroom has a growing research base that promotes methods of teaching and learning through oral language. These methods include cooperative learning, instructional scaffolding, and inquiry teaching.

In cooperative learning groups, students discuss and use language for learning that benefits both their content learning and skills in social interaction. Working in heterogeneous groups, students participate in their own learning and can extend their knowledge base and cultural awareness with students of different backgrounds. When students share information and ideas, they are completing difficult learning tasks, using divergent thinking and decision making, and developing their understanding of concepts. As issues are presented and responses are challenged, student thinking is clarified. Students assume the responsibility for planning within the group and for carrying out their assignments. When needed, the teacher models an activity with one group in front of the class, and when integrated with student questions, the modeling can become inquiry teaching. Activities can include any from a variety of heuristics (a heuristic is a tool used in solving a problem or understanding an idea), such as the following:

Brainstorming. Members generate ideas related to a key word and record them. Clustering or chunking, mapping, and the Venn diagram (all discussed in the following paragraphs) are variations on brainstorming.

Think-pair-share. Students are paired to discuss a concept that has been presented by the teacher. They share what they already know or have experienced about that concept, and then share that information with the rest of the class. This strategy is an excellent technique for preassessing and discovering students' prior notions.

Chunking or clustering. Groups of students apply mental organizers by clustering information into chunks for easier manipulation and remembering.

Memory strategies. The teacher and students model the use of acronyms, mnemonics, rhymes, or clustering of information into categories to promote learning. Sometimes, such as in memorizing the social security number, one must learn by rote information that is not connected to any prior knowledge. To do that it is helpful to break the information to be learned into smaller chunks, such as dividing the eight-digit social security number into smaller chunks of information (with, in this instance, each chunk separated by a hyphen). Learning by rote is also easier if one can connect that which is to be memorized to some prior knowledge. Strategies such as these are used to bridge the gap between rote learning and

Presentation of the Problem. In groups of three or four, students receive the following information.

Background. You (your group is considered as one person) are one of 120 passengers on the ship, the *Prince Charles.* You left England 12 weeks ago. You have experienced many hardships, including a stormy passage, limited rations, sickness, cold and damp weather, and hot, foul air below deck. Ten of your fellow immigrants to the New World, including three children, have died and been buried at sea. You are now anchored at an uncertain place, off the coast of the New World, which your captain believes to be somewhere north of the Virginia Grants. Seas are so rough and food so scarce that you and your fellow passengers have decided to settle here. A landing party has returned with a map they made of the area. You, as one of the elders, must decide at once where the settlement is to be located. The tradesmen want to settle along the river, which is deep, even though this seems to be the season of low water levels. Within ten months they expect deep-water ships from England with more colonists and merchants. Those within your group who are farmers say they must have fertile, workable land. The officer in charge of the landing party reported seeing a group of armed natives who fled when approached. He feels the settlement must be located so that it can be defended from the natives and from the sea.

Directions, step one: You (your group) are to select a site on the attached map that you feel is best suited for a colony. Your site must satisfy the different factions aboard the ship. A number of possible sites are already marked on the map (letters *A–G*). You may select one of these locations or use them as reference points to show the location of your colony. When your group has selected its site, list and explain the reasons for your choice. When each group has arrived at its tentative decision, these will be shared with the whole class.

Directions, step two: After each group has made its presentation and argument, a class debate is held about where the colony should be located.

Notes to teacher: For the debate, have a large map drawn on the writing board or on an overhead transparency, where each group's mark can be made for all to see and discuss. After each group has presented its argument for its location and against the others, we suggest that you then mark on the large map the two,

three, or more hypothetical locations (assuming that, as a class, there is no single favorite location yet). Then take a straw vote of the students, allowing each to vote on her own, independently, rather than as members of groups. At this time you can terminate the activity by saying that if the majority of students favor one location, then that, in fact, is the solution to the problem—that is, the colony is located wherever the majority of class members believe it should be. No sooner will that statement be made by you than someone will ask, "Are we correct?" or "What is the right answer?" They will ask such questions because, as students in school, they are used to solving problems that have right answers (Level I inquiry teaching). In real-world problems, however, there are no "right" answers, though some answers may seem better than others. It is the process of problem solving that is important. You want your students to develop confidence in their ability to solve problems and understand the tentativeness of "answers" to real-life problems.

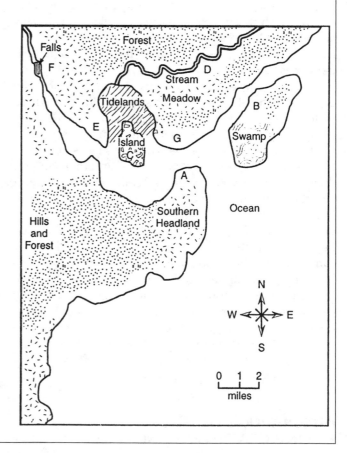

Figure 9.4
Locating a Colony: a Level II inquiry.
(*Source:* Adapted by permission from unpublished material provided by Jennifer Devine and Dennis Devine.)

240

meaningful learning and are known as *mnemonics*.[13] Sample mnemonics are:

- The notes on a treble staff are *FACE* for the space notes and *Empty Garbage Before Dad Flips (EGBDF)* for the line notes. The notes on the bass staff are *All Cows Eat Granola Bars* or *Grizzly Bears Don't Fly Airplanes (GBDFA)*.
- The order of the planets from the Sun are *My Very Educated Mother Just Served Us Nine Pizzas (Mercury, Venus, Earth, Mars, Jupiter, Saturn, Uranus, Neptune,* and *Pluto*—although, in reality, Pluto and Neptune alternate in this order because of their elliptical orbits).
- The names of the Great Lakes: HOMES for *Huron, Ontario, Michigan, Erie,* and *Superior.*
- Visual mnemonics are useful too, such as remembering that Italy is shaped in the form of a boot.

Comparing and contrasting. Similarities and differences between items are found and recorded.

Visual tools. A variety of terms for the visual tools useful for learning have been invented (some of which are synonymous) such as brainstorming web, mindmapping web, spider map, cluster, thinking map, cognitive map, semantic map, Venn diagram, visual scaffold, and graphic organizer. Visual tools are separated into three categories, according to purpose: (1) *brainstorming tools* (such as mind mapping, webbing, and clustering) for the purpose of developing one's knowledge and creativity; (2) *task-specific organizers* (such as life cycle diagrams used in biology, decision trees used in mathematics, and text structures in reading); and (3) *thinking maps* for encouraging cognitive development across disciplines.[14] It is the latter about which we are interested here.

Based on Ausubel's theory of meaningful learning,[15] thinking process mapping has been found useful for helping students in changing prior notions—their misconceptions, sometimes referred to as *naive views*. It can help students in their ability to organize and to represent their thoughts, as well as to help them connect new knowledge to their past experiences and precepts.[16]

Simply put, concepts can be thought of as classifications that attempt to organize the world of objects and events into a smaller number of categories. In everyday usage, the term *concept* means idea, as when someone says, "My concept of love is not the same as yours." Concepts embody a meaning that develops in complexity with experience and learning over time. For example, the concept of love that is held by a second grader is unlikely to be as complex as that held by a eleventh grader. Thinking process mapping is a graphical way of demonstrating the relationship between and among concepts.

Typically, a thinking map refers to a visual or graphic representation of concepts with bridges (connections) that show relationships. Figure 9.5 shows a partially complete thinking map in social studies, where students have made connections of concept relationships related to fruit farming and marketing. The general procedure for thinking process mapping is to have the students: (1) identify important concepts in materials being studied, often by circling those concepts; (2) rank order the concepts from the most general to the most specific; and (3) arrange the concepts on a sheet of paper, connect related ideas with lines, and define the connections between the related ideas.

Inferring. For instance, students assume the roles of people (real or fictional) and infer their motives, personalities, and thoughts.

Outlining. Each group completes an outline that contains some of the main ideas but with subtopics omitted.

Paraphrasing. In a brief summary, each student restates a short selection of what was read or heard.

Reciprocal teaching. In classroom dialogue, students take turns at generating questions, summarizing, clarifying, and predicting.[17]

Study strategies. Important strategies that should be taught explicitly include vocabulary expansion, reading and interpreting graphic information, locating resources, using advance organizers, adjusting one's reading rate, and skimming, scanning, and study reading.[18]

Textbook study strategies. Students use the *SQ4R* or related study strategies (see Chapter 5).

Vee mapping. A kind of road map is completed by students, as they learn, showing the route they follow from prior knowledge to new and future knowledge.

[13]See, for example, M. A. Mastropieri et al., "Using Mnemonic Strategies to Teach Information about U.S. Presidents: A Classroom-Based Investigation," *Learning Disability Quarterly* 20(1):13–21 (Winter 1997), and J. G. van Hell and A. C. Mahn, "Keyword Mnemonics Versus Rote Rehearsal: Learning Concrete and Abstract Foreign Words by Experienced and Inexperienced Learners," *Language Learning* 47(3):507–546 (September 1997).

[14]D. Hyerle, *Visual Tools for Constructing Knowledge* (Alexandria, VA: Association for Supervision and Curriculum Development, 1996).

[15]D. P. Ausubel, *The Psychology of Meaningful Learning* (New York: Grune & Stratton, 1963).

[16]About thinking process mapping, see J. D. Novak, "Concept Maps and Vee Diagrams: Two Metacognitive Tools to Facilitate Meaningful Learning," *Instructional Science* 19(1):29–52 (1990); J. D. Novak and B. D. Gowin, *Learning How to Learn* (Cambridge, England: Cambridge

University Press, 1984); and, E. Plotnick, *Concept Mapping: A Graphical System for Understanding the Relationship Between Concepts.* (Syracuse, NY: ERIC Clearinghouse on Information and Technology ED407938, 1997.)

[17]See C. J. Carter, "Why Reciprocal Teaching?" *Educational Leadership* 54(6):64–68 (March 1997).

[18]J. S. Choate and T. A. Rakes, *Inclusive Instruction for Struggling Readers,* Fastback 434 (Bloomington, IN: Phi Delta Kappa Educational Foundation, 1998).

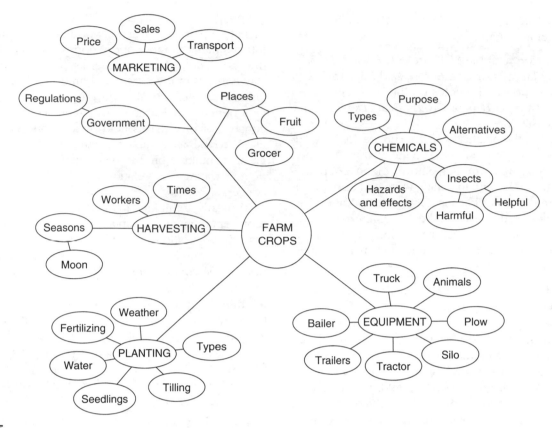

Figure 9.5

Venn diagramming. This is a technique for comparing two concepts or, for example, two stories, to show similarities and differences. Using stories as an example, a student is asked to draw two circles that intersect and to mark the circles one and two and the area where they intersect three. In circle one, the student lists characteristics of one story, and in circle two she or he lists the characteristics of the second story. In the area of the intersection, marked three, the student lists characteristics common to both stories.

Visual learning log (VLL). This is another kind of road map completed by students showing the route they follow from prior knowledge to new and future knowledge, except that the VLL consists of pictograms (free-form drawings) that each student makes and that are maintained in a journal.

LEARNING BY EDUCATIONAL GAMES

Devices classified as educational games include a wide variety of learning activities, such as simulations, role-play and sociodrama activities, mind games, board games, computer games, and sporting games, all of which provide valuable learning experiences for partic-

ipants. That is, they are experiences that tend to involve several senses and several learning modalities, tend to engage higher-order thinking skills, and tend to be quite effective as learning tools.

Of all the arts, drama involves the learner-participant most fully—intellectually, emotionally, physically, verbally, and socially. Interactive drama, which is role-playing, a simplified form of drama, is a method by which students can become involved with literature. Studies show that students' comprehension increases and they are highly motivated to read if they are involved in analyzing and actively responding to the characters, plot, and setting of the story being read.[19] For example, to help his students see how the world was and how it might have been different, a social science teacher at Pleasant Valley High School (Chico, CA) sets up a role-play for his students where they are to mediate a Texas land dispute between native Americans and white settlers. Obtained from the Internet, primary source documents present the issue from

---

[19]R. Coney and S. Kanel, "Opening the World of Literature to Children through Interactive Drama Experiences," paper presented at the Annual International Conference and Exhibition of the Association for Childhood Education (Portland, OR, April 9–12, 1997).

an Native American perspective, a white perspective, and a 19th-century Quaker perspective.[20]

Simulations, a more complex form of drama, serve many of the developmental needs of adolescents. They provide for interaction with peers and allow students of differences to work together on a common project. They engage students in physical activity and give them the opportunity to try out different roles, which helps them to better understand themselves. Role-play simulations can provide concrete experiences that help students understand complex concepts and issues, and they provide opportunities for exploring values and developing skill in decision-making.

Educational games can play an integral role in interdisciplinary teaching and serve as valuable resources for enriching the effectiveness of students' learning. As with any other instructional strategy, the use of games should follow a clear educational purpose, have a careful plan, and be congruent with the instructional objectives.

Classification of Educational Games

What are educational games? Seven types of games fall under the general heading of "educational games." Table 9.2 shows the seven types, with characteristics and examples of each. Certain types have greater educational value than do others. Games that do not empha-

size the element of competition—that are not "contest"—are particularly recommended for use in the academic classroom (types 1, 3, and 5 in Table 9.2).

Purposes of Educational Games

Games can be powerful tools for teaching and learning. A game can have one to several of the following purposes: (a) add variety and change of pace, (b) assess student learning, (c) enhance student self-esteem, (d) motivate students, (e) offer a break from the usual rigors of learning, (f) provide learning about real-life issues through simulation and role-playing, (g) provide learning through tactile and kinesthetic modalities, (h) provide problem-solving situations and experiences, (i) provide skill development and motivation through computer usage, (j) provide skill development in inductive thinking, (k) provide skill development in verbal communication and debate, (l) reinforce convergent thinking, (m) review and reinforce subject matter learning, (n) encourage learning through peer interaction, (o) stimulate critical thinking, (p) stimulate deductive thinking, (q) stimulate divergent and creative thinking, and (r) teach both content and process.

Sources of Educational Games

Sources for useful educational games include professional journals (see Figure 9.6) and the Internet. Sources of commercially available educational games for use in teaching are shown in Figure 9.7. Now do Exercise 9.2.

---

[20]B. Tally and M. Burns, "Mining Gold in a Mountain of Online Resources," *Harvard Education Letter* 16(2):6–7 (March/April 2000).

Table 9.2 Classification of Educational Games

Type	Characteristics	Examples
1. Pure game*	Fun	*Ungame, New Games*
2. Pure contest	Stimulates competition; built-in inefficiency[‡]	Political contests (e.g., U.S. presidential race)
3. Pure simulation*	Models reality	Toddler play
4. Contest/game	Stimulates competition; fun; built-in inefficiency	Gold; bowling; *Trivial Pursuit*
5. Simulation/game*	Models reality; fun	*SIMCITY; Our Town's Planning Commission Meeting*[§]
6. Contest/simulation	Stimulates competition; models reality; built-in inefficiency	Boxcar Derby of Akron, OH
7. Simulation/game/contest	Models reality; fun; stimulates competition; built-in inefficiency	*Monopoly, Life, Careers*

*These game types do not emphasize competition and thus are particularly recommended for use in the classroom as learning tools.
[‡] This means that rules for accomplishing the game objective make accomplishment of that objective less than efficient. For example, in **golf** the objective is to get the ball into the hole with the least amount of effort, but to do that, one has to take a peculiarly shaped stick (the club) and hit the ball, find it, and hit it again, continuing that sequence until the ball is in the hole. Yet, common sense tells us that the best way to get the ball into the hole with the least amount of effort would be to simply pick up the ball and place it by hand into the hole.
[§] See J. V. Vort, "Our Town's Planning Commission Meeting," *Journal of Geography* 96(4):183–190 (July–August 1997).

Figure 9.6

Sample professional journals with educational games.

- J. Bassett, "The Pullman Strike of 1894," *OAH Magazine of History* 11(2):34–41 (Winter 1997). Role-play simulation.
- D. Bogan and D. Wood, "Simulating Sun, Moon, and Earth Patterns," *Science Scope* 21(2):46, 48 (October 1997). Role-play simulation.
- C. Collyer, "Winter Secrets: An Instant Lesson Plan," *Pathways: The Ontario Journal of Outdoor Education* 9(2):18–20 (April 1997). Instructions for two games about predator-prey relationships.
- S. A. Farin, "Acting Atoms," *Science Scope* 21(3):46 (November/December 1997). Role-play.
- J. Gorman, "Strategy Games: Treasures from Ancient Times," *Mathematics Teaching in the Middle School* 3(2):110–116 (October 1997). Games for integrating history and mathematics.
- S. Hightshoe, "Sifting Through the Sands of Time: A Simulated Archaeological Special Feature," *Social Studies and the Young Learner* 9(3):28–30 (January/February, 1997).
- M. J. Howle, "Play-Party Games in the Modern Classroom," *Music Educators Journal* 83(5):24–28 (March 1997). Introduces games that were popular on the 19th-century American frontier.
- T. Levy, "The Amistad Incident: A Classroom Reenactment," *Social Education* 59(5):303–308 (September 1995).
- T. M. McCann, "A Pioneer Simulation for Writing and for the Study of Literature," *English Journal* 85(3):62–67 (March 1996).
- H. Morris, "Universal Games from A to Z," *Mathematics in School* 26(4):35–40 (September 1997). See also F. Tapson, "Mathematical Games," pp. 2–6 of the same issue.
- K. D. Owens et al., "Playing to Learn: Science Games in the Classroom," *Science Scope* 20(5):31–33 (February 1997).

Figure 9.7

Sources of educational games.

- Ampersand Press, 750 Lake St., Port Townsend, WA 98368. (800) 624–4263
- Aristoplay, 450 S. Wagner Rd., Ann Arbor, MI 48103. (800) GR8-GAME
- Carolina Biological Supply Company, 2700 York Road, Burlington, NC 27215. (800) 334–5551
- Creative Teaching Associates, P.O. Box 7766, Fresno, CA 93747. (800) 767–4282
- Dawn Publications, 14618 Tyler-Foote Rd., Nevada City, CA 95959. (800) 545–7475
- Delta Educational, 5 Hudson Park Dr., PO Box 915, Hudson, NH 03051. (800) 258–1302
- Harcourt Brace School Publishers, 6277 Sea Harbor Dr., Orlando, FL 32887. (800) 346–8648
- Higher-Order Thinking Company, 1733 N.E. Patterson Dr., Lee's Summit, MO 64086. (816) 524–2701.
- Latz Chance Games, P.O. Box 72308, Marietta, GA 30007–2308. (888) LCH-GAME
- Novostar Designs, 317 S. Main St., P.O. Box 1328, Burlington, NC 27216–1328. (800) 659–3197
- Optical Data School Media, 512 Means St., NW, Atlanta, GA 30318. (800) 524–2481
- Other Worlds Educational Enterprises, P.O. Box 6193, Woodland Park, CO 80866–6193. (719) 687–3840
- Summit Learning, P.O. Box 493, Fort Collins, CO 80522. (800) 777–8817
- Teacher Created Materials, 6421 Industry Way, Westminster, CA 92683. (800) 662–4321
- Young Naturalist Company, 1900 N. Main St., Newton, KS 67114. (316) 283–9108

EXERCISE 9.2

Developing a Lesson Using Level II Inquiry, Thinking Skill
Development, a Demonstration, or an Interactive
Lecture—Micro Peer Teaching II

Instructions: The purpose of this exercise is to provide the opportunity for you to create a brief lesson (about 20 minutes of instructional time but to be specified by your instructor) designed for a specific grade level and subject and to try it out on your peers for their feedback in an informal (i.e., nongraded) micro peer teaching demonstration.

Divide your class into four groups. The task of members of each group is to prepare lessons (individually) that fall into one of the four categories: Level II inquiry; thinking level; demonstration; interactive lecture. Schedule class presentations so that each class member has the opportunity to present her or his lesson and to obtain feedback from class members about it. For feedback, class members who are the "teacher's" audience can complete the assessment rubric shown after this exercise (by circling one of the three choices for each of the 10 categories) and give their completed form to the teacher for use in analysis and self-assessment. Before your class starts this exercise you may want to review the scoring rubric and make modifications to it that the class agrees on.

To structure your lesson plan, use one of the sample lesson plan formats presented in Chapter 6; however, each lesson should be centered around one major theme or concept and be planned for about 20 minutes of instructional time.

Group 1: Develop a level II inquiry lesson.

Group 2: Develop a lesson designed to raise the level of student thinking.

Group 3: Develop a lesson that involves a demonstration.

Group 4: Develop a lesson that is an interactive lecture.

PEER AND SELF-ASSESSMENT RUBRIC FOR USE WITH EXERCISE 9.2

For: _____   Group: _____

	1	0.5	0
1. Lesson beginning Comment:	effective	less effective	not effective
2. Sequencing Comment:	effective	less effective	rambling
3. Pacing of lesson Comment:	effective	less effective	too slow or too fast
4. Audience involvement Comment:	effective	less effective	none
5. Motivators (e.g., analogies, verbal cues, humor, visual cues, sensory cues) Comment:	effective	less effective,	not apparent
6. Content of lesson Comment:	well chosen	interesting	boring or inappropriate
7. Voice of teacher Comment:	stimulating	minor problem	major problems
8. Vocabulary used Comment:	well chosen	appropriate	inappropriate
9. Eye contact Comment:	excellent	average	problems
10. Closure Comment:	effective	less effective	unclear or none

Other Comments:

SUMMARY

Central to your selection of instructional strategies should be those strategies that encourage students to become independent thinkers and skilled learners who can help in the planning, structuring, regulating, and assessing of their own learning and learning activities.

Important to helping students construct their understandings are the cognitive tools that are available for their use. There is a large variety of useful and effective aids, media, and resources from which to draw as you plan your instructional experiences—the topic of the next and final chapter of Part III.

ADDITIONAL EXERCISES

See the companion website http://www.prenhall.com/ kellough for the following exercises related to the content of this chapter:

- A Study of Inquiry and Strategy Integration
- What Must Be Memorized in My Discipline

QUESTIONS FOR CLASS DISCUSSION

1. Many cognitive researchers agree that students should spend more time actively using knowledge to solve problems and less time reading introductory material and listening to teachers. Describe the meaning of this statement and how you feel about it with respect to your decision to become a secondary school teacher.
2. Explain why you would or would not like to teach by inquiry (Level II or III).
3. Explain the meaning of integrating strategies for integrated learning.
4. Are there any cautions that teachers need to be aware of when using games for teaching? If there are, describe them.
5. Explain specific ways you can help students develop their skills in thinking and learning. Explain how you will determine that students have raised their skill level in thinking and learning.
6. Select one of the characteristics of intelligent behavior and (for a grade level of your choice and time limit as decided by your class) write a lesson plan for helping students develop that behavior. Share or teach your lesson to others in your class for their analysis and suggestions.
7. Select one of the Reflective Thoughts from the opening of Part III that is specifically related to the content of this chapter, research it, and write a one-page essay explaining why you agree or disagree with the thought. Share your essay with members of your class for their thoughts.
8. Describe any prior concepts you held that changed as a result of your experiences with this chapter. Describe the changes.
9. From your current observations and field work as related to this teacher preparation program, clearly identify one specific example of educational practice that seems contradictory to exemplary practice or theory as presented in this chapter. Present your explanation for the discrepancy.
10. Do you have questions generated by the content of this chapter? If you do, list them along with ways answers might be found.

FOR FURTHER READING

Abdullah, M. H. *Problem-Based Learning In Language Instruction: A Constructivist Model.* (Bloomington, IN: ED423550, ERIC Clearinghouse on Reading, English, and Communication, 1998).

Allsopp, D. H. "Using Modeling, Manipulatives, and Mnemonics with Eighth-Grade Math Students." *Teaching Exceptional Children* 32(2):74–81 (November/December 1999).

Bellanca, J. "Teaching for Intelligence: In Search of Best Practices." *Phi Delta Kappan* 79(9):658–660 (May 1998).

Bockler, D. "Let's Play Doctor: Medical Rounds in Ancient Greece." *American Biology Teacher* 60(2):106–111 (February 1998).

Boston, J. A. "Unequal Resources: A Group Simulation." *Social Studies Review* 37(2):33–37 (Spring/Summer 1998).

Boston, J. A. "Using Simulations." *Social Studies Review* 37(2):31–32 (Spring/Summer 1998).

Callison, D. "Inquiry." *School Library Media Activities Monthly* 15(6):38–42 (February 1999).

Clemens-Walatka, B. "Amusement Park Inquiry." *Science Teacher* 65(1):20–23 (January 1998).

Collom, J. "Illot-Mollo and Other Games." *Teachers & Writers* 30(5):12–13 (May/June 1999).

Como, R. M., and O'Connor, J. S. "History on Trial: The Case of Columbus." *OAH Magazine of History* 12(2):45–48 (Winter 1998).

Eflin, J. C., and Eflin, J. T. "Thinking Critically about Global Environmental Issues." *Journal of Geography* 98(2):68–78 (March/April 1999).

Ford, B. "Critically Evaluating Scientific Claims in the Popular Press." *American Biology Teacher* 60(3):174–180 (March 1998).

Foster, S. J., and Padgett, C. S. "Authentic Historical Inquiry in the Social Studies Classroom." *Clearing House* 72(6):357–363 (July 1999).

Hannel, G. I., and Hannel, L. "The Seven Steps to Critical Thinking: A Practical Application of Critical Thinking Skills." *NASSP* (National Association of Secondary School Principals) *Bulletin* 82(598):87–93 (May 1998).

Harris, B., Kohlmeier, K., and Kiel, R. D. *Crime Scene Investigation.* Englewood, CO: Teacher Ideas Press, 1999.

Jongsma, K. "Vocabulary and Comprehension Strategy Development." *Reading Teacher* 53(4):310–312 (December 1999/January 2000).

Kwon, Y-J, and Lawson, A. E. "Linking Brain Growth with the Development of Scientific Reasoning Ability and Conceptual Change during Adolescence." *Journal of Research in Science Teaching* 37(1):44–62 (January 2000).

Martino-Brewster, G. "Reversing the Negative." *Voices from the Middle* 6(3):11–14 (March 1999).

Marzano, R. J., Pickering, D. J., and Pollock, J. E. *Classroom Instruction that Works: Research-Based Strategies for Increasing Student Achievement.* Alexandria, VA: Association for Supervision and Curriculum Development, 2001.

Mayer, R. H. "Two Actors in Search of a Story: Using Primary Documents to Raise the Dead and Improve History Instruction." *OAH Magazine of History* 13(3):66–72 (Spring 1999).

Novak, J. D. *Learning, Creating, and Using Knowledge: Concept Maps as Facilitative Tools in Schools and Corporations.* Mahwah, NJ: Lawrence Erlbaum, 1998.

O'Reilly, K. "What Would You Do? Constructing Decision-Making Guidelines Through Historical Problems." *Social Education* 62(1):46–49 (January 1998).

Presseisen, B. Z. (ed.). *Teaching for Intelligence: A Collection of Articles.* Arlington Heights, IL: Skylight, 1999.

Quinn, R. J., and Wiest, L. R. "Exploring Probability through an Evens-Odds Dice Game." *Mathematics Teaching in the Middle School* 4(6):358–362 (March 1999).

Rulf, B. "A Geometric Puzzle That Leads to Fibonacci Sequences." *Mathematics Teacher* 91(1):21–23 (January 1998).

Schug, T. "Teaching DNA Fingerprinting using a Hands-on Simulation." *American Biology Teacher* 60(1):38–41 (January 1998).

Shiveley, J. M., and VanFossen, P. J. "Critical Thinking and the Internet: Opportunities for the Social Studies Classroom." *Social Studies* 90(1):42–46 (January/February 1999).

Sutman, F. X. "We Need a Better Understanding of Inquiry in Instruction." *Harvard Education Letter* 16(5):8 (September/October 2000).

Sweeney, E. S., and Quinn, R. J. "Concentration: Connecting Fractions, Decimals, and Percents." *Mathematics Teaching in the Middle School* 5(5):324-328 (January 2000).

10

Using Media and Other Instructional Aids and Resources

Important to helping students construct their understandings are the cognitive tools that are available for their use. You will be pleased to know that there is a large variety of useful and effective media, aids, and resources from which to draw as you plan your instructional experiences. On the other hand, you could also become overwhelmed by the sheer quantity of different materials available—textbooks, supplementary texts, pamphlets, anthologies, paperbacks, encyclopedias, tests, programmed instructional systems, dictionaries, reference books, classroom periodicals, newspapers, films, records and cassettes, computer software, transparencies, realia, games, film-

strips, audio- and videotapes, slides, globes, manipulatives, CD-ROMs, DVDs, and graphics. You could spend a great deal of time reviewing, sorting, selecting, and practicing with the materials and tools for your use. Although nobody can make the job easier for you, information in this chapter may expedite the process.

Specifically, upon completion of this chapter you should be able to:

1. Demonstrate an awareness of electronic media available for teaching your subject field, how they can be evaluated and used, and how and where they can be obtained.

2. Demonstrate an awareness of the variety of materials and resources for use in your teaching.
3. Demonstrate an understanding about using community resources, speakers, and field trips.
4. Demonstrate competency in using standard classroom tools for teaching.
5. Demonstrate knowledge of copyright laws for using printed and media materials for teaching.

PRINTED MATERIALS, VISUAL DISPLAYS, AND THE INTERNET

Historically, of all the materials available for instruction, the printed textbook has had, and still has, the most influence on teaching and learning. In addition to the student textbook and perhaps an accompanying workbook, there is a vast array of other printed materials available for use in teaching, many of which are available without cost. Printed materials include books, workbooks, pamphlets, magazines, brochures, newspapers, professional journals, periodicals, and duplicated materials including those materials copied from Internet sources.

In reviewing printed materials, factors to be alert for include: (a) appropriateness of the material in both content and reading level; (b) articles in newspapers, magazines, and periodicals, related to the content that your students will be studying, or to the skills they will be learning; (c) assorted workbooks available from tradebook publishers that emphasize thinking and problem solving rather than rote memorization—with an assortment of workbooks you can have students working on similar but different assignments depending upon their interests and abilities—an example of multilevel teaching; (d) pamphlets, brochures, and other duplicated materials that students can read for specific information and viewpoints about particular topics; and (e) inexpensive paperback books that would provide multiple book readings for your class and that make it possible for students to read primary sources.

Sources of Free and Inexpensive Printed Materials

For free and inexpensive printed materials, look for sources in your college or university, or public library, in the resource center at a local school district, and through connections on the Internet (see Figure 10.1). When considering using materials that you have obtained free or inexpensively, you will want to assure that the materials are appropriate for use with your students, and that they are free of bias or an unwanted message. The National Education Association (NEA) has published guidelines for teachers to consider before purchasing or using commercial materials; for a free copy,

- Educators Progress Service, Inc., 214 Center Street, Randolph, WI 53956. (414) 326–3126. *Educator's Guide to Free Materials; Educator's Guide to Free Teaching Aids.*
- *Freebies: The Magazine with Something for Nothing.* PO Box 5025, Carpenteria, CA 93014–5025.
- *Video Placement Worldwide (VPW).* Source of free, sponsored educational videos and print materials on the Internet at http://www.vpw.com.

Figure 10.1
Resources for free and inexpensive printed materials.

contact NEA communications, 1201 16th Street, NW, Washington, DC 20036; phone (202) 822–7200.

The Internet

Originating from a Department of Defense (DOD) project in 1969 (called ARPAnet, from the DOD's Advanced Research Projects Agency, ARPA) to establish a computer network of military researchers, its successor, the federally funded Internet, has become an enormous, steadily expanding, global system of connected computer networks. Also known as the *Net,* the *Information Superhighway,* and *cyberspace,* the Internet provides literally millions of resources to explore, with thousands more added daily. You can surf the Internet and find many sources about how to use it, and you can walk into most any bookstore and find hundreds of recent titles, most of which give their authors' favorite websites on the Internet. (*Note: Website* refers to a location on the World Wide Web, which is, in turn, a component or subset of the network of computers called the Internet.) However, new technologies are steadily emerging and the Internet changes every day, with some sites and resources disappearing or not kept current, others having changed their location and undergone reconstruction, and new ones appearing; it would be superfluous for us in this book, which will be around for several years, to emphasize too strongly sites that we personally have viewed and can recommend as teacher resources. Nevertheless, Figure 10.2 includes available Internet resources that we have recently surfed and can recommend. Other sites have been mentioned in the text throughout this book, still others are listed in Figures 1.9 and 8.4 of Chapters 1 and 8 respectively. Perhaps you have found others that you can share with your classmates.

Cautions and Guidelines for Using the Internet

If you have yet to learn to use the Internet, we shall leave the mechanics of that to the many resources available to you, including the experts that can be found among your peers, on your college or university staff,

- *Electronic Reference Formats Recommended by the American Psychological Association* http://www.apa.org/journals/webref.html
- *ERIC Documents Online* http://ericir.syr.edu
- *Hewlett Packard E-Mail Mentor Program* http://www.telementor.org
- *Interactive Frog Dissection* http://teach.virginia.edu/go/frog
- *Learn the 'Net* http://www.learnthenet.com
- *Mathematics Archives* http://archives.math.utk.edu/
- *MLA-Style Citations of Electronic Sources* http://www.columbia.edu/cu/cup/cgos/idx_basic.html
- *National Archives and Records Administration* http://www.nara.gov
- *National Education Association (NEA)* http://www.nea.org/resources/refs.html
- *National Geographic Map Machine* http://www.nationalgeographic.com
- *School Match* http://schoolmatch.com
- *School Page* http://www.theschoolpage.com
- *Science Stuff* http://www.sciencestuff.com
- *Telementoring Young Women in Science, Engineering, and Computing* http://www.edc.org/CCT/telementoring
- *Teacher's Network* http://www.teachnet.org. A teacher's exchange
- *United States Copyright Office* http://lcweb.loc.gov/copyright
- *WWW4Teachers* http://4teachers.org/home/index.shtml

Figure 10.2
Additional Internet sites: materials and technology.

and among members of any public school faculty. The remaining pages of this section address the "how" of using the Internet from an academic perspective. Let's begin with the fictitious although feasible Teaching Scenario: Natural Disasters.

TEACHING SCENARIO
Natural Disasters

Let us suppose that the students from your "house" have been working nearly all year on an interdisciplinary thematic unit titled "Surviving Natural Disasters". As culmination to their study they published a document titled *Natural Disaster Preparation and Survival Guide for (name of their community)* and proudly distributed the guide to their parents and members of the community.

Long before preparing the guide, however, the students had to do research. To learn about the history of various kinds of natural disasters that had occurred or might occur locally and about the sorts of preparations a community should take for each kind of disaster, the students searched sources on the Internet, such as federal documents, scientific articles, and articles from newspapers around the world where natural disasters had occurred. They also searched in the local library and the local newspaper's archives to learn of floods, tornadoes, and fires that had occurred during the past 200 years. Much to their surprise, they also learned that

their community is located very near the New Madrid Fault and did, in fact, experience a serious earthquake in 1811, although none since. As a result of that earthquake, two nearby towns completely disappeared; the Mississippi River reportedly flowed in reverse, and its course changed and even caused the formation of a new lake.

From published and copyrighted sources, including websites, the students found many useful photographs, graphics, and articles, and they included those in whole or in part in their survival guide. They did so without obtaining permission from the original copyright holders or even citing those sources.

You and the other members of your teaching team and other people were so impressed with the students' work that students were encouraged to offer the document for publication on the school's website. In addition, the document was received with so much acclaim that the students decided to place it for sale in the local library and retail outlets. This would help defray the original cost of duplication and enable them to continue the supply of guides.

To the "natural disasters" scenario, there is both a desirable aspect and a not-so-desirable aspect. It was good that the students were able to use a modern technological tool (the Internet) to research a variety of sources, including many primary ones. But when they published their document on the Internet and when they made copies of their guide to be sold, they did so without permission from original copyright holders, and thus were infringing copyright law. Although it would take an attorney to say for sure, with this scenario it is probable that the students, teacher, school, and the school district would be liable. As is true for other documents (such as published photos, graphics, and text), unless there is a clear statement that materials taken from the Internet are public domain, it is best to assume that they are copyrighted and should not be republished for profit or on another website.

There is such a proliferation of information today, from both printed materials and from information on the Internet, that except for the obvious reliable sites such as the *New York Times* and the Library of Congress, how can a person determine the validity and currency of a particular piece of information? When searching for useful and reliable information on a particular topic, how can one be protected from wasting valuable time sifting through all the information? People need to know that just because information is found on a printed page or is published on the Internet doesn't necessarily mean that the information is accurate or current. Using a checklist, such as found on the Internet at http://www.infopeople.org/bkmk/select.html or at http://lib.nmsu.edu/instruction/eval.html, and provided with examples of materials that meet and do not meet the criteria of the checklist, students can learn how to assess materials and information found on the Internet.

Teaching all students how to access and assess websites adds to their repertoire of skills for lifelong learning. Consider allowing each student or teams of students to become experts on specific sites during particular units of study. It might be useful to start a chronicle of student-recorded log entries about particular websites to provide comprehensive, long-term data about those sites. Such data would be useful to share with students of other schools around the world.

When students use information from the Internet, require that they print copies of sources of citations and materials so you can check for accuracy. These copies may be maintained in their portfolios.

Student work published on the Internet should be considered intellectual material and protected from plagiarism by others. Speaking of plagiarism, you may be interested to know that the prevention of plagiarism by students of materials found on the Internet is now a service available to teachers by several Internet providers. See, for example, http://plagiarism.org and http://www.canexus.com.[1]

Most school districts post a copyright notice on their home page. Usually someone at the school or from the district office is assigned to supervise the school website to see that district and school policy and legal requirements are observed.

Professional Journals and Periodicals

Figure 10.3 lists examples of the many professional periodicals and journals that can provide useful teaching ideas and website information and that carry information about instructional materials and how to get them. Some of these may be in your university or college library and accessible through Internet sources. Check there for these and other titles of interest to you.

The ERIC Information Network

The Educational Resources Information Center (ERIC) system, established by the United States Office of Education, is a widely used network providing access to information and research in education. Selected clearinghouses and their addresses are shown in Figure 10.4.

Copying Printed Materials

As a teacher you must be familiar with the laws about the use of copyrighted materials, printed and non-printed, including those obtained from sources on the Internet. Remember that although there is no notice on many web pages, the material is still copyrighted. Copyright law protects original material; that is just as true for the intellectual property created by a minor as it is for that of an adult.

Although space limitations preclude full inclusion in this book of United States legal guidelines, your local school district should be able to provide a copy of current district policies for compliance with copyright laws. District policies should include guidelines for teachers and students in publishing materials on the Internet. If no district guidelines are available, when using printed materials adhere to the guidelines shown in Figure 10.5.[2]

When preparing to make a copy, you must find out whether law under the category of "permitted use" permits the copying. If not allowed under "permitted use," then you must obtain from the holder of the copyright written permission to reproduce the material. If the address of the source is not given on the material, addresses may be obtained from various references, such as *Literary Market Place, Audio-Visual Market Place,* and *Ulrich's International Periodical's Directory.*

---

[1]See also L. Renard, "Cut and Paste 101: Plagiarism and the Net," *Educational Leadership* 57(4):38–42 (December 1999/January 2000).

[2]See also the *Copyright and Fair Use* website of Stanford University, at http://fairuse.stanford.edu/.

The American Biology Teacher	The Middle School Journal
American Educational Research Quarterly	Modern Language Journal
The American Music Teacher	Music Educator's Journal
American Teacher	NEA Today
The Art Teacher	The Negro Educational Review
The Computing Teacher	The New Advocate
The Earth Scientist	OAH Magazine of History
Educational Leadership	Phi Delta Kappan
English Journal	Physical Education
English Language Teaching Journal	The Physics Teacher
Hispania	The Reading Teacher
The History Teacher	Reading Today
Journal of Business Education	School Arts
Journal of Chemical Education	School Library Journal
Journal of Economic Education	The School Musician
Journal of Geography	School Science and Mathematics
Journal of Home Economics	School Shop
Journal of Learning Disabilities	Science
Journal of the National Association of Bilingual Educators	Science Activities
	Science Scope
Journal of Physical Education and Recreation	Social Education
Journal of Reading	The Science Teacher
Journal of Teaching in Physical Education	The Social Studies
Language Arts	Social Studies Review
Language Learning	Teacher Magazine
Learning	TESOL Quarterly
The Mathematics Teacher	Theory and Research in Social Education
Mathematics Teaching in the Middle School	Voices From the Middle

Figure 10.3
Selected professional journals and periodicals of interest to secondary school teachers.

- *Assessment and Evaluation.* University of Maryland, College Park, Department of Measurement, Statistics, and Evaluation, 1129 Shriver Laboratory, College Park, MD 20742. URL: http://ericae.net/
- *Counseling and Student Services.* University of North Carolina at Greensboro, School of Education, 201 Ferguson Building, P.O. Box 26171, Greensboro, NC 27402-6171. URL: http://ericcass.uncg.edu/
- *Disabilities and Gifted Education.* The Council for Exceptional Children (CEC), 1920 Association Drive, Reston, VA 20191-1589. URL: http://ericec.org/
- *Information & Technology.* Syracuse University, 621 Skytop Road, Suite 160, Syracuse, NY 13244-5290. http://ericir.syr.edu/ithome/
- *Languages and Linguistics.* Center for Applied Linguistics (CAL), 4646 40th Street, NW, Washington, DC 20016-1859. URL: http://www.cal.org/ericcll/
- *Reading, English, and Communication.* Indiana University, Smith Research Center, 2805 East 10th Street, Suite 140, Bloomington, IN 47408-2698. URL: http://www.indiana.edu/~eric_rec/
- *Rural Education and Small Schools.* Appalachia Educational Laboratory, Inc. (AEL, Inc.), 1031 Quarrier Street, P.O. Box 1348, Charleston, WV 25325-1348. URL: http://www.ael.org/eric/
- *Science, Mathematics, and Environmental Education.* Ohio State University, 1929 Kenny Road, Columbus, Ohio 43210-1080. URL: http://www.ericse.org/
- *Service Learning.* University of Minnesota, R-460 VoTech Building, 1954 Buford Avenue, St. Paul, MN 55108. URL: http://nicsl.jaws.umn.edu/
- *Social Studies/Social Science Education.* Indiana University Social Studies Development Center, 2805 East 10th Street, Suite 120, Bloomington, IN 47408-2698 URL: http://www.indiana.edu/~ssdc/eric-chess.html
- *Urban Education.* Teachers College, Columbia University, Institute for Urban and Minority Education, Main Hall, Room 303, Box 40, New York, NY 10027-6696. URL: http://eric-web.tc.columbia.edu/

Figure 10.4
Selected ERIC addresses.

Permitted Uses—You May Make:

1. Single copies of:
   - A chapter of a book
   - An article from a periodical, magazine, or newspaper
   - A short story, short essay, or short poem, whether or not from a collected work
   - A chart, graph, diagram, drawing, cartoon
   - An illustration from a book, magazine, or newspaper
2. Multiple copies for classroom use (not to exceed one copy per student in a course) of:
   - A complete poem if less than 250 words
   - An excerpt from a longer poem, but not to exceed 250 words
   - A complete article, story, or essay of less than 2,500 words
   - An excerpt from a larger printed work not to exceed ten percent of the whole or 1,000 words
   - One chart, graph, diagram, cartoon, or picture per book or magazine issue.

Prohibited Uses—You May *Not*:

1. Copy more than one work or two excerpts from a single author during one class term (semester or year).
2. Copy more than three works from a collective work or periodical volume during one class term.
3. Reproduce more than nine sets of multiple copies for distribution to students in one class term.
4. Copy to create or replace or substitute for anthologies or collective works.
5. Copy "consumable" works (e.g., workbooks, standardized tests, or answer sheets).
6. Copy the same work year after year.

Figure 10.5
Guidelines for copying printed materials that are copyrighted.
(*Source:* Section 107 of the 1976 Federal Omnibus Copyright Revision Act.)

The Classroom Writing Board

As is true for an auto mechanic or a brain surgeon or any other professional, a teacher needs to know when and how to use the tools of the trade. One of the tools available to most every classroom teacher is the writing board. Can you imagine a classroom without a writing board? In this section you will find guidelines for using this important tool.

They used to be, and in some schools still are, slate blackboards (slate is a type of metamorphic rock). In today's classroom, however, the writing board is more likely to be a board that is painted plywood (chalkboard), which, like the blackboard, is quickly becoming obsolete at least in part because of the need to be concerned about the dust created from using chalk; or a white or colored (light green and light blue are common) *multipurpose dry—erase board* on which you write with special marking pens and erase with any soft, dry cloth. In addition to providing a surface upon which you can write and draw, the multipurpose board can be used as a projection screen and as a surface to which figures cut from colored transparency film will stick. It may also have a magnetic backing.

Extending the purposes of the multipurpose board and correlated with modern technology is an *electronic whiteboard* that can transfer information that is written on it to a connected computer monitor, which in turn can save the material as a computer file. The electronic whiteboard uses dry—erase markers and special erasers that have op-tically encoded sleeves that enable the device to track their position on the board. The data are then converted into a display for the computer monitor that may be printed, cut and pasted into other applications, sent as an e-mail or fax message, or networked to other sites.

Each day, each class, and even each new idea should begin with a clean board, except for announcements that have been placed there by you or another teacher. At the end of each class, clean the board, especially if another teacher follows you in that room (simple professional courtesy).

Use colored chalk or marking pens to highlight your board talk. This is especially helpful for students with learning difficulties. Beginning at the top left of the board, print or write neatly and clearly, with the writing intentionally positioned to indicate content relationships (e.g., causal, oppositional, numerical, comparative, categorical, and so on).

Use the writing board to acknowledge acceptance and to record student contributions. Print instructions for an activity on the board, in addition to giving them orally. At the top of the board frame you may find clips for hanging posters, maps, and charts.

Learn to use the board without having to turn your back entirely on students and without blocking their view of the board. When you have a lot of material to put on the board, do it before class and then cover it, or better yet, put the material on transparencies and use the overhead projector rather than the board, or use both. Be careful not to write too much information.

Airport
Apiary
Aquarium
Archeological site
Art gallery
Assembly plant
Bakery
Bird and wildlife sanctuary
Book publisher
Bookstore
Broadcasting and TV station
Building being raised
Building under construction
Canal lock
Cemetery
Chemical plant
City or county planning commission
Courthouse
Dairy
Dam and floodplain
Dock and harbor
Factory
Farm
Fire department
Fish hatchery
Flea market
Foreign embassy
Forest and forest preserve
Freeway under construction
Gas company
Geological site
Health department and hospital
Highway construction site

Highway patrol station
Historical sites and monuments
Industrial plant
Legislature session
Levee and water reservoir
Library and archive
Mass transit authority
Military installation
Mine
Museum
Native American Indian reservation
Newspaper plant
Observatory
Oil refinery
Park
Poetry reading
Police station
Post office and package delivery company
Recycling center
Retail store
Sanitation department
Sawmill or lumber company
Shopping mall
Shoreline (stream, lake, wetland, ocean)
Telecommunications center
Town meeting
Universities and colleges
Utility company
Warehouse
Water reservoir and treatment plant
Weather bureau and storm center
Wildlife park and preserve
Zoo

Figure 10.6
Community resources for speakers, materials, and field trips.

The Classroom Bulletin Board

Bulletin boards also are found in nearly every classroom, and, although sometimes poorly used or not used at all, they can be inexpensively transformed into attractive and valuable instructional tools. Among other uses, the bulletin board is a convenient location for posting reminders, assignments and schedules, commercially produced materials, and to celebrate and display model student work and anchor papers.

To plan, design, and prepare bulletin board displays, some teachers use student assistants or committees, giving those students guidance and responsibility for planning, preparing, and maintaining bulletin board displays. When preparing a bulletin board display, keep these guidelines in mind: the display should be simple, emphasizing one main idea, concept, topic, or theme, and captions should be short and concise; illustrations can accent learning topics; verbs can vitalize the captions; phrases can punctuate a student's thoughts; and alliteration can announce anything you wish on the board. Finally, as in all other aspects of the classroom learning environment, remember to ensure that the board display reflects gender and ethnic equity.

THE COMMUNITY AS A RESOURCE

One of the richest resources for learning is the local community and the people and places in it. You will want to build your own file of community resources—speakers, sources for free materials, and field trip locations. Your school may already have a community resource file available for your use. However, it may need updating. A community resource file (see Figure 10.6) should contain information about (a) possible field trip locations, (b) community resource people who could serve as guest speakers or mentors, and (c) local agencies that can provide information and instructional materials.

There are many ways of utilizing community resources, and quite a variety have been demonstrated by the schools specifically mentioned throughout this book (see Schools in index). Here, the discussion is limited to two often used, although sometimes abused, instructional tools: (a) guest speakers and (b) out-of-classroom and off-campus excursions, commonly called *field trips*.

Guest Speakers

Bringing outside speakers into your classroom can be a valuable educational experience for students, but not automatically so. In essence, guest speakers can be classified within a spectrum of four types, two of which should not be used. (1) A speaker is both informative and inspiring. (2) A speaker may be inspiring but with nothing substantive to offer, except for the possible diversion it might offer from the usual rigors of classroom work. (3) The speaker might be informative but boring to students. (4) At the worst end of this spectrum is the guest speaker who is both boring and uninformative. So, just like any other instructional experience, to make a guest speaker experience most effective takes careful planning on your part. To make sure that the experience is beneficial to student learning, consider the following guidelines.

- If at all possible, meet and talk with the guest speaker in advance to inform the speaker about your students and your expectations for the presentation, and to gauge how motivational and informative the speaker might be. If you believe the speaker might be informative but boring, then perhaps you can help structure the presentation in some way to make the presentation a bit more inspiring. For example, stop the speaker every few minutes and involve the students in questioning and discussions of points made.
- Prepare students in advance with key points of information that you expect students to obtain.
- Prepare students in advance with questions to ask the speaker, things the students want to find out, and information you want them to inquire about.
- Follow up the presentation with a thank-you letter to the guest speaker and perhaps further questions that developed during class discussions subsequent to the speaker's presentation.

Field Trips

What is the most memorable field trip that you were ever on as a student? What made it memorable? You may want to discuss these questions and others like them with your students.

Today's schools often have very limited funds for the transportation and liability costs for field trips. In some cases, there are no funds at all. At times, parent–teacher groups, business, and civic organizations help by providing financial resources so that students get valuable first-hand experiences that field trips so often can offer.

To prepare for and implement a successful field trip, there are three important stages of planning—before, during, and after—and critical decisions to be made at each stage. Consider the following guidelines.

Before the Field Trip

When the field trip is your idea (and not the students'), discuss the idea with your teaching team, principal, or department chair (especially when transportation will be needed) *before* mentioning the idea to your students. There is no cause served by getting students excited about a trip before you know if it is feasible.

Once you have obtained the necessary, but tentative, approval from school officials, take the trip yourself (or with team members), if possible. A previsit allows you to determine how to make the field trip most productive and what arrangements will be necessary. For this previsit you might consider taking a couple of your students along for their ideas and help. If a previsit is not possible, you still will need to arrange for travel directions, arrival and departure times, parking, briefing by the host, if there is one, storage of students' personal items, such as coats and lunches, provisions for eating and rest rooms, and fees, if any.

If there are fees, you need to talk with your administration about who will pay the fees. If the trip is worth taking, the school should cover the costs. If that is not possible, perhaps students can plan a fund-raising activity or financial assistance can be obtained from some other source. If this does not work, you might consider an alternative experience that does not involve costs.

Arrange for official permission from the school administration. This usually requires a form for requesting, planning, and reporting field trips. After permission has been obtained, you can discuss the field trip with your students and arrange for permissions from their parents or guardians. You need to realize that although parents or guardians sign official permission forms allowing their children to participate in the trip, these only show that the parents or guardians are aware of what will take place and give their permission for their child to participate. Although the permission form should include a statement that the parent or guardian absolves the teacher and the school from liability should an accident occur, it *does not* lessen the teacher's and the school's responsibilities should there be negligence by a teacher, driver, or chaperone.

Arrange for students to be excused from their other classes while on the field trip. Using an information form prepared and signed by you and perhaps by the appropriate administrator, the students should then assume responsibility for notifying their other teachers of the planned absence from classes and assure them that they will make up whatever work is missed. In addition, you will need to make arrangements for your own teaching duties to be covered. In some schools, teachers cooperate by filling in for those who will be gone. In other schools, substitute teachers are hired. Sometimes teachers have to hire their own substitute.

Arrange to have a cell phone available for your use during the trip. Some schools have a cell phone available for just that purpose. If not, and you don't have one yourself, perhaps one of the drivers or other adult chaperones might.

Arrange for whatever transportation is needed. Your principal, or the principal's designee, will help you with the details. In many schools, this detail is done by someone else. In any case, the use of private automobiles is ill advised, because you and the school could be liable for the acts of the drivers.

Arrange for the collection of money that is needed for fees. If there are out-of-pocket costs to be paid by students, this information needs to be included on the permission form. No students should ever be excluded from the field trip because of a lack of money. This can be a tricky issue, because there may be some students who would rather steal the money for a field trip than to say they don't have it. Try to anticipate problems; hopefully the school or some organization can pay for the trip so that fees need not be collected from students and therefore potential problems of this sort are avoided.

Plan details for student safety and the monitoring of their safety from departure to return. Included should be a first-aid kit and a system of student control, such as a "buddy system" whereby students must remain paired throughout the trip. The pairs sometimes are given numbers that are recorded and kept by the teacher and the chaperones, and then checked at departure time, periodically during the trip, and again upon return. Use adult chaperones. As a very general rule, there should be one adult chaperone for every ten students. Some districts have a policy regarding this. While on a field trip, at all times all students should be under the direct supervision of an adult.

Plan the complete route and schedule, including any stops along the way. If transportation is being provided, you will need to discuss the plans with the provider.

Establish and discuss, to the extent you believe necessary, the rules of behavior your students should follow. Included in this might be details of the trip, its purpose, directions, what they should wear and bring, academic expectations (consider, for example, giving each student a study guide), and follow-up activities. Also included should be information about what to do if anything should go awry, for example, if a student is late for the departure or return, loses a personal possession along the way, gets lost, is injured, becomes sick, or misbehaves. For the latter, *never* send a misbehaving stu-

dent back to school alone. Involve the adult chaperones in the previsit discussion. All of this information should also be included on the parental permission form.

If a field trip is supposed to promote some kind of learning, as is probably the case, then to avoid leaving it to chance, the learning expectations need to be clearly defined and the students given an explanation of how and where they may encounter the learning experience. Before the field trip, students should be asked questions such as, "What do we already know about _____? What do we want to find out about _____? How can we find out?" and then, with their assistance, an appropriate guide can be prepared for the students to use during the field trip.

To further ensure learning and individual student responsibility for that learning, you may want to assign different roles and responsibilities to students, just as would be done in cooperative learning (see, for example, the lesson plan of Figure 6.15 in Chapter 6), assuring that each student has a role with responsibility.

You may want to take recorders and cameras so the field trip experience can be relived and shared in class upon return. If so, roles and responsibilities for the equipment and its care and use can be assigned to students as well.

During the Field Trip

If your field trip has been carefully planned according to the preceding guidelines, it should be a valuable and safe experience for all. Enroute, while at the trip location, and on the return to school, you and the adult chaperones should monitor student behavior and learning just as you do in the classroom.

After the Field Trip

Plan the follow-up activities. As with any other lesson plan, the field trip lesson is complete only when there is both a proper introduction and a well-planned closure. All sorts of follow-up activities can be planned as an educational wrap-up to this educational experience. For example, a bulletin board committee can plan and prepare an attractive display summarizing the trip. Students can write about their experiences in their journals or as papers. Small groups can give oral reports sharing what they did and learned. Their reports can then serve as springboards for further class discussion, and perhaps further investigations. Finally, for future planning, all who were involved should contribute to an assessment of the experience.

MEDIA TOOLS

Your attention is now focused on teaching tools that depend upon electricity to project light and sound and to focus images on screens. Included are projectors of various sorts, computers, CD-ROMs, sound recorders, video recorders, and laser videodisc players. The aim here is *not* to provide instruction on how to operate modern equipment but to help you develop a philosophy for using it and to provide strategies for using media tools in your teaching. Consequently, to conserve space in this book, we devote no attention to traditional AV equipment, such as 16mm film, opaque, and slide projectors. There are staff members on any school faculty who gladly will assist you in locating and using those tools.

It is important to remember that the role of media tools is to aid student learning, not to teach *for* you. You must still select the objectives, orchestrate the instructional plan, tweak the instruction according to the needs of individual students, assess the results, and follow up the lessons, just as you have learned to do with various other instructional strategies. If you use media tools prudently, your teaching and students' learning will benefit. As said earlier, like a competent brain surgeon or a competent auto mechanic, a competent teacher knows when and how to select and use the right tools at the right time. Would you want your child operated on by a surgeon who was unfamiliar with the tools used in surgery? The education of youth should be no less important.

When Equipment Malfunctions

When using media equipment, it is usually best to set up the equipment and have it ready to go before students arrive. That helps avoid problems in classroom management that can occur when there is a delay because the equipment is not ready. After all, if you were a surgeon ready to begin an operation and your tools and equipment weren't ready, your patient's life would likely be placed in extra danger. Like any other competent professional, a competent teacher is ready when the work is to begin.

Of course, delays may be unavoidable when equipment breaks down, or if a videotape breaks. Remember "Murphy's law," which says if anything can go wrong, it will? It is particularly relevant when using audiovisual equipment. You want to be prepared for such emergencies. Effectively planning for and responding to this eventuality is a part of your system of movement management and takes place during the preactive stage of your planning. That preparation includes consideration of a number of factors.

When equipment malfunctions, three principles should be kept in mind: (a) you want to avoid dead time in the classroom, (b) you want to avoid causing permanent damage to equipment, and (c) you want to avoid losing content continuity of a lesson. So, what do you do when equipment breaks down? Again, the answer is: Be prepared for the eventuality.

If a projector bulb goes out, quickly insert another. That means that you should have an extra bulb on hand. If a tape breaks, you can do a quick temporary splice with cellophane tape. That means that tape should be readily available. If you must do a temporary splice, do it on the film or videotape that has already run through the machine rather than on the end yet to go through, so as not to mess up the machine or the film. Then, after class or after school, be sure to notify the person in charge of the tape that a temporary splice was made, so the tape can be permanently repaired before its next use. If, during direct, whole-class instruction, the computer screen freezes, you should probably quickly move to an alternate activity. If it happens during multilevel instruction, then while maintaining your classroom withitness, you can probably take the time to treat this as a teachable moment and show the student who is working with the computer what to do, which probably would be to restart the computer.

If a patient's cerebral artery suddenly and unexpectedly breaks during surgery, the surgeon and the surgical team are ready for that eventuality and makes the necessary repair. If, while working on an automobile, a part breaks, the mechanic gets a replacement part. If, while teaching, a computer program freezes or aborts on the screen, or if a fuse blows or you lose power for some other reason and you feel that there is going to be too much dead time before the equipment is working again, that is the time to go to an alternate lesson plan. You have probably heard the expression "go to Plan B." It is a useful phrase; what it means is that without missing a beat in the lesson, to accomplish the same instructional objective or another objective, you immediately and smoothly switch to an alternate learning activity. For you, the beginning teacher, it does not mean that you must plan *two* lessons for every one, but that when planning a lesson that utilizes media equipment, you should plan in your lesson an alternative activity, just in case. Then, you move your students into the planned alternative activity quickly and smoothly.

The Overhead Projector

In addition to a writing board and a bulletin board, nearly every classroom is equipped with an overhead projector. The overhead projector is a versatile, effective, and reliable teaching tool. Except for the bulb burning out, not much else can go wrong with an overhead projector. There is no film to break or program to crash.

The overhead projector projects light through objects that are transparent (see Figure 10.7). A properly functioning overhead projector usually works quite well in a fully lit room. Truly portable overhead projectors are available that can be carried easily from place to place in their compact cases.

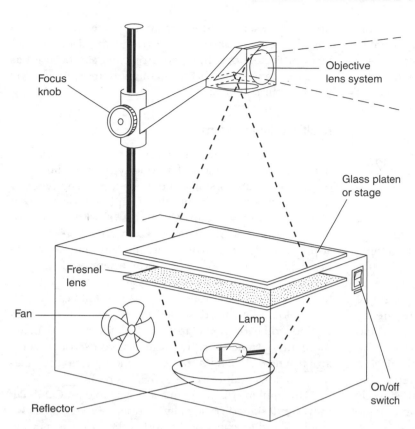

Figure 10.7
Overhead projector, cutaway view.

Other types of overhead projectors include rear-projection systems that allow the teacher to stand off to the side rather than between students and the screen and overhead video projectors that use video cameras to send images that are projected by television monitors. Some schools use overhead video camera technology that focuses on an object, pages of a book, or a demonstration, while sending a clear image to a video monitor with a screen large enough for an entire class to clearly see.

In some respects, the overhead projector is more practical than the writing board, particularly for a beginning teacher who is nervous. Using the overhead projector rather than the writing board can help avoid tension by decreasing the need to pace back and forth to the board. And by using an overhead projector rather than a writing board, you can maintain both eye contact and physical proximity with students, both of which are important for maintaining classroom control.

Guidelines for Using the Overhead Projector

As with any projector, find the best place in your classroom to put it. If there is no classroom projection screen, you can hang white paper or a sheet, use a white multipurpose board, or use a white or near-white wall.

Have you ever attended a presentation by someone who was not using an overhead projector properly? It

can be frustrating to members of an audience when the image is too small, out of focus, partially off the screen, or partially blocked from view by the presenter. To use this teaching tool in a professional manner:

- *Turn on the projector (the switch is probably on the front), and place it so the projected white light covers the entire screen and hits the screen at a 90-degree angle, then focus the image to be projected.*
- *Face the students while using the projector.* The fact that you do not lose eye contact with your audience is a major advantage of using the overhead projector rather than a writing board. What you write as you face your students will show up perfectly (unless out of focus or off the screen).
- *Lay the pencil flat onto the transparency with the tip of the pencil pointing to the detail being emphasized* rather than tilting the pencil, using your finger to point to detail, or pointing directly to the screen (thereby turning away from your students).
- *To lessen distraction, turn the overhead projector off when you want the students to shift attention back to you.*

To preserve the life of the projector's bulb, it is best not to move the projector until the bulb has cooled. In addition, bulbs will last longer if you avoid touching them with your fingers.

For writing on overhead projector transparencies, ordinary felt-tip pens are not satisfactory. Select a transparency-marking pen available at an office supply store. The ink of these pens is water-soluble, so keep the palm of your hand from resting on the transparency or you will have ink smudges on your transparency and on your hand. Non-water-soluble pens—permanent markers—can be used, but the transparency must be cleaned with an alcohol solvent or a plastic eraser. When using a cleaning solvent, you can clean and dry with paper toweling or a soft rag. To highlight the writing on a transparency and to organize student learning, use pens in a variety of colors. Transparency pens tend to dry out quickly, and they are relatively expensive, so the caps must be taken on and off frequently, which is something of a nuisance when working with several colors. Practice writing on a transparency, and also practice making overlays. You can use an acetate transparency roll or single sheets of flat transparencies. Flat sheets of transparency come in different colors—clear, red, blue, yellow, and green—which can be useful in making overlays.

Some teachers prepare lesson outlines in advance on transparencies, which allows more careful preparation of the transparencies and means that they are then ready for reuse at another time. Some teachers use an opaque material, such as a 3 × 5″ notecard, to block out prewritten material and then uncover it at the moment it is being discussed. For preparation of permanent transparencies you will probably want to use permanent marker pens rather than those that are water-soluble and easily smudged. Heavy paper frames are available for permanent transparencies; marginal notes can be written on the frames. Personal computers with laser printers and thermal processing (copy) machines, probably located in the teacher's workroom or in the school's main office, can be used to make permanent transparencies.

Other transparent objects can be shown on an overhead projector, such as transparent rulers, protractors, and Petri dishes for science activities; even opaque objects can be used if you want simply to show silhouette, as you might in math and art activities. Calculators, too, are available specifically for use on the overhead projector, as is a screen that fits onto the platform and is circuited to a computer, so whatever is displayed on the computer monitor is also projected onto the classroom screen.

Commercial transparencies are available from a variety of school supply houses. For sources, check the catalogs available in your school office or at the audiovisual and resources centers in your school district.

The overhead projector can also be used for tracing transparent charts or drawings into larger drawings on paper or on the writing board. The image projected onto the screen can be made smaller or larger by moving the projector closer or farther away, respectively, and then traced when you have the size you want. Also, an overhead projector (or a filmstrip projector) can be used as a light source (spotlight) to highlight demonstrations by you or your students.

Multimedia Program

A multimedia program is a collection of teaching/learning materials involving more than one type of medium and organized around a single theme or topic. The types of media involved vary from rather simple kits—perhaps a videotape, a game, activity cards, student worksheets, and a manual of instructions for the teacher—to very sophisticated packages involving building-level site licensed computer software, student handbooks, reproducible activity worksheets, classroom wall hangings, and an on-line subscription to a telecommunication network. Some kits are designed for teacher's use, others by individual or small groups of students, and many more are designed for the collaborative use of students and teachers. Teachers sometimes incorporate multimedia programs with learning activity centers.

Many multimedia programs are available on CD-ROM; they are designed principally as reference resources for students and teachers but include other aspects as well. One example is National Geographic's *Mammals: A Multimedia Encyclopedia,* which provides a lesson-planning guide, facts on more than 200 animals, 700 still color photos, range maps, animal vocalizations, full-motion movie clips, an animal classification game, glossary, and a printing capability. Selected sources of programs are shown in Figure 10.8.

Everyone knows that television, videos, and videodiscs represent a powerful medium. Their use as teaching aids, however, may present scheduling, curriculum, and physical problems that some school systems are yet unable to handle adequately.

For purposes of professional discussion, television programming can be divided into three categories: Instructional television, educational television, and general commercial television. Instructional television refers to programs specifically designed for classroom instruction. Educational television refers to programs of cable television and public broadcasting designed to educate in general, but not aimed at classroom instruction. Commercial television programs include the entertainment and public service programs of the television networks and local stations.

Watch for announcements for special educational programs in professional journals. And, of course, television program listings can be obtained from your local commercial, educational, or cable companies or by writing directly to network stations. Some networks sponsor Internet websites.

Combined with a television monitor, the VCR (video-cassette recorder) is one of the most popular and frequently used tools in today's classroom. Videotaped programs can do nearly everything that the former 16mm films could do. In addition, the VCR, combined with a video camera, makes it possible to record student activities, practice, projects, and demonstrations, as well as yourself when teaching. It gives students a marvelous opportunity to self-assess as they see and hear themselves in action.

Entire course packages, as well as supplements, are now available on videocassettes or on computer discs. The schools where you student teach and where you eventually are employed may have a collection of such programs. Some teachers make their own.

Carefully selected programs, tapes, discs, films, and slides enhance student learning. For example, videodiscs and CD-ROMs offer quick and efficient accessibility to thousands of visuals, thus providing an appreciated boost to teachers of students with limited language proficiency. With the use of frame control, students can observe phenomena, in detail, that previous students only read about.

Check school supplies catalogs and Internet resources for additional titles and sources for videodiscs. Generally, companies that sell computer software and CD-ROMs, also sell videodiscs. Figure 10.8 provides sample web addresses from which you may obtain information.

- **A.D.A.M. Software, Inc.** http://www.adam.com
- **Agency for Instructional Technology** http:www.ait.net
- **AIMS Multimedia** http://www.aimsmultimedia.com
- **Apex Learning, Inc.** http://www.apexlearning.com
- **Bigchalk** http://www.bigchalk.com
- **Boxer Learning** http://www.boxerlearning.com
- **Broderbund Software** http://www.broderbund.com
- **Cognitive Concepts** http://www.earobics.com
- **Educational Insights** http://www.educationalinsights.com
- **Pitsco, Inc.** http://www.pitsco.com
- **Riverdeep Interactive Learning** http://www.riverdeep.net
- **Sunburst.Com** http://www.sunburst.com
- **SVE & Churchill Media** http://www.SVEmedia.com
- **Tom Snyder Productions** http://www.tomsnyder.com
- **Videodiscovery** http://www.videodiscovery.com

Figure 10.8
Selected Internet resources for videotapes, computer software, CD-ROMs, and interactive multimedia.

COMPUTERS AND COMPUTER-BASED INSTRUCTIONAL TOOLS

As a secondary school teacher, you must be **computer literate**—you must understand and be able to use computers as well as you can read and write. The computer can be valuable to you in several ways. For example, the computer can help you manage the instruction by obtaining information, storing and preparing test materials, maintaining attendance and grade records, and preparing programs to aid in the academic development of individual students. This category of uses of the computer is referred to as *computer-managed instruction* (CMI), or a *computer performance system* (CPS).

The computer can also be used for instruction by employing various instructional software programs, and it can be used to teach about computers and to help students develop their metacognitive skills as well as their skills in computer use. When the computer is used to assist students in their learning, it is called *computer-assisted instruction* (CAI) or *computer-assisted learning* (CAL).

The Placement and Use of Computers: The On-line Classroom

Teachers looking to make their classrooms more student-centered, collaborative, and interactive, continue to increasingly turn to telecommunications networks. Webs of connected computers allow teachers and students from around the world to reach each other directly and gain access to quantities of information previously unimaginable. Students using networks learn new inquiry and analytical skills in a stimulating environment, and they can also gain an increased awareness of their role as world citizens.

How you use the computer for instruction is determined by several factors, including your knowledge of and skills in its use, the number of computers that you have available for instructional use, where computers are placed in the school, the software that is available, printer availability, and the telecommunications capabilities (i.e., wiring and phone lines, modems, and servers).

Schools continue to purchase or to lease computers and to upgrade their telecommunications capabilities. Regarding computer placement and equipment available, here are some possible scenarios and how classroom teachers work within each.

SCENARIO 1. With the assistance of a computer lab and the lab technician, computers are integrated into the whole curriculum. In collaboration with members of interdisciplinary teaching teams, in a computer lab students use computers, software, and sources on the Internet as tools to build their knowledge, to write stories with word processors, to illustrate diagrams with paint utilities, to create interactive reports with hypermedia, and to graph data they have gathered using spreadsheets.

SCENARIO 2. In some schools, students take "computers" as an elective or exploratory course. Students in your classes who are simultaneously enrolled in such a course may be given special computer assignments by you that they can then share with the rest of the class.

SCENARIO 3. Some classrooms have a computer connected to a large-screen video monitor. The teacher or a student works the computer, and the monitor screen can be seen by the entire class. As they view the screen, students can verbally respond to and interact with what is happening on the computer.

SCENARIO 4. You may be fortunate enough to have one or more computers in your classroom for all or part of the school year, computers with Internet connections, with CD-ROM playing capabilities, a videodisc player, an overhead projector, and a LCD (liquid crystal display) projection system. Coupled with the overhead projector, the LCD projection system allows you to project onto your large wall screen (and TV monitor at the same time) any image from computer software or a videodisc. With this system, all students can see and verbally interact with the multimedia instruction.

SCENARIO 5. Many classrooms have at least one computer with telecommunications capability, and some have many. When this is the case in your classroom, then you most likely will have one or two students working at the computer while others are doing other learning activities (multilevel teaching). Computers can be an integral part of a learning center and an important aid in your overall effort to personalize the instruction within your classroom.

Programs are continually being developed and enhanced to meet the new and more powerful computers being made available. (Videodiscs, computer software, and CD-ROMs are usually available from the same companies, addresses of which are listed in Figure 10.8.) There are many forms available for evaluating computer software programs and testing them for their compatibility with your instructional objectives. Forms are usually available from the local school district or from the state department of education and from professional associations.

For computers there are three types of storage disks—floppy disks of various storage capacities, the hard disk, and the **CD-ROM,** which is an abbreviation for "compact disc–read only memory." Use of a CD-ROM disc requires a computer with a CD-ROM drive. Newer computers have built in CD-ROM drives, while others may be connected to one. As with floppy and hard disks, CD-ROMs are used for storing characters in a digital format, while images on a videodisc are stored in an analog format. The CD-ROM is capable of storing some 20,000 images or the equivalent of approximately 250,000 pages of text—the capacity of 1,520 360K floppy disks or eight 70MB hard disks—and therefore is ideal for storing large amounts of information such as dictionaries, encyclopedias, and general reference works full of graphic images that you can copy and modify.

Having superior sound and visual performance, the DVD may replace CDs, VCR tapes, and computer CD-ROMs. Although in appearance it resembles the CD-ROM, the DVD can store nearly 17 gigabytes of information, provide a faster retrieval of data, and can be made interactive.

Sources of Free and Inexpensive Audiovisual Materials

For free and inexpensive audiovisual materials check Internet sources and your college or university library for sources listed in Figure 10.9.

Using Copyrighted Video, Computer, and Multimedia Programs

You must be knowledgeable about the laws on the use of copyrighted videos and computer software materials. Although space here prohibits full inclusion of U.S. legal guidelines, your local school district undoubtedly can provide a copy of current district policies to ensure your compliance with all copyright laws. As discussed earlier in regard to the use of printed materials that are copyrighted, when preparing to make any copy you must find out whether the copying is permitted by law under the category of "permitted use." If not allowed under "permitted use," then you must get written permission

---

- Professional periodicals and journals.
- *Catalog of Audiovisual Materials: A Guide to Government Sources* (ED 198 822). Arlington, VA: ERIC Documents Reproduction Service.
- Educator's Progress Service, Inc., 214 Center Street, Randolph, WI 53956 (414) 326–3126: *Educator's Guide to Free Audio and Video Materials; Educator's Guide to Free Films; Educator's Guide to Free Filmstrips; Guide to Free Computer Materials; Educator's Guide to Free Science Materials.*
- *Video Placement Worldwide (VPW).* Source of free-sponsored educational videos on Internet at http://www.vpw.com.

Figure 10.9
Resources for free and inexpensive audiovisual materials.

Permitted Uses—You May:

1. Request your media center or audiovisual coordinator to record a program for you if you cannot or if you lack the equipment.
2. Keep a videotaped copy of a broadcast (including cable transmission) for 45 calendar days, after which the program must be erased.
3. Use the program in class once during the first ten school days of the 45 calendar days, and a second time if instruction needs to be reinforced.
4. Have professional staff view the program several times for evaluation purposes during the full 45 day period.
5. Make a few copies to meet legitimate needs, but these copies must be erased when the original videotape is erased.
6. Use only a part of the program if instructional needs warrant.
7. Enter into a licensing agreement with the copyright holder to continue use of the program.

Prohibited Uses—You May *Not:*

1. Videotape premium cable services such as HBO without express permission.
2. Alter the original content of the program.
3. Exclude the copyright notice on the program.
4. Videorecord before a request for use is granted—the request to record must come from an instructor.
5. Keep the program, and any copies, after 45 days.

Figure 10.10
Copyright law for off-air videotaping.
(*Source:* From *Instructional Media and Technologies for Learning,* 6th ed., p. 389, by Robert Heinich, Michael Molenda, James D. Russell, and Sharon E. Smaldino, 1999. Copyright 1999 by Merrill/Prentice Hall, Upper Saddle River, NJ: Merrill/Prentice Hall. Reprinted by permission.)

Permitted Uses—You May:

1. Make a single back-up or archival copy of the computer program.
2. Adapt the computer program to another language if the program is unavailable in the target language.
3. Add features to make better use of the computer program.

Prohibited Uses—You May *Not:*

1. Make multiple copies.
2. Make replacement copies from an archival or back-up copy.
3. Make copies of copyrighted programs to be sold, leased, loaned, transmitted, or given away.

Figure 10.11
Copyright law for use of computer software.
(*Source:* December, 1980, Congressional amendment to the 1976 Copyright Act.)

from the holder of the copyright to reproduce the material. Figures 10.10 and 10.11 present guidelines for the copying of videotapes and computer software.

Usually, when purchasing CD-ROMs and other multimedia software packages intended for use by schools, you are also paying for a license to modify and use its contents for instructional purposes. However, not all CD-ROMs include copyright permission, so always check the copyright notice on any disk you purchase and use. Whenever in doubt, don't use it until you have asked your district media specialists about copyrights or have obtained necessary permissions from the original source.

As yet, there are no guidelines for fair use of films, filmstrips, slides, and multimedia programs. A general rule of thumb for use of any copyrighted material is to treat the work of others as you would want your own material treated were it protected by a copyright (see Figure 10.12).

DISTANCE LEARNING

Distance learning (or *distance education*) is the popular term for describing any instructional situation in which the learner is separated in time or space from the

1. For portions of copyrighted works used in your own multimedia production for use in teaching, follow normal copyright guidelines (e.g., the limitations on the amount of material used, whether it be motion media, text, music, illustrations, photographs, or computer software).
2. You may display your own multimedia work using copyrighted works to other teachers, such as in workshops. However, you may *not* make and distribute copies to colleagues without obtaining permission from copyright holders.
3. You may use your own multimedia production for instruction over an electronic network (e.g., distance learning) provided there are limits to access and to the number of students enrolled. You may *not* distribute such work over any electronic network (local area or wide area) without expressed permission from copyright holders.
4. You must obtain permissions from copyright holders before using any copyrighted materials in educational multimedia productions for commercial reproduction and distribution or before replicating more than one copy, distributing copies to others, or for use beyond your own classroom.

Figure 10.12
Fair use guidelines for using multimedia programs.

point of instruction. Long a means of providing courses (e.g., by mail correspondence) and workshops (e.g., by video) for industry training, medical organizations, and higher education, developments in telecommunications technologies have created a renewed interest in distance learning. In fact, some experts predict that learning and instruction over the Internet will be the driving force for educational changes in the twenty-first century, along with an accompanying change in the role of the classroom teacher from less of a deliverer of instruction to more of a facilitator of learning by providing individual tutoring and helping students work together in groups.

With the technology of distance learning, students in small rural schools can receive instruction in courses that because of limited local resources might otherwise be unavailable to them; via the Internet all students can interact in real time with people from around the world.

SUMMARY

You have learned of the variety of tools available to supplement your instruction. When used wisely, these tools will help you to reach more of your students more of the time. As you know, teachers must meet the needs of a diversity of students—many of who are linguistically and culturally different. The material selected and presented in this chapter should be of help in doing that. The future will undoubtedly continue to bring technological innovations that will be even more helpful—compact discs, computers, and telecommunications equipment have only marked the beginning of a revolution for teaching. As we enter a new millennium, new instructional delivery systems made possible by microcomputers and multimedia workstations will likely fundamentally alter what had become the traditional role of the classroom teacher during the twentieth century.

You should remain alert to developing technologies for your teaching. DVD, CD-ROMs interfaced with computers (i.e., the use of multimedia), telecommunications, digitized textbooks, and hand-held computers offer exciting technologies for learning. New instructional technologies are advancing at an increasingly rapid rate. You and your colleagues must maintain vigilance over new developments, constantly looking for those that will not only help make student learning meaningful and interesting, and your teaching effective, but that are cost effective as well.

ADDITIONAL EXERCISES

See the companion website http://www.prenhall.com/kellough for the following exercises related to the content of this chapter:

- Internet Sites of Use to Secondary School Teachers
- Collecting and Evaluating Free Materials
- Observations of Teacher's Use of Audiovisual Materials
- The Classroom Teacher and the Purchase of Materials for Teaching.

QUESTIONS FOR CLASS DISCUSSION

1. Explain how your effective use of the writing board and bulletin board can help students see relationships among verbal concepts or information.
2. Describe what you should look for when deciding whether material that you have obtained free or inexpensively is appropriate for use in your teaching.
3. Share with others in your class your knowledge, observations, and feelings about the use of multimedia and telecommunications for teaching. From your discussion, what more would you like to know about the use of multimedia and telecommunications for teaching? How might you learn more about these things?

4. In 1922, Thomas Edison predicted that "the motion picture is destined to revolutionize our educational system and . . . in a few years it will supplant largely, if not entirely, the use of textbooks." In 1945, William Levenson of the Cleveland public schools' radio station claimed that "the time may come when a portable radio receiver will be as common in the classroom as is the blackboard." In the early 1960s, B. F. Skinner believed that with the help of the new teaching machines and programmed instruction, students could learn twice as much in the same time and with the same effort as in a standard classroom. Did motion pictures, radio, programmed instruction, and television revolutionize education? Will computers become as much a part of the classroom as writing boards? What do you predict the public school classroom of the year 2050 will be like? Will the role of a teacher be different in any way than it is today?

5. Select and identify one instructional tool that is *not* discussed in this chapter and explain to your classmates its advantages and disadvantages for use in teaching a subject and grade level of your choice.

6. Has the purchase of new textbooks and library books become stagnated as schools increase their spending on leading-edge technology? Have traditional shop classes given way to technology education programs? Have music and art programs suffered as a result of increased expenditures on technology? How are school districts finding funds necessary for the cost of technology, such as for the cost of wiring classrooms for networking and for updated computers, and for the planning, installation, and maintenance of complex computer networks? Or are districts finding the necessary funds? In this respect, are some districts worse off or better off than others? Is this an issue? An issue for which every classroom teacher need be aware?

7. Select one of the Reflective Thoughts from the opening of Part III (page 220) that is specifically related to the content of this chapter, research it, and write a one-page essay explaining why you agree or disagree with the thought. Share your essay with members of your class for their thoughts.

8. Describe any prior concepts you held that changed as a result of your experiences with this chapter. Describe the changes.

9. From your current observations and field work as related to this teacher preparation program, clearly identify one specific example of educational practice that seems contradictory to exemplary practice or theory as presented in this chapter. Present your explanation for the discrepancy.

10. Do you have questions generated by the content of this chapter? If you do, list them along with ways answers might be found.

FOR FURTHER READING

Abdullah, M. H. *Guidelines for Evaluating Websites.* ERIC Digest 426440 98. Bloomington, IN: ERIC Clearinghouse on Reading, English, and Communications, 1998.

Andrews, K., and Marshall, K. "Making Learning Connections Through Telelearning." *Educational Leadership* 58(2):53–56 (October 2000).

Barron, A. E., and Ivers, K. S. *The Internet and Instruction: Activities and Ideas.* 2d ed. Englewood, CO: Libraries Unlimited, 1998.

Butler, D. "Gender, Girls, and Computer Technology: What's the Status Now?" *Clearing House* 73(4):225–229 (March/April 2000).

Churma, M. *A Guide to Integrating Technology Standards into the Curriculum.* Upper Saddle River, NJ: Merrill Prentice Hall, 1999.

Cotton, E. G. *The Online Classroom: Teaching with the Internet.* 3d ed. Bloomington, IN: EDINFO Press, 1998.

Curchy, C., and Kyker, K. *Educator's Survival Guide to TV Production Equipment and Setup.* Englewood, CO: Libraries Unlimited, 1998.

Donlevy, J. G., and Donlevy, T. R. "wNetSchool." *International Journal of Instructional Media* 26(1):9–10 (1999).

Ertmer, P. A., Hruskocy, C., and Woods, D. M. *Education on the Internet.* Upper Saddle River, NJ: Merrill Prentice Hall, 2000.

Foshay, J. D. *Project-Based Multimedia Instruction.* Fastback 445. Bloomington, IN: Phi Delta Kappa Educational Foundation, 1999.

Gardiner, S. "Cybercheating: A New Twist on an Old Problem." *Phi Delta Kappan* 83(2):172–174 (October 2001).

Gruber, S. (ed.). *Weaving a Virtual Web: Practical Approaches to New Information Technologies.* Urbana, IL: National Council of Teachers of English, 2000.

Harris, J. *Design Tools for the Internet-Supported Classroom.* Alexandria, VA: Association for Supervision and Curriculum Development, 1998.

Heide, A., and Stillborne, L. *The Teacher's Complete & Easy Guide to the Internet.* 2d ed. New York: Teachers College Press, 1999.

Jonassen, D. H., Peck, K. L., and Wilson, B. G. *Learning With Technology: A Constructivist Perspective.* Upper Saddle River, NJ: Merrill Prentice Hall, 1999.

Kahn, J. *Ideas and Strategies for the One-Computer Classroom.* Eugene, OR: International Society for Technology in Education, 1998.

Leu, D. J., Jr., Leu, D. D., and Leu, K. R. *Teaching with the Internet: Lessons from the Classroom.* Norwood, MA: Christopher-Gordon, 1999.

McCullen, C. "Copyright Issues in a Digital World." *Middle Ground* 3(2):7–9, 52 (October 1999).

McCullen, C. "The Hows and Whys of Conducting Desktop Teleconferences." *Middle Ground* 2(3):7–8 (February 1999).

Means, B. "Technology in America's Schools: Before and After Y2K." Chap. 8 in R. S. Brandt (ed.). *Education in a New Era.* Alexandria, VA: ASCD Yearbook, Association for Supervision and Curriculum Development, 2000. pp. 185–210.

Newby, T. J., Stepich, D. A., Lehman, J. D., and Russell, J. D. *Instructional Technology for Teaching and Learning.* 2d ed. Upper Saddle River, NJ: Merrill/Prentice Hall, 2000.

Owens, K. D. "Scientists and Engineers in the Middle School Classroom." *Clearing House* 73(3):150–152 (January/February 2000).

Pinhey, L. A. *Global Education: Internet Resources.* ERIC Digest 417124. Bloomington, IN: ERIC Clearinghouse for Social Studies/Social Science Education, 1998.

Rekrut, M. D. "Using the Internet in Classroom Instruction: A Primer for Teachers." *Journal of Adolescent & Adult Literacy* 42(7):546–557 (April 1999).

Renard, L. "Cut and Paste 101: Plagiarism and the Net." *Educational Leadership* 57(4):38–42 (December 1999/January 2000).

Roblyer, M. D., and Edwards, J. *Integrating Educational Technology into Teaching.* 2d ed. Upper Saddle River, NJ: Merrill Prentice Hall, 2000.

Roblyer, M. D. *Integrating Technology Across the Curriculum: A Database of Strategies and Lesson Plans.* Upper Saddle River, NJ: Merrill Prentice Hall, 1999.

Tally, B., and Burns, M. "Mining for Gold in a Mountain of Online Resources." *Harvard Education Letter* 16(2):6–7 (March/April 2000).

Tanner, C. K. "Into the Woods, Wetlands, and Prairies." *Educational Leadership* 64–66 (April 2001).

Tapscott, D. "Educating the Net Generation." *Educational Leadership* 56(5):6–11 (February 1999).

Teicher, J. "An Action Plan for Smart Internet Use." *Educational Leadership* 56(5):70–74 (February 1999).

Wassermann, S. "Curriculum Enrichment With Computer Software." *Phi Delta Kappan* 82(8):592–597 (April 2001).

Weinman, J., and Haag, P. "Gender Equity in Cyberspace." *Educational Leadership* 56(5):44–49 (February 1999).

IV

ASSESSMENT AND CONTINUING PROFESSIONAL DEVELOPMENT

Part IV responds to your needs concerning:

- Assessing student learning
- Finding a teaching job
- Grading and reporting student achievement
- Meeting with parents and guardians

- Performance assessment
- Remaining an alert and effective teacher
- Scoring rubrics
- Self-assessment through micro peer teaching
- Student teaching

Reflective Thoughts

When assessing for student achievement, it is important to use procedures that are compatible with the instructional objectives.

Performance-based assessment procedures require students to produce rather than to select responses.

That which separates the professional teacher from "anyone off the street" is the teacher's ability to go beyond mere description of a student's behavior.

For students' continued intellectual and emotional development, your comments about their work should be useful, productive, analytical, diagnostic, and prescriptive.

You must provide opportunities for students to think about what they are learning, how they are learning it, and how far they have progressed in learning it.

It is unprofessional to place a student teacher into a "sink-or-swim" situation.

Teaching is such an electrifying profession that it is not easy to remain energetic and to stay abreast of changes and trends in research and practice.

A teacher's concern should not be with deciding which students are better than others but to helping all of them succeed.

A student should never need to ask the question, "What's going to be on the test?"

Important decisions that affect an individual student's educational career should not rest on one test score alone but on multiple sources of data.

11

Assessment

Measuring Achievement and Growth in the Block

Authentic classroom assessments provide teachers with a repertoire of tools to measure student growth. . . . [T]eachers need to create vivid, colorful, and true moving pictures of a student as he or she develops and grows over the course of a year.
—Kay Burke 1994, *xxi*

THE RIGHT STUFF

One of the assessment tools that will continue to be used is objective testing. Practical alternatives and sound arguments exist, however, for a new brain-compatible and au-

thentic means of measuring student achievement. Grant Wiggins (1989) suggests that educators should actually teach to the test, but the tests to which they teach need to be very different from what they are now. The *right* kind of assessment is central to the learning process and engages students in real-life situations and applications. Kay Burke defines assessment as the "process of gathering evidence" (Burke 1994, *xvi*). If this is so, then clearly, the more diverse the sources of evidence, the more accurate the picture one can create of student strengths, abilities, and learning differences. In addition, by addressing assessment *during* the instructional-design stage—what Ferrar and McTighe (1996) and Wiggins (1989) call "backward planning"—the entire curricular process is shaped for the better. More brain-compatible assessments actually promote the instructional process like those in the *process phase* of a four-phase lesson plan. Conversely, the practice of teaching to the rigidity of the conventional standardized test with its set of mysterious "correct" answers is outdated and counterproductive. Figure 11.1 illustrates the differences between standardized test formats and their brain-compatible counterparts.

Surface knowledge, fact-based rather than context-based learning (the type most often measured by standardized tests), "does not prepare students to solve complex problems and apply the knowledge to unexpected and complex real-life situations" (Caine, Caine, and Crowell 1994, 47). What is called for is the development within students of dynamic thinking that can adapt to changing circumstances and conditions. Complex thinking is a journey into ambiguous, messy arenas of facts and opinions, which calls for very different kinds of assessment tools. Fogarty and Stoehr (1995) offer the "tri-assessment model," which suggests a combination of three approaches to assessment:

- Traditional test and quiz assessment
- Gathering samples of actual ongoing work into a portfolio
- Observations of students actually carrying out processes, demonstrations, and performances

The key to the tri-assessment model is varying the types of assessment a teacher uses, much the same way a teacher needs to vary instructional strategies. Evidence from various assessment approaches provides a multidimensional view—a "moving" picture, so to speak—that more accurately depicts a student's knowledge, understanding, and capability than can any one type alone. In addition, higher levels of thinking are best measured by authentic, less-traditional forms of assessment. Figure 11.2 "Forms of Assessment" suggests the benefits and characteristics of three forms of assessment.

CAUGHT IN THE ACT OF LEARNING: AUTHENTIC ASSESSMENT

As discussed in previous chapters, there is a necessity for students to perceive a connection between the curriculum and their real lives. Without some kind of rela-

tionship, there is little motivation to become involved with course content. The same can be said of the form of assessment used to determine what a student has learned. It is not that quizzes, multiple-choice, and standardized tests are ineffective; rather, it is that these forms are not enough to give witness to what students "know." Alternative, authentic forms of assessments can be utilized to gain a clear understanding of student learning.

Authentic assessments are those evaluative tools that are relevant and connected to real-life situations. In addition, they recognize the myriad of different student learning styles and provide repeated and various opportunities for students to demonstrate what they have learned. The important connection between "authentic" classroom learning tasks and "authentic" assessment techniques needs to exist. Using the first without the second runs counter to common sense. In the same vein, if educators are facilitating the acquisition of higher-level thinking skills, then the assessment itself needs to be rigorous enough to measure the depth of understanding such an approach brings about (Burke 1994).

Authentic assessments are an excellent system for providing students with a natural and immediate feedback loop. Students using an authentic assessment tool are aware of the performance requirements as they rehearse; they are assessed according to the very requirements they have been rehearsing, and then they are provided feedback regarding how closely they have met the requirements. With the feedback that is part of every assessment tool, students can make immediate alterations in their performance or emerging understanding. Feedback that is specific and immediate is essential to ensure that knowledge or skills are integrated into an appropriate schema and successfully stored in long-term memory. Without consistent and effective feedback, mistakes or "bugs" may be rehearsed over and over again, creating an inappropriate schema stored in long-term memory. Students who have created a malformed schema may never realize their mistake. If and when a misunderstanding or mispatterning is realized, students may have to exert an exhaustive effort to modify their schema. In addition, the timing of feedback needs to be consistent and immediate. Delays in feedback are not harmful as long as students are provided feedback at a time when they can recall their performance clearly and accurately. Authentic assessment tools are ideal for providing students with immediate, consistent, and accurate feedback.

A pleasant by-product of authentic assessment is the emotional context in which the assessment takes place. Emotion plays a central role not only in learning and memory but also in the conditions under which a person is best able to recall and apply information. Because

Standardized Tests vs. Brain-Compatible Assessment

Standardized Testing	Brain-Compatible Assessment
• results based on a mythical standard or norm, which requires that a certain percentage of children fail	• establishes an environment where each child has the opportunity to succeed
• pressures teachers to narrow their curriculum so that they can specifically concentrate on the test material	• allows teachers to develop meaningful curricula and assess within the context of that program
• emphasizes a single-instance assessment, which has no relation to the learning taking place in the classroom	• assessment is ongoing throughout the unit of study and provides an accurate picture of student achievement
• focuses on errors and mistakes rather than on what has been accomplished	• puts the emphasis on student strengths rather than weaknesses
• focuses too much importance on single sets of data (i.e. test scores) in making educational decisions	• provides multiple sources of evaluation that give an in-depth view of student progress
• treats all students in a uniform way	• treats each student as a unique human being
• discriminates against some students because of cultural background and learning style	• provides the opportunity to eliminate cultural bias and gives everyone an equal chance to succeed
• regards instruction and assessment as separate activities	• regards instruction and assessment as being a single, integrated activity
• answers are final, there is no opportunity for reflection or revision	• engages the student in a continual process of self-reflection, learning, and feedback, as well as revision
• focuses on the "right" answer without regard for understanding	• deals with comprehension and the learning process as much as the final product
• inexpensive and easy to administer and grade	• more difficult to achieve consistent, objective scoring results
• often provides results that can be simplified to a single numerical score	• data cannot easily be simplified as a single number
• easy to compare and contrast different populations of students	• difficult to compare different student populations

Figure 11.1
Adapted from *Brain-Compatible Assessments* by Diane Ronis. ©1999 by SkyLight Training and Publishing, Inc. Reprinted with permission of SkyLight Professional Development, Arlington Heights, IL.

authentic assessment is ongoing and an integral part of the instructional process, the test anxiety often associated with more traditional forms of assessment, most notably the standardized test, is not present. Students are relatively free from stress and are better able to demonstrate what they know.

Longer class times permit authentic assessment in ways that shorter class periods cannot. In a traditional fifty-minute class period, there is often barely enough

time for teachers to impart the *who, what,* and *when* of the curricular material. Larger blocks of time allow teachers to guide students to the *why* and *how* elements of the learning equation. Students have time to internalize the material and demonstrate that they know how to apply the material to real-life tasks and situations. Remembering Burke's (1994) definition of assessment as the process of gathering evidence; the question for teaching in the block becomes "What

Forms of Assessment

	Traditional Assessment	Portfolio Assessment	Performance Assessment
Definition	Written summaries of learnings	A collection of work samples from a unit or a semester or a year	Direct observation of a student's performance
Time Component	Periodically	Continually add evidence	Toward the end of a lesson or unit
Benefits	• Easy to grade • Answers are often right or wrong • Displays knowledge of details	• Shows growth and development	• Focuses on what a student does, or on skills a student can demonstrate
Intelligences	• Verbal/Linguistic • Logical/Mathematical • Visual/Spatial	• Visual/Spatial • Intrapersonal • Verbal/Linguistic • Logical/Mathematical • Interpersonal	• Visual/Spatial • Bodily/Kinesthetic • Verbal/Linguistic • Logical/Mathematical • Interpersonal • Musical/Rhythmic • Naturalist
Assessment Tool	**Answer sheet** • Graphic Organizers • Journals	**Rubric** • Standards • Criteria • Indicators • Checklist • Graphic Organizers • Reflections on Portfolio Contents	**Rubric** • Standards • Criteria • Indicators • Checklist

Figure 11.2
Adapted from *Best Practices for the Learner-Centered Classroom* by Robin Fogarty. ©1995 SkyLight Training and Publishing Inc. Reprinted with permission of SkyLight Professional Development, Arlington Heights, IL.

other methods can teachers use to obtain evidence of student understanding?" Skillful teachers expand the variety of assessment forms they use whenever possible. Employing conferences, graphic organizers, journals, logs, observation checklists, portfolios, and rubrics provides teachers *and* the students themselves with evidence that learning is occurring. Each is discussed below.

Conferences allow opportunities for the teacher to meet one on one with a student or a student team. While other class teams are working on projects or other tasks, the teacher can meet with students and verbally check on what learning is going on. Block scheduling offers the kind of multitask lesson flow that permits teacher-student conferencing.

Graphic Organizers are visual tools to help students organize and process a great deal of information.

Journals and Logs are ongoing writing opportunities that allow students to write and reflect upon ongoing learning. Journals are open-ended and contain more personal reflections than logs, which are used for more content-specific reflections, such as thoughts or observations about a science experiment, Internet search, field trip, or service learning experience. In addition, journals and logs offer the type of low-intensity activity essential to pulsed learning.

Observation Checklists are lists of specific criteria a teacher uses to determine a students level of mastery of an activity or concept. Such checklists can include performance criteria related to the following:

General Observations	*Specific Criteria*
• Social skills • Group dynamics • Presentation skills • Laboratory procedures • Steps in the writing and/or researching process	• Disagrees with ideas not the person • Encourages fellow students on his or her team • Speaks clearly and at a moderate rate • Uses appropriate visual tools while presenting • Gathers all the lab material before beginning the lab procedure • Documents each research source

Performance criteria are usually derived by the teacher, a teacher team, or a department from the broader content standards.

Portfolios are collections and samples of student work chosen by the teacher and the student to represent the student's growth and achievement. Portfolios are not just snapshots but moving pictures that illuminate achievement and growth over time. Like journals and logs, portfolio collection and reflection time are low-intensity activities that, in addition to their use in the assessment process, also serve as counterpoints to higher intensity activities. In its simplist form, the portfolio process has three stages: collection, selection, and reflection (Fogarty 1997a).

• *Collection.* Creating the work that may be appropriately placed in the portfolio or gathering artifacts or exhibits that add dimension to an entry or to the overall presentation of the portfolio.

• *Selection.* Determining what materials to include in the portfolio. It is important to note that not only "perfect" work is included. Work that reflects progress and illuminates the process of learning is not only appropriate but necessary to draw a full picture of achievement.

• *Reflection.* Like other activities, portfolio entries are thought about and looked back upon, which requires time to think about the content's purpose and meaning.

Rubrics use specific performance criteria to evaluate the level of student performance on a task or activity. Rubrics give clear guidelines to the student of what "good" and "good enough" look like before they undertake a task. The teacher then uses the rubric to ascertain student achievement. The student isn't left guessing what the teacher is looking for.

Figure 11.3 shows an open "Rubric Template" that teachers may use themselves or with students when constructing such an assessment tool. The column on the far left side of the template is where performance elements such as communication, organization, teamwork, accuracy, originality, and presentation can be listed. The person or persons constructing the rubric generally selects one or two labels for each performance level ("accomplished" and "B," for example). Students may want to use more trendy or informal language to label the levels. Teachers need to make sure the terms are positive ones such as (from lowest to highest level):

Rubric Template

Essential Elements of Performance	Performance Levels			
	Proficient Excellent/ Advanced "A" "4"	Accomplished Good "B" "3"	Basic Acceptable "C" "2"	Novice Not Yet "D" "1"
	Specific Performance Criteria ————————————————→			

Figure 11.3

First Base—Second Base—Third Base—Home Run!
Apprentice—Expert—Master
Needs more thought—Awesome!

The template shows four levels, but rubrics can have as few as two levels—acceptable and unacceptable for example. Two-level rubrics are often constructed to evaluate journal entries. The specific performance criteria fill in the rest of the grid. It is perhaps easiest to begin with what the best possible work would look like. At the highest level, the criteria are challenging and akin to what may have been formerly considered "extra credit." It is only by going the extra mile, so to speak, that students can attain the highest level.

Figure 11.4 directs the reader to other figures in this book that illustrate the various assessment tools discussed above as part of the four-phase lesson plans at the end of chapters 1 though 5.

Students who underperform on traditional tests can communicate their mastery of material through projects, performances, or demonstrations. Further, authentic assessment is perhaps the best chance for students to show "how they are smart" in terms of their own unique development of the intelligences. This presents a real challenge to teachers accustomed to working within the confines of the traditional time and assessment structure. Therefore, ongoing staff development is a necessary ingredient of successful block scheduling.

TESTING MATTERS

For better or worse, schools and their programs are often judged by the outcomes of standardized tests. Testing is a fact of life. While standardized tests will no doubt remain an educational constant, how schools and teachers relate to the tests will have a huge impact on their students. In an alternative scheduling context, the question of standardized testing is all the more pro-

nounced. The success of alternative scheduling is often judged by the performance of students in the block relative to their peers learning under a traditional schedule (Benton-Kupper 1999). Perhaps the two biggest perceived challenges to the efficacy of a block schedule are scope and recency of materials covered. "If the focus remains on surface learning and low-level recall, then the recency of exposure is critical!" (Rettig and Canady 1996, 10). But if the material is covered in depth, greater retention for longer periods can be achieved. Teachers experienced in the block report they can discern little educational significance between the difference in retention of students who recently completed a class over those students with greater time lapses between courses. So, once again, the question appears not so much to be one of the assessment or testing process but one of curricular material and instructional approaches.

The greatest predictor of student performance is what actually takes place in the classroom, whether it takes place in the block or within a conventional schedule. Students taught with strategies that tap into their long-term memory have a better chance to recall material on standardized tests than they would if their short-term memory were the focus. (See chapter 1 for a discussion of memory.) "Not surprisingly, students given instruction aimed at conceptual understanding do better on skills tests than students drilled on the skills directly" (Carpenter and others 1988). In addition to teaching to long-term memory, teachers need to employ the best practices in structuring extended class time. If teachers fail to use the time in the block efficiently, a decrease in standardized test scores can result.

By postponing higher-order thinking goals, skills remediation classes have a deleterious effect on the standarized test scores of students placed in these classes. Low-achieving students suffer most from a proficiency-driven curriculum (measured by standardized tests) because they are consigned indefinitely to dull and repetitive skills instruction that does not enable them to grasp

Evaluation Tools Modeled	
Tool	**As Illustrated in Figures**
Four-Level Rubric	2.8, 4.12, 5.3 (template), 5.5
Group Presentation Rubric	1.5
Teacher Observation	3.6
Portfolio Evaluation Rubric	4.11
Student Self-Assessment	3.9

Figure 11.4

underlying concepts (Levin, Glass, and Meister 1987). Luckily, brain-compatible learning approaches can have a dramatic impact even on students who have previously been labeled "low achieving." When instructional approaches are varied, when the curriculum content is made relevant and applicable to real-life situations, learning moves from mere rote memorization to deeply internalized, usable information. When this occurs, the material can be retained far longer than previously thought possible. Longer class times allow teachers more occasions to discern how well the material is being absorbed and to decide whether any reteaching strategies are needed to enable students to better grasp the material (Fitzgerald 1996).

IRON OUT THE "FORGETTING CURVE"

Some schools teaching in the block prepare their students for standardized tests by scheduling *structured review sessions*. Such sessions are scheduled three or four weeks before the tests are given. Their purpose is to help students recall the significant details needed for the test. If the original class work has emphasized the frameworks and the concepts, then the review sessions need only remind the students of these frameworks and concepts and then help the students get on top of the details again. On the other hand, if the original class work neglected sense-making frameworks and concepts, then it is as if the students are just beginning to absorb the details needed for the tests. This will make preparing for the standardized tests doubly difficult (College Boards Online 1999).

Extended time formats permit the teacher to spend time teaching the concepts and the overall frameworks of the material being presented. Probing questions that help students make connections to other material can be just the connections needed to push the material into long-term memory.

While student performance on standardized tests isn't the purpose of teaching, brain-compatible teaching methodologies that lay out frameworks and concepts as containers for crucial facts and information greatly enable peak student performance on such tests (Burke 1992). The more brain-compatible the structured review sessions are, the more powerful and long-lasting their effect will be. Students working within a system that harnesses the power of cooperative learning, recognizes multiple intelligences, facilitates the expansion of higher-order thinking skills, and provides adequate time for learning and metacognition retain information for use on standardized tests and beyond.

Tests Are Changing

Today, some standardized tests are very different from the simple multiple-choice tests of years ago (Burke 1992). Thinking and the ability to transfer and connect information are increasingly becoming part of standardized tests. Because the tests are changing, it is even more important than ever that teaching in the block emphasize concepts, frameworks, higher-order thinking skills, and applications to real life. Details are important. Discrete pieces of information will continue to be tested; however, much more is demanded of students in the real world than recollection of isolated bits of information. The brain-compatible pedagogy that alternative scheduling facilitates and encourages is well-suited to meet the rigorous demands society and the economy place on the educational system.

MEASURE UP

The ultimate reason and perhaps the only valid reason for implementing a program such as alternative block scheduling is because it has a positive impact on student achievement. Possibly the easiest way to "judge" (or at least the most frequently used way) student success and program success is testing. So naturally, the first trial block scheduling must undergo is how it fares under the glare of standardized testing. Studies have shown that students in the block have fared as well on such tests as their counterparts in traditionally scheduled classes (Baylis 1983). Several studies have found that both student conduct (attendance, attention, and morale) and academic performance (content mastery, post-test versus pre-test gains, and standardized test scores) are improved when block scheduling is instituted (Baylis 1983, Carroll 1994, Benton-Kupper 1999).

ASSESSMENT IN FOUR-PHASE LESSON AND UNIT DESIGN

When teachers use the Four-Phase Lesson design with its repeated "attend-experience-reflect" cycle they have an automatic, built-in format for providing students with thoughtful feedback in the form of authentic assessment. The design provides teachers with a structure for helping students process their learning, evaluate their respective levels of performance, and use authentic assessment as a natural part of the learning process.

The assessment process is integral to the learning process. Students need to engage in defining the performance criteria and working toward attaining high standards. Authentic assessment helps students achieve "excellence" because they know in advance what it looks like from the rubric or other format for the criteria.

Sample Four-Phase Lesson Plan # 5 is a structured review lesson in preparation for students taking a college advanced-placement (AP) test and, as stated above, is a method for "ironing out," or recalling information previously stored in long-term memory. *Science Schmience or Who Framed Sir Isaac Newton?* is offered here as a sample of what could be included in a unit taught in a mini session. The purposes of the lesson are to assist students in remembering important information, identifying ways to associate the information, and familiarizing themselves with the AP test question format. The curriculum connection is science. The AP European history teacher may want to invite one or more of the science teachers (physics, psychology, chemistry, biology, physiology) to act as a resource person during this lesson. While science was selected as the focus of this lesson, the focus could be any of the broad topics covered in AP European history such as art, music, literature, economics, government, war, or any other applicable topic.

Notice how students manipulate the course content in a variety of ways. Students do all of the talking and discussing during this lesson. Since students are reviewing in preparation for a major test, it is critical for them to share their knowledge and insights with each other, to practice saying things they might actually write, and to hear how others have connected the information to clarify their own understanding and to remember details and concepts.

Sample Four-Phase Lesson Plan

Sample Lesson 5

SCIENCE SCHMIENCE OR WHO FRAMED SIR ISAAC NEWTON?

Level: Secondary

Curriculum Integration: European History and Science

Multiple Intelligences

☑ Bodily/Kinesthetic   ❑ Musical
☑ Interpersonal   ❑ Naturalist
❑ Intrapersonal   ☑ Verbal/Linguistic
☑ Logical/Mathematical   ☑ Visual/Spacial

Content Standards

World History (European)

Understands major trends, technological advances, cultural innovations, and political, social, and cultural redefinitions in Europe from 4000 BCE to 20th century

Understands the impact of scientific and technological innovations on 20th century society

Understands major reasons for the great disparities between scientifically advanced industrialized nations and developing nations

Science

Understands the nature of scientific knowledge
Understands the scientific enterprise

INQUIRE PHASE
20 MINUTES

Inquire Activity Option A

Objective: To recall events from European history and arrange them in chronological order.

Attend

The teacher begins a dialogue in the following way . . .

- Today is a review of European history from the scientists' point of view.
- Think about all the scientific advances and issues that have had an impact on the political, economic, social, religious, intellectual, and artistic development of Europe.
- Discuss some of your thoughts with a classmate next to you.

Experience: "Human Timeline"

Each student . . .

- Independently chooses an event from European history.
- Draws a picture or other visual representation of the event on a 5- by 7-inch card or blank sheet of paper.
- Secures their completed card or paper to the front of their shirt with tape.
- Moves about the room to find one or more other students who have depicted the same event or an event that influenced or was influenced by their event.
- Lines up in chronological order with those they have identified as being somehow related to their topic.
- Discusses their event within their small group and then shares the events they depicted with the rest of the class.

Reflect

Students . . .

- Write in their metacognitive journals about their perceptions of how recent scientific discoveries have impacted today's culture, society, and government.

Inquire Activity Option B

Objective: Students recall and relate historical events having to do with science and the course of European history.

Attend

Teachers ask the following questions to start a class discussion . . .

- Do you think you have a good memory? Why or why not?
- Is a good memory important in an age when computers contain trillions of bits of information? Why or why not?

Experience: "Where Science and History Collide"

Students . . .

- Working alone, list every issue or event that comes to mind related to European history and science.
- Compare their lists in pairs or triads.

The teacher . . .

- Leads a whole-class discussion following each brainstorm and small-group sharing.
- Repeats the process two or three times.

Reflect

The teacher asks the class . . .

- What reminders were there for you during the Human Timeline activities?
- What did you hear that became clearer, made more sense, or introduced new connections to you?
- What can you do to remember this information?

GATHER PHASE
25 MINUTES

Gather Activity Option A

Objective: Students "gather," from other students and their own memory, specific elements of European history that were affected by scientific discoveries.

Attend

The teacher begins a class discussion that will introduce the students to the experience . . .

- In our next experience you will have to think like a detective.
- Does anybody know what *deductive reasoning* means?
- When would it be used? And by whom?
- If I told you that *inductive reasoning* uses the opposite method of determining information of deductive reasoning, what do you think the term means?

Experience: "Roving Investigators"

The teacher . . .

- Writes one person, place, event, or issue on a 3- by 5-inch card, filling out as many cards as there are ideas generated in the *inquire* phase (at least one for every student).
- Randomly places one card on the back of each student without the student knowing what item is on his or her back.

Students . . .

- Meander around the room asking "yes or no" or "true or false" questions of each other to determine the entry on their backs.
- May not give hints and must answer truthfully.
- Determine who or what is on their backs, then turn in their cards to the teacher and receive a different card.
- Continue investigating until every card is identified or until time is up.

Gather Activity Option B

Objective: Students design memory aids.

Attend

The teacher asks the following questions to begin a class discussion . . .

- When you were younger, how did you memorize spelling words?
- Do you or did you go about studying for a test on the plot and meaning of a novel differently than you would have studied for a spelling test?

Experience: "Left to Their Own Devices"

Students . . .

- In groups of three or four, design mnemonics and visuals, write lyrics to familiar tunes, or invent other ways to help them remember details about the names, places, and events on the cards.

Reflect
"Talking Circles"

Students . . .

- Stand in two concentric circles, with half the students on the inside circle, the other half on the outside circle.
- Face each other to talk with another student. One circle moves clockwise, while the other moves counterclockwise, moving ahead by one person each time the teacher asks one of the questions below. Each new pair exchanges their answer with the person they encountered on the circle.

The teacher asks . . .

- Of all the information you talked about today, what do you think are the most critical points for you to remember? Why?
- Why is it important to remember this information, beyond taking the AP exam?
- How is your world different today because of what happened in Europe?
- Enough other pertinent questions to complete the circle's cycle once.

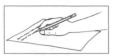

PROCESS PHASE
30 MINUTES

Process Activity

Objective: Students create mock AP test questions.

Attend

The teacher focuses student attention on the next experience by beginning a discussion . . .

- You are going to create some questions that are AP test quality. What do you think makes an excellent AP question? Share with a partner.
- Look at some sample questions in the AP European history test preparation book. What is the quality of these questions? Share with the class.
- Let's decide what makes a good AP question.

Students and teachers create a checklist for writing test questions.
Students . . .

- Working in groups of three, look through the AP test preparation manual to become familiar with the types of questions posed on the test.
- Determine characteristics of the test questions and the accompanying multiple-choice options.
- Share their findings with the class in order to develop a master set of criteria for use in evaluating the questions the student triads create. The rubric can be used for student self-evaluation, as refined directions for the activity, and as the instrument with which the students are evaluated on the experience.)

Experience: "Mock Questions"

Students . . .

- Working in the same groups and using the established criteria (see Figure 11.5) generate mock questions with a focus on science (three multiple-choice questions that include answer options and one essay question).
- Join another group and answer each other's test questions. Answers are discussed and groups give feed-

back to each other on the quality of the questions they created.
- Move to a different group and repeat the process one or two more times.
- Submit their test questions to the teacher.

The teacher . . .

- Randomly selects questions to ask the whole class.
- Facilitates a discussion on each question, reinforcing appropriate responses and eliciting multiple answers.
- Evaluates each group's questions using the rubric.

Reflect

The teacher asks the following questions, prompting student discussion . . .

- What do you think makes a good test question?
- How will knowing how good test questions are written help you be a better test taker?
- What procedure should you follow when answering multiple-choice and essay questions to improve the quality of your answers?

APPLY PHASE
15 MINUTES

Apply Activity

Objective: Students make meaning from the material by making connections between its various elements.

Attend

Students . . .

- Identify practical reasons for understanding and remembering information taught in AP European history.
- Write in their personal reflection journal their thoughts on the following questions:
    - What are some legitimate reasons for U.S. high school students to study European history?
    - In what ways are you a different person from the person who began this structured review class?
    - What long-term impact will what you learned about European history and test-taking have on your life?

Experience: "Cross-Content Connections"

Students . . .

- In small groups, create a graphic organizer, chart, graph, or other visual that demonstrates the relationship between science and any one of the following as it pertains to European history: visual arts, music, literature, economics, social systems, religion, war, government, or agriculture.

Mock Question Criteria				
	Performance Levels			
	Novice	**Adequate**	**Accomplished**	**Advanced**
Directions Clarity	Difficult to understand	Not entirely clear	Clearly stated	Very clearly and concisely stated
Questions Precision Accuracy Coverage	Did not evidence understanding of the material	Drawn too narrowly or too broadly and/or contained inaccurate references	Careful and accurate	Precise, accurate, and dealt with appropriate and challenging content that sought application of higher-level thinking skills
Options Number provided Length Accuracy	Do not reflect a serious attempt to construct useful and valid options	Provided four options for most Length of options "telegraphed" correct answer Some inaccuracies	Demonstrated understanding of material	Provided five challenging options of equal length for each with a clearly correct answer
Mechanics Spelling Grammar Punctuation	Substantial mechanical errors or repeated misspelling or inconsistently rendering proper names	Some mechanical errors, which in places detracted from question quality	Provided five options for most, some "decoy" options were too obvious and/or answer was too "tricky" Accurate Any errors in mechanics did not significantly detract from question quality	No spelling, grammar or punctuation errors

Figure 11.5

- Prepare to share their visual during the next class.

Reflect

The teacher poses the following questions . . .

- What is one thing that worries you most about taking the AP exam?
- What would you like to review before you take the exam?
- Who is in the best position to help you prepare for the exam?

HOMEWORK ASSIGNMENT

Students . . .

- Individually review their notes, books, or other sources to add information to their copy of the group visual they have started.

12

Assessing and Reporting Student Achievement

While preceding parts of this book addressed the *why* (Part I), *what* (Part II), and *how* (Part III) of teaching, Part IV focuses on the fourth and final component—the *how well*, or assessment, component. Together, these four components are the essentials of effective instruction.

Teaching and learning are reciprocal processes that depend on and affect one another. Thus, the assessment component deals with both how well the students are learning and how well the teacher is teaching. This chapter addresses the first.

Assessment is an integral part of an ongoing process in the educational arena. Curricula, buildings, materials, specific courses, teachers, supervisors, administrators, equipment—all must be periodically assessed in relation to student learning, the purpose of the school. When gaps between anticipated results and student achievement exist, efforts are made to eliminate those factors that seem to be limiting the educational output or in some other way to improve the situation. Thus, educational progress occurs.

Much concern today is expressed over the use of what is referred to as *high-stakes assessments*. An assessment is called *high stakes* if the assessment's results carry serious consequences, such as, a student's grade promotion rests on the student's performance on the test, or a student's graduation from high school rests on the student's performance on one administration of a single test. We agree with the many educators who argue that important decisions that affect a student's educational career should not rest on one test score alone but on multiple sources of data. In our opinion, placing too high a reliance on a single source of data is likely to result in an increase, rather than in an improvement, in the school dropout rate.

To learn effectively, students need to know how they are doing. Similarly, to be an effective teacher, you must be informed about what the student knows, feels, and can do so that you can help the student build on her or his skills, knowledge, and attitudes. Therefore you and your students need continuous feedback on their progress and problems in order to plan appropriate learning activities and to make adjustments to those already planned. If this feedback says that progress is slow, you can provide alternative activities; if it indicates that some or all of the students have already mastered the desired learning, you can eliminate unnecessary activities and practice for some or all of the students. In short, assessment provides a key for both effective teaching and learning.

The importance of continuous assessment mandates that you know various principles and techniques of assessment. This chapter explains some of those and shows you how to construct and use assessment instruments. It defines terms related to assessment, suggests procedures to use in the construction of assessment items, points out the advantages and disadvantages of different types of assessment items and procedures, and explains the construction and use of alternative assessment devices.

In addition, this chapter discusses grading (or marking) and reporting of student achievement, two professional responsibilities that can consume much of a teacher's valuable time. Grading is time-consuming and frustrating for many teachers. What should be graded? Should grades or marks represent student growth, level of achievement in a group, effort, attitude, general behavior, or a combination of these? What should determine grades—homework, tests, projects, class participation and group work, or some combination of these? And, what should be their relative weights? These are just a few of the questions that plague teachers, parents, and, indeed the profession, and have for a century or more in this country.

Still today, in too many secondary schools, the grade progress report and final report card are about the only

communication between the school and the student's home. Unless the teacher and the school have clearly determined what grades or marks represent and unless such understanding is periodically reviewed with each set of new parents or guardians, these reports may create unrest and dissatisfaction on the parts of parents and guardians and prove to be alienating devices. The grading system and reporting scheme, then, instead of informing parents and guardians may separate even further the home and the school, which do have a common concern—the intellectual, physical, social, and emotional development of the adolescent student.

The development of the adolescent student encompasses growth in the cognitive, affective, and psychomotor domains. Traditional objective paper-and-pencil tests provide only a portion of the data needed to indicate student progress in those domains. Many experts today, as indeed they have in the past, question the traditional sources of data and encourage the search for, development of, and use of alternative means to assess more authentically the students' development of thinking and higher-level learning. Although many things are not yet clear, one thing that is clear is that various techniques of assessment with the resultant multiple kinds of data must be used to determine how the student works, what the student is learning, and what the student can produce as a result of that learning. As the teacher, you must develop a repertoire of means of assessing learner behavior and academic progress.

Although marks and grades have been a part of school for about 100 years, and although it is clear to many experts that the conventional report card with marks or grades falls short of being a developmentally appropriate procedure for reporting the academic performance or progress of learners, and although some schools are experimenting with other ways of reporting student achievement in learning, letter grades for secondary schools still seem firmly entrenched—parents, students, colleges, and employers have come to expect grades as evaluations. Today's interest is (or should be) more on what the student can do (performance testing) as a result of learning than merely on what the student can recall (memory testing) from the experience.

In addition, there have been complaints about subjectivity and unfair practices. As a result of these concerns, a variety of systems of assessment and reporting has evolved, is still evolving, and will likely continue to evolve throughout your professional career.

When teachers are aware of alternative systems, they may be able to develop assessment and reporting processes that are fair and effective for particular situations. So, after beginning with assessment, the final focus in this chapter considers today's principles and practices in grading and reporting student achievement at the secondary school level.

Specifically, upon completion of this chapter you should be able to:

1. Demonstrate an understanding of the importance of assessment in teaching and learning.
2. Explain the concept of authentic assessment.
3. Explain the value of and give an example of a performance assessment that could be used in teaching your subject.
4. Explain why criterion-referenced grading is preferred over norm-referenced grading.
5. Explain how rubrics, checklists, portfolios, and journals are used in the assessment of student learning.
6. Differentiate among diagnostic assessment, summative assessment, and formative assessment, with examples of when and how each can be used at a particular grade level or discipline.
7. Describe the importance of and place for self-assessment in teaching and learning.
8. Describe the importance of and manner by which parents and guardians can be involved in the education of their children.

PURPOSES AND PRINCIPLES OF ASSESSMENT

Assessment of achievement in student learning is designed to serve the following seven purposes:

1. To *assist in student learning.* This is the purpose usually first thought of when speaking of assessment, and it is the principal topic of this chapter. For the classroom teacher it is (or should be) the most important purpose.
2. To *identify students' strengths and weaknesses.* Identification and assessment of students' strengths and weaknesses are necessary for two reasons: to structure and restructure the learning activities and to restructure the curriculum. Concerning the first, for example, data on student strengths and weaknesses in content and process skills are important in planning activities appropriate for both skill development and intellectual development. This is diagnostic assessment (known also as preassessment). For the second, data on student strengths and weaknesses in content and skills are useful for making appropriate modifications to the curriculum.
3. To *assess the effectiveness of a particular instructional strategy.* It is important for you to know how well a particular strategy helped accomplish a particular goal or objective. Exemplary teachers continually reflect on and evaluate their strategy choices, using a number of sources: student achievement as measured by assessment instruments, their own intuition, informal feedback given by the students, and, sometimes, informal feedback given by colleagues, such as members of a teaching team or mentor teachers.

4. To *assess and improve the effectiveness of curriculum programs.* Committees composed of teachers and administrators and sometimes parents/guardians students, and other members of the school and community continually assess components of the curriculum. The assessment is done while students are learning (i.e., formative assessment) and afterward (summative assessment).
5. To *assess and improve teaching effectiveness.* To improve student learning, teachers are periodically evaluated on the basis of: (a) their commitment to working with students, (b) their ability to work with students in a particular subject at a particular grade level, and (c) their ability to show mastery of appropriate instructional techniques articulated throughout this book.
6. To *provide data that assist in decision making about a student's future.* Assessment of student achievement is important in guiding decision making about course and program placement, promotion, school transfer, class standing, eligibility for honors and scholarships, graduation, and career planning.
7. To provide data in order to *communicate with and involve parents and guardians in their children's learning.* Parents and guardians, communities, and school boards all share in accountability for the effectiveness of the learning of the children. Today's secondary schools are reaching out more than ever and engaging parents, guardians, and the community in their young people's education. All teachers play an important role in the process of communicating with, reaching out to, and involving parents and guardians and the community.

Because the welfare and, indeed, the future of so many people depend on the outcomes of assessment, it is impossible to overemphasize its importance. For a learning endeavor to be successful, the learner must have answers to basic questions: Where am I going? Where am I now? How do I get where I am going? How will I know when I get there? Am I on the right track for getting there? These questions are integral to a good program of assessment. Of course, in the process of teaching and learning, the answers may be ever-changing, and the teacher and students must continue to assess and adjust plans as appropriate and necessary. As you have been reminded many times in this book, the exemplary school is in a mode of continuous change and progress.

Based on the preceding questions, there are eight principles that guide the assessment program and that are reflected in the discussions in this chapter.

- A teacher's responsibility is to facilitate student learning and to assess student progress in that learning, and for that the teacher is, or should be, held accountable.
- Assessment is a continuous process. The selection and implementation of plans and activities require

that teachers continue to monitor and assess progress and to change or adopt strategies to promote desired behavior.

- Assessment is a reciprocal process, which includes assessment of teacher performance as well as student achievement.
- Students need to know how well they are doing.
- Teachers need to know how well they are doing.
- Evidence and input data for knowing how well the teacher and students are doing should come from a variety of sources and types of data-collecting devices.
- Reflection and self-assessment are important components of any successful assessment program. Reflection and self-assessment are important if students are to develop the skills necessary for them to assume increasingly greater ownership of their own learning. Reflection and self-assessment are important for the continued and increasing effectiveness of a teacher.
- The program of assessment should aid teaching effectiveness and contribute to the intellectual and psychological growth of students.

TERMS USED IN ASSESSMENT

When discussing the assessment component of teaching and learning it is easy to be confused by the terminology. The following clarification of terms is offered to aid your reading and comprehension.

Assessment and Evaluation

Although some authors distinguish between the terms **assessment** (the process of finding out what students are learning, a relatively neutral process) and **evaluation** (making sense of what was found out, a subjective process), in this text we do not. We consider the difference too slight to matter; we consider the terms to be synonymous.

Measurement and Assessment

Measurement refers to quantifiable data about specific behaviors. Tests and the statistical procedures used to analyze the results are examples. Measurement is a descriptive and objective process; that is, it is relatively free from human value judgments.

Assessment includes objective data from measurement but also other types of information, some of which are more subjective, such as information from anecdotal records and teacher observations and ratings of student performance. In addition to the use of objective data (data from measurement), assessment includes arriving at value judgments made on the basis of subjective information.

An example of the use of these terms is as follows. A teacher may share the information that Penny Brown received a score in the 90th percentile on the eighth-grade state-wide achievement test in reading (a statement of measurement) but may add that "according to my assessment of her work in my language arts class, she has not been an outstanding student" (a statement of assessment).

Validity and Reliability

The degree to which a measuring instrument actually measures that which it is intended to measure is the instrument's **validity.** For example, when we ask if an instrument (such as a performance assessment instrument) has validity, key questions concerning that instrument are: Does the instrument adequately sample the intended content? Does it measure the cognitive, affective, and psychomotor knowledge and skills that are important to the unit of content being tested? Does it sample all the instructional objectives of that unit?

The accuracy with which a technique consistently measures that which it does measure is its **reliability.** If, for example, you know that you weigh 118 pounds, and a scale consistently records 118 pounds when you stand on it, then that scale has reliability. However, if the same scale consistently records 105 pounds when you stand on it, we can still say the scale has reliability. By this example, then, it should be clear to you that an instrument could be reliable (it produces similar results when used again and again) although not necessarily valid. In this second instance, the scale is not measuring what it is supposed to measure, so although it is reliable, it is not valid. Although a technique might be reliable but not valid, a technique must have reliability before it can have validity. The greater the number of test items or situations on a particular content objective, the higher the reliability. The higher the reliability, the more consistency there will be in students' scores measuring their understanding of that particular objective.

Authentic Assessment: Advantages and Disadvantages

When assessing for student achievement, it is important that you use procedures compatible with the instructional objectives. This is referred to as authentic assessment. Other terms used for authentic assessment are *accurate, active, aligned, alternative,* and *direct.* Although *performance* assessment is sometimes used, performance assessment refers to the type of student response being assessed, whereas authentic assessment refers to the assessment situation. Although not all performance assessments are authentic, assessments that are authentic are most assuredly performance assessments.

In English/language arts, for example, though it may seem fairly easy to develop a criterion-referenced test, administer it, and grade it, tests often measure language *skills* rather than language use. It is extremely difficult to measure students' communicative competence with a test. Tests do not measure listening and talking very well, and a test on punctuation marks, for example, does not indicate students' ability to use punctuation marks correctly in their own writing. Instead, tests typically evaluate students' ability to add punctuation marks to a set of sentences created by someone else or to proofread and spot punctuation errors in someone else's writing. An alternative and far better approach is to examine how students use punctuation marks in their own writing.[1] An authentic assessment of punctuation, then, would be an assessment of a performance item that involves students in writing and punctuating their own writing. For the authentic assessment of the student's understanding of that which the student has been learning, you would use a performance-based assessment procedure.

In another example: "If students have been actively involved in classifying objects using multiple characteristics, it sends them a confusing message if they are then required to take a paper-and-pencil test that asks them to 'define classification' or recite a memorized list of characteristics of good classifications schemes."[2] An authentic assessment technique would be a performance item that actually involves the students in classifying objects. In other words, to obtain an accurate assessment of a student's learning, the teacher uses a performance-based assessment procedure, that is, a procedure that requires students to produce rather than to select a response.

Advantages claimed for the use of authentic assessment include (a) the direct (also known as performance-based, criterion-referenced, outcome-based) measurement of what students should know and can do and (b) an emphasis on higher order thinking. On the other hand, disadvantages of authentic assessment include a higher cost, difficulty in making results consistent and usable, and problems with validity, reliability, and comparability.

Unfortunately, for the teacher who may never see a particular student again after a given school semester or year is over, the effect a teacher has had on a student's values and attitudes may never be observed by that teacher at all. In schools where groups or teams of teachers remain with the same cohort of students—as in the school-within-a-school programs and looping or banding (discussed in Chapter 1)—those teachers often do have an opportunity to observe the positive changes in their students' values and attitudes.

[1] G. E. Tompkins and K. Hoskisson, *Language Arts: Content and Teaching Strategies* (Upper Saddle River, NJ: Prentice Hall, 1991), p. 63.
[2] S. J. Rakow, "Assessment: A Driving Force," *Science Scope* 15(6):3 (March 1992).

Assessing Student Achievement: Diagnostic, Formative, and Summative

Assessing a student's achievement is a three-stage process. These three stages are: (1) *diagnostic assessment* (sometimes called preassessment)—the assessment of the student's knowledge and skills *before* the new instruction; (2) *formative assessment*—the assessment of learning *during* the instruction; and (3) *summative assessment*—the assessment of learning *after* the instruction, ultimately represented by the student's final term, semester, or year's achievement grade.

Grades (or marks) shown on unit tests, progress reports, deficiency notices, and interim reports are examples of formative evaluation reports. However, an end-of-chapter test or a unit test is summative when the test represents the absolute end of the student's learning of material for that instructional unit.

ASSESSING STUDENT LEARNING: THREE AVENUES

The three general avenues available for assessing a student's achievement in learning are: (1) assess what the student *says*—for example, the quantity and quality of a student's contributions to class discussions; (2) assess what the student *does*—for example, a student's performance, or the amount and quality of a student's participation in the learning activities; and (3) assess what the student *writes*—for example, as shown by items in the student's portfolio of homework assignments, checklists, project work, and written tests.

Importance and Weight of Each Avenue

Although your own situation and personal philosophy will dictate the levels of importance and weight you give to each avenue of assessment, you should have a strong rationale if you do not see the three avenues for assessment as having equal values.

Assessing What a Student Says and Does

When evaluating what a student says, you should listen to the student's oral reports, questions, responses, and interactions with others, and observe the student's attentiveness, involvement in class activities, creativeness, and responses to challenges. Notice that we say you should *listen* and *observe*. While listening to what the student is saying, you should also be observing the student's nonverbal behaviors. For this you can use narrative observation forms (see Figure 12.1), observations with checklists and scoring rubrics of the student's performance in learning activities (see sample checklists in Figures 12.2, 12.4, and 12.5, and sample scoring rubrics

Objective	Desired Behavior	What Student Did, Said, or Wrote

Student _____   Course _____   School _____

Observer _____   Date _____   Period _____

Teacher's (Observer's) comments:

Figure 12.1
Sample form for evaluating and recording student verbal and nonverbal behaviors.

in Figures 12.1, 12.2, 12.3, 12.10, 12.11, and 12.12), and periodic conferences with the student.

With each technique used, you must proceed from your awareness of anticipated learning outcomes (the instructional objectives), and you must assess a student's progress toward meeting those objectives. That is referred to as **criterion-referenced assessment.**

Observation Form

Figure 12.1 illustrates a sample, generic form for recording and evaluating teacher observations of a student's verbal and nonverbal behaviors. With modern technology, such as is afforded, for example, by the software program *Learner Profile,* a teacher can record observations electronically anywhere at any time.[3]

Checklist versus Scoring Rubric

As you can see from the sample rubric and sample checklist shown in Figure 12.2, there is little difference between what is a checklist and what is a rubric: The difference is that rubrics show the degrees for the desired characteristics while checklists usually show only the desired characteristics. The checklist could easily be made into a scoring rubric and the rubric could easily be made into a checklist.

---

[3]For information about Learner Profile, contact Sunburst, 101 Castleton Street, PO Box 100, Pleasantville, NY 10570-0100. Phone (800) 321-7511. See http://www.sunburst-store.com.

Sample rubric for assessing a student's skill in listening.

Score Point 3—Strong listener:
  Responds immediately to oral directions
  Focuses on speaker
  Maintains appropriate attention span
  Listens to what others are saying
  Is interactive
Score Point 2—Capable listener:
  Follows oral directions
  Usually attentive to speaker and to discussions
  Listens to others without interrupting
Score Point 1—Developing listener:
  Has difficulty following directions
  Relies on repetition
  Often inattentive
  Has short attention span
  Often interrupts the speaker

Sample checklist for assessing a student's skill in map work:

Check each item if the map comes up to standard in this particular category.

_____ 1. Accuracy

_____ 2. Neatness

_____ 3. Attention to details

Figure 12.2
Checklist and rubric compared.

Guidelines for Assessing What a Student Says and Does

When assessing a student's verbal and nonverbal behaviors in the classroom you should:

- Maintain an anecdotal record book or folder (teacher's log), with a separate section in it for your records on each student.
- For a specific activity, list the desirable behaviors.
- Check the list against the specific instructional objectives.
- Record your observations as quickly as possible following your observation. Audio or video recordings, and, of course, computer software programs, can help you maintain records and check the accuracy of your memory, but if this is inconvenient, you should spend time during school, immediately after school, or later that evening recording your observations while they are still fresh in your memory
- Record your professional judgment about the student's progress toward the desired behavior, but think it through before transferring it to a permanent record.
- Write comments that are reminders to yourself, such as, "Discuss observation with the student," "Check validity of observation by further testing," "Discuss observations with student's mentor" (e.g., an adult representative from the community), and "Discuss observations with other teachers on the teaching team."

Assessing What a Student Writes

When assessing what a student writes, you can use worksheets, written homework and papers, student journal writing, student writing projects, student portfolios, and tests (all discussed later in this chapter). In many schools, portfolios, worksheets, and homework assignments are the tools usually used for the formative evaluation of each student's achievement. Tests, too, should be a part of this evaluation, but tests are also used for summative evaluation at the end of a unit and for diagnostic purposes.

Your summative evaluation of a student's achievement and any other final judgment made by you about a student can have impact upon the psychological and intellectual development of that student. Special attention is given to this later in the section titled Recording Teacher Observations and Judgments.

Guidelines for Assessing Student Writing

Use the following guidelines when assessing what a student writes.

Student writing assignments, test items, and scoring rubrics (see Figure 12.3) *should be criterion-referenced,* that is, they should correlate with and be compatible with specific instructional objectives. Regardless of the avenue chosen, and their relative weights given by you, you must evaluate against the instructional objectives. Any given objective may be checked by using more than one method and by using more than one instrument. Subjectivity, inherent in the assessment process, may be reduced as you check for validity, comparing results of one measuring strategy against those of another.

Read nearly everything a student writes [Note: We are not talking about student diaries and private journals which are just that—private—and in our opinion should be left at home, not brought to school.] Regarding schoolwork, if it is important for the student to do the work, then it is equally important that you give your professional attention to the product of the student's efforts. Of course, papers can be read with varying degrees of intensity and scrutiny, depending on the purpose of the assignment.

Provide written or verbal comments about the student's work, and be positive in those comments. Rather than just writing "good" on a student's paper, briefly state what it was that in your opinion made it good. Rather than simply saying or pointing out that the student didn't do it right, tell or show the student what is acceptable and how to achieve it. For reinforcement, use positive comments and encouragement as frequently as possible.

Think before writing a comment on a student's paper, asking yourself how you think the student (or a parent

---

Score Point 4—correct purpose, mode, audience; effective elaboration; consistent organization; clear sense of order and completeness; fluent
Score Point 3—correct purpose, mode, audience; moderately well elaborated; organized but possible brief digressions; clear, effective language
Score Point 2—correct purpose, mode, audience; some elaboration; some specific details; gaps in organization; limited language control
Score Point 1—attempts to address audience; brief, vague, unelaborated; wanders off topic; lack of language control; little or no organization; wrong purpose and mode

Figure 12.3
Sample scoring rubric for assessing student writing.
Source: Texas Education Agency, *Writing Inservice Guide for English Language Arts and TAAS* (Austin, TX: Author, 1993).

or guardian) will interpret and react to the comment and if that is a correct interpretation or reaction to your intended meaning.

Avoid writing evaluative comments or grades in student journals.[4] Student journals are for encouraging students to write, to think about their thinking, and to record their creative thoughts. In journal writing, students should be encouraged to write about their experiences in school and out of school and especially about their experiences related to what is being learned. They should be encouraged to write their feelings about what is being learned and how they are learning it. Writing in journals gives them practice in expressing themselves in written form and in connecting their learning and should provide nonthreatening freedom to do it. Comments and evaluations from teachers might discourage creative and spontaneous expression. You can write simple empathic comments such as "Thank you for sharing your thoughts," or "I think I understand what makes you feel that way."

When reading student journals, talk individually with students to seek clarification about their expressions. Student journals are useful to the teacher (of any subject) in understanding the student's thought processes and writing skills (diagnostic assessment) and should not be graded. For grading purposes, teachers may simply record whether the student is maintaining a journal and, perhaps, an assessment regarding the quantity of writing in it, but no judgment should be made about the quality.

When reviewing student portfolios, discuss with students individually the progress in their learning as shown by the material in their portfolios. As with student journals, the portfolio should not be graded or compared in any way with those of other students. Its purpose is for student self-assessment and to show progress in learning. For this to happen, students should keep in their portfolios all or major samples of papers related to the course. (Student portfolios are discussed later in the chapter.)

Assessment for Affective and Psychomotor Domain Learning

While assessment of cognitive domain learning lends itself to traditional written tests of achievement, the assessment of learning within the affective and psychomotor domains is best suited by the use of performance checklists where student behaviors can be observed in action. However, many educators today are encouraging the use of alternative assessment procedures (i.e., alternatives to traditional paper-and-pencil written testing). After all, in learning that is most important and that has the most meaning to students, the domains are inextricably interconnected. Learning that is meaningful to stu-

dents is not as easily compartmentalized as the taxonomies of educational objectives would imply. Alternative assessment strategies include the use of group projects, portfolios, skits, papers, oral presentations, and performance tests.

RUBRICS: A TOOL FOR ORGANIZING ASSESSMENT

The connection between performance assessment and rubrics. Since teaching and learning are interactive, it is important for teachers to use a variety of tools to gather information to assess and evaluate students. Good assessment tools also help teachers evaluate their teaching and provide information to help them adapt assignments to better meet students' needs. There is no reason to "surprise" students with the grading criteria. In fact, many teachers find enlisting students' help in developing grading criteria an integral part of planning.

When instructors want to dig deeper and systematically evaluate competencies and performance, one valuable, research-based tool is performance assessment. Performance assessment is a way to evaluate competency-based learning or outcomes-based learning. Performance assessment consists of two parts: a task and scoring criteria. Examples of tasks are works of art, products that result from projects, written compositions, speeches, and musical performances. Actually, almost any traditional assignment or activity can become a "task" as long as the planning includes establishing scoring criteria. The scoring criteria are organized into a grid or matrix called a **rubric.** (See example on next page.)

Not only is a rubric an assessment tool, a rubric can be a powerful communications tool. It communicates in a visual way and in concrete terms what a teacher values most. When created or shared with students, a rubric allows learners to develop analytical skills so they can critically evaluate their own work. While creating or adapting a rubric may take more "up front" planning time, rubrics will save time in the long run because students will have evaluated their own work using the same criteria the teacher uses, *before* they hand it in!

While all grading is subjective to a certain extent, having the criteria established from the beginning will focus both teachers' and students' efforts on what is most important in a particular assignment, thereby creating a more objective process. Using rubrics will also reduce the number of discussions about why or how a grade was assigned—everyone will know the grading criteria from the outset.

Once created, an established rubric can be used or slightly modified and applied to many activities. Reviewing, reconceptualizing, and revisiting the same concepts from different angles improves understanding of

---

[4]See, for example, A. Chandler, "Is This for a Grade? A Personal Look at Journals," *English Journal* 86(1):45–49 (January 1997).

Analyzing a Primary Source Rubric   This rubric is establishing grading criteria for the task of analyzing a primary source.

LIST OF EVALUATION CRITERIA	PERFORMANCE SCALE			
	Exemplary Performance	*Adequate*	*Minimal*	*Attempted*
Analysis of Document	Offers in-depth analysis and interpretation of the document; distinguishes between fact and opinion; explores reliability of author; compares and contrasts author's point of view with views of others	Offers accurate analysis of the document	Demonstrates only a minimal understanding of the document	Reiterates one or two facts from the document but does not offer any analysis or interpretation of the document
Knowledge of Historical Context	Shows evidence of thorough knowledge of period in which source was written; relates primary source to specific historical context in which it was written	Uses previous general historical knowledge to examine issues included in document	Limited use of previous historical knowledge without complete accuracy	Barely indicates any previous historical knowledge
Identification of Key Issus/ Main Points	Identifies the key issues and main points included in the primary source; shows understanding of author's goal(s)	Identifies most but not all of the key issues and main points in the primary source	Describes in general terms one issue or concept included in the primary source	Deals only briefly and vaguely with the key issues and main points in the document
Resources	Uses several outside resources in addition to primary source	Uses 1–2 outside resources in addition to primary source	Relies heavily on the material/information provided	Relies exclusively on the material/ information provided; no evidence of outside resources
Identification of Literary Devices	Analyzes author's use of literary devices such as repetition, irony, analogy, and sarcasm	Mentions author's use of literary devices but does not develop fully	Does not discuss author's use of literary devices	Does not discuss author's use of literary devices
Understanding of Audience	Shows strong understanding of author's audience	Shows some understanding of author's audience	Shows little understanding of author's audience	

the lesson for students. Think about a writing rubric—good writing does not change with the project. Because the essentials remain constant, it is not necessary to create a completely new rubric for every activity. Another way to develop a rubric quickly is to find one online or from another teacher that comes close to meeting your task's requirements and adapt it.

What Does a Rubric Define?

A rubric defines all of the elements in the assignment (or task), and the percentage of the assignment grade that relates to that element. As a general rule, any evaluated task (e.g., a test, an oral report, a project) that is worth more than 25% of the student's final grade should have a rubric. For example, a teacher who has assigned an oral report that will account for 30% of the final course grade may develop the following percentages for each element of the oral report:

- Organization—25%
- Subject knowledge—25%
- Use of Visuals—15%
- Presentation Skills—10%
- Appropriate Use of English—15%
- Modeling Positive Group Dynamics—10%

An effective rubric will:

- Help instructors define excellence and plan how to help students achieve it.
- Communicate to students what constitutes excellence and how to evaluate their own work.
- Communicate goals and results to others.
- Help teachers or other raters be more accurate, unbiased and consistent in scoring.
- Document the procedures used in making important judgments about students.

—Herman, Joan, Aschbacher, Pamela, and Winters, Lynn. *A Practical Guide to Alternative Assessment*. Alexandria, VA: Association for Supervision and Curriculum Development, 1999.

Steps in Rubric Development

Developing rubrics is not difficult if you follow a few simple steps.

1. Determine learning outcomes
2. Keep it short and simple (Include 4–10 items; use brief statements or phrases)
3. Each rubric item should focus on a different skill
4. Focus on how students develop and express their learning
5. Evaluate only measurable criteria
6. Ideally, the entire rubric should fit on one sheet of paper
7. Reevaluate the rubric (Did it work? Was it sufficiently detailed?)

Here are some words that can go across the top row of the rubric matrix. These words measure "performance."

Words Used in Performance Scales

Needs Improvement . . . Satisfactory . . . Good . . . Exemplary

Beginning . . . Developing . . . Accomplished . . . Exemplary

Needs work . . . Good . . . Excellent

Novice . . . Apprentice . . . Proficient . . . Distinguished

Adding a numeric scale ranging from 1 to 5, for example, also helps students and parents understand the performance measured by a rubric.

Here's a tip. After you write the first phrases describing the highest level, circle the words in that that **can vary.** These words will be the ones that you will change as you describe characteristics of the "less than top level" performances.

Some concept words that convey various degrees of performance include:

Depth . . . Breadth . . . Quality . . . Scope . . . Extent . . . Complexity . . . Degrees . . . Accuracy

Presence or absence of a skill

Many to some to none . . . Major to minor . . . Consistent to inconsistent

Frequency: always performs well, generally performs well, sometimes demonstrates competency or rarely demonstrates competency.

It is important to evaluate rubrics, too. Teachers need effective tools. Here are some criteria to use when evaluating rubrics.

1. Decide whether the rubric addresses the most important aspects of student performance.
2. Decide whether or not the rubric addresses the instructional outcome(s) to be measured.
3. Decide whether the rubric includes anything extraneous. If so, change the rubric or use a different one.
4. Don't pay too much attention to the rubric's stated grade level. It may be usable at other grades with little or no modification.
5. Sometimes a rubric from a different subject area can be adapted to fit your needs. Reading rubrics can often be used to assess listening, writing rubrics may be adapted to assess speaking, and fine arts rubrics can sometimes be applied to several different art forms.
6. Make sure the rubric is clear.
7. Try the rubric out on some actual samples of student work to see if you and your colleagues can usually arrive at consensus about what scores to assign a piece of student work.
8. Combine or modify rubrics to make them work better.

RUBRICS AND CHECKLISTS

Rubrics can sometimes be more accessible to students if they are converted to checklists. This does not mean that

EXEMPLARY	ACCOMPLISHED	DEVELOPING	BEGINNING
5	*4*	*3*	*1 or 2*
Skill 1			
Skill 2			

students should not see the grading criteria in a rubric format. Experience shows that until students get used to using and creating rubrics, the more familiar checklist format can often elicit a more active evaluation process.

Converting a Rubric to a Checklist

Step 1: Begin with a statement of the PURPOSE of the type of skill or product.

EXAMPLE: Purpose Statement for Collaboration Rubric

Collaboration is the process of working with a partner or a group. The purpose of collaboration is to use the strengths of all of the group members (and minimize individual weaknesses) in order to create a better or more effective product or outcome. Collaboration skills can be developed and are highly valued in the workplace.

Step 2: Organize your checklist using the headings from the left-hand column of the rubric. Keep the headings in the checklist in the same order as the headings on the rubric.

Step 3: You may choose to add the most important sub-topics that describe the evaluation criteria under each main heading on the checklist.

Step 4: Include the number of points or the percentage that will be attached to each heading/area of evaluation.

Here is an example of a collaboration checklist.

COLLABORATION CHECKLIST

EVALUATION CRITERIA: Understands group goals; demonstrates ability to perform an individual role within the group, demonstration of knowledge, opinions, skills; supports effective group process; demonstrates ability to change and be flexible.

5 points—Student Demonstrates Thorough (or Exemplary) Understanding by:

- Consistently and actively works toward group goals.
- Is sensitive to the feelings and learning needs of all group members.
- Willingly accepts and fulfills individual role within the group.
- Consistently and actively contributes knowledge, opinions, and skills.
- Values the knowledge, opinion and skills of all group members and encourages their contribution.
- Helps group identify necessary changes and encourages group action for change.

3-4 points—Good Understanding

- Works toward group goals without prompting.
- Accepts and fulfills individual role within the group.
- Contributes knowledge, opinions, and skills without prompting.
- Shows sensitivity to the feelings of others.
- Willingly participates in needed changes.

2-2.9 points—Satisfactory Understanding

- Works toward group goals with occasional prompting.
- Contributes to the group with occasional prompting.
- Shows sensitivity to the feelings of others.
- Participates in needed changes, with occasional prompting.

1.5 to 1.9 points—Needs Improvement

- Works toward group goals only when prompted.
- Contributes to the group only when prompted.
- Needs occasional reminders to be sensitive to the feelings of others.

.5 to 1 point = Attempted (Don't always have to have this scale; usually implemented for younger students)

Have each student hand in the checklist with the assignment, or have a partner or team member do a peer review and fill out the checklist and hand it back to the student. Be sure to give students time to evaluate the peer review and remedy any deficiencies before they submit their paper or make their presentation.

CONVERTING A CHECKLIST TO A RUBRIC. Some teachers find it easier to create a rubric if they create a checklist first. You may want to keep an electronic file of rubrics you create because many can be reused. It is often more efficient to edit an existing rubric than to create one. This is a great time to use a search engine on the internet and put in the type of rubric you want to use. Again, it is easier (and less time-consuming) to adapt an existing rubric than it is to create one. There is "rubric creation" software available. Some of this software has objectives correlated to national and state standards.

See the example on the next page of the Collaboration Checklist converted into a rubric format.

STUDENT INVOLVEMENT IN ASSESSMENT

Students' continuous self-assessment should be planned as an important component of the assessment program. If students are to progress in the understanding of their own thinking (metacognition) and their intellectual development, then they must receive instruction and guidance in how to become more responsible for their own

COLLABORATION RUBRIC

OBJECTIVE	THROUGH UNDERSTANDING OR 5	GOOD UNDERSTANDING 3 TO 4 POINTS	SATISFACTORY UNDERSTANDING 2 TO 3 POINTS	NEEDS IMPROVEMENT OR 0-1 POINT
Group Goals	Consistently and actively works toward group goals.	Works toward group goals without prompting.	Works toward group goals with occasional prompting.	Works toward group goals only when prompted.
Individual Role	Willingly accepts and fulfills individual role within the group.	Accepts and fulfills individual role within the group	Understands role in group, accepts role, but needs prompting and extra encouragement.	Does not accept or does not fulfill role within group.
Knowledge Opinions Skills	Consistently and actively contributes knowledge, opinions, and skills.	Contributes knowledge, opinions, and skills without prompting	Contributes to the group with occasional prompting.	Contributes to the group only when prompted.
Group Process	Shows sensitivity to the feelings of others. Values the knowledge, opinion and skills of all group members and encourages their contribution.	Shows sensitivity to the feelings of others. Values knowledge, opinion and skills of others most of the time.	Shows sensitivity to the feelings of others. Values knowledge, opinion and skills of others some of the time.	Needs occasional reminders to be sensitive to the feelings of others.
Change and Flexibility	Helps group identify necessary changes and encourages group action for change.	Willingly participates in needed changes	Participates in needed changes, with occasional prompting	Unwilling to change or demonstrate flexibility.

Another example of a rubric is displayed in Figure 12.10 and 12.11.

learning. During that empowerment process they learn to think better of themselves and of their individual capabilities. To achieve this self-understanding and improved self-esteem requires the experiences afforded by successes, along with guidance in self-understanding and self-assessment.

To meet these goals, teachers provide opportunities for students to think about what they are learning, how they are learning it, and how far they have progressed. Specifically, to engage students in the assessment process you can provide opportunities for the students to identify learning targets that are especially valued by the students; to help in the design of assessment devices for the units of study; to evaluate the tests that are furnished by the textbook publisher in terms of how well they match learning targets identified by you and the students; and to help interpret assessment results. To aid in the interpretation of results students can maintain portfolios of their work, using rating scales or checklists periodically to self-assess their progress.

Using Student Portfolios

Portfolios are used by teachers as a means of instruction and by teachers and students as one means of assessing student learning. Although there is little research evidence to support or to refute the claim, educators believe that the instructional value comes from the process of the student's assembling and maintaining a personal portfolio. During that creative process the student is expected to self-reflect, to think critically about what has and is being learned, and is assuming some responsibility for his or her own learning.

Student portfolios fall into four general categories, and the purpose in a given situation may transcend some combination of all four. The categories are: (a) *selected works portfolio*, in which students maintain samples of their work as prompted by the teacher; (b) *longitudinal* or *growth portfolio*, which is oriented toward outcome-driven goals and includes samples of student work from the beginning and the end of the school term (or thematic unit of study) to exemplify achievement toward the goals; (c) *passport* or *career portfolio,* which contains samples of student work that will enable the student to transition, such as from one grade level to the next or from school to work or college; and (d) *exit portfolio,* samples of student work as evidence for qualification for high school graduation.

Student portfolios should be well organized and, depending on the purpose (or category), should contain assignment sheets, class worksheets, the results of homework, project binders, forms for student self-assessment and reflection on their work, and other class materials thought important by the students and teacher.[5] As a model of a real-life portfolio, you can show students your personal career portfolio.

Portfolio Assessment: Knowing and Dealing with Its Limitations

Although portfolio assessment as an alternative to traditional methods of evaluating student progress has gained momentum in recent years, establishing standards has been difficult. Research on the use of portfolios for assessment indicates that validity and reliability of teacher evaluation are often quite low. In addition, portfolio assessment is not always practical for use by every teacher. For your assessment of student learning, the use of checklists, rubrics, and student self-assessment may be more practical.

Before using portfolios as an alternative to traditional testing, you are advised to carefully consider and clearly understand the reasons for doing it and its practicality in your situation. Then decide carefully the portfolio content, establish rubrics or expectation standards, anticipate grading problems, and consider and prepare for reactions from parents and guardians. Rather than an alternative to traditional testing, some teachers have found it beneficial to use both portfolios and traditional testing, where test results are one source of data maintained by students in their portfolios.

While emphasizing the criteria for assessment, rating scales and checklists provide students with means of expressing their feelings and give the teacher still another source of input data for use in assessment. To provide students with reinforcement and guidance to improve their learning and development, teachers can meet with individual students to discuss their self-assessments. Such conferences should provide students with understandable and achievable short-term goals as well as help them develop and maintain an adequate self-esteem.[6]

Although almost any instrument used for assessing student work can be used for student self-assessment, in some cases it might be better to construct specific instruments with the student's understanding of the instrument in mind. Student self-assessment and self-reflection should be done on a regular and continuing basis so comparisons can be made periodically by the student. You will need to help students learn how to analyze these comparisons. Comparisons should provide a student with information previously not recognized about his or her own progress and growth.

Using Checklists

One of the items that can be maintained by students in their portfolios is a series of checklists. Checklist items can be used easily by a student to compare with previous self-assessments. Items on the checklist will vary depending on your purpose, subject, and grade level. (See sample forms, Figures 12.4 and 12.5.) Open-ended questions allow the student to provide additional information as well as to do some expressive writing. After a student has demonstrated each of the skills satisfactorily, a check is made next to the student's name, either by the teacher alone or in conference with the student.

Guidelines for Using Portfolios for Assessment

Here are general guidelines for using student portfolios in the assessment of learning.

- Contents of the portfolio should reflect course goals and objectives.
- Determine what materials should be kept in the portfolio and announce clearly (post schedule in room) when, how, and by what criteria portfolios will be reviewed by you.
- Give responsibility for maintenance of the portfolios to the students.
- Portfolios should be kept in the classroom.
- Students should date everything that goes into their portfolios.
- The portfolio should not be graded or compared in any way with those of other students. Its purpose is for student self-assessment and for showing progress in learning. For this to happen, students should keep in their portfolio all papers, or major sample papers, related to the course. For grading purposes, you can

---

[5]Software packages for the development of student electronic portfolios are available, such as *Classroom Manager* from CTB Macmillan/McGraw-Hill (Monterey, CA), *Electronic Portfolio* from Learning Quest (Corvallis, OR), and *Grady Profile* from Aurbach and Associates (St. Louis, MO).

[6]For a discussion of the biological importance and educational benefits of positive feedback, student portfolios, and group learning, see R. Sylwester, "The Neurobiology of Self-Esteem and Aggression," *Educational Leadership* 54(5):75–79 (February 1997).

Checklist: Oral Report Assessment

Student: _____   Date: _____

Teacher: _____   Time: _____

Did the student:	Yes	No	Comments
1. Speak so that everyone could hear?	_____	_____	_____
2. Finish sentences?	_____	_____	_____
3. Seem comfortable in front of the group?	_____	_____	_____
4. Give a good introduction?	_____	_____	_____
5. Seem well informed about the topic?	_____	_____	_____
6. Explain ideas clearly?	_____	_____	_____
7. Stay on the topic?	_____	_____	_____
8. Give a good conclusion?	_____	_____	_____
9. Use effective visuals to make the presentation interesting?	_____	_____	_____
10. Give good answers to questions from the audience?	_____	_____	_____

Figure 12.4
Sample checklist: Assessing a student's oral report.

Checklist: Interdisciplinary Thematic Unit Learning

Student: _____   Date: _____

Teacher: _____   Time: _____

The student:	Yes	No	Comments/Evidence
1. Can identify theme, topic, main idea of the unit	_____	_____	_____
2. Can identify contributions of others to the theme	_____	_____	_____
3. Can identify problems related to the unit study	_____	_____	_____
4. Has developed skills in:	_____	_____	_____
Applying knowledge	_____	_____	_____
Assuming responsibility	_____	_____	_____
Classifying	_____	_____	_____
Categorizing	_____	_____	_____
Decision making	_____	_____	_____
Discussing	_____	_____	_____
Gathering resources	_____	_____	_____
Impulse control	_____	_____	_____
Inquiry	_____	_____	_____
Justifying choices	_____	_____	_____
Listening to others	_____	_____	_____
Locating information	_____	_____	_____

Figure 12.5
Sample checklist: Student learning assessment for use with interdisciplinary thematic instruction.

4. Has developed skills in:	Yes	No	Comments/Evidence
Metacognition	_____	_____	_____
Ordering	_____	_____	_____
Organizing information	_____	_____	_____
Problem recognition/identification	_____	_____	_____
Problem solving	_____	_____	_____
Reading text	_____	_____	_____
Reading maps and globes	_____	_____	_____
Reasoning	_____	_____	_____
Reflecting	_____	_____	_____
Reporting to others	_____	_____	_____
Self-assessing	_____	_____	_____
Sharing	_____	_____	_____
Studying	_____	_____	_____
Summarizing	_____	_____	_____
Thinking	_____	_____	_____
Using resources	_____	_____	_____
Working with others	_____	_____	_____
Working independently	_____	_____	_____
(Others unique to the unit)	_____	_____	_____

Additional teacher and student comments:

simply record whether or not the portfolio was maintained and, by checklist, whether all items required are in the portfolio.

MAINTAINING RECORDS OF STUDENT ACHIEVEMENT

You must maintain well-organized and complete records of student achievement. You may do this in a written record book or on an electronic record book. At the very least, the record book should include attendance records and all records of scores on tests, homework, projects, and other assignments.

Daily interactions and events occur in the classroom that may provide informative data about a student's intellectual, emotional, and physical development. Maintaining a dated log of your observations of these interactions and events can provide important information that might otherwise be forgotten. At the end of a unit

and again at the conclusion of a grading term, you will want to review your records. During the course of the school year, your anecdotal records (and those of other members of your teaching team) will provide important information about the development of each student and ideas for attention to be given to individual students.

Recording Teacher Observations and Judgments

You must think carefully about any written comments that you intend to make about a student. Teenagers can be quite sensitive to what others say about them, and most particularly to comments about them made by a teacher.

Additionally, we have seen anecdotal comments in students' permanent records that said more about their teachers who made the comments than about the recipient students. Comments that have been carelessly, hurriedly, and thoughtlessly made can be detrimental to a student's welfare and progress in school. Teacher comments must be professional; that is, they must be diagnostically useful to the continued intellectual and psychological development of the student. This is true for any comment you make or write, whether on a student's paper, on the student's permanent school record, or on a message sent to the student's home.

As an example, consider the following unprofessional comment observed in one student's permanent record. A teacher wrote, "John is lazy." Describing John as "lazy" could be done by anyone; it is nonproductive, and it is certainly not a professional diagnosis. How many times do you suppose John needs to receive such negative descriptions of his behavior before he begins to believe that he is lazy and as a result acts that way even more often? Written comments like that can also be damaging because they may be read by the teacher who next has John in class and lead that teacher to perpetuate the same expectation of John. To say that John is lazy merely describes behavior as judged by the teacher who wrote the comment. More important, and more professional, would be for the teacher to try to analyze why John is behaving that way, then to *prescribe* activities that are likely to motivate John to assume more constructive charge of his own learning behavior.

For students' continued intellectual and emotional development, your comments should be useful, productive, analytical, diagnostic, and prescriptive. The professional teacher makes diagnoses and prepares prescriptions; a professional teacher does not label students as "lazy," "vulgar," "slow," "stupid," "difficult," or "dumb." The professional teacher sees the behavior of a student as being goal-directed. Perhaps "lazy" John found that particular behavioral pattern won him attention. John's goal, then, was attention (don't we all need attention?), and John assumed negative, perhaps even self-destructive, behavioral patterns to reach that goal. The professional task of any teacher is to facilitate the learner's understanding (perception) of a goal and help the student identify acceptable behaviors positively designed to reach that goal.

That which separates the professional teacher from "anyone off the street" is the teacher's ability to go beyond mere description of behavior. Always keep that in mind when you write comments that will be read by students, by their parents or guardians, and by other teachers. Now check your understanding of this concept by doing Exercise 12.1.

EXERCISE 12.1

An Evaluation of Written Teacher Comments about Students—A Self-Check Exercise

---

Instructions: The following comments were selected from student records written by teachers about their students. Check *yes* for those you consider to be professionally useful and *no* for those you do not. Then compare your responses against the key that follows. Discuss the results with your classmates and instructor.

Professionally Useful Comments?	*Yes*	*No*
1. Sonja performs her writing assignments much better when done in class than when done as homework.	____	____
2. Lucretia was very disruptive in class during our unit on westward expansion.	____	____
3. Aram has a lot of difficulty staying in his seat.	____	____
4. Arthur seems more responsive during science experiments than during my lectures.	____	____
5. Razmik seems to have an excess of nervous energy, and I have a concern about his nutritional health.	____	____

6. Su Chin did very well this year in laboratory activities but seems to have reading difficulties. _____ _____

7. Catalina does not get along well with her peers during group learning activities. _____ _____

8. Angela seems unable to understand my verbal instructions. _____ _____

9. I am recommending special remediation for José, perhaps through tutoring. _____ _____

10. I do not appreciate Dan's use of vulgarity.

Answer Key

1. This is useful information.
2. Not useful, because there are no helpful specifics. "Disruptive" is merely descriptive, not prescriptive. Also, it could cause Lucretia's future teachers to be biased against her.
3. Could be useful to future teachers.
4. Useful.
5. Useful.
6. Useful, although additional specifics would help more.
7. Useful, although additional specifics would help more.
8. Not very useful; it may tell more about the teacher than it does about Angela.
9. Useful.
10. Not useful.

Note: It can be argued that those identified as "not useful," although not prescriptive, could be signals that the student might benefit from a session with the school counselor.

GRADING AND MARKING STUDENT ACHIEVEMENT

If conditions were ideal (which they are not), and if teachers did their job perfectly well (which many of us do not), then all students would receive top marks (the ultimate in mastery or quality learning), and there would be less of a need to talk about grading and marking. Mastery learning implies that some end point of learning is attainable, but there probably isn't an end point. In any case, because conditions for teaching are never ideal and we teachers are mere mortals, let us continue with this topic of grading that is undoubtedly of special interest to you, to your students, to their parents or guardians, and to school counselors, administrators and school boards, potential employers, providers of scholarships, and college admissions officers.

We frequently use the term *achievement*. What is meant by this term? Achievement means accomplishment, but is it accomplishment of the instructional objectives against preset standards, or is it simply accomplishment? Most teachers probably choose the former, where the teacher subjectively establishes a standard that must be met in order for a student to receive a certain grade for an assignment, project, test, quarter, semester, or course. Achievement, then, is decided by degrees of accomplishment.

Preset standards are usually expressed in percentages (degrees of accomplishment) needed for marks or *ABC* grades. If no student achieves the standard required for an *A* grade, for example, then no student receives an *A*. On the other hand, if all students meet the preset standard for the *A* grade, then all receive *A*s. Determining student grades on the basis of preset standards is referred to as criterion-referenced grading.

Criterion-Referenced vs. Norm-Referenced Grading

While criterion-referenced (or competency-based) grading is based on preset standards, norm-referenced grading measures the relative accomplishment of individuals in the group (e.g., one classroom of tenth-grade English students) or in a larger group (e.g., all students enrolled in tenth-grade English) by comparing and ranking students, and is commonly known as "grading on a [normal] curve." Because it encourages competition and discourages cooperative learning, for the determination of student grades *norm-referenced grading is not recommended*. Norm-referenced grading is educationally dysfunctional. For your personal interest, after several years of teaching, you can produce frequency-distribution studies of grades you have given over a period of time, but *do not* give students grades that are based on a curve. That grading and reporting should always be done in reference to learning criteria, and never using "on a curve" is well supported by research studies and authorities on the matter.[7] Grades for student achievement should be tied to performance levels and determined on the basis of each student's achievement toward preset standards. As stated by Stiggins, "Teachers who develop success-oriented partnerships with students have no use for grading on a curve. They know they are not the best teacher they can be until every student attains an A by demonstrating the highest possible achievement on rigorous, high-quality assessments."[8]

In criterion-referenced grading, the aim is to communicate information about an individual student's progress in knowledge and work skills in comparison to that student's previous attainment or in the pursuit of an absolute, such as content mastery. Criterion-referenced grading is featured in continuous-progress curricula, competency-based curricula, and other programs that focus on quality learning and individualized education.

Criterion-referenced grading is based on the level at which each student meets the specified objectives (standards) for the course or grade level. The objectives must be clearly stated to represent important student learning outcomes. This approach implies that effective teaching and learning result in high grades (*A*s) or marks for most students. In fact, when a mastery concept is used, the student must accomplish the objectives before being allowed to proceed to the next learning task. The philosophy of teachers who favor criterion-referenced procedures recognizes individual potential. Such teachers accept the challenge of finding teaching strategies to help students progress from where they are to the next designated level. Instead of wondering how Sally compares with Juanita, the comparison is between what Sally could do yesterday and what she can do today and

how well these performances compare to the preset standard.

Most school systems use some sort of combination of both norm-referenced and criterion-referenced data usage. Sometimes both kinds of information are useful. For example, a report card for a student in the eighth grade might indicate how that student is meeting certain criteria, such as an *A* grade for addition of fractions. Another entry might show that this mastery is expected, however, in the sixth grade. Both criterion- and norm-referenced data may be communicated to the parents or guardians and the student. Appropriate procedures should be used: a criterion-referenced approach to show whether or not the student can accomplish the task, and if so, to what degree, and a norm-referenced approach to show how well that student performs compared to the larger group to which the student belongs. The later is important data for college admissions officers and for committees that appropriate academic scholarships.

Determining Grades

Once entered onto school transcripts, grades have significant impact upon the futures of students. When determining achievement grades for student performance, you must make several important and professional decisions. Although in a few schools, and for certain classes or assignments, only marks such as *E* (excellent), *S* (standard), and *I* (incomplete), or *HP* (highest proficiency), *H* (proficient with honors), and *P* (standard proficient), or "pass/no pass," are used, percentages of accomplishment and letter grades are used for most secondary schools.[9] And, even when traditional ABC grades are replaced with letters HP, H, and P, the school, in fact, is still using letter grades. For determining student grades, consider the guidelines presented in the following paragraphs.

At the start of the school term, explain your marking and grading policies *first to yourself,* then to your students and to their parents or guardians at back-to-school night, or by a written explanation that is sent home, or both. Share sample scoring and grading rubrics with students and parents. In addition, include your grading policy in the course syllabus.

When converting your interpretation of a student's accomplishments to a letter grade, be as objective as possible. For the selection of criteria for ABC grades, select a percentage standard, such as 92 percent for an A, 85 percent for a B, 75 percent for a C, and 65 percent for a D. Cutoff percentages used are your decision, al-

---

[7]See, for example, T. R. Guskey (ed.) *Communicating Student Learning* (Alexandria, VA: ASCD Yearbook, Association for Supervision and Curriculum Development, 1996), pp. 18–19, and R. L. Linn and N. E. Gronlund, *Measurement and Assessment in Teaching,* 8th ed. (Upper Saddle River, NJ: Merrill/Prentice Hall, 2000), p. 392.
[8]R. J. Stiggins, *Student-Involved Classroom Assessment,* 3rd ed. (Upper Saddle River, NJ: Prentice Hall, 2001), p. 444.

[9]For other methods being used to report student achievement see J. Bailey and J. McTighe, "Reporting Achievement at the Secondary Level: What and How," Chap. 10 in T. R. Guskey, *Communicating Student Learning.*

though the district, school, program area, or department may have established guidelines that you are expected to follow.

For the determination of students' final grades, many teachers use a point system, in which things that students write, say, and do, are given points (but not for journals or portfolios, except, perhaps, for whether the student does one or not); then the possible point total is the factor for grade determination. For example, if 92 percent is the cutoff for an *A* and 500 points are possible, then any student with 460 points or more (500 × .92) has achieved an *A*. Likewise, for a test or any other assignment, if the value is 100 points, the cutoff for an *A* is 92 (100 × .92). With a point system and preset standards, the teacher and students, at any time during the grading period, always know the current points possible and can easily calculate a student's current grade standing. Then, as far as a current grade is concerned, students always know where they stand in the course.

Build your grading policy around degrees of accomplishment rather than failure and where students proceed from one accomplishment to the next. This is *continuous promotion*, not necessarily the promotion of the student from one grade level to the next, but within the classroom. (However, some schools have eliminated grade-level designation and, in its place, use the concept of continuous promotion from the time of student entry into the school through the student's graduation or exit from it.)

Remember that *assessment* and *grading* are *not* synonymous. As you learned earlier, assessment implies the collection of information from a variety of sources, including measurement techniques and subjective observations. These data, then, become the basis for arriving at a final grade, which in effect is a final value judgment. Grades are one aspect of evaluation and are intended to communicate educational progress to students and to their parents or guardians. For grades to be valid as an indicator of that progress, you *must* use a variety of sources of data for determination of a student's final grade.

Decide beforehand your policy about makeup work. Students will be absent and will miss assignments and tests, so it is best that your policies about late assignments and missed tests be clearly communicated to students and to their parents or guardians. For makeup work, please consider the remaining paragraphs of this section.

HOMEWORK ASSIGNMENTS. We recommend that after due dates have been negotiated or set for assignments no credit or reduced credit be given for work that is turned in late. Sometimes, however, a student has legitimate reasons for not being able to complete the assignment by the due date, and the teacher must exercise a professional judgment in each instance. Although it is important that teachers have rules and procedures—and

that they consistently apply those—the teacher is a professional who must consider all aspects of a student's situation and, after doing so, show compassion, caring, and regard for the human situation.

TESTS. If a student is absent when tests are given, you have several options. Some teachers allow students to miss or discount one test per grading period. Another technique is to allow the student to substitute a written homework assignment or project for one missed test. Still another option is to give the student the choice of either taking a makeup test or having the next test count double. When makeup tests are given, the makeup test should be taken within a week of the regular test unless there is a compelling reason (e.g., medical or family problem) why this cannot happen.

It is not uncommon for secondary school students to miss a testing period, not because of being absent from school but because of involvement in other school activities. In those instances, the student may be able to arrange to come in and take the test during another of your class periods, or your prep period, on that day or the next. If a student is absent during performance testing, the logistics and possible diminished reliability of having to re-administer the test for one student may necessitate giving the student an alternate paper-and-pencil test or some other option.

QUIZZES. Many teachers give frequent and brief quizzes, as often as every day, sometimes for grades and sometimes for practice. As opposed to tests (see next section), quizzes are usually brief (perhaps taking only five minutes of class time) and intended to reinforce the importance of frequent study and review. (However, quizzes should be prepared using the same care and precision as presented in the guidelines for testing and preparation of assessment items.) When quizzes are given at frequent intervals, no single quiz should count very much toward the student's final grade; therefore, you will probably want to avoid having to schedule and give make-up quizzes for students who were absent during a quiz period. The following are reasonable options to administering make-up quizzes, and are presented here in order of our preference, the first (a) being our preferred choice: (a) give a certain number of quizzes during a grading period, say ten, but allow a student to discount a few quiz scores, say two of the ten, thereby allowing the student to discount a low score or a missed quiz due to absence or both; (b) count the next quiz double for a student who missed one due to absence. About the only problem with this option is when a student misses several quizzes; (c) if he or she misses several quizzes, count the unit test a certain and relative percentage greater for any student who missed a quiz during that unit. By the way, we see absolutely no educational value in giving "pop" or unannounced, graded quizzes.

Caution about assigning zero credit. Be very cautious before ever assigning a score of zero to a student for a missed or incomplete assignment, test, or quiz, or for cheating, specially when using a point system for grading. Depending on the weight of the assignment in relation to the total points possible for the grading period, the assigning of a zero grade can have an extreme negative affect on the student's total grade, thus becoming an act of punishment by the teacher rather than a fair representation of the grade earned (or, in this instance, not earned) by the student. This is another example where you, the teacher, must exercise your professional judgment. In addition to those mentioned above, alternatives to using a zero grade include ignoring the missing grade and calculating the student's final (quarter or semester) percentage grade using a lesser total points possible, or, if not counter to school policy, assigning a grade of "incomplete" that gives the student some additional time to complete the work.

TESTING FOR ACHIEVEMENT

One source of information used for determining grades is data obtained from testing for student achievement. There are two kinds of tests, those that are standardized and those that are not.

Standardized and Nonstandardized Tests

Standardized tests are those that have been constructed and published by commercial testing bureaus and used by states and districts to determine and compare student achievement, principally in the core subjects. At least 18 states now require the passing of a standardized test for high school graduation. Some educators today believe that too much emphasis is being placed on standardized testing, that too much valuable instructional time is being consumed preparing students for mandatory standardized testing, and that curriculum is becoming a reflection of the standardized assessment rather than assessment a reflection of the curriculum.

Space in this book does not allow a consideration of standardized achievement testing. Rather, our focus is on non-standardized tests that are designed by you, the classroom teacher, for your own unique group of students. Standardized norm-referenced tests are best for diagnostic purposes and should *not* be used for determining student grades.

Textbook publishers' tests, test item pools, and standardized tests are available from a variety of sources, but because schools, teachers, and students are different, most of the time you will be designing (or collabora-

tively participating in the designing, as is often the case within the departments of large high schools) and preparing tests for your own purposes for your distinct group of students.

Competent planning, preparing, administering, and scoring of tests is an important professional skill. You may want to refer to the guidelines that follow while you are student teaching, and again during your initial years as an employed teacher.

Purposes for Testing

Tests can be designed for several purposes, and a variety of kinds of tests and alternate test items will keep your testing program interesting, useful, and reliable. As a college student, you are probably most experienced with testing for measuring for achievement, but you will use tests for other reasons as well. Tests are also used to assess and aid in curriculum development; help determine teaching effectiveness; help students develop positive attitudes, appreciations, and values; help students increase their understanding and retention of facts, principles, skills, and concepts; motivate students; provide diagnostic information for planning for individualization of the instruction; provide review and drill to enhance teaching and learning; and serve as informational data for students and parents/guardians.

Frequency of Testing

First of all, assessment for student learning should be continual; that is, it should be going on every minute of every class day. For grading or marking purposes, it is difficult to generalize about how often to formally test for student achievement, but we believe that testing should be cumulative and frequent. By cumulative, we mean that each assessment should assess for the student's understanding of previously learned material as well as for the current unit of study; that is, it should assess for connected learning. By frequent, we mean as often as once a week. Advantages of assessment that is cumulative include the review, reinforcement, and articulation of old material with the most recent. The advantages of frequent assessment include a reduction in student anxiety over tests and an increase in the validity of the summative assessment.

Test Construction

After determining the reasons for which you are designing and administering a test, you need to identify the specific instructional objectives the test is being designed to measure. Thus, the first step in test construction is identification of the purpose(s) for the test. The second step is to identify the objectives to be measured, and the third step is to prepare the test items. The best time to prepare draft items is after you have prepared your instructional objectives—while the objectives are fresh in your mind, which means before the lessons are taught. After a lesson is taught you will then want to re-work your first draft of the test items that are related to that lesson to make any modifications that were a result of the instruction that occurred.

Administering Tests

For many students, test taking can be a time of high anxiety. Students demonstrate test anxiety in various ways. Just before and during testing some are quiet and thoughtful, while others are noisy and disruptive. To more accurately measure student achievement you will want to take steps to reduce their anxiety. To control or reduce student anxieties, consider the following discussion as a guideline for administering tests.

Since students respond best to familiar routine, plan your formative assessment program so tests are given at regular intervals and administered at the same time and in the same way. In some schools, days of the week are assigned to departments for administering major tests. For example, Tuesdays might be assigned for English/language arts and mathematics testing, while Wednesday is the day for social studies/history and science testing.

Avoid tests that are too long and that will take too much time. Sometimes beginning teachers have un-reasonable expectations of teenagers about their at-tention spans during testing. Frequent testing with frequent sampling of student knowledge is preferred over infrequent and long tests that attempt to cover everything.

Try to arrange the classroom so it is well-ventilated, the temperature is comfortable, and, when giving paper-and-pencil tests individually, the seats are well-spaced. If spacing is a problem, then consider group testing or using alternate forms of the test, where students seated adjacent to one another have different forms of the same test (e.g., multiple choice answer alternatives are arranged in different order).

Before test time, be certain that you have a sufficient number of copies of the test. Although this may sound trite, we mention it because we have known of too many instances in which the teacher started testing with an insufficient number of test copies. (Sometimes a test is duplicated for the teacher by someone else and a mis-take is made in the number run.)

Before distributing the test, be sure students know what they are to do when finished, such as quietly be-gin an anchor activity, because not all of the students will finish at the same time. It is unreasonable to expect most students to just sit quietly after finishing a test; they need something to do.

When ready to test, don't drag it out. Distribute tests quickly and efficiently. Once testing has begun, avoid interrupting the students. Items or announcements of important information can be written on the board or, if unrelated to the test, held until all are finished with the test. Stay in the room and visually monitor the students. If the test is not going to take an entire class period (and most shouldn't), and it's a major test, then give it at the beginning of the period, if possible, unless you are plan-ning a test review just prior to it. (That seems rather late to conduct a meaningful review, however.) It's improb-able that any teacher can effectively teach a lesson with a reasonable degree of student interest just prior to or immediately after a major test.

Controlling Cheating

Cheating by secondary school students does occur, some say more today than ever.[10] There are steps you can take to discourage cheating or to reduce the oppor-tunity and pressure that cause students to cheat on tests. Consider the following.

PREVENTING CHEATING. Space students or, as men-tioned before, use alternate forms of the test. Frequent testing and not allowing a single test to count too much toward a term grade reduce test anxiety and the pres-sure that can cause cheating. It can also increase student learning by "stimulating greater effort and providing in-termittent feedback" to the student.[11] Prepare test ques-tions that are clear, and unambiguous, thereby reducing student frustration that is caused by a question or in-structions that students do not understand. As said be-fore, avoid tests that are too long and that will take too much time. During long tests, some students get dis-couraged and restless, and that is a time when classroom management problems can occur.

By their sheer nature, performance tests can cause even greater pressure on students and can also provide greater opportunity for cheating. When administering performance tests to an entire class, it is best to have several monitors, such as members of your teaching team. If that isn't possible, consider testing groups of stu-dents, such as cooperative learning groups, rather than individuals. Evaluation of test performance, then, would be based on group rather than individual achievement.

Consider using open-text and open-notebook tests or allowing each student to prepare a page of notes to use during the test. When students can use their books and

---

[10]See, for example, K. Bushweller, "Generation of Cheaters," *American School Board Journal* 186(4):24–30, 32 (April 1999).
[11]H. J. Walberg, "Productive Teaching and Instruction: Assessing the Knowledge Base," *Phi Delta Kappan* 71(6):472 (February 1990).

notes, that not only reduces anxiety but it helps with their organization of information and the retention of what has been learned.

STOPPING CHEATING. The preceding paragraphs provide hints to prevent student cheating. If you suspect cheating *is* occurring, move and stand in the area of the suspected student. Usually that will stop it.

DEALING WITH CHEATING. When you suspect cheating has occurred, you are faced with a dilemma. Unless your suspicion is backed by solid proof, you are advised to forget it, but keep a close watch on the student the next time to prevent cheating from happening. Your job is not to catch students being dishonest but to discourage dishonesty. If you have absolute proof that a student has cheated, then you are obligated to proceed with school policy on student cheating, and that may call for a session with the counselor or the student and the student's parent or guardian, perhaps an automatic *F* grade on the test, and even a temporary suspension from class.

Determining the Time Needed to Take a Test

Again, avoid giving tests that are too long and that will take too much time. Preparing and administering good tests is a skill that you will develop over time. In the meantime, it is best to test frequently and to use tests that sample student achievement rather than try for a comprehensive measure of that achievement.

Some students take more time on the same test than do others. You want to avoid giving too much time, or classroom management problems will result. On the other hand, you don't want to cut short the time needed by students who can do well but need more time to think and to write. As a very general guide, use the table of time needed for different types of test items (Table 12.1). This is only a guide for determining the approxi-

Table 12.1 Approximate Time to Allow for Testing As Determined by the Types of Items.*

Type of Test Item	Time Needed per Item
Matching	30 seconds per matching item
Completion	30 seconds per item
Multiple-choice	1 minute per item
Completion drawing	2–3 minutes
Arrangement	2–3 minutes
Identification	2–3 minutes
Short explanation	2–3 minutes
Essay and performance	10 or more minutes

*Students with disabilities and ELL students, of course, may need more time per item, may need to have the test administered in briefer sessions, or need some other accommodation according to the individual's situation.

mate amount of time to allow students to complete a test. For example, for a test made up of ten multiple-choice items, five arrangement items, and two short-explanation items, you would want to allow about 30 minutes for students to complete the test.

PREPARING ASSESSMENT ITEMS

Preparing and writing good assessment items is yet another professional skill, and to become proficient it takes study, time, practice, and reflection. Because of the importance of an assessment program, please assume this professional charge seriously and responsibly. Although poorly prepared items take no time at all to construct, they will cause you more trouble than you can ever imagine. As a professional you should take time to study different types of assessment items that can be used and how best to write them, and then practice writing them. Remember, when preparing assessment items, ensure that they match and sufficiently cover the instructional objectives. In addition, you should prepare each item carefully enough to be reasonably confident that each item will be understood by the student in the manner that you anticipate its being understood. With the diversity of students in today's school classroom, especially with respect to their proficiency in oral and written English language and the inclusion of students with special needs, this is an especially important point. For your high-stakes tests, such as unit tests and semester exams, ask a trusted colleague to read your test for clarity and errors and to check the test's key for accuracy. Finally, after administering a test you must take time to analyze the results and reflect on the value of each item before ever using that item again.

Classification of Assessment Items

Assessment items can be classified as verbal (oral or written words), visual (pictures and diagrams), and manipulative or performance (handling of materials and equipment; performing). Written, verbal items are the ones that have traditionally been used in testing. However, visual items and visual tests are useful, for example, when working with students who lack fluency with the written word or when testing students who have limited or no proficiency in the English language.

Performance items and tests are useful when measuring for psychomotor skill development. Common examples are performance testing of a student's ability to carry a microscope or hold a jumping rope in place (gross motor skill) or to focus a microscope or to jump rope (fine motor skill). Performance testing also can and should be a part of a wider testing program that includes testing for higher-level thinking skills and knowledge, as, for example, when a student or small group of students are given the problem of creating from discarded materials a habitat for an imaginary animal and then display, write about, and orally present their product to the rest of the class.

As noted throughout this book, educators have taken a rekindled interest in this last described form of performance testing as a means of assessing learning that is closer to measuring for the real thing—that is authentic. In a program for teacher preparation, micro peer teaching and the student teaching experience are examples of performance assessment; that is, assessment practices used to assess the teacher candidate's ability to teach (to perform). It seems axiomatic that assessment of student teaching is a more authentic assessment of a candidate's ability to teach than would be a written (paper-and-pencil test) or verbal (oral test) form of assessment. Although less direct and perhaps less reliable than a checklist observation and analysis of a student teacher actually teaching, an observation of a student teacher's analysis of a video-recorded episode (i.e., with pictures) of another teacher's performance would be a better way of authentically assessing a teacher's ability to teach than a paper-and-pencil response item test.

Performance Testing Can Be Expensive and Time-Intensive

Performance testing is usually more expensive and time-consuming than is verbal testing, which in turn is more time demanding and expensive than is written testing. However, a good program of assessment will use alternate forms of assessment and not rely solely on one form (such as written) and one type of written item (such as multiple-choice).

The type of test and items that you use depend upon your purpose and objectives. Carefully consider the alternatives within that framework. To provide validity checks and to account for the individual differences of students, a good assessment program should include items from all three types. That is what writers of articles in professional journals are referring to when they talk about **alternative assessment.** They are encouraging the use of multiple assessment items, as opposed to the traditional heavy reliance on objective items such as multiple-choice questions.

General Guidelines for Preparing for Assessment

Consider the following general guidelines when preparing for assessment.

- Include several kinds of items and assessment instruments (see 12 types that follow).
- Assure that content coverage is complete (i.e., that all objectives are being measured).
- Assure that each item is reliable; that it measures the intended objective. One way to check item reliability is to have more than one item measuring for the same objective.

- Assure that each item is clear and unambiguous to all students.
- Plan each item to be difficult enough for the poorly prepared student but easy enough for the student who is well prepared.
- Because it is time-consuming to write good assessment items, you are advised to maintain a bank of items, with each item coded according to its matching instructional objective and according to its domain of learning (cognitive, affective, or psychomotor) and perhaps according to its level within the hierarchy of a particular domain. Another code could indicate whether the item requires thinking that is recall, processing, or application. Computer software programs are available for this. Ready-made test item banks are available on computer disks and accompany many programs or textbooks. If you use them, be certain that the items match your course objectives and that they are well written. It doesn't follow that because they were published they are well written or match what students were supposed to have learned. When preparing items for your test bank, use your creative thinking and best writing skills. Prepare items that match your objectives, put them aside, think about them, then work them over again.

Every test that you administer to your students should represent your best professional effort. It should be clean and sans spelling and grammar errors. A quickly and poorly prepared test can cause you more grief than you can imagine. One that is hurriedly prepared and wrought with spelling and grammar errors will quickly be frowned upon by discerning parents or guardians. If you are a student teacher, such sloppiness and unprofessional output will certainly bring about an admonishment from your university supervisor and, if it continues, your speedy release from the teacher preparation program.

Attaining Content Validity

To ensure that your test measures what is supposed to be measured, you can construct a table of specifications. A two-way grid indicates behavior in one dimension and content in the other (see Figures 12.6 and 12.7).

In this grid, behavior relates to the three domains: cognitive, affective, psychomotor. In Figure 12.6, the cognitive domain is divided, according to Bloom's taxonomy, into six categories: knowledge or simple recall, comprehension, application, analysis, synthesis (often involving an original product in oral or written form), and evaluation. The specifications table in Figure 12.6 does not specify levels within the affective and psychomotor domains.

To use a table of specifications, the teacher examining objectives for the unit decides what emphasis should be given to the behavior and to the content. For example, if vocabulary development is a concern for this

CONTENT	BEHAVIORS								TOTAL
SOCIAL STUDIES GRADE 8	**COGNITIVE**						**AFFEC-TIVE**	**PSYCHO-MOTOR**	
Ancient Greece	*Knowledge*	*Compre-hension*	*Appli-cation*	*Analysis*	*Synthesis*	*Evaluation*			
I. Vocabulary development		2 (1,2)	1 (2)						3
II. Concepts		2 (3,4)	2 (4)						4
III. Applications	1 (5)	1 (5)	1 (5)	1 (5)	1 (5)	1 (5)			6
IV. Problem solving		1 (6)		1 (6)					2
TOTAL	1	6	4	2	1	1			15

Figure 12.6
Specifications I.

CONTENT	BEHAVIORS							TOTAL
	COGNITIVE			**AFFECTIVE**		**PSYCHOMOTOR**		
	Input	*Processing*	*Application*	*Low*	*High*	*Low*	*High*	
I.								
II.								
III.								
IV.								
TOTAL								

Figure 12.7
Specifications II.

sixth-grade study of matter and energy, then probably 20 percent of the test on vocabulary would be appropriate, but 50 percent would be unsuitable. This planning enables the teacher to design a test that fits the situation rather than a haphazard test that does not correspond to the objectives either in content or behavior emphasis. Since this is to be an objective test and it is so difficult to write objective items to test affective and psychomotor behaviors, this table of specifications calls for no test items in these areas. If these areas are included in the unit objectives, some other assessment devices must be used to test learning in these domains. The teacher could also show the objectives tested, as indicated within parentheses in Figure 12.6. Then, a check later on inclusion of all objectives is easy.

Preferred by some teachers is the alternative table shown in Figure 12.7. Rather than differentiating among all six of Bloom's cognitive levels, this table separates cognitive objectives into just three levels: those that re-

quire simple low-level recall of knowledge, those that require information processing, and those that require application of new knowledge. In addition, the affective and psychomotor domains each are divided into low- and high-level behaviors. A third alternative, not illustrated here, is a table of specifications that shows all levels of each of the three domains.

TWELVE TYPES OF ASSESSMENT ITEMS: DESCRIPTIONS, EXAMPLES, AND GUIDELINES FOR PREPARING AND USING

In this section, we present descriptions of, advantages and disadvantages of, and guidelines for preparing and using 12 types of assessment items. When reading about the advantages and disadvantages of each, you will notice that some types are appropriate for use in direct or performance assessment, while others are not.

Arrangement

Description: Terms, photos, or real objects are to be arranged in a specified order.

Example 1: Arrange the following list of events on a timeline in order of their occurrence: Maximilian I elected King of Germany; Maximilian I becomes Holy Roman Emperor; Diet of Augsburg establishes Council of Regency, divides Germany into six regions; Charles I of Spain becomes Holy Roman Emperor; Ferdinand I assumes the title of Holy Roman Emperor.

Example 2: The assortment of balls on the table represents the planets in our solar system. (*Note:* The balls are of various sizes, such as marbles, golf balls, tennis balls, basketballs, and so on, each labeled with a planetary name, with a large beach ball that is labeled *Sun.*) Arrange the balls in their proper order around the sun.

Advantages: This type of item tests for knowledge of sequence and order and is good for review and for starting discussions and for performance assessment. Example 2 is also an example of a performance test item.

Disadvantages: Scoring could be difficult, so be cautious, meticulous, and open to lateral thinking (see Chapter 9) when using this type for grading purposes. For example, in the second example the student could rightfully place either Neptune or Pluto as the outermost planet in the solar system (because of the extreme oval shape of their orbits, Pluto and Neptune alternate in their relative positions from the Sun), or even omit Pluto because many scientists today believe that rather than being a planet Pluto is actually the largest or nearest member of a group of icy asteroids found in the outer solar system.

Guideline for use: To enhance reliability, you may need to include instructions to students to include the rationale for their arrangement, making it a combined arrangement and short-explanation type of assessment, allowing space for explanations on an answer sheet. Useful for small, heterogeneous group assessment to allow students to share and learn from their collaborative thinking and reasoning.

Completion Drawing

Description: An incomplete drawing is presented and the student is to complete it.

Example 1: Connect the following items with arrow lines to show the stages from introduction of a new bill until it becomes law (items not included here).

Example 2: In the following food web (not shown here), draw arrow lines indicating which organisms are consumers and which are producers.

Advantages: This type requires less time than would a complete drawing that might be required in an essay item. Scoring is relatively easy.

Disadvantages: Care needs to be exercised in the instructions so students do not misinterpret the expectation.

Guidelines for use: Use occasionally for diversion, but take care in preparing. This type can be instructive when assessing for student thinking and reasoning as it can measure conceptual knowledge. Consider making the item a combined completion-drawing, short-explanation type by having students include their rationales for their drawing completion. Be sure to allow space for their explanations. Useful for small, heterogeneous group assessment to allow students to share and learn from their collaborative thinking and reasoning.

Completion Statement

Description: Sometimes called a fill-in item, an incomplete sentence is presented and the student is to complete it by filling in the blank space(s).

Example 1: A group of words that have a special meaning, such as "a skeleton in the closet," is called a(n) _____.

Example 2: To test their hypotheses, scientists and social scientists conduct _____.

Advantages: This type is easy to devise, take, and score.

Disadvantages: When using this type, there is a tendency to emphasize rote memory and measure procedural knowledge only. Provision of a word bank of possible answers is sometimes useful, especially with mainstreamed students, to reduce dependency on rote memory. It is difficult to write this type of item to measure for conceptual knowledge and higher levels of cognition. You must be alert for a correct response different from the expected. For example, in Example 2, although the teacher's key has "experiments" as the correct answer, a student might answer the question with "investigations" or "tests" or some other response that is equally valid.

Guideline for use: Use occasionally for review or for preassessment of student knowledge. Avoid using this type for grading unless you can write quality items that extend student thinking beyond mere recall. In all instances, avoid copying items verbatim from the student book. As with all types, be sure to provide adequate space for students' answers, and large spaces for students with motor control difficulties. Try to use one only one blank per item. Try also to keep the blanks equal in length. Useful for small, heterogeneous group assessment to allow students to share and learn from their collaborative thinking and reasoning.

Correction

Description: This is similar to the completion type except that sentences or paragraphs are complete but with italicized or underlined words that can be changed to make the sentences correct.

Example 1: The work of the TVA was started by building <u>sand castles</u>. A <u>sand castle</u> is a wall built across a <u>kid</u> to stop its flow. The <u>sand castle</u> holds back the <u>football</u> so the <u>kids</u> do not overflow their <u>backpacks</u> and cause <u>tears</u>.

Example 2: 1, 1, 2, 3, 5, 8, <u>12</u>, 21, 34, <u>87</u>, 89

Advantages: Writing this type can be fun for the teacher for the purpose of preassessment of student knowledge or for review. Students may enjoy this type, especially when used only occasionally, for the tension relief afforded by the incorrect absurdities. This type can is useful for introducing words with multiple meanings.

Disadvantages: As with the completion type, the correction type tends to measure for low level recall and rote memory (although this is not necessarily the case in Example 2; if a student is unfamiliar with the Fibonacci number series in mathematics, it would be a relatively high-level question). The underlined incorrect items could be so whimsical that they might cause more classroom disturbance than you want.

Guidelines for use: Use occasionally for diversion and discussion. Try to write items that measure for higher-level cognition. Consider making it a combined correction, short-explanation type. Be sure to allow space for student explanations.

Essay

Description: A question or problem is presented, and the student is to compose a response in the form of sustained prose, using the student's own words, phrases, and ideas, within the limits of the question or problem.

Example 1: In the story just read, does the author elaborate the setting in great detail or barely sketch it? Explain your response.

Example 2: A healthy, green coleus plant sitting in front of you has been planted in fertile soil and sealed in a glass jar. If we place the jar on the window sill where it will receive strong sunlight and the temperature inside the jar is maintained between 60 and 80 degrees Fahrenheit, how long do you predict the plant will live? Justify your prediction.

Advantages: This type measures conceptual knowledge and higher mental processes, such as the ability to synthesize material and express ideas in clear and precise written language. It is especially useful in integrated thematic teaching. It provides practice in written expression and can be used in performance assessment, as is the case for Example 2.

Disadvantages: Essay items require a good deal of time to read and to score. They tend to provide an unreliable sampling of achievement and are vulnerable to teacher subjectivity and unreliable scoring. Furthermore, they tend to punish the student who writes slowly and laboriously, who has limited proficiency in the written language but who may have achieved as well as a student who writes faster and is more proficient in the language. Essay items tend to favor students who have fluency with words but whose achievement may not necessarily be better. In addition, unless the students have been given instruction in the meaning of key directive verbs and in how to respond to them, the teacher should not assume that all students understand such verbs (such as *explain* in the first example and *justify* in the second).

Guidelines for Using an Essay Item

1. When preparing an essay-only test, many questions, each requiring a relatively short prose response, are preferable to a smaller number of questions requiring long prose responses. Briefer answers tend to be more precise, and the use of many items provides a more reliable sampling of student achievement. When preparing short prose response, be sure to avoid using words verbatim from the student textbook.

2. Allow students adequate test time for a full response.

3. Different qualities of achievement are more likely comparable when all students must answer the same questions, as opposed to providing a list of essay items from which students may select those they answer.

4. After preparing essay items, make a tentative scoring key, deciding the key ideas you expect students to identify and how many points will be allotted to each.

5. Students should be informed about the relative test value for each item. Point values, if different for each item, can be listed in the margin of the test next to each item.

6. Inform students of the role of spelling, grammar, and sentence structure in your scoring of their essay items.

7. When reading student essay responses, read all student papers for one item at a time in one sitting, and, while doing that, make notes to yourself; then repeat and while reading that item again, score each student's paper for that item. Repeat the process for the next item but modify the order of the pile of papers so you are not reading them in the same order by student. While scoring essay responses, keep in mind the nature of the objective being measured, which may or may not include the qualities of handwriting, grammar, spelling, punctuation, and neatness.

8. To nullify the "halo effect" that can occur when you know whose paper you are reading, have students put their name on the back of the paper or use a number code rather than having students put their names on essay papers, so while reading the papers, you are unaware of whose paper is being read.

9. While having some understanding of a concept, many students are not yet facile with written expression, so you must remember to be patient, tolerant, positive, and prescriptive. Mark papers with positive and constructive comments, showing students how they could have explained or responded better.

10. Prior to using this type of test item, give instruction and practice to students in responding to key directive verbs that will be used (see Figure 12.8).

Grouping

Description: Several items are presented, and the student is to select and group those that are in some way related.

Example 1: Separate the following words into two groups (words are not included here); those that are homonyms, place in group A and those that are not homonyms, place in group B.

Example 2: Circle the figure that is least like the others (showing a wrench, screwdriver, saw, and swing).

Advantages: This type of item tests knowledge of grouping and can be used to measure conceptual knowledge, for higher levels of cognition, and to stimulate discussion. As Example 2 shows, it can be similar to a multiple-choice type item.

Disadvantage: Remain alert for the student who has an alternative but valid rationale for her or his grouping.

Guideline for use: To allow for an alternative correct response, consider making the item a combination grouping, short-explanation type, being certain to allow adequate space to encourage student explanations.

Identification

Description: Unknown "specimens" are to be identified by name or some other criterion.

Example 1: Identify each of the plant specimens on the table by their common names.

Example 2: Identify by style each of the three poems shown on the screen.

Advantages: Verbalization (i.e., the use of abstract symbolization) is less significant, as the student is working with real materials; should be measuring for higher level learning than simple recall. The item can also be written to measure for procedural understanding, such as for identification of steps in booting up a computer program. This is another useful type for authentic and performance assessments.

Disadvantages: Because of a special familiarity with the material, some students may have an advantage over others; to be fair, "specimens" used should be equally familiar or unfamiliar to all students. This type takes more time than many of the other items types, both for the teacher to prepare and for students to do.

Compare asks for an analysis of similarity and difference, but with a greater emphasis on similarities or likenesses.
Contrast asks more for differences than for similarities.
Criticize asks for the good and bad of an idea or situation.
Define means to express clearly and concisely the meaning of a term, as from a dictionary or in the student's own words.
Diagram means to put quantities or numerical values into the form of a chart, graph, or drawing.
Discuss means to explain or argue, presenting various sides of events, ideas, or situations.
Enumerate means to name or list one after another, which is different from "explain briefly" or "tell in a few words."
Evaluate means to express worth, value, and judgment.
Explain means to describe, with emphasis on cause and effect.
Generalize means to arrive at a valid generalization from provided specific information.
Identify means to state recognizable or identifiable characteristics.
Infer means to forecast what is likely to happen as a result of information provided.
Illustrate means to describe by means of examples, figures, pictures, or diagrams.
Interpret means to describe or explain a given fact, theory, principle, or doctrine within a specific context.
Justify means to show reasons, with an emphasis on correct, positive, and advantageous.
List means just that, to simply name items in a category or to include them in a list, without much description.
Outline means to give a short summary with headings and subheadings.
Prove means to present materials as witnesses, proof, and evidence.
Relate means to tell how specified things are connected or brought into some kind of relationship.
Summarize means to recapitulate the main points without examples or illustrations.
Trace means to follow a history or series of events, step by step, by going backward over the evidence.

Figure 12.8
Meaning of key directive verbs for essay item responses.

Guidelines for use: Whatever "specimens," are used, they must be familiar to all or to none of the students, and they must be clear, not confusing (e.g., fuzzy photographs or unclear photocopies, dried and incomplete plant specimens, and garbled music recordings can be confusing and frustrating to try and discern). Consider using dyad or team rather than individual testing.

Matching

Description: Students are to match related items from a list of numbered items to a list of lettered choices or in some way connect those items that are the same or related.

Example 1: In the blank space next to each description in Column A (stem or premises column) put the letter of the correct answer from Column B (answer or response column).

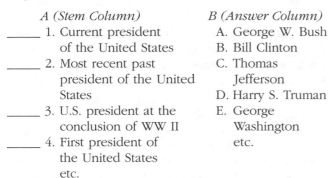

	A (Stem Column)	B (Answer Column)
_____	1. Current president of the United States	A. George W. Bush
_____	2. Most recent past president of the United States	B. Bill Clinton
		C. Thomas Jefferson
_____	3. U.S. president at the conclusion of WW II	D. Harry S. Truman
_____	4. First president of the United States etc.	E. George Washington etc.

Example 2: Match items in Column A (stem column) to those of Column B (answer column) by drawing lines connecting the matched pairs.

Column A	Column B
ann/enn	conquer
auto	large
min	self
vic/vinc	small
(etc.)	year
	(etc.)

Advantages: Matching items can measure for ability to judge relationships and to differentiate between similar facts, ideas, definitions, and concepts. They are easy to score and can test a broad range of content. They reduce guessing, especially if one group (e.g., answer column) contains more items than the other, are interesting to students, and are adaptable for performance assessment.

Disadvantages: Although the matching item is adaptable for performance assessment, items are not easily adapted to measuring for higher cognition. Because all parts must be homogeneous, it is possible that clues will be given, thus reducing item validity.

Guidelines for use: The number of items in the response or answer column should exceed the number in the stem or premises column. The number of items in the stem column to be matched should not exceed

ten. Less is better. Matching sets should have high homogeneity (i.e., items in both columns or groups should be of the same general category; avoid, for example, mixing dates, events, and names). Answers in the response column should be kept short, one or two words each, and ordered logically, such as alphabetically. If answers from the response column can be used more than once, and that is advised to avoid guessing by elimination, the directions should so state. Be prepared for the student who can legitimately defend an "incorrect" response. To eliminate the paper-and-pencil aspect and make the item more direct, use an item such as "of the materials on the table, pair up those that are most alike."

Multiple-Choice

Description: This type is similar to the completion item in that statements are presented (the stem), sometimes in incomplete form, but with several options or alternatives, requiring recognition or even higher cognitive processes rather than mere recall.

Example 1: Of four cylinders with the following dimensions, the one that would cause the highest-pitched sound would be

(a) 4 inches long and 3 inches in diameter
(b) 8 inches long and 3 inches in diameter
(c) 4 inches long and 1 inch in diameter
(d) 8 inches long and 1 inch in diameter

Example 2: Which one of the following is a pair of antonyms?

(a) loud–soft
(b) halt–finish
(c) absolve–vindicate
(d) procure–purchase

Advantages: Items can be answered and scored quickly. A wide range of content and higher levels of cognition can be tested in a relatively short time. This type is excellent for all testing purposes—motivation, review, and assessment of learning.

Disadvantages: Unfortunately, because multiple-choice items are relatively easy to write, there is a tendency to write items measuring only for low levels of cognition. Multiple-choice items are excellent for major testing, but it takes care and time to write quality questions that measure higher levels of thinking and learning.

Guidelines for Using Multiple-Choice Items

1. If the item is in the form of an incomplete statement, it should be meaningful in itself and imply a direct question rather than merely lead into a collection of unrelated true and false statements.

2. Use a level of language that is easy enough for even the poorest readers and those with limited proficiency in English to understand; avoid unnecessary wordiness.

3. If there is much variation in the length of alternatives, arrange the alternatives in order from shortest to longest (i.e., first alternative is the shortest, last alternative is the longest). For single-word alternatives, consistent use of arrangement of alternatives is recommended, such as by length of answer or alphabetically.

4. Arrangement of alternatives should be uniform throughout the test and listed in vertical (column) form rather than in horizontal (paragraph) form.

5. If there is more than one correct response, then students should be instructed to identify all responses they believe are correct. Questions that have more than a single correct response should be worth more than one point each, such as a point for each correct response.

6. Incorrect responses (distracters) should be plausible and related to the same concept as the correct alternative. Although an occasional humorous distracter may help relieve text anxiety, along with absurd distracters they should generally be avoided. They offer no measuring value and increase the likelihood of the student guessing the correct response.

7. It is not necessary to maintain a fixed number of alternatives for every item, but the use of less than three is not recommended. Although it is not always possible to come up with four or five plausible responses, the use of four or five reduces chance responses and guessing, thereby increasing reliability for the item. If you cannot think of enough plausible distracters, include the item on a test the first time as a completion item. As students respond, wrong answers will provide you with a number of plausible distracters that you can use the next time to make the item a multiple-choice type item.

8. Some mainstreamed students may work better when allowed to circle their selected response rather than writing its letter or number in a blank space.

9. Responses such as "all of these" or "none of these" should be used only when they will contribute more than another plausible distracter. Care must be taken that such responses answer or complete the item. "All of the above" is a poorer alternative than "none of the above" because items that use it as a correct response need to have four or five correct answers; also, if it is the right answer, knowledge of any two of the distracters will cue it.

10. Every item should be grammatically consistent. For example, if the stem is in the form of an incomplete sentence, it should be possible to complete the sentence by attaching any of the alternatives to it.

11. The stem should state a single and specific point.

12. The stem must mean the same thing to every student.

13. The item should be expressed in positive form. A negative form can present a psychological disadvantage to students. Negative items are those that ask what is *not* characteristic of something, or what is the *least* useful. Discard the item if you cannot express it in positive terminology.

14. The stem must not include clues that would clue the correct alternative. For example,

A four-sided figure whose opposite sides are parallel is called _____ .
    (a) a triangle
    (b) an octagon
    (c) a trapezoid
    (d) a parallelogram

Use of the word "parallel" clues the answer.

15. There must be only one correct or best response. However, this is easier said than done (refer to guideline 20).

16. Measuring for understanding of definitions is better tested by furnishing the name or word and requiring choice between alternative definitions than by presenting the definition and requiring choice between alternative words.

17. Avoid using alternatives that include absolute terms such as *never* and *always*.

18. Multiple-choice items need not be entirely verbal. Consider the use of realia, charts, diagrams, videos, and other visuals. They will make the test more interesting, especially to students with low verbal abilities or to those who have limited proficiency in English, and, consequently, they will make the assessment more direct.

19. Once you have composed a series of multiple-choice items or a test comprised completely of this item type, tally the position of answers to be sure they are evenly distributed, to avoid the common psychological habit (when there are four alternatives) of having the correct alternative in the third position. In other words, when alternative choices are A, B, C, and D, or 1, 2, 3, and 4, unless the test designer is aware and avoids it, more correct answers will be in the "C" or "3" position than in any other.

20. Consider providing space between test items for students to include their rationales for their response selections, thus making the test a combination multiple-choice and short-explanation item type. This provides for the measurement of higher levels of cognition and encourages writing. It provides for the student who can rationalize an alternative that you had not considered plausible, especially possible today with the diversity of cultural experiences represented by students. For example, we recall the story of the math question on a test which asked if a farmer saw eight crows sitting on a fence and shot three of them, how many would be left. Of course, the "correct" response on the answer key was five. However, one critical thinking student chose "none"

as his response, an answer that was marked "wrong" by the teacher. However, the student was thinking that those crows that weren't shot would be frightened and would all fly away, thus he selected "none" as his answer.

21. While scoring, on a blank copy of the test, for each item tally the incorrect responses. Analyze incorrect responses for each item to discover potential errors in your scoring key. If, for example, many students select B for an item for which your key says the correct answer is A, you may have made a mistake on your scoring key or in teaching the lesson.

22. Sometimes teachers attempt to discourage cheating by preparing several versions of the multiple-choice exam with the questions in different order. This could be giving one group of students an unfair advantage if the order of their questions are in the same sequence in which the information was originally presented and learned and for another group of students the questions are in a random order. To avoid this, questions should be in random order on every version of the exam.

Performance

Description: Provided with certain conditions or materials, the student solves a problem or accomplishes some other action.

Example 1: Write a retelling of your favorite fable and create a diorama to accompany it.

Example 2: (As a culminating project for a unit on sound, groups of students were challenged to design and make their own musical instruments.) The performance assessment included:

1. Play your instrument for the class.
2. Show us the part of the instrument that makes the sound.
3. Describe the function of other parts of your instrument.
4. Demonstrate how you change the pitch of the sound.
5. Share with us how you made your instrument.

Example 3: Demonstrate your understanding of diffusion by designing and completing an experiment using only those chemicals and materials located at this learning station.

Example 4: Measure and calculate to the nearest centimeter the "within bounds only" square footage of our football playing field.

Advantages: Performance test item types come closer to direct measurement (authentic assessment) of certain expected outcomes than do most other types. As has been indicated in discussions of the preceding question types, other types of questions can actually be prepared as performance-type items, that is, where the student actually does what he or she is being tested for.

Disadvantages: This type can be difficult and time consuming to administer to a group of students. Adequate supply of materials could be a problem. Scoring may tend to be subjective. It could be difficult to give make up tests to students who were absent.

Guidelines for use: Use your creativity to design and use performance tests, as they tend to measure well the important objectives. To reduce subjectivity in scoring, prepare distinct scoring guidelines (rubrics), as was discussed in scoring essay-type items and as shown in Figures 12.10 and 12.11. To set up a performance assessment situation, see the instructions in Figure 12.9.

Short Explanation

Description: The short explanation question is like the essay-type but requires a shorter answer.

Example 1: Briefly explain in a paragraph how you would end the story.

Example 2: Briefly explain why organ pipes are made to vary in length.

Advantages: As with the essay type, student understanding is assessed, but this type takes less time for the teacher to read and to score. By using several questions of this type, a greater amount of content can be covered than with a lesser number of essay questions. This type

Figure 12.9
Procedure for setting up a performance assessment situation.

1. Specify the performance objective.
2. Specify the test conditions.
3. Establish the standards or criteria (scoring rubric) for judging the quality of the process and/or product.
4. Prepare directions in writing, outlining the situation, with instructions that the students are to follow.
5. Share the procedure with a colleague for feedback before using it with students.

Professional Presentation	**14–15** Well organized; smooth transitions between sections; all enthusiastically participate and share responsibility.	**12–13** Well organized with transitions; students confer/present ideas; group shows ability to interact; attentive discussion of research.	**11** Shows basic organization; lacks transitions; some interaction; discussion focuses mostly on research.	**1–10** Unorganized, lacks planning; no transitions; reliance on one spokesperson; little interaction; disinterest; too brief.
Engagement of Audience	**14–15** Successfully and actively engages audience in more than one pertinent activity; maintains interest throughout.	**12–13** Engages audience in at least one related activity; maintains attention through most of presentation.	**11** Attempts to engage audience in at least one activity; no attempt to involve *entire* audience. May not relate in significant way.	**1–10** Fails to involve audience; does not maintain audience's attention; no connection with audience. No relationship between activity and topic.
Use of Literature	**18–20** Strong connection between literature and topic; significant, perceptive explanation of literature; pertinent to topic; at least two pieces used.	**16–17** Clear connection between literature and topic; clear explanation; appropriate to topic; two pieces used.	**14–15** Weak connection to topic; unclear explanation; one genre; one piece used.	**1–13** No connection to topic; no explanation; inappropriate literature; no literature.
Knowledge of Subject	**18–20** Strong understanding of topic; knowledge factually relevant, accurate, and consistent; solution shows analysis of evidence.	**16–17** Good understanding of topic; uses main points of information researched; builds solution on examination of major evidence.	**14–15** Shows general understanding; focuses on one aspect, discusses at least one other idea; uses research, attempts to add to it; solution refers to evidence.	**1–13** Little understanding or comprehension of topic; uses little basic information researched; forms minimal solution; relies solely on own opinions without support.
Use of Media	**18–20** Effectively combines and integrates three distinct forms with one original piece; enhances understanding; offers insight into topic.	**16–17** Combines two forms with one original piece; relates to topic; connection between media and topic is explained.	**14–15** Includes two or three forms but no original piece; media relates to topic; explanation may be vague or missing.	**1–13** One form; no original piece; connection between media and topic is unclear.
Speaking Skills	**9–10** Clear enunciation; strong projection; vocal variety; eye contact with entire audience; presentation posture; solid focus with no interruptions.	**8** Good enunciation; adequate projection; partial audience eye contact; appropriate posture.	**7** Inconsistent enunciation; low projection with little vocal variety; inconsistent posture.	**1–6** Difficult to understand; inaudible; monotonous; no eye contact; inappropriate posture; interruptions and distractions.

Figure 12.10
Sample of a scoring rubric for student project presentation.
(*Source:* Elk Grove School District, Elk Grove, CA.)
(Possible score = 100. Scorer marks a relevant square in each of the six categories—the horizontal rows—and student's score for that category is the small number within that square.)

	14–15	12–13	11	1–10
Parenthetical References	All documented correctly. Paper's references document a wide variety of sources cited—at least five from bibliography.	Most documented correctly. Few minor errors. At least three sources from bibliography are cited.	Some documented correctly. Some show no documentation at all. May not correlate to the bibliography.	Few to none are documented. Does not correlate to the bibliography. May be totally absent.
	14–15	**12–13**	**11**	**1–10**
Bibliography and Sources	Strong use of library research. Exceeds minimum of five sources. Bibliography is correctly formatted.	Good use of library research. Exceeds minimum of five sources. Bibliography has few or no errors in format.	Some use of library research. Meets minimum of five sources. Bibliography is present but may be problematic.	Fails to meet minimum standards for library research. Bibliography has major flaws or may be missing.
	14–15	**12–13**	**11**	**1–10**
Mechanics/Format	Correct format and pagination. Neat title page, near-perfect spelling, punctuation, and grammar.	Mostly correct format and pagination. Neat. Few errors in title page, spelling, punctuation, and grammar.	Errors in format and pagination. Flawed title page. Distracting errors in spelling, punctuation, and grammar.	Incorrect format. Title page is flawed or missing. Many errors in spelling, punctuation, and grammar. Lack of planning is obvious. Paper is difficult to read.
	9–10	**8**	**7**	**1–6**
Thesis	An original and comprehensive thesis that is clear and well thought out. All sections work to support it.	Comprehensive and well-focused thesis, which is clearly stated. All sections work to support it.	Adequate thesis that is understandable but may be neither clear nor focused. It covers the majority of the issues found in the sections.	Inadequate thesis that is disconnected from the research or may be too broad to support. May be convoluted, confusing, or absent.
	18–20	**16–17**	**14–15**	**1–13**
Completeness/Coherence	Paper reads as a unified whole. There is no repetition of information. All sections are in place, and transitions between them are clearly developed.	Paper reads as a unified whole with no repetition. All sections are in place, but transitions between them are not as smooth.	Paper has required sections. Repetitions may be evident. The paper does not present a unified whole. Transitions are missing or inadequate.	Paper lacks one or more sections and makes no attempt to connect sections as a whole unit. Sections may be grossly repetitive or contradictory.
	23–25	**20–22**	**17–19**	**1–16**
Thinking/Analyzing	Strong understanding of the topic. Knowledge is factually relevant, accurate, and consistent. Solutions show analysis of research discussed in paper.	Good understanding of the topic. Uses main points of information researched. Solutions build on examination of research discussed in paper.	General understanding of topic. Uses research and attempts to add to it; solutions refer to some of the research discussed.	Little understanding of topic. Uses little basic information researched. Minimal examination of the topic. Solutions may be based solely on own opinions, without support.

Figure 12.11

Sample of a scoring rubric for student research paper.

(*Source:* Elk Grove School District, Elk Grove, CA.)

(Possible score = 100. Scorer marks a relevant square in each of the six categories—the horizontal rows—and student's score for that category is the small number within that square.)

of question is good practice for students to learn to express themselves succinctly in writing.

Disadvantages: Some students will have difficulty expressing themselves in a limited fashion or in writing. They need practice, coaching, and time.

Guidelines for use: This type is useful for occasional reviews and quizzes and as an alternative to other types of questions. For scoring, establish a scoring rubric and follow the same guidelines as for the essay-type item.

True–False

Description: A statement is presented that students are to judge as being accurate or not.

Example 1: A suffix is any bound morpheme added to the end of a root word. T or F?

Example 2: Christopher Columbus discovered America in 1492. T or F?

Advantages: Many items can be answered in a relativly short time, making broad content coverage possible. Scoring is quick and simple. True–false items are good as discussion starters, for review, and for diagnostic evaluation (preassessment) of what students already know or think they know.

Disadvantages: It is sometimes difficult to write true–false items that are purely true or false or without qualifying them in such a way that clues the answer. In the second sample question, for example, the student may question whether Columbus really did discover America or misunderstand the meaning of "discovering America." Weren't there people already there when he landed? Where, in fact, did he land? What is meant by "America?" Example 2 is poor also because it tests for more than one idea—Columbus, America, and 1492.

Much of the content that most easily lends itself to the true–false type of test item is trivial. Students have a 50 percent chance of guessing the correct answer, thus giving this item type both *poor validity* and *poor reliability.* Scoring and grading give no clue about why the student missed an item. Consequently, the disadvantages of true–false items far outweigh the advantages; *pure true–false items should not be used for arriving at grades.* For grading purposes, you may use modified true–false items (see guideline 11 that follows), where space is provided between items for students to write in their explanations, thus making the item a combined true–false, short-explanation type.

Guidelines for Using True–False Items

1. For preparing a false statement, first write the statement as a true statement, then make it false by changing a word or phrase.
2. Try to avoid using negative statements since they tend to confuse students.
3. A true–false statement should include only one idea.
4. Use close to an equal number of true and false items.
5. Try to avoid using specific determiners (e.g., "always," "all," or "none"), because they usually clue that the statement is false. Also avoid words that may clue that the statement is true (e.g., "often," "probably," and "sometimes").
6. Avoid words that may have different meanings for different students.
7. Avoid using verbatim language from the student textbook.
8. Avoid trick items, such as a slight reversal of numbers in a date.
9. Rather than using symbols for the words *true* and *false* (sometimes teachers use symbols such as + and −) which might be confusing, or having students write the letters *T* and *F* (sometimes a student does not write the letters clearly enough for the teacher to be able to distinguish which it is), have students either write out the words true and false or, better yet, have them simply circle T and F in the left margin of each item as indicated by the two examples provided.
10. Proofread your items (or have a friend do it) to be sure that the sentences are well-constructed and are free from typographical errors.
11. To avoid "wrong" answers, caused by variations in thinking, and to make the item more valid and reliable, students should be encouraged to write in their rationale for selecting true or false, making the item a *modified true–false* item. For example,

    When a farmer saw eight crows sitting on the fence surrounding his cornfield, he shot three of them. Five were left on the fence. T or F? _____

    Explanation: _____

    _____

    _____

As stated earlier, for grading purposes, you may use modified true–false items thus making the item a combined true–false, short-explanation type, and allowing for divergent and critical thinking. Another form of modified true–false item is the "sometimes-always-never" item, where a third alternative, "sometimes," is introduced to reduce the chance for guessing.

Now do Exercise 12.2 to start the development of your skill in writing assessment items.

EXERCISE 12.2

Preparing Assessment Items

Instructions: The purpose of this exercise is to practice your skill in preparing the different types of assessment items discussed previously. For use in your own teaching, select one specific instructional objective and write assessment items for it. When completed, share this exercise with your colleagues for their feedback.

Objective: _____

Grade and subject: _____

1. Arrangement item: _____

   _____

   _____

   _____

2. Completion drawing item: _____

   _____

   _____

   _____

   _____

3. Completion statement item: _____

   _____

   _____

   _____

   _____

4. Correction item: _____

   _____

   _____

   _____

   _____

5. Essay item: _____

   _____

   _____

   _____

   _____

6. Grouping item: _____

_____

_____

_____

7. Identification item: _____

_____

_____

_____

8. Matching item: _____

_____

_____

_____

_____

9. Multiple-choice item: _____

_____

_____

_____

_____

10. Performance item: _____

_____

_____

_____

_____

11. Short-explanation item: _____

_____

_____

_____

_____

12. *Modified* true–false item: _____

_____

_____

_____

_____

REPORTING STUDENT ACHIEVEMENT

One of your responsibilities as a classroom teacher is to report student progress in achievement to parents or guardians as well as to the school administration for record keeping. In some schools the reporting is of student progress and effort as well as of achievement. As described in the discussions that follow, reporting is done in at least two, and sometimes more, ways. However, for secondary schools, letter grades on report cards are still the most widely used method for reporting student learning.[12]

The Grade Report

Periodically a grade report (report card) is issued (generally from four to six times a year, depending upon the school, its purpose, and its type of scheduling). Grade reports may be distributed during an advisory period or they may be mailed to the student's home. This grade report represents an achievement grade (formative evaluation). The final report of the semester is also the semester grade, and for courses that are only one semester long it also is the final grade (summative evaluation). In essence, the first and sometimes second reports are progress notices, with the semester grade being the one that is transferred to the student's transcript of records.

In addition to the student's academic achievement, you must report the student's social behaviors (classroom conduct) while in your classroom. Whichever reporting form is used, you must separate your assessments of a student's social behaviors from the student's academic achievement. Academic achievement (or accomplishment) is represented by a letter (sometimes a number) grade (A through E or F, or E, S, and U, or 1 to 5, and sometimes with minuses and pluses), and the social behavior by a "satisfactory" or an "unsatisfactory," or by more specific items, or supplemented by teacher-written or computer-generated comments. In some instances, especially for middle schools, there may be a location on the reporting form for teachers to check whether basic grade-level standards have been met in the core subjects.

In addition to grading and reporting on subject-matter knowledge and social behavior, some secondary schools are including a broader set of "workplace" or "life" skills that transcend particular subject areas. For example, Academy High School (Fort Myers, FL) uses a "work ethic checklist," which is part of the senior portfolio in the school's internship preparation program.[13]

In some instances, especially in middle schools, there may be a location on the reporting form for the teacher to check whether basic grade-level standards have been met in the core subjects. As an extension to that, some high schools use a two-tiered graduation diploma system, with a basic tier for the student who has reached only minimal standards of proficiency in the basic core subject areas (especially reading, science, and mathematics) for graduation, and a second tier for the student who has reached a standard higher than the minimal. Some may even use a third tier, for students who have reached the highest possible standard of proficiency in one or more areas of the curriculum. As a matter of fact, with the current and growing emphasis on high-stakes standardized testing of achievement and for graduation, and less emphasis on grade designation (especially grades 10, 11, and 12), we predict more schools will eliminate the use of grades for reporting and develop some sort of three-tiered reporting system instead.

MORE ABOUT PARENTAL/GUARDIAN INVOLVEMENT AND HOME–SCHOOL CONNECTIONS

Study after study shows that when parents (or guardians) are involved in their child's school and school work, students learn better and earn better grades, and teachers experience more positive feelings about teaching. As a result, schools constantly are searching for new and better ways to communicate with and to involve parents/guardians. What follows are additional suggestions and resources.

Contacting Parents/Guardians

Although it is not always obligatory, some teachers purposefully contact parents or guardians by telephone or by e-mail, especially when a student has shown a sudden turn for either the worse or the better in academic achievement or in classroom behavior. That initiative and contact by the teacher are usually welcomed by parents/guardians and can lead to productive conferences with the teacher. A telephone conference can save valuable time for both the teacher and the parent or guardian.

Another way of contacting parents/guardians is by letter, either faxed or mailed. Contacting a parent/guardian by letter gives you time to think and to make clear your thoughts and concerns to that parent/guardian and to invite the parent/guardian to respond at her or his convenience by letter, by phone, or by arranging to have a conference with you, thus affording the parent/guardian time to think before responding.

---

[12]T. R. Guskey, *Communicating Student Learning*, p. 121.
[13]J. Bailey and J. McTighe, "Reporting Achievement at the Secondary Level: What and How," in Guskey, *Communicating Student Learning*, p. 121.

Weekly Assessment Checklist for: _____

	Math	History	Science	Language Arts
Number of tardies				
Number of absences				
Academic grade				
Citizenship grade				

	Usually	Sometimes	Rarely	Never
Homework turned in on time				
Class work satisfactorily completed				
Exhibits acceptable classroom behavior				
Exhibits acceptable use of time in class				
Skill level is adequate to do work				
Participates orally in class discussions				
Participates in classroom learning activities				
Assumes responsibilities for own actions				
Avoids talking excessively or out of turn				
Comes to class prepared with supplies				
Is ready to start working when class begins				
Performs well on quizzes and tests				
Is attentive and focused during class				
Shows good listening skills				
Shows good organizational skills				
Shows up for assigned detentions				
Respects the property of others and of the school				
Respects the rights of others				

Other comments or concerns: _____

_____

_____

_____

_____

_____

_____

_____

_____

_____

Figure 12.12
Weekly assessment checklist: Sample with teacher input only.

Progress Report: Marina High School

Student: _Anthony von Hauser_   Course: _Algebra 1_   Date: _September 14, 2001_

This progress report form incorporates evaluation by student, teacher, and parent. The form will be completed by the student on Wednesday and by the teacher on Thursday and reviewed by the office and returned to the student on Friday. The student will take the form home for parental review, comments, and signature.

Section I: Self-Assessment: The student is asked to evaluate progress in the course in terms of goals and how closely these goals are being achieved. Do you feel you have made progress since the last progress report?

By taking this algebra class I achieved a greater understanding of it. I feel I have made a lot of progress since I took the class in 8th grade. It is also taught much better, which makes it easier.

Section II: Teacher Assessment: The teacher is asked to assess the student's entry, competency, and achievement to date and make recommendations.

Anthony is doing quite well. He has had to make some adjustments from previous work habits (ie., showing work), but he has made an excellent transition. Anthony has great skills and strong understanding of concepts.

Present Status: (Rated A–F)		*What Is Needed*
B+ Class work/ participation	A = Excellent	✔ Emphasis on homework
C+ Homework	B = Above average	___ Improve class participation
A Portfolio	C = Average	___ More careful preparation for tests
A Quizzes	D = Below average	✔ Keep up the good work
A Tests	F = Falling	___ Contact teacher
A Overall		___ Improve portfolio
		___ Other _____
		Office initial _CM_

Section III: Parent Evaluation and Comments: Parents are asked to respond and sign this progress report.

I thank you for this timely report. I am delighted that Anthony has started off well and is liking the class. He talks at home a lot about the class and the interesting activities; a tribute to good teaching. I can tell from our conversations at home that he is feeling much better about his math capability. I thank you.

Eric von Hauser

Figure 12.13
Progress report: Subject-specific with student and parent/guardian input.

Progress Reporting to Parents/Guardians

In absence of a computer-link assignment/progress report hotline, or in addition to that, most schools have a progress report form that, upon request by a parent/guardian, can be sent home as often as agreed upon by the teacher and the parent/guardian. The form may be similar to the one shown in Figure 12.12 showing the student's progress in each of the core subjects, or perhaps like the one in Figure 12.13 that requires student self-evaluation, teacher assessment, office signature, and parental/guardian response and signature.

Meeting Parents/Guardians

You will meet some of the parents/guardians early in the school year during back-to-school (or meet the teacher or curriculum night as it is variously called) and throughout the year in individual conferences and later in the year during spring open house. For the beginning teacher, these meetings with parents/guardians can be anxious times. The following paragraphs provide guidelines to help you with those experiences.[14]

Back-to-school night is the evening early in the school year when parents and guardians come to the school and meet their children's teachers. The parents and guardians arrive either at the student's homebase or in the auditorium for a greeting and a few words from various school officials and then proceed through a simulation of their sons' or daughters' school day; as a group, they meet each class and each teacher for a few minutes. Later, in the spring, many schools host an open house night where parents and guardians may have more time to talk individually with teachers, although the major purpose of the open house is for the school and teachers to celebrate and display the work and progress of the students.

At back-to-school night, parents/guardians are anxious to learn as much as they can about their children's teachers. You will meet each group of parents/guardians for a brief time, usually about ten minutes. During that meeting you will provide them with a copy of the course syllabus, make some straightforward remarks about yourself, and talk about the course, its requirements, your expectations of the students, and how they, the students' parents and guardians, might help.

Although there will be precious little time for questions from the parents/guardians, during your introduction the adults will be delighted to learn that you have your program well planned, are a "task master," appreciate their interest, and welcome their participation. They will be happy to hear your willingness to communicate with them. Parents/guardians will be pleased to know that you are "from the school of the three Fs"—that is, that you are firm, friendly, and fair. For any parent/guardian who indicates an urgent need to talk with you, try to schedule a mutually convenient private conference time in person or via telephone for later that evening or during the next few days.

Specifically, parents/guardians will expect to learn about your curriculum goals and objectives, about any long-term projects, class size, about when tests will be given, your procedures for late work and makeup work, and your grading procedures. They will want to know what you expect of them: Will there be homework, and if so, should they help their children with it? How can they contact you? Try to anticipate other questions. Your principal, department chair, or colleagues can be of aid in helping you anticipate and prepare for these questions.

tions. Of course, you can never prepare for the question or comment that comes from left field. Just remain calm and avoid being flustered (or at least appear so). Ten minutes will fly by quickly, and parents and guardians will be reassured to know you are in control.

As parents who have attended many back-to-school nights at our own children's schools, we continue to be both surprised and dismayed that so few teachers seem well prepared for the few minutes they have with the parents; that, considering how often we hear about teachers wanting more involvement of parents, so few seem delighted that parents have indeed come; and that so few teachers take full advantage of this time with parents to truly celebrate their programs. Consequently, we include a model handout (Figure 12.14) that demonstrates the kind of planning a teacher should do for back-to-school night with parents and the sort of information that parents appreciate receiving from their children's teachers.

Conferences with Parent/Guardian

When meeting parents or guardians for conferences, you should be as specific as possible when explaining to a parent/guardian the progress of that adult's child in your class. And, again, express your appreciation for their interest. Be helpful to his or her understanding, and don't saturate the parent/guardian with more information than he or she needs. Resist any tendency to talk too much. Allow time for the parent or guardian to ask questions. Keep your answers succinct. Never compare one student with another or with the rest of the class. If the parent or guardian asks a question for which you do not have an answer, tell the person you will try to find an answer and will phone him or her as quickly as you can. And do it. Have the student's portfolio and other work with you during the parent/guardian conference so you can show the parent/guardian examples of what is being discussed. Also, have your grade book on hand, or a computer printout of it, but be prepared to protect from the person the names and records of the other students.

Sometimes it is helpful to have a three-way conference, a conference with the parent/guardian, the student, and you, or a conference with the parent/guardian, the principal or counselor, and several or all of the student's teachers. If, especially as a beginning teacher, you would like the presence of an administrator at a parent/guardian–teacher conference as backup, don't be hesitant to arrange that.

Some educators prefer a student-led conference, arguing that "placing students in charge of the conference makes them individually accountable, encourages them to take pride in their work, and encourages student–parent/guardian communication about school perfor-

---

[14]For suggestions from a school administrator for "delivering powerful presentations to parents" at back-to-school night, see W. B. Ribas, "Tips for Reaching Parents," *Educational Leadership* 56(1):83–85 (September 1998).

Course:	Honors Precalculus (HP)
Instructor:	Mr. Charles Schwing
Text:	Advanced Mathematical Concepts
Description:	This is an accelerated class designed to prepare the student for calculus. As an Honors class (HP), the course requires a higher level of commitment on the part of the student. Grades of *A, B,* or *C* are awarded an extra grade point by St. Francis High School and by the University of California and California State University systems and are given extra weight by many other public and private colleges and universities. A partial listing of topics covered in this class includes analytic geometry, trigonometry, matrices and determinants, probability and statistics, and an introduction to calculus, including the epsilon-delta definition of limit.
Homework:	Homework is assigned daily (with very few exceptions) and should require approximately 30 to 40 minutes to complete. Success in this class is virtually impossible unless assignments are done in a timely and conscientious manner.
Grades:	Points are given for homework, quizzes, and major exams. Grades are computed based on total points, with quizzes and exams comprising 75% of those points. The grading scale is *A* = 88% or above, *B* = 75–87%, *C* = 60–74%, *D* = below 60%. To earn an *F* requires a special "effort" on the part of the student.
Citizenship:	Students begin this class with an *A* in citizenship. Demerits are earned for tardiness and inappropriate behavior. Three demerits result in a one letter drop in citizenship (e.g., from an *A* to a *B*).
Instructor Availability:	I am available for extra help from 7:45 until 8:10 each morning, during blocks C, D, and F, and after school until 4:00. I can be at school before 7:45 or after 4:00 if arranged in advance. It is your child's responsibility to seek me out—I will not chase after a student to come in for help. If extra help is obtained as soon as the need arises, it is usually only a matter of a 10- or 15-minute session. Hours at a time are rarely needed. There is most definitely a positive correlation between the students who come in for help and the grades they receive. If at any time you are concerned about your child's progress, please feel free to call me at school and leave a message. I will get back to you the same day if at all possible.

Figure 12.14
Handout for parents/guardians at back-to-school night.
(*Source:* Courtesy of Charles Schwing.)

mance."[15] But, like most innovations in education, the concept of student-led conferences has its limitations—the most important of which perhaps is the matter of time.[16]

---

[15]D. W. Johnson and R. T. Johnson, "The Role of Cooperative Learning in Assessing and Communicating Student Learning," in T. R. Guskey, *Communicating Student Learning,* p. 43.

[16]For a discussion of the pros and cons of using the student-led conference, and for a conference organizer tool, see J. Bailey and J. McTighe, "Reporting Achievement at the Secondary Level: What and How," of T. R. Guskey, *Communicating Student Learning,* pp. 137–139. See also L. Countryman and M. Schroeder, "When Students Lead Parent–Teacher Conferences," *Educational Leadership* 53(7):64–68 (April 1996), and D. G. Hackmann, *Student-Led Conferences at the Middle Level* (Champaign, IL: ED407171, ERIC Clearinghouse on Elementary and Early Childhood Education, 1997).

When a parent or guardian asks how she or he may help in the student's learning, the paragraphs that follow offer suggestions for your consideration. Many schools have made special and successful efforts to link home and school. At some schools, through homework hotlines, parents/guardians have phone access to their children's assignment specifications and to their progress in their schoolwork, and parents/guardians with a personal computer and a modem have access to tutorial services to assist students with assignments.

Helping students become critical thinkers is one of the aims of education and one that parents and guardians can help with by reinforcing the strategies being used in the classroom. Ways to do this are to ask "what if" questions; think aloud as a model for the student's thinking development; encourage the student's own metacognition by asking questions such as, "How did you arrive at that

- **Alliance for Parental Involvement in Education,** PO Box 59, East Chatham, NY 12060-0059 (518) 392-6900.
- **Center on Families, Communities, Schools & Children's Learning,** 3505 N. Charles St., Baltimore, MD 21218 (410) 516-8800.
- **National Coalition for Parent Involvement in Education,** Box 39, 1201 16th St., NW, Washington, DC 20036.
- **National Community Education Association,** 3929 Old Lee Highway, Suite 91A, Fairfax, VA 22030-2401 (703) 359-8973.
- **National PTA,** 330 North Wabash Ave., Ste. 2100, Chicago, IL 60611-3690 (312) 670-6782.
- **Parents for Public Schools,** PO Box 12807, Jackson, MS 39236-2807 (800) 880-1222.

Figure 12.15
Resources for developing home–school partnerships.

conclusion?" or "How do you feel about your conclusion now?" and asking these questions about the student's everyday social interactions, topics that are important to the student; ask the student to elaborate on his or her ideas; accepting the fact that the student may make mistakes but encourage the student to learn from them.

Many resources are available for parents/guardians to use at home. The United States government, for example, has a variety of free or low-cost booklets available. For information, contact the Consumer Information Center, Department BEST, Pueblo, CO 81009, or the website on http://www.pueblo.gsa.gov. Figure 12.15 presents addresses for additional ideas and resources for home–school partnerships.

Dealing with an Angry Parent or Guardian

If a parent or guardian is angry or hostile toward you and the school, the paragraphs that follow offer guidelines for dealing with that hostility.

Remain calm in your discussion with the adult, allowing the parent or guardian to talk out his or her hostility while you say very little; usually, the less you say the better off you will be. What you do say must be objective and to the point of the student's work in your classroom. The parent or guardian may just need to vent frustrations that might have very little to do with you, the school, or even the student.

Do *not* allow yourself to be intimidated, put on the defensive, or backed into a verbal corner. If the parent/guardian tries to do so by attacking you personally, do not press your defense at this point. Perhaps the parent/guardian has made a point that you should take time to consider, and now is a good time to arrange for another conference with the parent/guardian for about a week later. In a follow-up conference, if the parent/guardian agrees, you may want to consider bringing in a mediator, such as another member of your teaching team, an administrator, or a school counselor.

You must *not* talk about other students; keep the conversation focused on the progress of this parent or guardian's child. The adult is *not* your rival, or should

not be. You both share a concern for the academic and emotional well-being of the parent or guardian's child. Use your best skills in critical thinking and problem solving, trying to focus the discussion by identifying the problem, defining it, and then arriving at some decision about how mutually to go about solving it. To this end you may need to ask for help from a third party, such as the student's school counselor. If agreed to by the parent, please take that step.

Parents and guardians do *not* need to hear about how busy you are, about your personal problems, or about how many other students you are dealing with on a daily basis, unless, of course, a parent/guardian asks. Parents and guardians rightfully expect you to be the capable professional who knows what to do and is doing it.

SUMMARY

Whereas preceding parts of this book addressed the *why, what,* and *how* components of teaching, this chapter has focused your attention on the fourth and final component—the *how well* component—and on the first of two aspects of that component. Assessment is an integral and on-going factor in the teaching-learning process; consequently, this chapter has emphasized the importance of your including the following in your teaching performance:

- Use a variety of instruments to collect a body of evidence to most reliably assess the learning of students that focus on their individual development.
- Involve students in the assessment process; keep students informed of their progress. Return tests promptly, review answers to all questions, and respond to inquiries about marks given.
- Consider your assessment and grading procedures carefully, plan them, and explain your policies to the students.
- Make sure to explain any ambiguities that result from the terminology used, and base your assessments on the material that has been taught.

- Strive for objective and impartial assessment as you put your assessment plan into operation.
- Try to minimize arguments about grades, cheating, and teacher subjectivity by involving students in the planning, reinforcing individual student development, and providing an accepting, stimulating learning environment.
- Maintain accurate and clear records of assessment results so that you will have an adequate supply of data on which to base your judgmental decisions about achievement.

Because teaching and learning work hand in hand, and because they are reciprocal processes where one depends on and affects the other, the how well component deals with the assessment of both how well the students are learning and how well the teacher is teaching. This chapter has dealt with the first. In the next and final chapter of this book, your attention is directed to techniques designed to help you develop your teaching skills and assess that development, a process that is just beginning and will continue throughout your teaching career. For, as a teacher, you are a learner among learners.

QUESTIONS FOR CLASS DISCUSSION

1. Identify a problem in grading that you personally experienced as a student in school. What was your perceived cause of the problem? How might it have been avoided? What was the resolution and how was that resolution arrived at? Was the resolution satisfactory to all concerned? Why or why not?
2. Other than a paper-and-pencil test, identify three techniques for assessing student learning during or at completion of an instructional unit.
3. Investigate various ways that schools are experimenting today with assessing and reporting student achievement. Share what you find with your classmates. With your classmates, discuss the pros and cons of various systems of assessing and reporting.
4. When using a point system for determining student grades, is it educationally defensible to give a student a higher grade than that student's points call for? a lower grade? Give your rationale for your answers.
5. Describe any student learning activities or situations that you believe should *not* be graded but should or could be used for assessment of student learning.
6. Describe the roles and limitations of objectivity and subjectivity in the assessment of student learning.
7. Select one of the Reflective Thoughts from the opening of Part IV (page 340) that is specifically related to the content of this chapter, research it, and write a one-page essay explaining why you agree or disagree with the thought. Share your essay with members of your class for their thoughts.
8. Describe any prior concepts you held that changed as a result of your experiences with this chapter. Describe the changes.

9. From your current observations and field work as related to this teacher preparation program, clearly identify one specific example of educational practice that seems contradictory to exemplary practice or theory as presented in this chapter. Present your explanation for the discrepancy.
10. Do you have questions generated by the content of this chapter? If you do, list them along with ways answers might be found.

FOR FURTHER READING

Andrade, H. G. "Using Rubrics to Promote Thinking and Learning." *Educational Leadership* 57(5):13–18 (February 2000).

Asp, E. "Assessment in Education: Where Have We Been? Where Are We Headed?" Chap. 6 of R. S. Brandt (ed.). *Education in a New Era.* Alexandria, VA: ASCD Yearbook, Association for Supervision and Curriculum Development, 2000, pp. 123–157.

Birk, L. "Grade Inflation: What's Really Behind All Those A's?" *Harvard Education Letter* 16(1):1–3 (January/February 2000).

Bracey, G. W. *A Short Guide to Standardized Testing.* Fastback 459. Bloomington, IN: Phi Delta Kappa Educational Foundation, 2000.

Chase, C. I. *Contemporary Assessment for Educators.* New York: Addison Wesley Longman, 1999.

Cizek, G. J. *Cheating on Tests: How To Do It, Detect It, and Prevent It.* Mahway, NJ: Lawrence Erlbaum, 1999.

Colby, S. A. "Grading in a Standards-Based System." *Educational Leadership* 56(6):17–21 (March 1999).

Cole, K. A. "Walking Around: Getting More from Informal Assessment." *Mathematics Teaching in the Middle School* 4(4):224–227 (January 1999).

Conway, K. D. "Assessing Open-Ended Problems." *Mathematics Teaching in the Middle School* 4(8):510–514 (May 1999).

Danielson, C., and Marquez, E. *A Collection of Performance Tasks and Rubrics. High School Mathematics.* New York: Eye on Education, 1998.

Doran, R., Chan, F., and Tamir, P. *Science Educator's Guide to Assessment.* Arlington, VA: National Science Teachers Association, 1998.

Eilertsen, T. V., and Valdermo, O. "Open-Book Assessment: A Contribution to Improved Learning?" *Studies in Educational Evaluation* 26(2):91–103 (2000).

Geocaris, C., and Ross, M. "A Test Worth Taking." *Educational Leadership* 57(1):29–33 (September 1999).

Gredler, M. E. *Classroom Assessment and Learning.* New York: Addison Wesley Longman, 1999.

Gronlund, N. E. *Assessment of Student Achievement.* 6th Ed. Needham Heights, MA: Allyn & Bacon Longman, 1998.

Grosse, S. J., Gotts, S. L., Rath, C., and Cummings, M. "Physical Education Standards: Making Assessment Manageable in the Urban High School." *Strategies* 14(3):15–18 (January/February 2001).

Gustafson, C. "Phone Home." *Educational Leadership* 56(2):31–32 (October 1998).

Kelly, K. "Retention vs. Social Promotion: Schools Search for Alternatives." *The Harvard Education Letter* 15(1):1–3 (January/February 1999).

Kelly, K. "Seeking a Cure for Senior-Year Slump." *Harvard Education Letter* 17(4):1–4 (July/August 2001).

Libit, H. "Report Card Redux." *School Administrator* 56(10):6–10 (November 1999).

Madaus, G. F., and O'Dwyer, L. M. "A Short History of Performance Assessment." *Phi Delta Kappan* 80(9):688–695 (May 1999).

Marzano, R. J. *Transforming Classroom Grading.* Alexandria, VA: Association for Supervision and Curriculum Development, 2000.

Murdock, T. B. "Discouraging Cheating in Your Classroom." *Mathematics Teacher* 92(7):587–591 (October 1999).

Popham, W. J. *Classroom Assessment: What Teachers Need to Know.* 2nd Ed. Needham Heights, MA: Allyn & Bacon, 1999.

Popham, W. J. *The Truth About Testing.* Alexandria, VA: Association for Supervision and Curriculum Develolpment, 2001.

Ronis, D. *Brain Compatible Assessments.* Arlington Heights, IL: Skyline, 2000.

Schmoker, M. *The Results Fieldbook: Practical Strategies from Dramatically Improved Schools.* Alexandria, VA: Association for Supervision and Curriculum Development, 2001.

Stephens, D., and Story, J. (Eds.). *Assessment as Inquiry: Learning the Hypothesis-Test Process.* Urbana, IL: National Council of Teachers of English, 2000.

Stiggins, R. J. *Student-Involved Classroom Assessment.* 3rd ed. Upper Saddle River, NJ: Merrill/Prentice Hall, 2001.

Stoskopf, A. "Reviving Clio: Inspired History Teaching and Learning (Without High-Stakes Tests)." *Phi Delta Kappan* 9(4):468–473 (February 2001).

Zmuda, A., and Tomaino, M. "A Contract for the High School Classroom." *Educational Leadership* 56(6):59–61 (March 1999).

13

Assessing Teaching Effectiveness and Continued Professional Development

Although most of us are not born with innate teaching skills, *teaching skills can be learned and steadily improved.* Teachers who wish to improve their teaching can do so, and (in addition to this book) there are many resources that can help.

This chapter addresses the assessment and development of your effectiveness as a classroom teacher, a process that continues throughout your professional career. Teaching is such an electrifying profession that it is not easy to remain energetic and to stay abreast of changes and trends that result from research and

practice. You will need to make a continuous and determined effort to remain an alert and effective teacher.

One way to collect data and improve your effectiveness is through periodic assessment of your teaching performance, either by an evaluation of your teaching in the real classroom or, if you are in a program of teacher preparation, by a technique called *micro peer teaching.* The latter is the focus of the final section of this chapter and is an example of a type of final performance (authentic) assessment for this book.

Specifically, upon completion of this chapter you should be able to:

1. Demonstrate knowledge about the field components of teacher preparation.
2. Demonstrate knowledge of how to find a teaching job.
3. Demonstrate knowledge of how to remain an alert and effective classroom teacher throughout your teaching career.

PROFESSIONAL DEVELOPMENT THROUGH STUDENT TEACHING

You are excited about the prospect of being assigned as a student teacher to your first classroom, but you are also concerned. Questions linger in your mind. Will your host (cooperating) teacher(s) like you? Will you get along? Will the students accept you? Will you be assigned to the school, grade level, and subjects you want? What will the students be like? Will there be many classroom management problems? What about mainstreamed students, and students with only limited proficiency in English? Your questions will be unending.

Indeed, you *should* be excited and concerned, for this experience of student teaching is one of the most significant and important facets of your program of teacher preparation. In some programs, this practical field experience is planned as a coexperience with the college or university theory classes. In other programs, student teaching is the culminating experience. Different sequences are represented in different programs. For example, at some colleges, field teaching extends over two or three semesters. In other programs, teacher candidates first take theory classes followed by a full second semester of student teaching. Regardless of when and how your student teaching occurs, the experience is a bright and shining opportunity to hone your teaching skills in a real classroom. During this time, you will be supported by an experienced college or university supervisor and by carefully selected cooperating teachers who will share their expertise. Once you have started your student teaching, it can be helpful toward establishing a feeling of community, preventing a sense of isolation, and encouraging reflection if you and your college or university supervisor can communicate by e-mail over the Internet.

Everyone concerned in the teacher preparation program—your cooperating teacher, your university instructors, the school administrators, and your university supervisor—realize that this is your practicum in learning how to teach. During your student teaching, you will no doubt make errors, and with the understanding and guidance of those supervising your work you will benefit and learn from those errors. Sometimes your fresh approach to motivation, your creative ideas for learning activities, and your energy and enthusiasm make it possible for the cooperating teacher to learn from you. After all, teaching and learning are always reciprocal processes. What is most important is that the students who are involved with you in the teaching-learning process will benefit from your role as the teacher candidate in the classroom. The following guidelines are offered to help make this practical experience beneficial to everyone involved.

Student Teaching Is the Real Thing

Because you have a classroom setting for practicing and honing your teaching skills with active, responsive, young people, student teaching *is* the real thing. On the other hand, student teaching is *not* real in the sense that it is your cooperating teacher, not you, who has the ultimate responsibility and authority for the classroom.

Getting Ready for Student Teaching

To prepare yourself for student teaching, you must study, plan, practice, and reflect. You should become knowledgeable about your students and their developmental backgrounds. In your theory classes, you learned a great deal about students. Review your class notes and textbooks from those courses, or select some readings suggested in Part I. Perhaps some of the topics will have more meaning for you now.

First Impressions

First impressions are often lasting impressions. You have heard that statement before, and now, as you ready for this important phase of your professional preparation, you hear it again for it is crucial to your success. Remember it as you prepare to meet your school principal and cooperating teacher for the first time; remember it again as you prepare to meet your students for the first time; and remember it again as you prepare for your university supervisor's first observation of your teaching. In each case, you have only one opportunity to make a first impression.

Continuing to Get Ready for Student Teaching

In addition to the aforementioned preparations, you will need to be knowledgeable about your assigned school and the community that surrounds it. Review the subject areas you will be teaching and the curriculum content and standards in those areas. Carefully discuss with your cooperating teacher (or teachers, as you may have more than one) and your university supervisor all responsibilities that you will be expected to assume.

As a student teacher you may want to run through each lesson verbally, perhaps in front of a mirror, the night before teaching your lesson. Some student teachers read through each lesson, audiorecording the lesson, playing it back, and evaluating whether the directions are clear, the instruction is mind-grabbing (or at least interesting), the sequence is logical, and the lesson closure is concise. Still other student teachers always have a Plan B in mind in case Plan A turns out to be inappropriate.

Student Teaching from the Cooperating Teacher's Point of View

For your consideration, information about student teaching from the viewpoint of a cooperating teacher is presented here in a question-and-answer format. You may wish to share this section with your cooperating teacher.

What is my role? As the cooperating teacher, your role is to assist when necessary: to provide guidance, to review lesson plans before they are taught, to facilitate the learning and skill development of your student teacher, and to help your student teacher become and feel like a member of the school faculty and of the profession.

How can I prepare for the experience? Get to know your student teacher before he or she begins teaching. Develop a collegial rapport with the student teacher.

Who is my student teacher? Your student teacher is a person making the transition from another career or from the life of a college student to the profession of teaching. Your student teacher may be your age, older, or younger. In any case, your student teacher may be scared to death, anxious, knowledgeable, and, when it comes to teaching philosophy, somewhere between being a romantic idealist and a pragmatic realist. Do not destroy the idealism—help the student teacher to understand and deal with the realism of everyday teaching.

It is important that you learn about the kinds of teaching experiences that your student teacher has had prior to this assignment so the student teacher and you may build from those experiences. For example, this may be your student teacher's very first teaching experience, or he or she may have substitute teaching experience, experience teaching in another country, or may have had student teaching at another school prior to this term.

What kind of support, criticism, and supervision should I give? Much of this you will have to decide for yourself. On the other hand, some teacher preparation programs include seminars that train the cooperating teachers in techniques for supervising student teachers. Cooperating teachers are often selected not only because of their effectiveness in teaching but also because of their skill in working with other adults. It is likely that you will be working as a member of a team that includes you, the student teacher, and the university supervisor. Your student teacher may have more than one cooperating teacher who should be included as a member of this professional team. Whatever the situation, your student teacher needs support, helpful suggestions, and productive monitoring. It is unprofessional to place a student teacher into a total "sink-or-swim" situation.

What danger signs should I be alert for? Your student teacher may be quite different from you in both appearance and style of teaching but may be potentially just as effective a teacher. Be slow and cautious in judging your student teacher's effectiveness. Offer suggestions, but do not make demands.

A student teacher who is not preparing well is likely to be heading for trouble. The saying stands: Failing to prepare is preparing to fail. Be certain to ask for and to receive lesson plans before they are taught, especially in the beginning and whenever you feel the student teacher is not preparing well.

Another danger signal is when the student teacher seems to show no real interest in the school and the students beyond the classroom. The student teacher should be prompt, eager to spend extra time with you, attend faculty meetings, and be aware of the necessity of performing school clerical tasks. If you feel there is a lurking problem, then let the student teacher or the university supervisor know immediately. Trust your intuition. Poor communication between members of the teaching team is another danger signal.

What else should I know? Your student teacher may be employed elsewhere and have other demands on his or her time. Become aware of these other demands, but keep the educational welfare of your students paramount in your mind.

See that your student teacher is treated as a member of the faculty and invited to faculty functions. Your student teacher should have a personal mailbox (or share yours, with his or her name on it as well) and should understand school policies, procedures, and curriculum documents.

Once your student teacher is well grounded, he or she should be ready to gradually be alone with the students for increasingly longer periods of time. For a specified time, a student teacher's goal is to work toward a competency level that enables him or her to assume increasing responsibility for everything. This means that you are nearby and on call in case of an emergency, but out of sight of the students.

Comments from the University Supervisor

When is the supervisor coming? Is the supervisor going to be here today? Do you see a university or a college supervisor's observation of your student teaching as a pleasant experience or a painful one? Do you realize that classroom observations of your teaching continue during your beginning years of teaching? Being observed and evaluated does not have to be a painful, nerve-racking experience for you. You don't have to become a bundle of raw nerve endings when you realize the supervisor is coming to see you. Whether you are a student teacher being observed by your university supervisor, or a probationary teacher being evaluated by your principal, some professional suggestions may help you turn an evaluating observation into a useful, professionally satisfying experience.

What to Do Before an Observation

Successful teachers seem to be able to ameliorate tension and get through an evaluation with skill and tact. Prepare for your evaluative visit by deciding what you do well and plan to demonstrate your best skills, decorating your room and bulletin boards, especially by displaying student work, making sure your work area is orderly (this shows good organization), and select an academic aspect of the teaching day that demonstrates some of your best teaching skills. If your university supervisor has previously targeted some areas that need strengthening, plan to demonstrate growth in those teaching abilities.

What to Do During an Observation

Some supervisors and administrators choose to preannounce their visits. This is certainly true for *clinical supervision* practices. Clinical supervision is based on shared decision making between the supervisor and teacher, and focused on improving, rather than evaluating, teaching behaviors. With the use of clinical supervision, you know when the supervisor or administrator is coming, and you will probably look forward to the visit because of the rapport that has been established between members of your triad (in student teaching situations, your triad is composed of you, your cooperating teacher, and your university or college supervisor).

Features of effective clinical supervision include a preobservation conference, observation of teaching, and a postobservation conference. In the preobservation conference, the student teacher, cooperating teacher, and the supervisor meet to discuss goals, objectives, teaching strategies, and the evaluation process. During the observation of teaching, the supervisor collects data on the classroom students' performance of objectives and on the student teacher's performance of the teaching strategies. In the postobservation conference, the student teacher, cooperating teacher, and the supervisor discuss the performances. They may compare what happened with what was expected, make inferences about students' achievement of objectives, and discuss relationships between teaching performance and student achievement. The supervisor and cooperating teacher act as educational consultants and may discuss alternative strategies for teaching at this conference or at a later one.

Sometimes your supervisor or administrator may drop in unannounced. When that happens you can take a deep breath, count to ten (quietly), and then proceed with your lesson. You will undoubtedly do just fine if you have been following the guidelines set forth in this book. Additional guidelines for a classroom observation are: allow the observer to sit wherever he or she wishes; do not interrupt your lesson to introduce the observer, unless the observer requests it, but *do* prepare your students in advance by letting them know who may be visiting and why; do not put the observer on the spot by suddenly involving him or her in the lesson, but *do* try to discern in advance the level of participation desired by your observer.

If you have been assigned to a classroom for a student teaching experience, your university supervisor will meet with you and explain some of the tasks you should attend to when the supervisor visits your class. These may vary from the list presented. For instance, some supervisors prefer to walk into a classroom quietly and not interrupt the learning activities. Some prefer not to be introduced to the class or to participate in the activities. Some supervisors are already well known by the students and teaching staff from prior visits to the school. Other supervisors may give you a special form to be completed before he or she arrives for the visit. This form often resembles a lesson plan format and includes space for your objectives, lesson procedures, motivational strategies, related activities, and method of assessing how well the students learned from the lesson. Remember, keep the line of communication open with your supervisor so you have a clear understanding of what is expected of you when she or he visits your classroom to observe your teaching. Without "missing a beat" in your lesson, you may walk over and quietly hand the observer a copy of the lesson plan and the textbook (or any other materials being used), opened to the appropriate page.

In some teacher preparation programs the student teacher is expected to maintain a student teaching binder in the classroom. The binder is kept in a particular location so that the cooperating teacher may refer to it, and so the college or university supervisor can pick it up upon entering the classroom and refer to it during the observation. Organized in the binder are the current lesson plan, the current unit plan, previous lessons with reflections, tests and their results, assignments, classroom management plan, and a current seating chart with the students' names. The student teaching binder can, in fact, represent the start of your professional portfolio (discussed later in this chapter).

Soon after the observational visit, there should be a conference in which observations are discussed in a nonjudgmental atmosphere. It might be necessary for you to make sure that a conference is scheduled. The

---

purposes of this postobservation conference are: for you and the observer(s) to discuss, rather than to evaluate, your teaching; and, for you to exit the conference with agreements about areas for improvement and how to accomplish those improvements.

What to Do During an Observation Conference

Some supervisors will arrange to have a conference with you to discuss the classroom observation and to begin to resolve any classroom teaching problems. As a teacher or teacher candidate, you should be quite professional during this conference. For instance, one student teacher asks for additional help by requesting resources. Another takes notes and suggests developing a cooperative plan with the supervisor to improve teaching competencies. Still another discusses visiting other classrooms to observe exemplary teachers.

During other conferences, student teachers may ask for assistance in scheduling additional meetings with the supervisor. At such meetings, the teacher (or teacher candidate) views videos of selected teaching styles or methods, listens to audiotapes, or visits an outside educational consultant or nearby resource center.

Almost all supervisors conclude their conferences by leaving something in writing with the teacher or teacher candidate. This written record usually includes: a summary of teaching strengths or weaknesses, with a review of classroom management; the supervisor's recommendations; and, perhaps, steps in an overall plan for the teacher's (or student teacher's) continued professional growth and development.

What to Do After the Supervisor Leaves

In addition to observing the classes of other teachers, attending workshops and conferences, and conferring with college and university authorities, the following are ways to implement your plan for improvement. Be sure you debug your lesson plans by walking through them in advance of implementing them in the classroom. Do what you and your supervisor have agreed on. Document your activities with a record or diary with dated entries. If you maintain a supervisor's binder, this documentation may be kept in the binder along with the supervisor's written comments. If you have a problem with classroom management or organization, review your written classroom management plan and procedures, comparing your plan with the guidelines presented in Chapter 4. Review your plan and procedures with your cooperating teacher, a trusted teaching colleague, or your university supervisor. Obtain help when you need it. Write comments to parents or guardians about students' progress, and leave space for a return message from the adult (see, for example Figure 12.13 of Chapter 12). Keep positive responses that you receive

from these adults and share them with your supervisor at your next conference.

FINDING A TEACHING POSITION

As your successful student-teaching experience draws to a close, you will embark upon finding your first paid teaching job. The guidelines that follow are provided to help you accomplish your goal.

Guidelines for Locating a Teaching Position

To prepare for finding the position you want, you should focus on: (1) letters of recommendation from your cooperating teacher(s), your college or university supervisor, and, in some instances, the school principal; (2) your professional preparation as evidenced by your letters of recommendation and other items in your professional portfolio (discussed next); and (3) your job-interviewing skills.

First, consider the recommendations about your teaching. Most colleges and universities have a career center, usually called a *job* (or *career*) *placement center,* where there is probably a counselor who can advise you how to open the job placement file that will hold your professional recommendations. This enables prospective personnel directors or district personnel who are expecting to employ new teachers to review your recommendations. Sometimes there are special forms for writing these recommendations. It is your responsibility to request letters of recommendation and, when appropriate, to supply the person writing the recommendation with the blank form and an appropriately addressed stamped envelope. Sometimes the job placement files are confidential, so your recommendations will be mailed directly to the placement office. The confidentiality of recommendations may be optional, and, when possible, you may want to maintain your own copies of letters of recommendation and include them in your professional portfolio.

The letters of recommendation from educators at the school(s) where you did your student teaching should include the following information: the name of the school and district where you did your student teaching, the grade levels and subjects you taught, your proven skills in managing students of diversity in the classroom, your ability to teach the relevant subject(s), your skills in assessing student learning and in reflecting on your teaching performance and learning from that reflection, and your skills in communicating and interacting with students and adults.

Second, consider your preparation as a teacher. Teachers, as you have learned, represent a myriad of specialties. Hiring personnel will want to know how you see yourself—for example, as a specialist in middle school core, or as a high school music teacher. Or a high school social studies teacher who would also like to coach cross country track. Perhaps your interest is only teaching high school chemistry. You may indicate a special interest or skill, such as competency in teaching English as a foreign language. Or, perhaps, although your teaching field is mathematics, you also are bilingual and have had rich and varied crosscultural experiences. Have you had a rich and varied background of experience so that you will feel comfortable when you are hired and placed in the one assignment in which you were least interested? The hiring personnel who consider your application will be interested in your sincerity and will want to see that you are academically and socially impressive.

Last, consider your in-person interview with a district official. Sometimes you will have several interviews or you will be interviewed simultaneously with other candidates. There may be an initial screening interview by an administrative panel from the district, followed by an interview by a department chairperson, a school principal, or a school team composed of one or more teachers and administrators from the interested school or district. In all interviews, your verbal and nonverbal behaviors will be observed as you respond to various questions, including (1) factual questions about your student teaching, or about particular curriculum programs with which you would be expected to work, and (2) hypothetical questions, such as "What would you do if. . .?" Often these are questions that relate to your philosophy of education, your reasons for wanting to be a teacher, your approach to handling a particular classroom situation, and perhaps specifically the reasons for your interest in teaching at this particular school and in this district. Interview guidelines follow later in this section.

The Professional Career Portfolio (or How to Get Hired by Really Trying)

A way to be proactive in your job search is to create a personal professional portfolio to be shared with persons who are considering your application for employment. That is the objective of Exercise 13.1.

The professional career portfolio is organized to provide clear evidence of your teaching skills and to make you professionally desirable to a hiring committee. A professional portfolio is not simply a collection of your accomplishments randomly tossed into a folder. It is a deliberate, current, and organized collection of your skills, attributes, experiences, and accomplishments.

Because it would be impractical to send a complete portfolio with every application you submit, it might be advisable to have a minimum portfolio that could be sent with each application, in addition to a complete portfolio that you could make available upon request or that you would take with you to an interview. However it is done, the actual contents of the portfolio will vary depending on the specific job being sought; you will continually add and delete materials from your portfolio. Exercise 13.1 suggests categories and subcategories listed in the order that they may be best presented in portfolios A and B.[1]

---

[1] For further information, see K. Wolf, "Developing an Effective Teaching Portfolio," *Educational Leadership* 53(6):34–37 (March 1996), and Chap. 4, "Creating a Professional Portfolio," in C. Danielson, *Enhancing Professional Practice: A Framework for Teaching* (Alexandria, VA: Association for Supervision and Curriculum Development, 1996). See also the Internet at http://www.teachnet.com/. Preservice teachers in particular may be interested in several articles about portfolios in the theme issue of *Teacher Education Quarterly*, 25(1): (Winter 1998).

EXERCISE 13.1

Development of a Professional Portfolio

Instructions: The purpose of this exercise is to guide you in the creation of a personal professional portfolio that will be shared with persons who are considering your application for employment as a credentialed teacher.

Because it would be impractical to send a complete portfolio with every application you submit, you should consider developing a minimum portfolio (portfolio B) that could be sent with each application, in addition to a complete portfolio (portfolio A) that you could make available upon request and take with you to an interview. However it is done, the actual contents of the portfolio will vary depending on the specific job being sought: you will continually add and delete materials from your portfolio. Suggested categories and subcategories, listed in the order that they may be best presented in portfolios A and B are as follows.

1. Table of contents of portfolio (not too lengthy)—portfolio A only.

2. Your professional résumé—both portfolios.

3. Evidence of your language and communication skills (evidence of your use of English and of other languages, including American Sign)—portfolio A. (Also state this information briefly in your letter of application. See the résumé section that follows.)
   a. Your teaching philosophy (written in your own handwriting so to demonstrate your handwriting).
   b. Other evidence to support this category.

4. Evidence of teaching skills—portfolio A.
   a. For planning skills, include instructional objectives and a unit plan. (See Exercise 5.5)
   b. For teaching skills, include a sample lesson plan and a video of your actual teaching.
   c. For assessment skills, include a sample personal assessment and samples of student assessment.

5. Letters of recommendation and other documentation to support your teaching skills—both portfolios.

6. Other (for example, personal interests related to the position for which you are applying)—portfolio A.

Resources for Locating Teaching Vacancies

To locate teaching vacancies, you can establish contact with any of the following resources.

1. *Academic employment network.* A network employment page on the Internet at http://www.academploy.com/. Contact AEN, 2665 Gray Road, Windham, ME 04062. Phone (800) 890–8283. E-mail info@academploy.com.

2. *College or university placement office.* Establishing a career placement file with your local college or university placement service is an excellent way to begin the process of locating teaching vacancies.

3. *Local school or district personnel office.* You can contact school personnel offices to obtain information about teaching vacancies, and sometimes about open job interviews.

4. *County educational agency.* Contact local county offices of education about job openings.

5. *State departments of education.* Some state departments of education maintain information about job openings statewide. (See state departments of education Internet addresses later in the chapter.)

6. *Independent schools.* You can contact non-public-supported schools that interest you, either directly or through educational placement services such as:
   - IES (Independent Educational Services), 20 Nassau Street, Princeton, NJ 08540 (800)257–5102.
   - European Council of Independent Schools, 21B Lavant St., Petersfield, Hampshire, GU32 3EL, England.

7. *Commercial placement agencies.* Nationwide job listings and placement services are available from such agencies as:
   - Carney, Sandoe & Associates, 136 Boylston Street, Boston, MA 02116 (800)225–7986.
   - National Education Service Center, PO Box 1279, Department NS, Riverton, WY 82501–1279 (307)856–0170.
   - National Teachers Clearinghouse-SE, PO Box 267, Boston, MA 02118–0267 (617)267–3204.

8. *Out-of-country teaching opportunities.* Information regarding teaching positions outside the United States can be obtained from:
   - 313 East 43rd St., New York, NY 10017.
   - Department of Defense Dependent Schools, 4040 N. Fairfax Dr., Arlington, VA 22203–1634.

- European Council of Independent Schools, 21B Lavant St., Petersfield, Hampshire, GU32 3EL, England.
- International Schools Service, PO Box 5910, Princeton, NJ 08543.
- Peace Corps, Recruitment Office, 806 Connecticut Ave., NW, Washington, DC 20526.
- Teachers Overseas Recruitment Centers, National Teacher Placement Bureaus of America, Inc., PO Box 09027, 4190 Pearl Rd., Cleveland, OH 44109.
- YMCA of the USA, Attn: Teaching in Japan and Taiwan, 101 N. Wacker Dr., Chicago, IL 60606.

9. *Professional educational journals and other publications.* Professional teaching journals (as found in Figure 10.3 Chapter 10) often run advertisements of teaching vacancies, as do education newspapers such as *Education Week.* These can be found in your college or university library. See also *Education Week's* site on the Internet at http://www.edweek.org/.

State (and Territorial) Sources for Information about Credential Requirements

If you are interested in the credential requirements for other states and U.S. territories, check at the appropriate office of your own college or university teacher preparation program to see what information is available about requirements for states of interest to you, and whether the credential that you are about to receive has reciprocity with other states. Addresses and contact numbers for information about state credentials are available on the Internet at http://www.ed.gov/Programs/bastmp/SEA.htm.

The Professional Résumé

Résumé preparation is the subject of how-to books, computer programs, and commercial services, but a teacher's résumé is specific. Although no one can tell you exactly what résumé will work best for you, a few basic guidelines are especially helpful for the preparation for a teacher's résumé:

- The résumé should be no more than *two pages* in length. If it is any longer, it becomes a life history rather than a professional résumé.
- The presentation should be neat and uncluttered.
- Page size should be standard 8 1/2 × 11 inches. Over-sized and undersized pages can get lost.
- Stationery color should be white or off-white.
- Do *not* give information such as your age, height, weight, marital status, number or names of your children, or a photograph of yourself, because including personal data may make it appear that you are trying to prejudice members of the hiring committee, which is simply unprofessional.

- Sentences should be clear and concise; avoid educational jargon, awkward phrases, abbreviations, or unfamiliar words.
- Organize the information carefully, in this order: your name, address, and telephone number, followed by your education, professional experience, credential status, location of placement file, professional affiliations, and honors.
- When identifying your experiences—academic, teaching, and life—do so in *reverse chronological order,* listing your most recent degree or your current position first. (See sample résumé in Figure 13.1.)
- Be absolutely truthful; avoid any distortions of facts about your degrees, experiences, or any other information that you provide on your résumé.
- Take time to develop your résumé, and then keep it current. Do not duplicate hundreds of copies; produce a new copy each time you apply for a job. If you maintain your résumé on a computer disc, then it is easy to make modifications and print a current copy each time one is needed.
- Prepare a cover letter to accompany your résumé that is written *specifically* for the position for which you are applying. Address the letter personally but formally to the personnel director. Limit the cover letter to one page, and emphasize yourself, your teaching experiences and interests, and reasons that you are best qualified for the position. Show a familiarity with the particular school or district. Again, if you maintain a generic application letter on a computer disc, you can easily modify it to make it specific for each position.
- Have your résumé and cover letter edited by someone familiar with résumé writing and editing, perhaps an English-teaching friend. A poorly written, poorly typed, or poorly copied résumé fraught with spelling and grammar errors will guarantee that you will not be considered for the job.
- Be sure that your application reaches the personnel director by the announced deadline. If for some reason it will be late, then telephone the director, explain the circumstances, and request permission to submit your application late.

The In-Person Interview

If your application and résumé are attractive to the personnel director, you will be notified and scheduled for a personal or small-group interview, although in some instances the hiring interview may precede the request for your personal papers. Whichever the case, during the interview you should be honest, and you should be yourself. Practice an interview, perhaps with aid of a video camera. Ask a friend to role-play an interview with you and to ask you some tough questions. Plan your interview wardrobe and get it ready the night before. Leave

---

JENNIFER DAWSON
510 Newcomb Street, #309, Davis, CA 95616
(916) 552-8996
jdaw@aol.com

CREDENTIALS
_____

January 2001   California Preliminary Single Subject Credential in English
                        Supplemental authorization in Social Studies
May 2001   CLAD (Culture and Language Academic Development) Certificate
                        California State University, Sacramento

EDUCATION
_____

May 1995   Bachelor of Arts Degree in English Literature
                        Saint Olaf College, Northfield, Minnesota

TEACHING EXPERIENCE
_____

September 2001   **Douglass Junior High School (Woodland, CA).** *Two 7th-grade 2-hour block*
through   *interdisciplinary core classes, English and Social Studies.*
January 2001   • Worked with a team to develop interdisciplinary thematic lessons.
(Student Teaching III) • Conducted student-led parent conferences.
                        • Employed hands-on learning techniques and simulations.

February 2001   **Davis High School (Davis, CA).** *One period of college preparatory English*
through May 2001   *Literature for juniors.*
(Student Teaching II) • Developed book clubs, small-group forums for discussing three novels.
                        • Developed poetry unit in which students published their own poems for
                          class collection.

September 1999   **Los Cerros Middle School (Danville, CA).** *One period ESL—13 culturally*
through May 2000   *diverse 7th and 8th graders.*
(Student Teaching I) • Bilingual stories and activities; reader's theater presentations.

RELATED EXPERIENCE
_____

Summer of 2001   • Developed and taught a Summer Writing Workshop for small groups of 3rd
                          through 10th-grade students. Met with students and parents to establish
                          goals.
September 1999–May 2000 • Reader for English department at Valley High School.

OTHER EXPERIENCE
_____

• Volunteer in Juarez, Mexico, through YWAM (Youth with a Mission).
• Coordinator in Glacier National Park for the group, A Christian Ministry in the National Parks.

Figure 13.1
Sample professional résumé.

early for your interview so that you arrive in plenty of time. If possible, long before your scheduled interview, locate someone who works in the school district and discuss curriculum, classroom management policies, popular programs, and district demographics with that person. If you anticipate a professionally embarrassing question during the interview, think of diplomatic ways to respond. This means that you should think of ways to turn your weaknesses into strengths. For instance, if your cooperating teacher has mentioned that you need to continue to develop your room environment skills (meaning that you were sloppy), admit that you realize that you need to be more conscientious about keeping supplies and materials neat and tidy, but mention your concern about the students and the learning and that you realize you have a tendency to interact with students more than with objects. Assure someone that you will work on this skill, and then do it. The paragraphs that follow offer additional specific guidelines for preparing for and handling the in-person interview. As you peruse these guidelines please know that what may seem trite and obvious to one reader is not necessarily obvious to another.

You will be given a specific time, date, and place for the interview. Regardless of your other activities, accept the time, date, and location suggested, rather than trying to manipulate the interviewer around a schedule more convenient for you.

As a part of the interview you may be expected to do a formal but abbreviated (10–15 minute) teaching demonstration. You may or may not be told in advance of this expectation. So, it is a good idea to thoughtfully develop and rehearse a model one that you could perform on immediate request. Just in case it might be useful, some candidates carry to the interview a videotape of one of their best real-teaching episodes made during student teaching.

Dress for success. Regardless of what else you may be doing for living, take the time necessary to make a professional and proud appearance.

Avoid coming to the interview with small children. If necessary, arrange to have them taken care of by someone.

Arrive promptly, shake your dry hands firmly with members of the committee, and initiate conversation with a friendly comment, based on your personal knowledge, about the school or district.

Be prepared to answer standard-interview questions. Sometimes school districts will send candidates the questions that will be asked during the interview; at other times, these questions are handed to the candidate upon arrival at the interview. The questions that are likely to be asked will cover the following topics:

- *Your experiences with students of the relevant age.* The committee wants to be reasonably certain that you can effectively manage and teach at this level. You should answer this question by sharing specific successes that demonstrate you are a decisive and competent teacher.
- *Hobbies and travels.* The committee wants to know more about you as a person to ensure that you will be an interesting and energetic teacher to the students, as well as a congenial member of the faculty.
- *Extracurricular interests and experiences.* The committee wants to know about all the ways in which you might be helpful in the school and to know that you will promote the interests and cocurricular activities of students and the school community.
- *Classroom management techniques.* You must convince the committee that you can effectively manage a classroom of diverse learners in a manner that will help the students to develop their self-esteem.
- *Knowledge of the curriculum standards and the subject taught at the level for which you are being considered.* The committee needs to be reasonably certain that you have command of the subject and its place within the developmental stages of students at

this level. This is where you should show your knowledge of national standards and of state and local curriculum documents.
- *Knowledge of assessment strategies relevant for use in teaching at this level.* This is your place to shine with your professional knowledge about using rubrics and performance assessment.
- *Commitment to teaching at this level.* The committee wants to be assured that you are knowledgeable about and committed to teaching and learning at this level, as opposed to just seeking this job until something better comes along.
- *Your ability to reflect on experience and to grow from that reflection.* Demonstrate that you are a reflective decision maker and a life-long learner.
- *Your perceived weaknesses.* If you are asked about your weaknesses, you have an opportunity to show that you can effectively reflect and self-assess, that you can think reflectively and critically, and that you know the value of learning from your own errors and how to do it. Be prepared for this question by identifying a specific error that you have made, perhaps while student teaching, and explain how you turned that error into a profitable learning experience.

Throughout the interview you should maintain eye contact with the interviewer while demonstrating interest, enthusiasm, and self-confidence. When an opportunity arises, ask one or two planned questions that demonstrate your knowledge of and interest in this position and this community and school or district.

When the interview has obviously been brought to a close by the interviewer, that is your signal to leave. Do not hang around; this is a sign of lacking confidence. Follow the interview with a thank-you letter addressed to the personnel director or interviewer; even if you do not get the job, you will be better remembered for future reference.[2]

Once you are employed as a teacher, your professional development continues. The sections that follow demonstrate ways in which that can happen.

PROFESSIONAL DEVELOPMENT THROUGH REFLECTION AND SELF-ASSESSMENT

Beginning now and continuing throughout your career, you will reflect on your teaching (reflection is inevitable), and you will want to continue to grow as a professional as a result of those reflections (growth is not so inevitable unless self-initiated and systematically planned). The most competent professional is one who

---

[2]For additional suggestions for preparing for a teaching job interview, see the Internet web site http://www.teachnet.com/.

is proactive, that is, who takes charge and initiates his or her own continuing professional development. One useful way of continuing to reflect, self-assess, and grow professionally is by maintaining a professional journal, much as your students do when they maintain journals reflecting on what they are learning. Another is by continuing to maintain the professional career portfolio that you began assembling early in your preservice program and finalized for your job search (as discussed earlier in this chapter). Some teachers maintain professional logbooks, which serve not only as documentations of their specific professional contributions and activities, but also as documentation of the breadth of their professional involvement. Some teachers maintain research logs as a way of recording questions that come up during the busy teaching day, and of establishing a plan for finding answers.[3] The research log strategy can be of tremendous benefit to you in actively researching and improving your classroom work, but also can be of interest to colleagues. Finally, working in teams and sharing your work with team members is still another way of continuing to reflect, self-assess, and grow as a teacher.

PROFESSIONAL DEVELOPMENT THROUGH MENTORING

Mentoring, one teacher facilitating the learning of another teacher, can aid in professional development.[4] In what is sometimes called *peer coaching,* a mentor teacher volunteers or is selected by the teacher who wishes to improve or is selected by a school administrator, formally or informally. The mentor observes and coaches the teacher to help him or her improve in teaching. Sometimes the teacher simply wants to learn a new skill. In other instances, the teacher being coached remains with the mentor teacher for an entire school year, developing and improving old and new skills or learning how to teach with a new program. In many districts, new teachers are automatically assigned to mentor teachers for their first, and sometimes second, year, as a program of induction.

PROFESSIONAL DEVELOPMENT THROUGH INSERVICE AND GRADUATE STUDY

Inservice workshops and programs are offered for teachers at the school level, by the district, and by other agencies such as a county office of education or a nearby college or university. Inservice workshops and programs are usually designed for specific purposes, such as to train teachers in new teaching skills, update their knowledge in content, and introduce them to new teaching materials or programs. For example, Baltimore City Public School (MD) provides a systemwide professional development program for teachers of middle school grades, administrators, and staff at its Lombard Learning Academy Demonstration Center. The Lombard Learning Academy is a school-within-a-school located at Lombard Middle School. Cohorts of five to ten teachers from other schools in the district visit the Academy for five-day periods to observe instruction, practice strategies, and hone their skills in using technology.

University graduate study is yet another way of continuing your professional development. Some teachers pursue master's degrees in academic teaching fields, while many others pursue master's degrees in curriculum and methods of instruction or in educational administration or counseling. Some universities offer a Master of Arts in Teaching (MAT), a program of courses in specific academic fields that are especially designed for teachers.

PROFESSIONAL DEVELOPMENT THROUGH PARTICIPATION IN PROFESSIONAL ORGANIZATIONS

There are many professional organizations, local, statewide, national, and international. For secondary school teachers the organizations are usually discipline-specific, such as, the National Council of Teachers of Mathematics, the National Council for the Social Studies, the National Council of the Teachers of English, and the National Science Teachers Association (see Chapter 5). In most states there is a statewide organization, probably affiliated with a national organization. In addition, there are national teachers organizations, such as the ones shown in Figure 13.2. The NEA is the oldest and the AAE and the NAPE are more recent. The NEA and AFT have merged statewide in a few states and in a few large metropolitan areas.[5]

Local, district, state, and national organizations have meetings that include guest speakers, workshops, and

---

[3]For more on the professional portfolio and logs, see Chap. 4, "Creating a Professional Portfolio," of C. Danielson, *Enhancing Professional Practice: A Framework for Teaching* (Alexandria, VA: Association for Supervision and Curriculum Development, 1996), pp. 38–50.

[4]For additional information, see "The International Center for Information About New Teacher Mentoring and Induction" at http://www.teachermentors.com/MCenter%20Site/AdviceBegTchr.html, and a description of California's Beginning Teacher Support and Assessment (BTSA) Program at http://intergate.cccoe.k12.ca.us/coe/curins/sbtsa/description. See also A. Gratch, "Beginning Teacher and Mentor Relationships," *Journal of Teacher Education* 49(3):220–227 (May/June 1998).

[5]See A. Bradley, "Teachers' Unions To Merge in Two More States," *Education Week,* 19(30):3 (April 2000).

- American Federation of Teachers (AFT), AFL-CIO, 555 New Jersey Avenue, NW, Washington, DC 20001 http://www.aft.org
- Association of American Educators (AAE), 26012 Marguerite parkway #333, Mission Viejo, CA 92692 http://www.aaeteachers.org/info.html#board
- National Association of Professional Educators (NAPE), Suite 300, 900 17th Street, Washington, DC 20006 http://www.teacherspet.com/ napeindx.htm
- National Education Association (NEA), 1201 16th Street, NW, Washington, DC 20036-3290 http://www.nea.org

Figure 13.2
National professional associations for teachers.

publishers' displays. Professional meetings of teachers are educational, enriching, and fulfilling for those who attend. In addition, many other professional associations, such as those for reading teachers, supply speakers and publish articles in their journals that are often of interest to teachers other than the target audience.

Professional organizations publish newsletters and journals for their members, and these will likely be found in your college or university library. Sample periodicals were listed in Figure 11.3 (Chapter 11). Many professional organizations have special membership prices for teachers who are still college or university students, a courtesy that allows for an inexpensive beginning affiliation with a professional association. For information on special membership prices and association services, contact those of interest to you.

PROFESSIONAL DEVELOPMENT THROUGH COMMUNICATIONS WITH OTHER TEACHERS

Visiting teachers at other schools; attending inservice workshops, graduate seminars, and programs; participating in teacher study groups[6] and meetings of professional organizations; participation in teacher networks[7] and sharing with teachers by means of electronic bulletin boards are all valuable experiences, if for no other reason than talking and sharing with teachers from across the country and around the world. These discussions include not only a sharing of "war stories" but of ideas and descriptions of new programs, books, materials, and techniques that work.

As in other process skills, the teacher practices and models skill in communication, in and out of the classroom. This includes communicating with other teachers to improve one's own repertoire of strategies and knowledge about teaching as well as sharing one's experiences with others. Teaching other teachers about your own special skills and sharing your experiences are important components of the communication and professional development processes.

PROFESSIONAL DEVELOPMENT THROUGH SUMMER AND OFF-TEACHING WORK EXPERIENCE

In many areas of the country there are special programs of short-term employment available to interested teachers. These are offered by public agencies, private industry, foundations, and research institutes. These institutions are interested in disseminating information and providing opportunities for teachers to update their skills and knowledge, with an ultimate hope that the teachers will stimulate in more students a desire to develop their physical fitness, understand civic responsibilities, and consider careers in science and technology. Participating industries, foundations, governments, and institutes provide on-the-job training with salaries or stipends to teachers who are selected to participate. During the program of employment and depending on the nature of that work, a variety of people (e.g., scientists, technicians, politicians, businesspersons, social workers, and sometimes university educators) meet with teachers to share experiences and discuss what is being learned and its implications for teaching and curriculum development.

Some of the programs for teachers are government-sponsored field-centered and content-specific. For example, a program may concentrate on geology, anthropology, mathematics, or reading. At another location, a program may concentrate on teaching or using a specific new or experimental curriculum. These programs, located around the country, may have university affiliation, which means that university credit may be available. Room and board, travel, and a stipend are sometimes granted to participating teachers.

Sources of information about the availability of programs include professional journals, the local chamber of commerce, and meetings of the local or regional teacher's organization. In areas where there are no organized programs of part-time work experience for teachers, some teachers have had success in initiating their own by establishing contact with management personnel of local businesses or companies.

---

[6]See, for example, G. Cramer et al., *Teacher Study Groups for Professional Development,* Fastback 406 (Bloomington, IN: Phi Delta Kappa Educational Foundation, 1996).

[7]See, for example, A. Lieberman and M. Grolnick, "Networks, Reform, and the Professional Development of Teachers," Chap. 10 of A. Hargreaves (ed.), *Rethinking Educational Change With Heart and Mind* (Alexandria, VA: ASCD 1997 Yearbook, Association for Supervision and Curriculum Development, 1997). pp. 192–215.

PROFESSIONAL DEVELOPMENT THROUGH MICRO PEER TEACHING

Micro peer teaching (MPT) is a skill-development strategy used for professional development by both preservice (prior to credentialing) and inservice (credentialed and employed) teachers. Micro peer teaching (to which you were introduced in Exercises 7.1 and 9.2) is a scaled-down teaching experience involving a:

- Limited objective
- Brief interval for teaching a lesson
- Lesson taught to a few (8–10) peers (as your students)
- Lesson that focuses on the use of one or several instructional strategies

Micro peer teaching can be a predictor of later teaching effectiveness in a regular classroom. More importantly, it can provide an opportunity to develop and improve specific teaching behaviors. A videotaped MPT allows you to see yourself in action for self-evaluation and diagnosis. Evaluation of an MPT session is based on:

- The quality of the teacher's preparation and lesson implementation
- The quality of the planned and implemented student involvement
- Whether the instructional objective(s) was reached
- The appropriateness of the cognitive level of the lesson

Whether a preservice or inservice teacher, you are urged to participate in one or more MPT experiences. Formatted differently from previous exercises in this book, Exercise 13.2 can represent a summative performance assessment for the course for which this book is being used.

FOR YOUR NOTES

EXERCISE 13.2
Pulling It All Together—Micro Peer Teaching III

Instructions: The purpose of this exercise is to learn how to develop your own MPT experiences. You will prepare and teach a lesson that is prepared as a lesson presentation for your peers, at their level of intellectual maturity and understanding (i.e., as opposed to teaching the lesson to peers pretending that they are public school students).

This experience has two components:

1. Your preparation and implementation of a demonstration lesson.

2. Your completion of an analysis of the summative peer assessment and the self-assessment, with statements of how you would change the lesson and your teaching of it were you to repeat the lesson.

You should prepare and carry out a 15- to 20-minute lesson to a group of peers. The exact time limit for the lesson should be set by your group, based on the size of the group and the amount of time available. When the time limit has been set, complete the time-allowed entry (item 1) of Form A of this exercise. Some of your peers will serve as your students; others will be evaluating your teaching. (The process works best when "students" do not evaluate while being students.) Your teaching should be videotaped for self-evaluation.

For your lesson, identify one concept and develop your lesson to teach toward an understanding of that concept. Within the time allowed, your lesson should include both teacher talk and a hands-on activity for the students. Use Form A for the initial planning of your lesson. Then complete a lesson plan, selecting a lesson plan format as discussed in Chapter 5. Then present the lesson to the "students." The peers who are evaluating your presentation should use Form B of this exercise.

After your presentation, collect your peer evaluations (the Form B copies that you gave to the evaluators). Then review your presentation by viewing the videotape. After viewing the tape, prepare:

- A tabulation and statistical analysis of the peer evaluations of your lesson.
- A self-evaluation based on your analysis of the peer evaluations, your feelings after having taught the lesson, and your thoughts after viewing the videotape.
- A summary analysis that includes your selection and a description of your teaching strengths and weaknesses as indicated by this peer-teaching experience, and how you would improve were you to repeat the lesson.

Tabulation of Peer Evaluations

The procedure for tabulating the completed evaluations received from your peers is as follows:

1. *Use a blank copy of Form B for tabulating.* In the left margin of that copy, place the letters N (number) and σ (total) to prepare for two columns of numbers that will fall below each of those letters. In the far right margin, place the word *Score*.

2. *For each item (a through y) on the peer evaluation form, count the number of evaluators who gave a rating (from 1 to 5) on the item.* Sometimes an evaluator may not rate a particular item, so although ten peers may have been evaluating your micro peer teaching, the number of evaluators giving you a rating on any one particular item could be less than ten. For each item, the number of evaluators rating that item we call N. Place this number in the N column at the far left margin on your blank copy of Form B, next to the relevant item.

☞

3. *Using a calculator, obtain the sum of the peer ratings for each item.* For example, for item a, Lesson Preparation, you add the numbers given by each evaluator for that item. If there were ten evaluators who gave you a number rating on that item, then your sum on that item will not be more than 50 (5 × 10). Because individual evaluators will make their X marks differently, you sometimes must estimate an individual evaluator's number rating—that is, rather than a clear rating of 3 or 3.5 on an item, you may have to estimate it as being a 3.2 or a 3.9. In the left margin of your blank copy of Form B, in the σ column, place the sum for each item.

4. *Now obtain a score for each item, a through y.* The score for each item is obtained by dividing σ by N. Your score for each item will range between 1 and 5. Write this dividend in the column in the right margin under the word *Score* on a line parallel to the relevant item. This is the number you will use in the analysis phase.

Procedure for Analyzing the Tabulations

Having completed the tabulation of the peer evaluations of your teaching, you are ready to proceed with your analysis of those tabulations.

1. To proceed, you need a blank copy of Form C of this exercise, your self-analysis form.

2. On the blank copy of Form C, there are five items: Implementation, Personal, Voice, Materials, and Strategies.

3. In the far left margin of Form C, place the letter σ for the sum. To its right, and parallel with it, place the word *Average*. You now have arranged for two columns of five numbers each—a σ column and an *Average* column.

4. For each of the five items, get the total score for that item, as follows:
   a. *Implementation.* Add all scores (from the right margin of blank Form B) for the four items a, c, x, and y. The total should be 20 or less (4 × 5). Place this total in the left margin under σ (to the left of "1. Implementation").
   b. *Personal.* Add all scores (from the right margin of blank Form B) for the nine items f, g, m, n, o, p, q, s, and t. The total should be 45 or less (9 × 5). Place this total in the left margin under σ (to the left of "2. Personal").
   c. *Voice.* Add all scores (from the right margin of blank Form B) for the three items h, i, and j. The total should be 15 or less (3 × 5). Place this total in the left margin under σ (to the left of "3. Voice").
   d. *Materials.* Add all "scores" (from the right margin of blank Form B) for item k. The total should be five or less (1 × 5). Place this total in the left margin under s (to the left of "4. Materials").
   e. *Strategies.* Add all "scores" (from the right margin of blank Form B) for the eight items b, d, e, l, r, u, v, and w. The total should be 40 or less (8 × 5). Place this total in the left margin under s (to the left of "5. Strategies").

5. Now, for each of the five categories, divide the sum by the number of items in the category to get your peer evaluation average score for that category. For item 1 you will divide by 4; for item 2, by 9; for item 3, by 3; for item 4, by 1; and for item 5, by 8. For each category you should then have a final average peer evaluation score of a number between 1 and 5. If correctly done, you now have average scores for each of the five categories: Implementation, Personal, Voice, Materials, and Strategies. With those scores and evaluators' comments you can prepare your final summary analysis.

The following table includes three sample analyses of MPT lessons based *only* on the scores—that is, without reference to comments made by individual evaluators, although peer evaluators' comments are important considerations for actual analyses.

Sample Analyses of MPTs Based Only on Peer Evaluation Scores

| Teacher | Category/Rating | | | | | Possible Strengths and Weaknesses |
	1	2	3	4	5	
A	4.2	2.5	2.8	4.5	4.5	Good lesson, weakened by personal items and voice
B	4.5	4.6	5.0	5.0	5.0	Excellent teaching, perhaps needing a stronger start
C	2.5	3.0	3.5	1.0	1.5	Poor strategy choice, lack of student involvement

EXERCISE 13.2 FORM A

MPT Preparation

Form A is to be used for initial preparation of your MPT lesson. (For preparation of your lesson, study Form B.) After completing Form A, proceed with the preparation of your MPT lesson using a lesson plan format as discussed in Chapter 6. A copy of the final lesson plan should be presented to the evaluators at the start of your MPT presentation.

1. Time allowed: _____

2. Title or topic of lesson I will teach: _____

3. Concept: _____

4. Specific instructional objectives for the lesson:

    Cognitive: _____

    _____

    Affective: _____

    _____

    Psychomotor: _____

    _____

5. Strategies to be used, including approximate time plan: _____

    Set introduction: _____

    _____

    Transitions: _____

    _____

    Closure: _____

    _____

    Others: _____

    _____

6. Student experiences to be provided (i.e., specify for each—visual, verbal, kinesthetic, and tactile experiences):

    _____

    _____

7. Materials, equipment, and resources needed:

    _____

    _____

FOR YOUR NOTES

EXERCISE 13.2 FORM B
Peer Evaluation

Evaluators use Form B, making an *X* on the continuum between 5 and 1. Far left (5) is the highest rating; far right (1) is the lowest. Completed forms are collected and given to the teacher upon completion of that teacher's MPT and are reviewed by the teacher prior to reviewing his or her videotaped lesson.

To evaluators: Comments as well as marks are useful to the teacher.

To teacher: Give one copy of your lesson plan to the evaluators at the start of your MPT. (Note: It is best if evaluators can be together at a table at the rear of the room.)

Teacher: _____ Date: _____

Topic: _____

Concept: _____

1. Organization of Lesson	5	4	3	2	1
a. Lesson preparation evident	very		somewhat		no
b. Lesson beginning effective	yes		somewhat		poor
c. Subject-matter knowledge apparent	yes		somewhat		no
d. Strategies selection effective	yes		somewhat		poor
e. Closure effective	yes		somewhat		poor

Comments:_____

_____

_____

_____

_____

_____

_____

2. Lesson Implementation	5	4	3	2	1
f. Eye contact excellent	yes		somewhat		poor
g. Enthusiasm evident	yes		somewhat		no
h. Speech delivery	articulate		minor problems		poor
i. Voice inflection; cueing	effective		minor problems		poor
j. Vocabulary use	well chosen		minor problems		poor

☞

k. Aids, props, and materials	effective	okay	none
l. Use of examples and analogies	effective	need improvement	none
m. Student involvement	effective	okay	none
n. Use of overlapping skills	good	okay	poor
o. Nonverbal communication	effective	a bit confusing	distracting
p. Use of active listening	effective	okay	poor
q. Responses to students	personal and accepting	passive or indifferent	impersonal and antagonistic
r. Use of questions	effective	okay	poor
s. Use of student names	effective	okay	no
t. Use of humor	effective	okay	poor
u. Directions and refocusing	succinct	a bit vague	confusing
v. Teacher mobility	effective	okay	none
w. Use of transitions	smooth	a bit rough	unclear
x. Motivating presentation	very	somewhat	not at all
y. Momentum (pacing) of lesson	smooth and brisk	okay	too slow or too fast

Comments: _____

_____

_____

_____

_____

_____

_____

_____

_____

_____

_____

_____

_____

_____

_____

_____

_____

EXERCISE 13.2 FORM C
Teacher's Summative Peer Evaluation

See instructions within Exercise 12.2 for completing this form.

1. Implementation (items a, c, x, y)	5	4	3	2	1
2. Personal (items f, g, m, n, o, p, q, s, t)	5	4	3	2	1
3. Voice (items h, i, j)	5	4	3	2	1
4. Materials (item k)	5	4	3	2	1
5. Strategies (items b, d, e, l, r, u, v, w)	5	4	3	2	1

Total = _____

Comments: _____

_____

_____

_____

_____

_____

_____

_____

_____

_____

_____

_____

_____

_____

_____

_____

_____

_____

_____

_____

_____

FOR YOUR NOTES

SUMMARY

Because teaching and learning go hand in hand, and the effectiveness of one affects that of the other, the final two chapters of this book have dealt with both aspects of the *how well* component of teacher preparation—how well the students are learning and how well the teacher is teaching.

In addition, you have been presented with guidelines about how to obtain your first teaching job and how to continue your professional development. Throughout your teaching career you will continue improving your knowledge and skills in all aspects of teaching and learning.

We wish you the very best in your new career. Be the very best teacher you can be. The nation and its youth need you.

—Richard Kellough and Noreen Kellough

ADDITIONAL EXERCISE

See the companion website http://www.prenhall.com/ kellough for the following exercise related to the content of this chapter:

- Attending a Back-to-School Night

QUESTIONS FOR CLASS DISCUSSION

1. Discover what professional teacher organizations there are in your geographical area. Share what you find with others in your class. Attend a local, regional, or national meeting of a professional teachers' association, report to your class what it was like and what you learned, and share with your class any free or inexpensive teaching materials you obtained.
2. Talk with experienced teachers and find out how they remain current in their teaching fields. Share what you find with others in your class.
3. Select one of the Reflective Thoughts from the opening of Part IV that is specifically related to the content of this chapter, research it, and write a one-page essay explaining why you agree or disagree with the thought. Share your essay with members of your class for their thoughts.
4. Describe any prior concepts you held that changed as a result of your experiences with this chapter. Describe the changes.
5. From your current observations and field work related to this teacher preparation program, clearly identify one spe-

cific example of educational practice that seems contradictory to exemplary practice or theory presented in this chapter. Present your explanation for the discrepancy.
6. Congratulations! You have reached the end of this book, but there may be questions lingering in your mind. As before, list them and try to find answers.

FOR FURTHER READING

Backes, C. E., and Backes, L. S. "Making the Best of a Learning Experience." *Techniques: Making Education and Career Connections* 74(5):23–24 (May 1999).

Bradford, J. J. "How to Stay in Teaching (When You Really Feel Like Crying)." *Educational Leadership* 56(8):67–68 (May 1999).

Cramer, G., and Hurst, B. *How to Find a Teaching Job: A Guide for Success.* Upper Saddle River, NJ: Merrill Prentice Hall, 2000.

Duck, L. "The Ongoing Professional Journal." *Educational Leadership* 57(7):42–45 (May 2000).

Graham, P., et al. (eds.) *Teacher/Mentor.* New York: Teachers College Press, 1999.

Keller, J. D. "Deciphering Teacher Lounge Talk." *Phi Delta Kappan* 81(4):328–329 (December 1999).

Kellough, R. D. *Surviving Your First Year of Teaching: Guidelines for Success.* 2d ed. New Jersey: Merrill/Prentice Hall, 2001.

Kramer, M. C. "Triumph Out of the Wilderness: A Reflection on the Importance Of Mentoring." *Phi Delta Kappan* 82(5): 411–412 (January 2001).

Lowenhaupt, M. A., and Stephanik, C. E. *Making Student Teaching Work: Creating a Partnership.* Fastback 447. Bloomington, IN: Phi Delta Kappa Educational Foundation, 1999.

Martin, D. B. *The Portfolio Planner: Making Professional Portfolios Work for You.* Upper Saddle River, NJ: Merrill Prentice Hall, 1999.

McEwan, E. K. *How To Deal with Parents Who Are Angry, Troubled, Afraid, or Just Plain Crazy.* Thousand Oaks, CA: Corwin Press, 1998.

Notman, T. S., and Megyeri, K. A. "To Student Teach." *English Journal* 88(4):20–25 (March 1999).

Sillmaer, K., and Smith, T. "Creating a Professional Development Opportunity Within the Supervisor-Student Teacher Relationship." *Science Educator* 9(1):19–26 (Spring 2000).

Sparks, D. "What Teachers Know and Don't Know Matters." *Harvard Education Letter* 15(4):8 (July/August 1999).

Torreano, J. M. *500 Q&A for New Teachers: A Survival Guide.* Norwood, MA: Christopher-Gordon, 2000.

Wilder, A., and Croker, D. L. "How Can We Better Train Our Student Teachers?" *English Journal* 88(3):17–21 (January 1999).

Glossary

ability grouping   The assignment of students to separate classrooms or separate activities within a classroom according to their perceived academic abilities. *Homogeneous grouping* is the grouping of students of similar abilities, while *heterogeneous grouping* is the grouping of students of mixed abilities.

accommodation   The cognitive process of modifying a schema or creating new schemata.

accountability   Reference to the concept that an individual is responsible for his or her behaviors and should be able to demonstrate publicly the worth of the activities carried out.

adolescence   The period of life from the onset of puberty to maturity terminating legally at the age of majority, generally the ages of 12 to 20.

advance organizer   Preinstructional cues that encourage a mental set, used to enhance retention of materials to be studied.

advisor–advisee   A homeroom or advisory program that provides each student the opportunity to interact with peers about school and personal concerns and to develop a meaningful relationship with at least one member of the school staff.

affective domain   The area of learning related to interests, attitudes, feelings, values, and personal adjustment.

alternative assessment   Assessment of learning in ways that are different from traditional paper-and-pencil objective testing, such as a portfolio, project, or self-assessment. See *authentic assessment*.

American Federation of Teachers (AFT)   A national professional organization of teachers founded in 1916, and currently affiliated with the American Federation of Labor and Congress of Industrial Organizations (AFL-CIO).

anticipatory set   See *advance organizer*.

assessment   The relatively neutral process of finding out what students are or have learned as a result of instruction. See also *evaluation*.

assignment   A statement telling the student what he or she is to accomplish.

assimilation   The cognitive process by which a learner integrates new information into an existing schema.

at risk   General term given to a student who shows a high potential for not completing school.

authentic assessment   The use of evaluation procedures (usually portfolios and projects) that are highly compatible with the instructional objectives. Also referred to as *accurate, active, aligned, alternative, direct,* and *performance assessment*.

behavioral objective   A statement of expectation describing what the learner should be able to do upon completion of the instruction, and containing four components: the audience (learner), the overt behavior, the conditions, and the level or degree of performance. Also referred to as *performance* and *terminal objective*.

behaviorism   A theory that equates learning with changes in observable behavior.

benchmark   defines the prescribed quality level of student work.

block scheduling   The school programming procedure that provides large blocks of time (e.g., two hours) in which individual teachers or teacher teams can organize and arrange groupings of students for varied periods, thereby more effectively individualizing the instruction for students with various needs and abilities.

brain model (also, brain schema or mental schema) the picture or concept the brain comes up with to make sense out of material that has been input.

brainstorming   An instructional strategy used to create a flow of new ideas, during which judgments of the ideas of others are forbidden.

CD-ROM (compact disc-read only memory)   Digitally encoded information permanently recorded on a compact disc.

classroom control   The process of influencing student behavior in the classroom.

classroom management   The teacher's system of establishing a climate for learning, including techniques for preventing and handling student misbehavior.

closure   In a lesson, the means by which a teacher brings the lesson to an end.

coaching   See *mentoring.*

cognition   The process of thinking.

cognitive disequilibrium   The mental state of not yet having made sense out of a perplexing (discrepant) situation.

cognitive domain   The area of learning related to intellectual skills, such as retention and assimilation of knowledge.

cognitive psychology   A branch of psychology devoted to the study of how individuals acquire, process, and use information.

cognitivism   A theory that holds that learning entails the construction or reshaping of mental schemata and that mental processes mediate learning. Also known as *constructivism.*

common planning time   A regularly scheduled time during the school day when teachers who teach the same students meet for joint planning, parent conferences, materials preparation, and student evaluation.

compact disc (CD)   A 4.72-inch disc on which a laser has recorded digital information.

competency-based instruction   See *performance-based instruction.*

comprehension   A level of cognition that refers to the skill of understanding.

computer-assisted instruction (CAI)   Instruction received by a student when interacting with lessons programmed into a computer system. Known also as computer-assisted learning (CAL).

computer literate   The ability at some level on a continuum to understand and use computers.

computer-managed instruction (CMI)   The use of a computer system to manage information about learner performance and learning-resources options in order to prescribe and control individual lessons.

concept map   A visual or graphic representation of concepts and their relationships; words related to a key word are written in categories around the key word, and the categories are labeled.

conferences   a form of gathering evidence of what a student or a group of students have learned.

constructivism   See *cognitivism.*

constructivist Learning Theory   the notion that learners construct their own unique concepts through active participation and meaning making.

continuous progress   An instructional procedure that allows students to progress at their own pace through a sequenced curriculum.

convergent thinking   Thinking that is directed to a preset conclusion.

cooperative learning   A genre of instructional strategies that use small groups of students working together and helping each other on learning tasks, stressing support for one another rather than competition.

copernican plan   perhaps the most flexible and most complex of the block scheduling models; allows some courses to be taught in thirty or sixty days with very extended time formats.

core curriculum   Subject or discipline components of the curriculum considered absolutely necessary. Traditionally these are English/language arts, mathematics, science, and social science.

covert behavior   A learner behavior that is not outwardly observable.

criterion   A standard by which behavioral performance is judged.

criterion-referenced assessment   Assessment in which standards are established and behaviors are judged against the preset guidelines, rather than against the behaviors of others.

critical thinking   The ability to recognize and identify problems and discrepancies, to propose and test solutions, and to arrive at tentative conclusions based on the data collected.

curriculum   Originally derived from a Latin term referring to a race course for the chariots, the term still has no widely accepted definition. As used in this text, curriculum is that which is planned and encouraged for teaching and learning. This includes both school and nonschool environments, overt (formal) and hidden (informal) curriculums, and broad as well as narrow notions of content—its development, acquisition, and consequences.

deductive learning   Learning that proceeds from the general to the specific. See also *expository learning.*

detracking   An effort to minimize or eliminate separate classes or programs for students according to their differing abilities.

developmental characteristics   A set of common intellectual, psychological, physical, and social characteristics that, when considered as a whole, indicate an individual's development relative to others during a particular age span.

developmental needs   A set of needs unique and appropriate to the developmental characteristics of a particular age span.

diagnostic assessment See *preassessment.*

didactic teaching See *direct teaching.*

direct experience Learning by doing (applying) that which is being learned.

direct instruction Teacher-centered instruction, typically with the entire class, where the teacher controls student attention and behaviors as opposed to permitting students greater control over their own learning and behaviors.

direct intervention Teacher use of verbal reminders or verbal commands to redirect student behavior, as opposed to nonverbal gestures or cues.

direct teaching Teacher-centered expository instruction.

discipline The process of controlling student behavior in the classroom. The term has been largely replaced by the terms *classroom control* or *classroom management.* It is also used in reference to the subject taught (e.g., language arts, science, mathematics, and so forth).

discovery learning Learning that proceeds from identification of a problem, through the development of hypotheses, the testing of the hypotheses, and the arrival at a conclusion. See also *critical thinking.*

divergent thinking Thinking that expands beyond original thought.

DVD (digital video disc or digital versatile disc) A compact disc format for displaying motion video.

early adolescence The developmental stage of young people as they approach and begin to experience puberty. This stage usually occurs between 10 and 14 years of age and deals with the successful attainment of the appropriate developmental characteristics for this age span.

eclectic Utilizing the best from a variety of sources.

effective school A school where students master basic skills, seek academic excellence in all subjects, demonstrate achievement, and display good behavior and attendance. Known also as an *exemplary school.*

elective High-interest or special-needs courses that are based on student selection from various options.

empathy The ability to understand the feelings of another person.

equality Considered to be the same in status or competency level.

equilibration The mental process of moving from disequilibrium to equilibrium.

equilibrium The balance between assimilation and accommodation.

equity Fairness and justice, with impartiality.

evaluation Like assessment, but includes making sense out of the assessment results, usually based on criteria or a rubric. Evaluation is more subjective than is assessment.

exceptional child A child who deviates from the average in any of the following ways: mental characteristics, sensory ability, neuromotor or physical characteristics, social behavior, communication ability, or multiple handicaps. Also known as a *special-needs child* or *special education student.*

exemplary school See *effective school.*

exploratory course A course designed to help students explore curriculum experiences based on their felt needs, interests, and abilities.

expository learning The traditional classroom instructional approach that proceeds as follows: presentation of information to the learners, reference to particular examples, and application of the information to the learner's experiences.

extended-year school Schools that have extended the school year calendar from the traditional 180 days to a longer period such as 200 days.

extrinsic motivators Motivation of learning by rewards outside of the learner, such as parent and teacher expectations, gifts, certificates, and grades.

facilitating behavior Teacher behavior that makes it possible for students to learn.

facilitative teaching See *indirect teaching.*

family See *school-within-a-school.*

feedback Information sent from the receiver to the originator that provides disclosure about the reception of the intended message.

flexible scheduling Organization of classes and activities in a way that allows for variation from day to day, as opposed to the traditional fixed schedule that does not vary from day to day.

formative assessment Evaluation of learning in progress.

goal, course A broad, generalized statement about the expected outcomes of a course.

goal, educational A desired instructional outcome that is broad in scope.

goal, teacher A statement about what the teacher hopes to accomplish.

graphic organizer simple pictures or images that serve as tools to organize information.

hands-on learning Learning by doing, or active learning.

Hawthorne effect Says that no matter what, try something new and it will show positive effects at first simply because of the interest demonstrated when something new is tried. Name derived from first notice of the effect in 1962 at the Hawthorne plant of Western Electric in Cicero, IL.

heterogeneous grouping   A grouping pattern that does not separate students into groups based on their intelligence, learning achievement, or physical characteristics.

high school   A school that houses students in any combination of grades 9–12.

holistic learning   Learning that incorporates emotions with thinking.

homogeneous grouping   A grouping pattern that usually separates students into groups based on their intelligence, school achievement, or physical characteristics.

house   See *school-within-a-school*.

inclusion   The commitment to the education of each special-needs learner, to the maximum extent appropriate, in the school and classroom he or she would otherwise attend.

independent study   An instructional strategy that allows a student to select a topic, set the goals, and work alone to attain them.

indirect teaching   Student-centered teaching using discovery and inquiry instructional strategies.

individualized instruction   See *individualized learning*.

individualized learning   The self-paced process whereby individual students assume responsibility for learning through study, practice, feedback, and reinforcement with appropriately designed instructional packages or modules.

inductive learning   Learning that proceeds from specifics to the general. See also *discovery learning*.

inquiry learning   Like discovery learning, except here the learner designs the processes to be used in resolving the problem, thereby requiring higher levels of cognition.

inservice teacher   Term used when referring to credentialed and employed teachers.

instruction   Planned arrangement of experiences to help a learner develop understanding and to achieve a desirable change in behavior.

instructional module   Any freestanding instructional unit that includes these components: rationale, objectives, pretest, learning activities, comprehension checks with instructive feedback, and posttest.

integrated (interdisciplinary) curriculum   Curriculum organization that combines subject matter traditionally taught separately.

interdisciplinary team   An organizational pattern of two or more teachers representing different subject areas. The team shares the same students, schedule, areas of the school, and the opportunity for teaching more than one subject.

interdisciplinary thematic unit (ITU)   A thematic unit that crosses boundaries of two or more disciplines.

intermediate grades   Term sometimes used to refer to grades 4–6. An intermediate school, for example, is an elementary school that houses children of grades 4–6.

internalization   The extent to which an attitude or value becomes a part of the learner. That is, without having to think about it, the learner's behavior reflects the attitude or value.

interscholastic sports   Athletic competition between teams from two or more schools.

intervention   A teacher's interruption to redirect a student's behavior, either by direct intervention (e.g., by a verbal command) or by indirect intervention (e.g., by eye contact or physical proximity).

intramural program   Organized activity program that features events between individuals or teams from within the school.

intrinsic motivation   Motivation of learning through the student's internal sense of accomplishment.

intuition   Knowing without conscious reasoning.

junior high school   A school that houses grades 7–9 or 7–8 and that has a schedule and curriculum that resemble those of the traditional senior high school (grades 9–12 or 10–12) more than those of the elementary school.

lead teacher   The member of a teaching team who is designated to facilitate the work and planning of that team.

learning   The development of understandings and the change in behavior resulting from experiences. For different interpretations of learning, see *behaviorism* and *cognitivism*.

learning center (LC)   An instructional strategy that utilizes activities and materials located at a special place in the classroom and that is designed to allow a student to work independently at his or her own pace to learn one area of content.

learning modality   The way a person receives information. Four modalities are recognized: visual, auditory, tactile (touch), and kinesthetic (movement).

learning resource center   The central location in the school where instructional materials and media are stored, organized, and accessed by students and staff.

learning style   The way a person learns best in a given situation.

log   notebook in which student reflections on content material read or studied in class can be written.

looping   An arrangement in which the cohort of students and teachers remain together as a group for several or for all the years a child is at a particular school. Also referred to as multiyear grouping, multiyear instruction, multiyear placement, and teacher–student progression.

magnet school A school that specializes in a particular academic area, such as science, mathematics and technology, the arts, or international relations. Also referred to as a *theme school*.

mainstreaming Placing an exceptional child in regular education classrooms for all (inclusion) or part (partial inclusion) of the school day.

mandala A diagram, usually circular, with spiritual and ritual significance.

mastery learning The concept that a student should master the content of one lesson before moving on to the content of the next.

measurement The process of collecting and interpreting data.

mentoring One-on-one coaching, tutoring, or guidance to facilitate learning.

metacognition The ability to plan, monitor, and evaluate one's own thinking.

metacognitive journal notebook of sorts in which one writes personal reflections on life and/or learning experiences.

micro peer teaching (MPT) Teaching a limited objective for a brief period to a small group of peers for the purpose of evaluation and improvement of particular teaching skills.

middle grades Grades 5–8.

middle level education Any school unit between elementary and high school.

middle school A school that has been planned and organized especially for students of ages 10–14, and that generally has grades 5–8, with grades 6–8 being the most popular grade-span organization, although many varied patterns exist. For example, a school might include only grades 7 and 8 and still be called a middle school.

minds-on learning Learning in which the learner is intellectually active, thinking about what is being learned.

misconception Faulty understanding of a major idea or concept. Also known as a *naïve theory* and *conceptual misunderstanding*.

modeling The teacher's direct and indirect demonstration, by actions and by words, of the behaviors expected of students.

multicultural education A deliberate attempt to help students understand facts, generalizations, attitudes, and behaviors derived from their own ethnic roots as well as others. In this process students unlearn racism and biases and recognize the interdependent fabric of society, giving due acknowledgment for contributions made by its members.

multilevel teaching See *multitasking*.

multimedia The combined use of sound, video, and graphics for instruction.

multiple intelligences A theory of several different intelligences, as opposed to just one general intelligence; other intelligences that have been described are verbal/linguistic, musical, logical/mathematical, naturalist, visual/spatial, bodily/kinesthetic, interpersonal, and intrapersonal.

multipurpose board A writing board with a smooth plastic surface used with special marking pens rather than chalk. Sometimes called a visual aid panel, the board may have a steel backing and then can be used as a magnetic board as well as a screen for projecting visuals.

multitasking The simultaneous use of several levels of teaching and learning in the same classroom, with students working on different objectives or different tasks leading to the same objective. Also called *multilevel teaching*.

naïve theory See *misconception*.

National Education Association (NEA) The nation's oldest professional organization of teachers, founded in 1857 as the National Teachers Association and changed in 1879 to its present name.

norm-referenced Individual performance is judged relative to overall performance of the group (e.g., grading on a curve), as opposed to being criterion-referenced.

observation checklist a list of targeted behaviors or activities that are being taught or assessed at a particular time.

orientation set See *advance organizer*.

overlapping A teacher behavior where the teacher is able to attend to more than one matter at once.

overt behavior A learner behavior that is outwardly observable.

partial inclusion Placing special-needs children in a regular education classroom part of the day.

peer tutoring An instructional strategy that places students in a tutorial role in which one student helps another learn.

performance assessment See *authentic assessment*.

performance-based instruction Instruction designed around the instruction and assessment of student achievement against specified and predetermined objectives.

performance learning curricular framework in which students enact or carry out a specific process or task such as a musical piece, a dance step, a scientific lab process, a speech, an individual or group presentation, a role play about a particular period in history, a dramatic re-creation of a Shakespearean play in modern times, etc.

performance objective See *behavioral objective*.

portfolio a collection of student samples that reveal the learning and growth that has taken place over a period of time.

portfolio assessment An alternative approach to evaluation that assembles representative samples of a student's work over time as a basis for assessment.

positive reinforcer A means of encouraging desired student behaviors by rewarding those behaviors when they occur.

preassessment Diagnostic assessment of what students know or think they know prior to the instruction.

preservice Term used when referring to teachers in training, as opposed to inservice teachers (i.e., teachers who are employed).

probationary teacher An untenured teacher. After a designated number of years in the same district, usually three, upon rehire the probationary teacher receives a tenure contract.

procedure A statement telling the student how to accomplish a task.

project learning curricular framework from which the student completes a specific objective task such as a model of an ancient Roman village, a video on an environmental project on river clean-up, a brochure about travel opportunities in the country of the foreign language being studied, etc.

psychomotor domain The domain of learning that involves locomotor behaviors.

pulsed activities alternating higher-intensity activities with lower-intensity activities to allow for processing of the material.

realia Real objects used as visual props during instruction, such as political campaign buttons, plants, memorabilia, art, balls, and so forth.

reciprocal teaching A form of collaborative teaching where the teacher and the students share the teaching responsibility and all are involved in asking questions, clarifying, predicting, and summarizing.

reflection The conscious process of mentally replaying experiences.

reflective abstraction See *metacognition*.

reliability In measurement, the consistency with which an item or instrument is measured over time.

rubric An outline of the criteria used to assess a student's work.

rubric a set of criteria with progressive indicators used to assess a student's performance or project. The criteria and indicators are specific enough that both the teacher and the student are crystal clear ahead of time about what is expected in the performance or project.

schema (plural: schemata) A mental construct by which the learner organizes his or her perceptions of situations and knowledge.

school-within-a-school Sometimes referred to as a *house, cluster, village, pod,* or *family,* it is a teaching arrangement where one team of teachers is assigned to work with the same group of about 125 students for a common block of time, for the entire school day, or, in some instances, for all the years those students are at that school.

secondary school Traditionally, any school housing students for any combination of grades 7–12.

selective abandonment the setting aside of curriculum material in order to create a more workable amount of curriculum for the semester, the trimester, or the unit.

self-contained classroom Commonly used in the primary grades, it is a grouping pattern where one teacher teaches all or most all subjects to one group of children.

self-paced learning See *individualized learning*.

senior high school Usually a high school that houses only students in grades 9–12 or 10–12.

sequencing Arranging ideas in logical order.

simulation An abstraction or simplification of a real-life situation.

special needs student See *exceptional child*.

standardized test a test prepared by a regionally or nationally central office to determine how a student or a school is doing compared to other students or schools in the region or in the nation. Traditionally such tests have emphasized the memorization of curriculum details assessed through multiple-choice or true-false questions.

student teaching A field experience component of teacher preparation, often the culminating experience, where the teacher candidate practices teaching children while under the supervision of a credentialed teacher and a university supervisor.

summative assessment Assessment of learning after instruction is completed.

teacher leader See *lead teacher*.

teaching See *instruction*.

teaching style The way teachers teach; their distinctive mannerisms complemented by their choices of teaching behaviors and strategies.

teaching team A team of two or more teachers who work together to provide instruction to the same group of students, either alternating the instruction or team teaching simultaneously.

team teaching Two or more teachers working together to provide instruction to a group of students.

tenured teacher   After serving a designated number of years in the same school district (usually three) as a probationary teacher, upon rehire the teacher receives a tenure contract, which means that the teacher is automatically rehired each year thereafter unless the contract is revoked by either the district or the teacher and for specific and legal reasons.

terminal behavior   That which has been learned as a direct result of instruction.

thematic unit   A unit of instruction built on a central theme or concept.

theme school   See *magnet school.*

think time   See *wait time.*

tracking   The practice of the voluntary or involuntary placement of students in different programs or courses according to their ability and prior academic performance.

traditional teaching   Teacher-centered direct instruction, typically using lectures, discussions, textbooks, and worksheets.

transescence   A no longer popular term referring to the stage of human development, usually thought of as ages 9–14, the middle school years, which begins before the onset of puberty and extends through the early stages of adolescence. Students in this stage of development have been referred to variously as the *transescent, preadolescent, pre-teen, in-betweenager,* and *tweenager.*

transition   In a lesson, the planned procedures that move student thinking from one idea to the next or that move their actions from one activity to the next.

untracking   See *detracking.*

validity   In measurement, the degree to which an item or instrument measures that which it is intended to measure.

village   See *school-within-a-school.*

wait time   In the use of questioning, the period of silence between the time a question is asked and the inquirer (teacher) does something, such as repeats the question, rephrases the question, calls on a particular student, answers the question him- or herself, or asks another question.

whole-language learning   A point of view with a focus on seeking or creating meaning that encourages language production, risk-taking, independence in producing language, and the use of a wide variety of print materials in authentic reading and writing situations.

withitness   The teacher's timely ability to intervene and redirect a student's inappropriate behavior.

year-round school   A school that operates as traditional, that is with 180 school days, but the days are spread out over 12 months rather than the more traditional ten. Most common is a nine weeks on, three weeks off format.

Name Index

Subject Index

The Tiger Part of Me: I Like Action!
Adventurer Behavioral Strengths

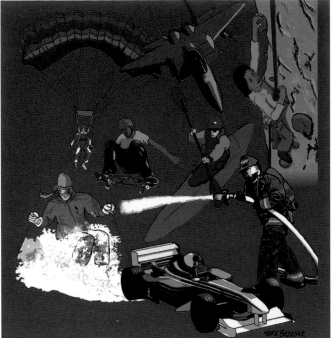

Words that describe me: Play, Perform, Take Chances, Fast Machines, Do It Now, Learn By Doing, Fun, Tell Jokes.

Communication Keys: Freedom of Action, Spur of the Moment, Challenge, Pushing the Limits, Excitement, Act it Out.

© 2004 Stefan

The Bull and Bear Part of Me: I Like Leading!
Builder Behavioral Strengths

Words that describe me: Results, Traditional, Responsible, Productive, Control, Decisive, Leadership, Give Directions.

Communication keys: Bottom-Line, Awards, Rules, Respect, Power, Obedience, First is Important.

© 2004 Stefan

The Fox Part of Me: I Like Thinking!
Planner Behavioral Strengths

Words that describe me: Imaginative, Perfectionist, Analytical, Thinker, Dreamer, Logical, New Ideas, Independent.

Communication Keys: Individual Freedom, Understand, Budget, Improve, Mystery, New Ways, Creative.

© 2004 Stefan

The Dolphin Part of Me: I Like Being Part of a Team!
Relater Behavioral Strengths

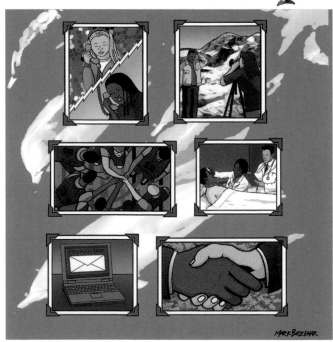

Words that describe me: Team Builder, Sympathetic, Concern for Others, Want People to Like Me, Like to Talk.

Communication Keys: Personal Interaction, Friendly, Honest, Work Together, Respect for Feelings, Romantic, Want Harmony.

© 2004 Stefan

My Builder Behavioral Strengths

If I emphasize the **Bull and Bear Part of Me (brown)**, I usually enjoy leading and being "up front" with people. I express myself openly and directly. I prefer taking a leadership role in a group or situation. I know what I ought to do and do not hesitate to remind other people about their responsibilities and commitments. I want status, recognition and power. I have a deep respect for traditions. I strive to be leader of any group. I believe in preparing and saving, thus building life on a rock-solid foundation, which will stand when the winds and rains come. I am a strong-willed, organized person who stands as a fortress for all to see, desiring respect and appreciation for the ways I help others to be their best.

Bull and Bear Vocabulary includes the following, in addition to those on the front of this card:

◆ results ◆ control ◆ at one's command ◆ reliable ◆
◆ law abiding ◆ duty ◆ dependable ◆ obedient ◆ organized ◆
◆ builder ◆ prepared ◆ accountable ◆ clear-cut ◆

People who show these behaviors in public: Condoleezza Rice (Planner Behaviors also), Bill O'Reilly (all four strengths), Frankie (Shark Tale), Senator Hillary Clinton (all four strengths), General Colin Powell (all four strengths), George W. Bush (President), The Lion King, Buffy the Vampire Slayer, General Patton, Hillary Clinton, President Ronald Reagan, Lucy (Peanuts), Susie (Rugrat), Head Master Dumbledore (also a Planner), Banking Industry, Queen Elizabeth, Germany (as a country), U.S.A. (all four strengths), I.R.S. and the "Star Spangled Banner" (song).

Financial and personal success is not an accident!

Created by Stefan Neilson, MA.   Illustration: Mark Bezenar

Contact us for:

◆ Train-the-Trainer ◆ Keynotes ◆ Character Education ◆
◆ Seminars ◆ Violence Prevention ◆ Career Selection ◆
◆ Videos ◆ Leadership/Team Building ◆ Communication ◆

© 2007 Stefan   Financial and Personal Success, Inc.
P.O. Box 96, Mountlake Terrace, WA 98043
(425) 672 8222

winningcolors@mindspring.com
web sites: winningcolors.com & financialsuccessinc.com

Value at least $ 1,000,000.00. Your investment $ 10.00

My Adventurer Behavioral Strengths

If I emphasize the **Tiger Part of Me (red)**, I just do it. I usually enjoy being where the action is and bring the fun and thrills into the routine of daily life. I am the entrepreneur and enjoy the excitement of taking chances. In times of crisis, I am at my best! I believe that people are free and make no bones about enjoying life without being bound by rules and regulations. I want excitement! I believe that money should be spent freely. The present moment is most important. Yesterday is easily forgotten and tomorrow is not relevant. Fast machines are an important part of my action world. I have fun flying over the rainbow rather than finding the pot of gold at the end. I am a free-spirited person for the entire world to see.

Tiger Vocabulary includes the following, in addition to those on the front of this card:

◆ thrill ◆ perform ◆ climb to the top ◆ games ◆ light-hearted ◆
◆ buy and sell ◆ stir the blood ◆ gamble ◆
◆ Shop 'til I drop ◆ fast machines ◆ good time ◆ danger ◆

These behaviors are exhibited in public by: General Colin Powell (all four behaviors), President Clinton, Eddie Murphy, Michael Jordan (also a blue), Lil Bow-Wow, Marion Jones, Jackie Chan, Arnold Schwarzenegger, Robin Williams, Madonna, Ricky Martin, Richard Dean Anderson (Stargate SG1), Whoopi Goldberg, Garth Brooks, Elvis, Jim Carrey, Michael Andretti, Tiger Woods (also a blue), Backstreet Boys, Bart Simpson, Angelica (Rugrat), Fred and George Weasley, Hagrid, Nelly, 'N Sync, The Road Runner, SpongeBob Square Pants, Oscar (Shark Tale), Australia (as a country), U.S.A. (all four strengths), and "Foot Loose" (song).

Financial and personal success is not an accident!

Created by Stefan Neilson, MA.   Illustration: Mark Bezenar

Contact us for:

◆ Train-the-Trainer ◆ Keynotes ◆
◆ Seminars ◆ Violence Prevention ◆ Career Selection ◆
◆ Videos ◆ Leadership/Team Building ◆ Communication ◆

© 2007 Stefan   Financial and Personal Success, Inc.
P.O. Box 96, Mountlake Terrace, WA 98043
(425) 672 8222

winningcolors@mindspring.com
web sites: winningcolors.com & financialsuccessinc.com

Value at least $ 1,000,000.00. Your investment $ 10.00

My Relater Behavioral Strengths

If I emphasize the **Dolphin Part of Me (blue)**, I usually enjoy being with people and have a high regard for emotions. I am the team builder, the basic ingredient for success. I know that feelings are very important and will bend my needs to those of others. People are the most important part of my decision making. I like to work in a team. I want unity with others, am a romantic at heart and a sympathetic person by nature. I want opportunities to communicate and socialize with others. I believe that care and consideration are the rock-solid foundation of a successful and prosperous life. I have strong emotions, based on honesty and sincerity. I feel that I can help others become productive and happy.

Dolphin Vocabulary includes the following, in addition to those on the front of this card:

◆ team building ◆ harmony ◆ sympathy ◆ sharing ◆
◆ group projects ◆ brotherly love ◆
◆ concern for people ◆ honesty with others ◆ friendly ◆

People who show these behaviors in public: General Colin Powell (all four strengths), Oprah Winfrey, Bill Cosby, Billy Graham, Jimmy Carter, Celine Dion, Rosie O'Donnell, Michael Jordan (also a red), Reba McEntire, Ronald McDonald (McDonald's), Snoopy, Chuckie (Rugrat), Lenny (Shark Tale), Mexico/Italy (as a country), U.S.A. (all four strengths) and "We are the World" (song).

Financial and personal success is not an accident!

Created by Stefan Neilson, MA.   Illustration: Mark Bezenar

Contact us for: ◆ Train-the-Trainer ◆ Keynotes ◆
◆ Seminars ◆ Violence Prevention ◆ Career Identification ◆
◆ Videos ◆ Leadership/Team Building ◆ Communication ◆

Financial and Personal Success, Inc.   © 2007 Stefan
P.O. Box 96, Mountlake Terrace, WA 98043
(425) 672 8222

winningcolors@mindspring.com
web sites: winningcolors.com & financialsuccessinc.com

Value at least $ 1,000,000.00. Your investment $ 10.00

My Planner Behavioral Strengths

If I emphasize the **Fox Part of Me (green)**, I usually enjoy thinking about new and better ways for creating and doing things. I know that underlying details are important. I make sure that everything is brought into consideration before making an important decision. I want know-how. I want to do things right. I want to know new things. I am a thinker by nature. I believe in using time and money wisely. I am curious about the inner world of people. I want to understand nature. I am a creative person of reason and wisdom. I desire the ability to prepare for the future so that society might not only survive but also prosper.

Fox Vocabulary includes the following, in addition to those on the front of this card:

◆ magic ◆ intuitive ◆ imaginative ◆ cautious ◆
◆ dreamer ◆ creative ◆ new and better ways ◆
◆ theoretical ◆ science fiction ◆

People who show these behaviors in public: General Colin Powell (all four strengths), Laura Bush, Steven Spielberg, Prince William, Alexander G. Bell, John F. Kennedy, Jr., Bill Gates, Gloria Estevan, Thomas Edison, Marge Simpson, James Earl Jones, Martin Luther King, Noriyuki Morita, Harry Potter, Hermione, Canada or France (as a country), U.S.A. (all four strengths) and "The Impossible Dream" (song).

Financial and personal success is not an accident!

Created by Stefan Neilson, MA.   Illustration: Mark Bezenar

Contact us for:

◆ Train-the-Trainer ◆ Keynotes ◆ Character Education ◆
◆ Seminars ◆ Violence Prevention ◆ Career Selection ◆
◆ Videos ◆ Leadership/Team Building ◆ Communication ◆

© 2007 Stefan   Financial and Personal Success, Inc.
P.O. Box 96, Mountlake Terrace, WA 98043
(425) 672 8222

winningcolors@mindspring.com
web sites: winningcolors.com & financialsuccessinc.com

Value at least $ 1,000,000.00. Your investment $ 10.00